Hebrews, the General Letters, and Revelation

Hebrews, the General Letters, and Revelation

An Introduction

CHARLES B. PUSKAS

CASCADE *Books* • Eugene, Oregon

HEBREWS, THE GENERAL LETTERS, AND REVELATION
An Introduction

Copyright © 2016 Charles B. Puskas. All rights reserved. Except for brief quotations in critical publications or reviews, no part of this book may be reproduced in any manner without prior written permission from the publisher. Write: Permissions, Wipf and Stock Publishers, 199 W. 8th Ave., Suite 3, Eugene, OR 97401.

Cascade Books
An Imprint of Wipf and Stock Publishers
199 W. 8th Ave., Suite 3
Eugene, OR 97401

www.wipfandstock.com

paperback ISBN: 978-1-62564-830-3
hardcover ISBN: 978-1-4982-8777-7
ebook ISBN: 978-1-4982-8639-8

Cataloging-in-Publication data:

Names: Puskas, Charles B.

Title: Hebrews, the general letters, and Revelation : an introduction / Charles B. Puskas

Description: Eugene, OR: Cascade Books. | Includes bibliographical references and index.

Identifiers: ISBN: 978-1-62564-830-3 (paperback). | 978-1-4982-8777-7 (hardcover). | 978-1-4982-8639-8 (ebook)

Subjects: LCSH: Bible. Hebrews—Crticism, interpretation, etc. | Bible. Catholic Epistles—Criticism, interpretation, etc. | Bible. Revelation—Criticism, interpretation, etc.

Classification: BS2775.2 P90 2016 (print). | BS2775.2 (ebook)

Manufactured in the USA

Scripture texts in this work are taken from the *New Revised Standard Version Bible* © 1989, Division of Christian Education of the National Council of the Churches of Christ in the United States of America. Used by permission. All rights reserved.

Credit Lines for Figures

Map A: Communities of Christ-followers in the first century. Used by permission, from Kurt A. Richardson, *James* (New American Commentary 36), Nashville: Broadman & Holman, 1997) 50.

Figure 1: Papyrus 12, third century, Hebrews 1:1. New York: Pierpont Morgan Library. Wikimedia Commons.

Figure 2: "Tabernacle Schematic" by Epictatus. Wikimedia Commons.

Figure 3: The caves near Khirbet Qumran, where the Dead Sea Scrolls were discovered. Photo by S. Puskas.

Figure 4: Levitical Priests of the Tabernacle. Illustration from the 1897 *Bible Pictures and What They Teach Us: With Brief Descriptions by Charles Foster.* Public Domain.

Figure 5: *Sermon on the Mount.* Woodcut on vellum by Christian Rohlfs (1849–1938). Wikimedia Commons.

Figure 6: Sculpture bust of Seneca (first century CE). Antiquities Collection, Berlin. Photo by C. B. Puskas.

Map B: Map of Roman Empire, first century CE. Used with permission from Walter A. Elwell, ed., *Baker Encyclopedia of the Bible* (Grand Rapids: Baker Book House, 1988) 393.

Figure 7: Arch of Titus, 81 CE, celebrating the Roman victory over the Judeans in war (66–70 CE). Photo by C. B. Puskas.

Figure 8: Denarius of Augustus Caesar wearing a laurel wreath. Photo from Rasiel Suarez of Tantalus Coins. Used with permission.

CREDIT LINES FOR FIGURES

Figure 9: A Roman couple holding hands. Heliograph by Arents after E. Guillame. Iconographic Collections. Wikimedia Commons.

Figure 10: Papyrus 72, Conclusion of 1 Peter (recto) and beginning of 2 Peter (verso) from the third century CE, Papyrus Bodmer VIII, original in the Biblioteca Apostolica Vaticana. Wikimedia Commons.

Figure 11: Early Christian painting of a baptism. Saint Calixte Catacomb (third century). Public domain.

Figure 12: Folio 32 of Nag Hammadi Codex II, with the ending of the Apocryphon of John, and the beginning of the Gospel of Thomas. Photo from *The Facsimile Edition of the Nag Hammadi Codices, 1974*. Used with permission of the Yale Divinity School Library.

Figure 13: Epicurean philosopher Metrodorus (331–278 BCE). Pergamum Museum, Berlin. Wikimedia Commons.

Figure 14: Library of Tiberius Julius Celsus Polemaeanus (Roman senator, consul, and governor of Asia), Ephesus, financed by him and erected by his son, 110 CE. It stored twelve thousand scrolls. Wikimedia Commons.

Map C: The cities of the seven churches of Asia Minor in the book of Revelation, first century CE. Used with permission from D. A. Carson and Douglas J. Moo, *An Introduction to the New Testament* (Grand Rapids: Zondervan, 2005) 711.

Figure 15: Model of Pergamum, second century CE, with Roman additions, constructed by K. Stephanowitz, 1965, based on original by H. Schleif, 1930. Scale 1:300. Photo by C. B. Puskas.

Figure 16: Denarius of Emperor Domitian (81–96 CE). Wikimedia Commons. Photo from Rasiel Suarez of Tantalus Coins. Used with permission.

Figure 17: Papyrus 24, fourth century, Rev 5:5–8; 6:5–8. Franklin Trask Library, Andover Newton Theological School. Used with permission.

Figure 18: *The Whore of Babylon*, Rev 17. One of a series of woodblocks made by the German artist Albrecht Dürer (1471–1528). Public domain.

Contents

Credite Lines for Figures | v
List of Figures | ix
List of Tables | x
Abbreviations | xi
Preface | xxi

Introduction | 1
1. The Letter to the Hebrews | 10
2. The Letter of James | 40
3. The First Letter of Peter | 67
4. Jude and 2 Peter | 92
5. The Letters of John | 115
6. The Book of Revelation | 141

Glossary | 165
Bibliography | 173
Index | 211

List of Figures

Map A	Communities of Christ-followers in the first century	9
Figure 1	Papyrus 12, Heb 1:1 (third century)	14
Figure 2	Tabernacle Schematic by Epictatus	20
Figure 3	C. B. Puskas at the caves near Khirbet Qumran	23
Figure 4	Levitical Priests of the Tabernacle	29
Figure 5	*Sermon on the Mount* (woodcut by Christian Rohlfs)	46
Figure 6	Sculpture bust of Seneca, Berlin	55
Map B	Map of Roman Empire (first century CE)	66
Figure 7	Arch of Titus, Roman Forum (81 CE)	70
Figure 8	Denarius of Caesar Augustus	74
Figure 9	Roman couple holding hands	75
Figure 10	Papyrus 72, of 1 and 2 Peter	77
Figure 11	Christ-follower painting of a baptism (third century)	84
Figure 12	Folio 32 of Nag Hammadi Codex II	99
Figure 13	Epicurean philosopher Metrodorus	104
Figure 14	Library of Tiberius Julius Celsus Polemaeanus	126
Map C	Cities of the seven churches in Revelation	140
Figure 15	Model of Pergamum (second century CE)	147
Figure 16	Denarius of Emperor Domitian (81–96 CE)	149
Figure 17	Papyrus 24, Rev 5:5–8; 6:5–8 (fourth century)	153
Figure 18	*The Whore of Babylon* (woodcut by A. Dürer)	161

List of Tables

Table 2.1	James and Acts Parallels | 44
Table 2.2	James and the Old Testament Parallels | 45
Table 2.3	James and the Sermon on the Mount Parallels | 47
Table 2.4	James and Paul Parallels | 50
Table 2.5	James and First Peter Parallels | 51
Table 2.6	James and Shepherd of Hermas Parallels | 52
Table 3.1	First Peter and Acts Parallels | 68
Table 3.2	First Peter and the Old Testament Parallels | 78
Table 4.1	Jude and Second Peter Parallels | 92
Table 4.2	Second Peter, Jude, and Israelite History Parallels | 95
Table 5.1	First John and the Gospel of John Parallels | 118

Abbreviations

Abbreviations for journals (*JBL*, *NTS*), major reference works (*NIDB*), and series (LCL, NIGTC) follow those of *The SBL Handbook of Style: For Ancient Near Eastern, Biblical and Early Christian Studies*, 2nd ed., Billie Jean Collins, project director (Atlanta: SBL Press, 2014), and also *The Chicago Manual of Style*, 16th ed. (Chicago: University of Chicago Press, 2010).

Aland, *Text of NT* (1989)	Kurt Aland and Barbara Aland, *The Text of the New Testament*. Translated by E. F. Rhodes. 2nd ed. Grand Rapids: Eerdmans, 1989
AnBib	Analecta Biblica
AB	Anchor Bible
AYB	Anchor Yale Bible
AYBD	*Anchor Yale Bible Dictionary*. Edited by David Noel Freedman (formerly *Anchor Bible Dictionary*)
ANF	*The Ante-Nicene Fathers: Translations of the Writings of the Fathers down to AD 325*. 10 vols. Edited by A. Roberts, J. Donaldson, et al. Buffalo, NY: Christian Literature Co., 1884–86
ANTC	Abingdon New Testament Commentaries
Aune, *Literary Environment*	David E. Aune, *The New Testament in Its Literary Environment*. LEC. Philadelphia: Westminster, 1987

ABBREVIATIONS

Aune, *Literature and Rhetoric*	David E. Aune, ed. *The Westminster Dictionary of New Testament and Early Christian Literature and Rhetoric.* Louisville: Westminster John Knox, 2003
AUSS	Andrews University Seminary Studies (Berrien Springs, MI)
BAFC	The Book of Acts in Its First Century Setting
BDAG	Walter Bauer, Frederick W. Danker, W. F. Arndt, and F. W. Gingrich, eds., *A Greek-English Lexicon of the New Testament and Other Early Christian Literature.* 3rd ed. University of Chicago Press, 2000
BHGNT	Baylor Handbook on the Greek New Testament. Baylor University Press
Biblical Criticism	*Biblical Criticism: Historical Literary, and Textual.* Edited by R. K. Harrison et al. Contemporary Evangelical Perspectives. Grand Rapids: Zondervan, 1978
BJS	Brown Judaic Studies
BR	*Biblical Research: Papers of the Chicago Society of Biblical Research*
BTB	*Biblical Theology Bulletin*
BTCB	Brazos Theological Commentary on the Bible
BBR	*Bulletin for Biblical Research*
BJRL	*Bulletin of the John Rylands University Library of Manchester*
CAH	S. A. Cook et al., eds., *The Cambridge Ancient History.* Vols. 7–12. Cambridge: Cambridge University Press, 1928–39
CBET	Contributions to Biblical Exegesis and Theology
CBQ	*Catholic Biblical Quarterly*
CCSS	Catholic Commentary on Sacred Scripture

ABBREVIATIONS

CHB	*The Cambridge History of the Bible: From the Beginnings to Jerome*. Vol. 1. Edited by P. R. Ackroyd and C. F. Evans. Cambridge: Cambridge University Press, 1970
Charlesworth, OTP	James H. Charlesworth, *The Old Testament Pseudepigrapha*. 2 vols. Garden City, NY: Doubleday, 1983, 1985
CTJ	*Calvin Theological Journal*
Current Issues	*Current Issues in Biblical and Patristic Interpretation*. Edited by Gerald F. Hawthorne. Grand Rapids: Eerdmans, 1975
Deissmann, LAE	Adolf Deissmann, *Light from the Ancient East: The New Testament Illustrated by Recently Discovered Texts of the Graeco-Roman World*. Translated by Lionel R. M. Strachan, 1927. Reprinted, Grand Rapids: Baker, 1978
DJBP	*Dictionary of Judaism in the Biblical Period*. Edited by Jacob Neusner and William Scott Green. Peabody, MA: Hendrickson, 1999
DLNTD	*Dictionary of the Later New Testament & Its Developments*. Edited by Ralph P. Martin and Peter H. Davids. Downers Grove, IL: InterVarsity, 1997
DMBI	*Dictionary of Major Biblical Interpreters*. Edited by Donald K. McKim. Downers Grove, IL: InterVarsity, 2007.
DSS	Garcia Martinez, Florentino and Eibert J. C. Tigchelaar, eds. *The Dead Sea Scrolls: Study Edition*. 2 vols. 2nd ed. Leiden: Brill, 1997. Grand Rapids: Eerdmans, 1999.
Early Judaism (2010)	*Eerdmans Dictionary of Early Judaism*. Edited by John J. Collins and Daniel C. Harlow Grand Rapids: Eerdmans, 2010
Encyclopedia Judaica	*Encyclopedia Judaica*. Edited by C. Roth et al. 16 vols. Jerusalem: Keter; New York: Macmillan, 1971–72

ABBREVIATIONS

Eusebius, *Hist. eccl.*	Eusebius Pamphilus, *Ecclesiastical History*.
ExBC	The Expositor's Bible Commentary.
ExpT	*Expository Times*
Farmer and Farkasfalvy, NT Canon	William R. Farmer and Denis M. Farkasfalvy, *The Formation of the New Testament Canon: An Ecumenical Approach*. New York: Paulist, 1983
GBS	Guides to Biblical Scholarship.
GNB	Good News Bible
GNS	Good News Studies
Greenlee, *Textual Criticism*	J. Harold Greenlee, *Introduction to New Testament Textual Criticism*. Rev. ed. Peabody, MA: Hendrickson, 1995
Guthrie, *NT Introduction*	Donald Guthrie, *New Testament Introduction*. 4th ed. Downers Grove, IL: InterVarsity, 1990
HBD	*Harper's Bible Dictionary*. Edited by Paul J. Achtemeier. San Francisco: Harper & Row, 1985
Hellenistic Commentary	*Hellenistic Commentary to the New Testament*. Edited by M. Eugene Boring, Klaus Berger, and Carlsten Colpe. Nashville: Abingdon, 1995
HNT	Handbuch zum Neuen Testament
HNTC	Harper's New Testament Commentaries
HTR	*Harvard Theological Review*
HUT	Hermeneutische Untersuchungen zur Theologie
ICC	International Critical Commentary
IDB	*The Interpreter's Dictionary of the Bible*. 4 vols. Edited by George Arthur Buttrick. Nashville: Abingdon, 1962
IDBSup	*The Interpreter's Dictionary of the Bible Supplementary Volume*. Edited by K. Crim. Nashville: Abingdon, 1976

ABBREVIATIONS

Interpretation	*Interpretation: A Bible Commentary for Teaching and Preaching*
JANT	*Jewish Annotated New Testament: New Revised Standard Version*. Edited by Amy-Jill Levine and Marc Zvi Brettler. New York: Oxford University Press, 2011
JBL	*Journal of Biblical Literature*
Josephus, *Ant.*; *War*	Josephus, *Antiquities of the Jews*; *The Jewish War*
JSNT	*Journal for the Study of the New Testament*
JSNTSup	Journal for the Study of the New Testament Supplement Series
JTS	*Journal of Theological Studies*, New Series
Kennedy, *NT Rhetorical Criticism*	George A. Kennedy, *New Testament Interpretation through Rhetorical Criticism*. Chapel Hill: University of North Carolina Press, 1984
Kümmel, *NTHIP*	Werner Georg Kümmel, *The New Testament: The History of the Investigation of Its Problems*. Translated by S. MacLean Gilmour and Howard Clark Kee. Nashville: Abingdon, 1972
LCBI	Literary Currents in Biblical Interpretation
LCL	Loeb Classical Library
LEC	Library of Early Christianity
LNTS	Library of New Testament Studies
Longenecker, *Biblical Exegesis*	Richard N. Longenecker, *Biblical Exegesis in the Apostolic Period*. 2nd ed. Grand Rapids: Eerdmans, 1999
LW	*Luther's Works*, 55 vols. Philadelphia: Fortress; St. Louis: Concordia, 1957–

ABBREVIATIONS

Marjanen & Luomanen,
Second-Century — Antti Marjanen and Petri Luomanen, eds. *A Companion to Second-Century Christian "Heretics."* Leiden: Brill, 2008

Malina and Pilch,
Revelation — Bruce J. Malina and John J. Pilch, *Social-Science Commentary on the Book of Revelation*. Minneapolis: Fortress, 2000

Metzger, *Text of NT* — Metzger, B. *The Text of the New Testament*. 3rd ed. New York: Oxford University Press, 1992

NA^{28} — Novum Testamentum Graece, Nestle-Aland, 28th ed. Stuttgart: Biblelgesellschaft, 2012.

NAB — New American Bible

NCBC — New Century Bible Commentary

New Documents — *New Documents Illustrating Early Christianity. A Review of the Greek Inscriptions and Papyri.* Edited by G. H. R. Horsely, S. R. Llewelyn, et al. The Ancient History Documentary Research Centre of Macquire University, North Ryde, NSW, Australia, 1981–2002

NIBCNT — New International Bible Commentary of the New Testament

NICNT — New International Commentary of the New Testament

NIDB — *The New Interpreter's Dictionary of the Bible*. Edited by Katherine Doob Sakenfeld et al. 5 vols. Nashville, Abingdon Press, 2001–2009

NIDNTT — *The New International Dictionary of New Testament Theology*. Edited by Colin Brown. 3 vols. Grand Rapids: Zondervan, 1975, 1976, 1978

NIGTC — New International Greek Testament Commentary

NIV — New International Version of the Bible

ABBREVIATIONS

NJBC	*The New Jerome Biblical Commentary*. Edited by Ramond E. Brown, Joseph A. Fitzmyer, and Roland E. Murphy. Englewood Cliffs, NJ: Prentice-Hall, 1990
NovT	*Novum Testamentum*
NovTSup	Novum Testamentum Supplements
NRSV	New Revised Standard Version of the Bible
NTS	*New Testament Studies*
OTS	*Old Testament Studies*
Oxford Classical Dictionary	*The Oxford Classical Dictionary*. Edited by Simon Hammond and Anthony Spawforth. 3rd ed. Oxford: University Press, 1996
Perkins, *Gnosticism and NT*	Pheme Perkins, *Gnosticism and the New Testament*. Minneapolis: Fortress, 1993
PNTC	Pillar New Testament Commentary
Porter, *Classical Rhetoric*	Stanley E. Porter, ed., *Handbook of Classical Rhetoric in the Hellenistic Period, 330 B.C.–A.D. 400*. Leiden: Brill, 2001
PrC	Proclamation Commentaries
Puskas and Crump, *Gospels and Acts*	Charles B. Puskas and David Crump. *An Introduction to the Gospels and Acts*. Grand Rapids: Eerdmans, 2008.
Puskas and Reasoner, *Letters*	Charles B. Puskas and Mark Reasoner, *An Introduction to the Letters of Paul*. 2nd ed. Collegeville, MN: Liturgical, 2013
Puskas and Robbins, *Introduction*	Puskas, Charles B., and C. Michael Robbins. *An Introduction to the New Testament*. 2nd ed. Eugene, OR: Cascade Books, 2011
RBS	Resources for Biblical Study

ABBREVIATIONS

RSV	Revised Standard Version Bible
SP	Sacra Pagina
SBLDS	Society of Biblical Literature Dissertation Series.
Schürer and Vermes, *Jewish People*	Emil Schürer, *The History of the Jewish People in the Age of Jesus Christ* (175 BC–AD 135). Revised and edited by Geza Vermes, Fergus Millar, et al. 3 vols. Edinburgh: T & T Clark, 1973, 1979, 1986
SE	*Studia Evangelica*
Semeia	*Semeia: An Experimental Journal for Biblical Criticism*
S&HBC	Smith & Helwys Bible Commentary
SNTSMS	Society for New Testament Studies Monograph Series
Soulen and Soulen, *Biblical Criticism*	Richard N. Soulen and R. Kendell Soulen, *Handbook of Biblical Criticism*. 4th ed. Louisville: Westminster John Knox, 2011
TDNT	*Theological Dictionary of the New Testament*. 10 vols. Edited by Gerhard Kittel and Gerhard Friedrich. Translated by Geoffrey W. Bromiley. Grand Rapids: Eerdmans 1964–76
TNTC	Tyndale New Testament Commentary
Trebilco, *Ephesus* (2007)	Paul Trebilco, *The Early Christians in Ephesus from Paul to Ignatius*. Grand Rapids: Eerdmans, 2007.
Turner, *Style* (1976)	Nigel Turner, *Style*. Vol. 4 (1976) of Moulton, James Hope. *A Grammar of New Testament Greek*. 4 vols. Edinburgh: T. & T. Clark, 1908–76
USQR	Union Seminary Quarterly Review
Vermes, *Scrolls* (1997)	Geza Vermes, ed. and trans. *The Complete Dead Sea Scrolls in English*. New York: Penguin, 1997

ABBREVIATIONS

WA	Weimar Ausgabe, Weimar edition of Luther's Works in German, 73 vols. (1885–2009)
WBC	Word Biblical Commentary
WUNT	Wissenschaftliche Untersuchungen zum Neuen Testament
Women's Bible Commentary (2012)	*Women's Bible Commentary*. Rev. and updated. Edited by Carol A. Newsom, Sharon H. Ringe, Jacqueline E. Lapslely. Louisville, Westminster John Knox, 2012
Women in Scripture	*Women in Scripture: A Dictionary of Names and Unnamed Women in the Hebrew Bible, The Aprocryphal/Deuterocanonical Books, and the New Testament*. Edited by Carol Meyers. Grand Rapids: Eerdmans, 2000
WBC	Word Biblical Commentary
ZNW	*Zeitschrift für die neutestamentliche Wissenschaft und die Kunde der älteren Kirche*
ZPEB (1975)	*The Zondervan Pictorial Encyclopedia of the Bible*. 5 vols. Edited by Merrill C. Tenney. Grand Rapids: Zondervan, 1975

Preface

THE WRITING OF THIS book was begun in the 1980s as part of an *Introduction to the New Testament*, but much was not included, to keep the introduction to a reasonable page limit.[1] The explanation underscores the importance of publishing this book. Most New Testament (NT) introductions, because of page limitations and other reasons, tend to scale down or minimize their treatment of the last nine books of the Christian Bible (from Hebrews to Revelation). In most cases the focus in these introductions is on the four Gospels and the Letters of Paul. As important as these books are, one should not neglect, with only a brief survey, the treatment of Hebrews, the General Letters, and the Book of Revelation. The title given later to the collection, Catholic Epistles or General Letters, for example, is a reminder of its general appeal to the whole church, despite its slow "canonical" recognition and authorship issues (e.g., who wrote?). Nevertheless, these writings from Hebrews to Revelation continue to capture our attention and ignite our imagination. An introduction to this collection therefore meets an identifiable need as either a supplement for classes in NT Introduction or as a textbook for classes focusing on the later NT writings.

My purpose for this Introduction is to focus on specific questions related to each NT book: When and why was it written? By whom and to whom? What are some of its special features (genre, structure, style)? How soon (or late) was it included in the NT collection? Answers to many of these questions are tentative. The "assured results of scholarship" are in continual need of reevaluation. Since the 1980s a host of diverse cultural, historical, ideological, sociorhetorical, literary, and contextual

---

1. Puskas and Robbins, *Introduction to the New Testament* (2nd ed.; Eugene, OR: Cascade Books, 2011) is 374 pages including indexes plus twenty pages of front matter. The first edition, published by Hendrickson Publishers, Peabody, MA, in 1989 was 297 pages including indexes with twenty pages of front matter.

studies have emerged, and I have to endeavored include them when relevant to the topic of discussion.

This book includes a glossary of terms, a bibliography divided into three sections: 1) reference works, 2) commentaries, and 3) essays, monographs and related works. It concludes with a general index of major topics, authors, and references.

Many thanks to my editor, K. C. Hanson, and the staff at Cascade Books, for encouragement, direction, and support. I am grateful to the universities in Missouri (Evangel, Drury, MSU) and Minnesota (Bethel, St. Catherine, Metro State) that gave me opportunities to teach these NT books in the classroom and also to several congregations (UMC, ELCA) that asked me to teach interested laypeople NT books that inspire, encourage, and motivate to action. Special thanks and appreciation to my wife, Susan, for her encouragement and support.

Introduction

THE LAST NINE BOOKS of the NT are worthy of our investigation and thoughtful consideration. Much attention has been given to the four Gospels and Paul's writings, but these controversial books from Hebrews to Revelation continue to intrigue, fascinate, and mystify us.

The melodious language of Hebrews permeated with Israel's Scriptures, the vital hope for tough times offered by 1 Peter, and the prophetic visions of future destiny in Revelation, are just a few highlights from this group of writings that can awaken our curiosity and capture our imagination in surprising ways. What follows is an overview of key features and concerns.

Hebrews opens with a grand announcement of the glorified Son higher in rank than the angels (illustrated from the Scriptures) and demonstrating his divine sonship and authority (ch. 1). Intertextuality in the service of Christology is the focus here. The enthronement of the Son forever with God as a high priest greater than Aaron and Moses (vv. 2–5, 7) recalls the Levitical cult and raises for us the issue of a new theology replacing it. Hebrews 4 makes relevant an old covenant idea: those who trust in the Son enter God's rest and await a final Sabbath with God. Exhortations to maturity, faithfulness, and service (ch. 6) are typical of the book's hortatory style (13:22). The author draws heavily on the Scriptures, with over sixty quotations. He interprets most of these ancient texts in light of the death and resurrection of Christ.

Is Hebrews 8 about covenant renewal or new covenant (Jer 31:31–34)? The sacrifice of Christ, once for all, that provides access to God for all believers (9–10) recalls other NT texts. At this point another question can be asked: Are the analogies between shadow and reality (8:5; 10:1), the earthly and the heavenly (8:1–4; 9:23–24), the created and the uncreated (9: 11), the transitory and the enduring (7:23–24; 10: 34) indicators of some kind of Platonic dualism? Finally, the encomium of Israel's faithful (11) is a basis for further exhortations (12–13) on faith, endurance, discipline, the pursuit of peace, mutual love, prayer, and communal worship.

James confidently begins with some wisdom on how trials can build character, produce maturity (cf. Rom 5:3–4; 1 Pet 1:6–7), and strengthen faith in God the source of every good gift. The divided self lacks faith and accuses God of being a tempter but does not know that temptation arises from surrendering to one's selfish desires. James exhorts his readers to be practioners of the word, not just listeners, that true devotion to God expresses itself in the action of helping the needy and remaining separate from worldly values that are hostile to God (Jas 1; cf. 4:4). His readers are not to be partial, except to the poor. Faith must be demonstrated by action if it is to prove itself as useful and beneficial (2). Angry words against one's neighbor dishonors people and God. They arise from worldly wisdom focused on jealously and selfish ambition, wisdom from God is even-tempered, fair, and conciliatory (3).

The source of all conflict lies within humans, who harbor jealousy and evil intentions. One needs to humble oneself, be separate from worldly ambition, and order oneself under God (4:1–16). James's readers are not to become arrogant planners, ignoring God's providence, because life is short. Also, one does not want to receive the judgment that God will bring upon those wealthy who oppress their workers (4:17—5:6). The faithful are to wait patiently for God's arrival as the prophets did, bearing much suffering. Live together honorably in worship and facing adversity (James commands) for one who returns a sinner from his error will save his soul and cover many sins (5:7–20; cf. Prov 10:12; 1 Pet 4:8). The author of James quotes from the Scriptures at least eight times, with many more allusions and echoes. Some commentators even claim that the book of James is a sermon on the Sermon on the Mount (Matt 5–7; cf. Luke 6:17–47): at least twelve passages in James parallel Jesus's so-called sermon.

First Peter 1:1 is addressed to five specific provinces of Asia Minor (modern Turkey), not to the church "catholic." Is it really then a "general letter"? With a lengthy prayer of blessing and thanksgiving (similar to Eph 1:3–14), 1 Pet 1:3–12 intensifies a common allegiance to the foreknowing Father and the sanctifying Spirit, for obedience to the Son who consecrates the hearers and readers with his blood in a covenant relationship (v. 2; cf. Exod 24:8) for an inheritance of eternal salvation. As

INTRODUCTION

the Letter of James states (1:2–4, 12), so the First Letter of Peter notes that the "various trials" readers will face are to prove that their faith is genuine. The prophets awaited this day of revelation, and their prophecies find fulfillment in the time of Peter's audience (cf. "this is that": Acts 2:16). The lengthy thanksgiving (1 Pet 1:3–12) functions like a musical overture before an opera, announcing themes to be developed later in the book (e.g., new birth, hope, mercy, chosenness, a fiery ordeal, sufferings of Christ, and the bringing or showing of honor).

The liturgical and baptismal material in 1 Peter is noteworthy. Comparisons can be made between the rituals of mystery cults and early liturgies of Christ-followers—comparisons that can lead to reading of 1 Peter as a Roman baptismal service. Along with the baptismal language and imagery, there are indications in 1 Peter of a liturgical rite in progress (1:21–22). The exhortations in 1 Pet 2:3–3:7 may have functioned as a specific address to baptismal candidates, and those in 4:12—5:11 as a general address to the congregation.

Concerning the interpretation of 1 Pet 3:18–22 some observations can also be made. Perhaps Christ's proclamation to the spirits in prison is an image of the risen Christ's triumph over the powers of evil, and not a descent into hades. Also, it seems unlikely that the water of baptism itself or alone accomplishes salvation, but it is the chosen means used to effect salvation through the resurrection of Christ (3:20–21).

First Peter begins and ends like a Pauline letter, with numerous literary forms of earliest churches wedged within the book (e.g., hymns, catecheses, ethical lists, household duties). The household rules concerning "wives" (1 Pet 3:1–6) have a conservative, patriarchal tone. What could have prompted these injunctions? One theory suggests that the women Christ-followers of Asia Minor (e.g., Priscilla, Phoebe, Junia), with their own kind of "liberated behavior" might have occasioned some stereotypical Hellenistic slander: e.g., "only 'loose women' dressed fashionably and spoke in public." Their "liberated behavior" (cf. Gal 3:28) may have prompted these patriarchal instructions to dress conservatively and to behave with the quiet demeanor of a Greco-Roman matron (1 Pet 3:3–4). What do you think of this theory? Here is a related question: Were such household codes (2:13—3:7) written to *protect* the identity of Christ-followers or to seek to *uphold* Greco-Roman expectations?

The audience of 1 Peter may have been experiencing or anticipating various kinds of trials or suffering. Perhaps it was persecution, slander, or discrimination for their faith (1 Pet 1:6; 2:12; 2:21; 3:9, 14, 17; 4:12–19;

5:9–10). As we will see also in Revelation, it is difficult to determine the specific situation. By 110 CE in Bithynia (1 Pet 1:1; 2:12), locals were sometimes arrested for worshipping Christ. They could be released if they denounced their faith and invoked the gods. Pliny the Younger, the Roman governor of Bithynia, wrote to Emperor Trajan on this matter, and the emperor supported him but Trajan cautioned against using any anonymous informants or accusers (Pliny, *Letters* 10.96–97). Earlier, under Domitian (81–96), we have no evidence of any official and empire-wide persecution of Christ-followers. Emperor Decius (249–51) was the first to initiate an empire-wide persecution of "Christians."

Nevertheless, any reluctance and hesitation shown by Peter's community regarding the observance of the imperial cult or the local gods so prevalent in Greco-Roman society might have aroused the suspicion of local citizens, who could have interpreted these hesitant actions as disloyalty to Rome or even a threat to the local cult (cf. Acts 19:23–27).

Departing from the canonical order of the NT, I have placed Jude and 2 Peter together in this study. Both contain a large amount of almost identical words and phrases. Both also maintain similar views of "the Way" and its opponents. Both were late in receiving recognition as NT books. What type of literary relationship exists between Jude and 2 Peter? What are their similarities and differences? Why was their authenticity questioned for so many centuries?

Jude's opening thesis is concerned with the salvation that he and his readers share; it exhorts readers to contend for the faith once for entrusted to the saints (v. 3). Although the polemical aspects of Jude reflect a concern for the justice of past wrongdoings, the thesis (vv. 3–4) and closing exhortations (vv. 20–23) underscore the need to intensify present adherence to common values. A dual feature of this kind of rhetoric is the praise of common virtues and the censure of characteristic vices (vv. 3–4). Readers of Jude are to build themselves up in the most holy faith, pray in the Holy Spirit, keep themselves in the love of God, to look forward to the mercy of the Lord Jesus Christ that leads to eternal life, and have mercy on those who waver (vv. 20–23; cf. Jas 5:19–20).

Second Peter extols the many blessings that God has bestowed on those that God called to partake of his glory, virtue, and divine nature (1:3–4). They are to add moral excellence to faith, with knowledge, self-control, endurance, and love. Those who confirm their call and election in this way will receive a rich welcome in the everlasting kingdom of the Lord (1:4–10). Like Jude, 2 Peter seeks to intensify adherence to common values; but 2 Peter also has the appearance of a last testament (in epistolary form). Specific examples of this form of rhetoric are the farewell address of Jesus in John 13:31—17:26, and Paul's farewell speech in Acts 20:17-38.

The call to remember in 2 Peter (1:12-13,15; 3:1) appears in other farewell speeches (e.g., John 14:26; 2 Tim 1:3, 5) and forms of display rhetoric (e.g., Rom 15:14-15; Jude 17). The censure of opponents (2 Peter), as mentioned in Jude, is the negative counterpart of praising common values. The autobiographical allusions (1:12-18), typical of farewell addresses (Acts 20; John 13-17; 2 Tim), also provide narrative background for the thesis (1:12-15).

A final observation regarding the relationship of Jude and 2 Peter will be noted. Concerning Hebrew history, Jude ignores chronological order (wilderness wandering, fallen angels, Sodom and Gomorrah, Cain, Balaam, Korah), whereas 2 Peter carefully observes the events as they appear in biblical sequence (fallen angels, flood, Sodom and Gomorrah, Balaam), and omits some characters found in Jude (Cain, Korah). Although Jude freely draws illustrations from 1 Enoch 60:8 (Jude 14) and the Assumption/Testament of Moses (Jude 9), 2 Peter seems to maintain a stricter view of Scripture and omits these popular but "apocryphal" references even at the expense of obscuring the meaning of the passage! Is the author of 2 Peter using Jude as a source and improving on it for his own purposes?

The order of the Johannine letters in the NT is probably based upon their size. Like the Pauline writings which begin with Romans (the longest) and end with Philemon (the shortest), so also are the Johannine letters arranged: 1 John (the longest), next 2 John (245 words); then 3 John (219 words). Other reasons for favoring the traditional sequence can be substantiated. Although 2 and 3 John are chronologically close, because of their similar epistolary features (opening, closing, similar travel plans), some clues hint at a 2 John–3 John sequence. The actions of Diotrephes (3 John 9-10) suggest a reaction to the secession (leaving the church) in 1 and 2 John. Third John 9 ("I have written something to the church") may be referring to 2 John.

Similar contents with analogous denouncements of similar adversaries (1 John 2:18, 22; 4:1-3; 2 John 7, 9) suggest that 1 and 2 John were written about the same time; however, the opponents are denounced at great length in 1 John and only briefly in 2 John. Perhaps the false teachers had not yet arrived at the community of 2 John, whereas in 1 John they are already present. Some have suggested that the instruction to exclude false teachers in 2 John 10–11 provoked the secession described in 1 John 2:19. Yet these differences may stem from geography, rather than a chronological interval. The danger presented by the secessionist teachers may not have reached the outlying Johannine church addressed in 2 John.

The author of 1 John seems to live close to his addressees, whereas in 2 John he appears more distant (12b). If the author of 1 John belongs to the central locale of Johannine churches, and the addressees of 2 and 3 John are in the outlying churches, this situation could substantiate our suggested sequence of 1, 2, and 3 John. Either 2 John served as a circulating cover letter for 1 John, which has no address information or 3 John, perhaps carried by Demetrius (12). The author of 3 John commends Gaius to receive his missionaries, and opposes Diotrephes, who has refused any hospitality (3 John 9–10). Both 2 and 3 John are addressed to specific audiences and *not* to the church "catholic" (cf. 1 Pet 1:1).

Was the author of the Johannine letters also the author of the Fourth Gospel? The numerous similarities in content and structure have likened both 1 John and the Gospel of John to Luke and Acts, 1 and 2 Thessalonians, or Colossians and Ephesians. Extensive lists of parallels can also be drawn up between the Johannine letters (mostly 1 John) and the Fourth Gospel (e.g., "word," "life," "truth," "in the flesh," union of Father and Son, "joy," light and darkness, abiding in God/Christ, "new commandment," "born of God," "love one another").

With what literary categories do we equate the Johannine letters? The writings of 2 and 3 John share most of the characteristics of ancient letters (cf. Philemon) whereas 1 John does not. The many parallels noted above suggest that 1 John is an exposition of the Fourth Gospel to refute the secessionists (in 1 John) who also revered the Gospel. Certain books of the Dead Sea Scrolls called *pesharim* ("commentaries") are midrashic expositions of biblical books (e.g., Habbakkuk, Nahum, Isaiah). They read the biblical prophecies as referring to the last days in which the community finds itself living. Except for only a few *pesharim* (e.g., Kittim as Gentile oppressors, Wicked Priest, Man of Lies), most lack the polemics of 1 John, and an apocalyptic focus is lacking in 1 John. A commentary on John by the Valentinian gnostic called Heracleon and the gnostic Gospel of Truth may serve as parallels because both seek to update and apply the Fourth Gospel to their own situation, but the author of 1 John is not as speculative or mythological as the gnostics. We might also suggest as

INTRODUCTION

examples of this type of genre, Ephesians, which makes use of Colossians, or even 2 Peter, which utilizes Jude for polemical and hortatory reasons. Ephesians, however, lacks the polemics, and 2 Peter the homiletical exhortations, of 1 John.

The ancient book of Revelation, with its complex and bizarre imagery (e.g., a monstrous red dragon, a seven-headed beast, cosmic warfare) has been a source of fascination and perplexity for almost two millennia. What type of literature is the book of Revelation? How do we interpret its bizarre visions and dire warnings? Most who read Revelation are either impressed or confounded by the book's composite nature. It has many diverse forms found in the Gospels, Acts, and early letters from Christ-followers. Revelation also shows more dependency on the Scriptures (OT) for its images and phraseology than any other NT book. Numerous allusions to the Hebrew prophetic writings and the apocalyptic book of Daniel also appear. In comparisons with early NT letters, Revelation is enveloped by a letter form and contains seven letters to churches in Asia Minor. Like the early NT letters, Revelation includes hymns ("odes," Rev 5:9; 15:3), creeds, catechetical material, and ethical exhortation.

One noteworthy technique used to achieve this interwoven texture of the book is that of numbers and numerical structures. The book has two scroll visions (Rev 5; 10) and four septets, or cycles of seven (seven letters, 2:1—3:22; seven seals, 4:1—8:1; seven trumpets, 8:2—9:21; 11:15–19; seven bowls, 15:1 with 15:5—16:21). The three plague septets are related to each other as prelude, crescendo, and climax, whereas the letter septet points forward to the visions of eschatological salvation.

A common stock of symbols and images is employed throughout the book. For example, readers must see the image of the throne in connection with other expressions and symbols of kingship in order to grasp its full-impact symbolic colors—e.g., purple as royalty or luxury. See also other symbolic colors (e.g., black as death, white as joy or victory, red as slaughter or war, gold as divine splendor) as well as symbolic numerals (e.g., seven for perfection or completeness, twelve for the twelve tribes or the people of God, three and a half years as an interval of persecution, two as a number for witnesses, olive trees, and lampstands). Revelation also contrasts the beast and the Lamb, the great harlot and the woman of chapter 12.

The book does not appear to follow any chronological or linear order. The literary techniques and structure of Revelation have some similarities with Greek drama (e.g., a prologue; plot: complication, *crisis*, denouement; choruses; epilogue). Following these insights and detecting a structure called chiasm or inverted parallelism (represented by this scheme: A B C D D' C' B' A')—a structure found elsewhere in the NT (e.g., in John 16:28; Rom 2:6–11; 2 Cor 10–13) as well as in the OT and non-Judean writings—a case can be made for outlining the book of Revelation in this chiastic manner (although several different attempts to do this have been made).

The affliction faced or anticipated by the author and his readers might be, e.g., local persecution, poverty, famine, or political unrest. We have no evidence of an official and empire-wide persecution of Christ-followers under Domitian (81–96 CE). Whatever the situation, the author is certain that compromise with Rome's imperial culture is not to be tolerated (Rev 2:13; 13:15–16).

Despite the words of comfort and hope for the faithful, Revelation does not refrain from using vengeful language (19:20–21; 20:10, 13–15; 21:8) and some "misogynist stereotyping" (2:20–23; 17:15–17) typical of the very imperial order it opposes. Much of the language condemning spiritual adultery as idolatry, however, is borrowed from Israel's prophetic tradition (e.g., Isa 57:3; Jer 3:6–25; Ezek 16:32–43). The vengeful language is also nuanced, because the symbol of the conquering lion is replaced by the Lamb who was slain (Rev 5:5–14; 17:14). Finally, the language of misogyny is balanced (somewhat) by more positive female imagery: the woman (cf., daughter of Zion, Zeph 3:14), who, despite the dragon's opposition, gives birth (Jer 4:31) to the messiah (Rev 12:5; Ps 2:7), and both woman and child are under God's protective care (Rev 12:13–17; Exod 19:4). In contrast to Babylon, mother of prostitutes (17:1–6), the New Jerusalem is presented as a bride clothed in the fine linen of righteous deeds (19:7–8; 21:9; Isa 61:10; Ezek 16:9–13).

As I mentioned earlier, the book of Revelation does contain hope, especially the hope of Christ's return (22:12, 20). This "yet-to-come" hope makes living in the now more fulfilling and purposeful, because the present Lord of the church is the coming Lord of the universe.

In the chapters that follow this one, attention will be given to some of the questions raised in this overview. Special focus will be on canonical recognition (or the lack of it), authorship, date, historical and social context, audience, genre, rhetorical style, structure, and problematic texts or related issues. Join me in a learning adventure that has intrigued and inspired readers for almost two millennia!

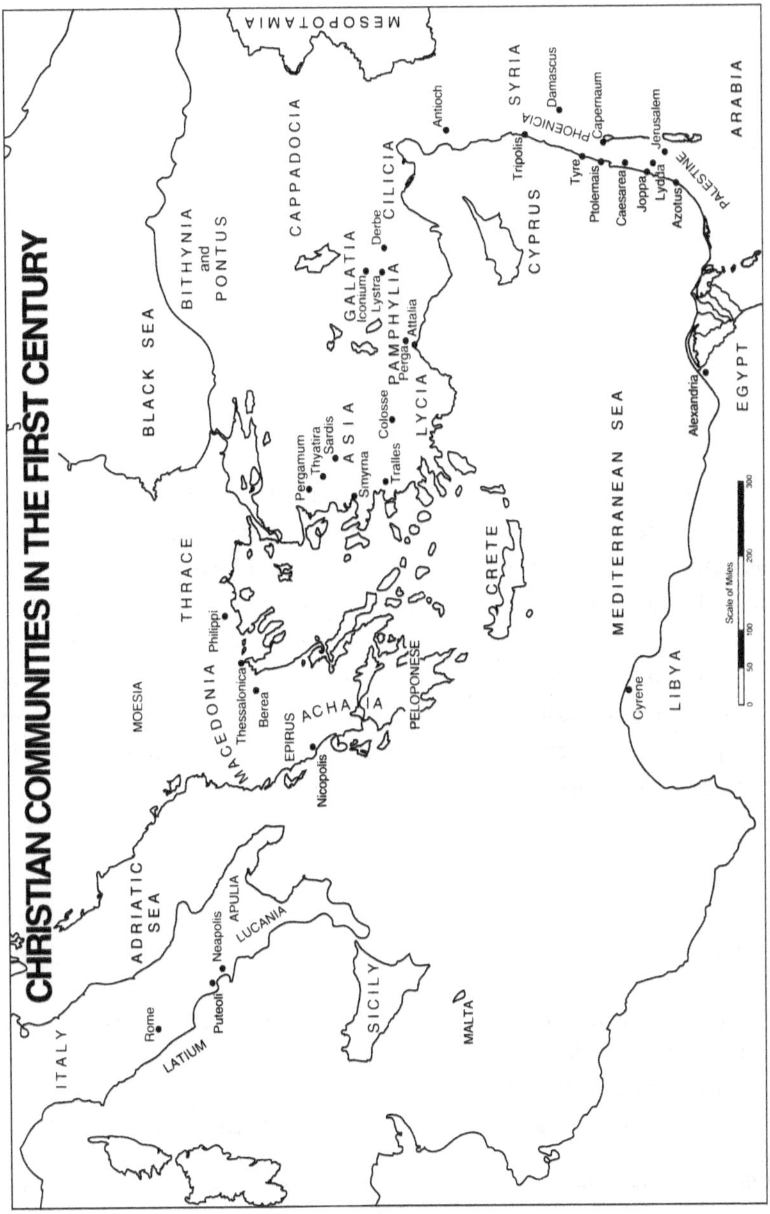

INTRODUCTION

Map A: Communities of Christ-followers in the first century.

1

Hebrews

Introduction

IT HAS BECOME FASHIONABLE to characterize Hebrews by its own description of Melchizedek, "without father or mother or genealogy" (7:3), because there is so much doubt about who wrote it, who received it, and when.[1] The early theologian Origen tersely summed up the authorship question with the statement: "only God knows who wrote this epistle."[2] Even the literary form is a mystery since it begins like a treatise, proceeds like a sermon, and closes like a letter. Let us now examine the following topics: genre, rhetorical structure, faith and worship contexts, authorship, place of composition, audience, destination, and date.[3]

---

1. The statement, originally attributed to Franz Overbeck (1875), is from Brown and Meier, *Antioch and Rome*, 139. See also Horton, *Melchizedek Tradition*.

2. Cited in Eusebius, *Hist. eccl.* 6.25.14.

3. For commentaries and other studies, see Attridge, *Epistle to the Hebrews*; Bateman, *Early Jewish Hermeutic and Hebrews 1:5–13*; Bauckham, et al., *Hebrews and Christian Theology*; Bauckham, et al., *Cloud of Witnesses*; Lane, *Hebrews 1–8*; Lane, *Hebrews 9–13*; Cockerill, *Epistle to the Hebrews*; DeSilva, *Despising Shame*; DeSilva, *Perseverance in Gratitude*; Hagner, *Hebrews*; Johnson, *Hebrews*; Käsemann, *Wandering People of God*; C. R. Koester, *Hebrews*; Koester, *Dwelling of God*; McKnight and Church, *Hebrews–James*; Montefiore, *Hebrews*; O'Brien, *Letter to the Hebrews*; Scholer, *Proleptic Priests*; Smith, *Hebrews*.

HEBREWS

The Genre[4]

As do John's Gospel and 1 John, Hebrews opens with a majestic prose introduction of the divine Son of God (1:1-4).[5] It proceeds with further expositions of doctrinal themes (in indirect discourse: 1:5-14; 2:5—3:6; 5:1-10; 7:1—10:18; 11:1-40; 12:18-24; 13:8,10-12), that are interchanged with practical exhortations (in direct discourse: 2:1-4; 3:7—4:16 [14:1-16 mixed]; 5:11—6:20; 10: 19-39; 12:1-17; 13:1-23 [13:7-21 mixed]). It then concludes as an early NT letter: paraenesis (exhortation and admonition, 13:1-19), closing prayer and doxology (vv. 20-21), postscript with a "personal" word (v. 22), brief travelogue (v. 23), final greeting (v. 24), and benediction (v. 25).[6]

Despite the likelihood that Hebrews was put into written form for circulation among the author's readers (e.g., 13:12, "I have written to you"), the work lacks too many epistolary features to be classed as a letter. There is no letter opening, no sender identified, no addressee designated (the title "to the Hebrews" was no later than 200 CE), and the epistolary closing is a postscript.

Almost all ancient writings were intended to be read aloud;[7] Hebrews is explicit on this point. It seems to be written as a spoken address, probably as a sermon or collection of sermons. First, the author seems to identify his document as a "word of exhortation" (*paraklēsis*, 13:22; cf. 6:18; 12:5). In Acts, a homily (or sermon) given in a synagogue after the reading of Scripture is identified as a "word of exhortation" (*paraklēsis*, Acts 13:15; cf. 15:31).[8] See also the related usage of the Greek verb,

---

4. "Genre" is the French word for the Latin *genus* (from Greek *genos*) used in English as a technical term in scientific classification and sometimes translated with the gloss "species." So literary genre is a species of literature, having characteristics in common with other literary works with which it can then be understood as "kin." But the difficulty is just what kinds of characteristics a species of literature must have to be "kin" to another. Almost every literary work is composed of numerous genres and literary forms in combination. (See also p. 142n4 of this book). Nevertheless, it is helpful to know "what kind of fruit we are picking" and "in whose orchard we are picking it."

5. Bauckham, "On the Divinity of Christ in the Epistle to the Hebrews"; and also J. Webster, "One Who Is Son," 69-94.

6. The First Letter of Peter ends in a similar manner: paraenesis (5:6-10), doxology (v. 11), postscript with personal comments (v. 12), and final greeting (vv. 13-14).

7. See Aune, *Literary Environment*, 158-61, 192, 197; Gamble, *Books and Readers*, 203-8, 321-22.

8. Even if Acts 13:15 reflects the situation of the narrator instead of the situation of the audience (i.e., the actual preaching situation), it still is a contemporary parallel

parakaleō (Heb 3:13; 10:25; 13:19,22).⁹ Second, allusions to speaking and hearing in Hebrews support its oratorical nature. Here are examples: "about this matter we have much to say that is hard to explain since you have become dull of hearing" (5:11); "though we speak this" (6:9); "now the main point in what we are saying is this" (8:1; cf. 2:1,5; 9:5; 11:32). All these statements exemplify direct address between the speaker and his audience.

A third clue about the hortatory nature of Hebrews is that it contains many practical exhortations that are typical of early homilies by Judeans and Christ-followers (on my nomenclature, see pp. 19n30, 166, 169). In the Greek text they are distinctly marked by the use of the first-person-plural hortatory subjunctive, "let us" (4:1, 11, 14, 16; 6:1; 10:22, 23, 24; 12:1, 28; 13:13, 15). Also, these practical exhortations are combined with doctrinal expositions that are based on passages from the Hebrew Scriptures (e.g., Heb 2:1–9/Ps 8:4–6; Heb 3:7—4:3/Ps 95; Heb 7/Gen 14 and Ps 110; Heb 8/Jer 31:31–34).

The combinations in Hebrews of doctrinal exposition of Scripture (e.g., 1:5–14; 4:14—5:10; 8:1—10:18) with practical exhortation (2:1–4; 5:11—6:20; 10:19–25) is characteristic of early homilies by Judeans and Christ-followers in late antiquity. This practice occurs in a variety of Judean hortatory literature: e.g., T. 12 Patr.; the introduction to Wis 1–5; Tob 4; the opening exhortations in the Damascus Document of Qumran, CD 1–8. It is not characteristic only of the speeches in Acts (e.g., Acts 2:14–36; 3:12–26; 7:2–53; 10:34–43; 13:15–43; 17:22–31) but also of early homilies by Christ-followers (e.g., 1 Pet, 2 Clem., Letter to Diognetus 11–12).¹⁰

Therefore, because of the hortatory clues in the text, Hebrews should be classed with early sermons like 1 Peter, 2 Clement, Diognetus 11–12, and the kerygmatic speeches of Acts. There are five reasons for this classification. (1) All make use of the Israelite Scriptures to expound their doctrines. (2) Each combines doctrinal exposition derived from

---

to Heb 13:22. This comment assumes that the author of Hebrews wrote in the late first century, as did the author of Luke-Acts (see my discussion of "The Date" on pp. 37–38 of this chapter). On Hebrews as a hortatory sermon, see Lane, *Hebrews 1–8*, lxx–lxxi; O'Brien, *Hebrews*, 20–22.

9. On the similar usage of the verb *parakaleō*, see: Acts 2:40; 11:23; 14:22; 15:32; 20:2; Rom 15:30; 16:7; 1 Cor 1:10; BDAG 764–66.

10. For other primary sources (e.g., Epictetus) and discussion on *protreptic* (persuasive) speech and paraenesis (exhortation), see Elliott and Reasoner, *Documents and Images*, 68–74. See also Malherbe, *Cynic Epistles*.

the Scriptures with practical exhortations. (3) Each has the deliberative rhetorical function to persuade or dissuade the listeners/readers.[11] (4) All presuppose an oratorical setting (real or fictional) between the speaker and his audience.[12] (5) All are concerned with the rhetorical effects of the message upon the intended audience.

The classification of Hebrews as an early sermon, however (e.g., 3:1—4:13; 8:1—10:18; 12:1–13), does not undervalue the diverse influences that produced this hortatory genre. The sections of biblical exposition have affinities with both rabbinic argumentation[13] and the pesher exegesis of Qumran.[14] Furthermore, Judean missionary propaganda (e.g., Philo, Sib. Or., Aristob.)[15] and Hellenistic rhetoric (e.g., Aristotle, Cynic-Stoic dialogues) both may have influenced it. Finally, hymns and

---

11. Information on deliberative (symbouleutic) rhetoric can be found in Aristotle, *Rhetorica*; Cicero, *de Inventione*; Quintilian, *Institutia Oratia*. Examples of deliberative rhetoric are *The Third Philippic* of Demosthenes (341 BCE), where the famous statesman advises the Athenian assembly to unite with other Greek city-states in opposition to Philip of Macedon. Isocrates, in his *On Peace* (355 BCE), proposes before the political assembly of Athens a policy of lasting peace between Athens and her neighbors; and there are responses by teachers (in letter form) to questions asked by their students: Epicurus, Letter II, *To Pythocles*; and Plutarch, *On the Tranquility of the Mind* (in *Moralia* 1012B1030C). See 1 Cor 1–8; 10–16; 2 Cor 8–9; Eph 4–6; James. See also Puskas, "Apostolic Advice." Texts like 1 Cor 9 and Acts 7 are forms of judicial rhetoric, e.g., indicting critics or opponents on issues of the past. See discussion in Lane, *Hebrews 1–8*, lxxv–lxxx; Aune, *Literature and Rhetoric*, 418–25; and Aune, *Literary Environment*, 158–61, 197–99.

12. By "fictional" we mean that certain speeches and their settings, like those in Acts, are primarily the work of the author, not the original speaker.

13. For e.g., the rabbinic inference from minor to major (*qal wahomer* "light and heavy") is used in Heb 9:14; 12:9, 25 (cf. Luke 11: 13; 12:28) and the catchword linkage of similar words between two texts (*gezeira sheva* "comparison of equals") in Heb 4:3–4, 10 (Israel's "rest" and God's "Sabbath"). These are two examples of the rabbinic middoth ("rules"), the original seven may date back to Hillel (first century BCE), see Bakhos, "Midrash, Midrashim," in *Early Judaism* (2010), 944–49. For other examples in Hebrews, see Bateman, *Charts on the Book of Hebrews*, 163–66.

14. Pesher (Heb., "interpretation, commentary," cf. Eccl 8:1) is sometimes called "midrash pesher" (Vermes) to convey the idea of a nonliteral biblical interpretation, see Aune, "Pesharim," in Aune, *Literature and Rhetoric*, 347–50; Longenecker prefers a separate treatment of rabbinic midrash and Qumran pesher (although a NT book could employ both). See Longenecker, *Biblical Exegesis*, 18–30, on Hebrews and OT, see ibid., 140–65.

15. For discussion of Philo, see later in this chapter, "Judean Tradition of Alexandria" (pp. 21–23). An excellent introduction and translation of the *Sibylline Oracles* is found in Charlesworth, *OTP*, 1:317–472. Some of the teachings of Aristobulus, the Judean teacher of Ptolemy (2 Macc 1: 10), are mentioned in Eusebius *Praep. Ev.* vii. 14; xiii. 12.

kerygma concerning Jesus, the Greek OT (e.g., Genesis, Deuteronomy, Pss 2; 8; 22; 110; Isaiah; Jer 31), and Near Eastern wisdom traditions also determined the hortatory genre among Christ-followers.

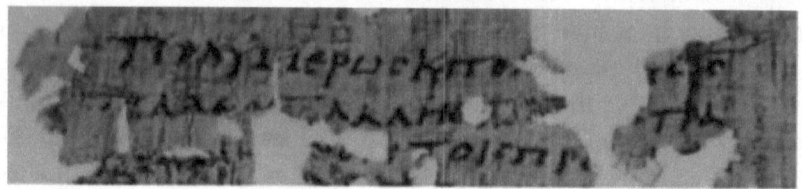

Figure 1: Papyrus 12, Hebrews 1:1 (third century)

The Rhetorical Function

Now that Hebrews has been identified as a NT homily, we will consider its rhetorical function. The use of rhetoric and its intended effect on the audience were important concerns in homilies and speeches. What type of rhetoric was employed? Although much of the doctrinal sections of Hebrews contain encomia, praising Christ or the virtues of famous people, the exhortations give it a deliberative function: to persuade its readers in the faith and dissuade them from unacceptable views and practices.[16] As 1 Cor 7–8 and 2 Cor 8–9 do, so Hebrews focuses on expedient courses of action for the future, although praiseworthy virtues in the present (encomium) are included. The types of rhetoric employed in Hebrews will be helpful in determining its function and purpose, as well as its structure. In my outline of the rhetorical structure,[17] attention will be given to both the doctrinal prose sections and the hortatory discourses (which often overlap).

Related to paraenetic (hortatory) language, but perhaps more forceful or intentional, is protreptic rhetoric, promoting a *particular course* of action (Gk. *protreptein*, "to urge, impel"). In a speech attributed to the

---

16. Johnson, *Hebrews*, 33–34, argues that Hebrews is deliberative rhetoric; so also O'Brien, *Letter to the Hebrews*, 20–22; Small, *Characterization of Jesus in Hebrews*, 105. Attridge favors epideictic or demonstrative rhetoric with his highlighting of the supremacy of Christ and the encomium of the faithful (Heb 11) punctuated by hortatory appeals, in his *Hebrews*, 17–27. According to C. R. Koester, *Hebrews*, 82, those readers who are committed to Christ will find Hebrews epideictic, but for those who are drifting away from the faith, it is deliberative; see also C. R. Koester, "Hebrews, Rhetoric, and the Future of Humanity," 100.

17. For alternative outlines of Hebrews, see Cockerill, *Epistle to the Hebrews*, 79–81; McKnight and Church, *Hebrews–James*, 25; and O'Brien, *Letter to the Hebrews*, 22–34.

Stoic Epictetus (first–second century CE), he contrasts it with those who would flatter people rather than to recommend for them the *right* way to live (Arrian, *Epict. Diss.* 3.23). A good Cynic is to teach and live by those sober realities of life (Dio Chrysostom, *Or.* 77/78.38; Crates, *Letter* 35).[18] In a similar manner, Hebrews reminds his readers to heed and obey the oracles of God (2:1–4; 3:7–15; 4:1–13), hold fast to their confession with boldness (4:14–16; 10:19–25, 35–39), and grow/progress in the faith together (5:11—6:8; 12:1—13:19).

The Rhetorical Structure of Hebrews

I. Proem: Christ as a superior mediator   1:1—4:16
   A. Doctrine
      1. A final revelation of God[19]   1:1–4
      2. Superior to the angels   1:5—2:18
         Announced with OT support[20] (1:5–14)
         Hortatory application (2:1–4)
         Appeal to necessity of correct action (2:3a)
         First *prolepsis*[21] on a faithful high priest (2:17)
      3. Superior to Moses   3:1–6
         Second *prolepsis* on Jesus the high priest (3:1)
   B. Ethical exhortations on heeding God's voice
      and entering his heavenly rest   3:7—4:16
      Exposition of Psalm 95 (3:7–11, 15)
      Rhetorical questions (3:16–18)
      Third *prolepsis* on a great high priest (4:14–15)

---

18. Examples of the protreptic style (mentioned above) are found in Elliott and Reasoner, *Documents and Images*, 70–73. For discussion, see Stowers, *Letter Writing in Greco-Roman Antiquity*, 91–92.

19. For Heb 1:1–4 as a chiasm (A B C D C' B' A') see O'Brien, *Letter to the Hebrews*, 45–47. Hebrews 1:1 also employs a fivefold alliteration with *polumerōs* ("various portions") *polutropōs* ("various ways") *palai . . . tois patrasin en tois prophētais*, ibid., 49n30. See Aune, *Literature and Rhetoric*, 33; Lanham, *Handlist of Rhetorical Terms*, 9–10. See also my discussion of chiasm in 1 John and Revelation (pp. 133–34, 158–60).

20. Vanhoye, *Different Priest*, 78, finds in Heb 1:11–12 a chiasm of "concentric symmetry" (A B C D C' B' A').

21. The word *prolepsis* (Gk. "taking beforehand") is used here to denote a statement which anticipates some objection or precedes further clarification and amplification.

II. Diegesis (narration of the case):
    The superior high priesthood of Christ .... 5:1—6:20
    A. Doctrine: Christ & the qualifications of the priesthood 5:1–10
        First *prolepsis* on Melchizedek (v. 10)
        Topics to be developed later (5:11) in chs. 7–10
    B. Exhortations on maturity (5:12—6:3), apostasy (6:4–8),
        service (vv. 9–12), and hope (vv. 13–20) .... 5:12—6:20
        First *prolepsis* on heroes of faith (6:13–18; cf. ch. 11)
        Second *prolepsis* of Melchizedek (v. 20)

III. *Apodeixis* or demonstration of evidence concerning
    Christ's superiority over the Levitical system .... 7:1—10:18
    (devlopment of topics)
    A. On the priesthood of Melchizedek: A superior order
        (Ps 110 references in Heb 7:3, 11, 17, 21)[22] 7:1–28
        1. It continues for ever and is superior to that
            of the Levites 3–11
        2. It is not based on physical descent,
            since Christ also belongs to this order 12–22
        3. Christ, who offered the ultimate sacrifice for sin,
            holds this office permanently 23–28
    B. Christ serves as high priest of the heavenly sanctuary
        and is the mediator of the new covenant 8:1–13
    C. The worship conducted in the wilderness tent was
        imperfect and temporary 9:1–10
    D. Christ as high priest and mediator of the new covenant
        offered himself as the eternal sacrifice for sin .... 9:11—10:18
        1. Thesis: He performed a final sacrifice in a more
            perfect tent for eternal redemption (9:11–12),
            and his death ratifies the new covenant (vv. 15–22)[23] ..9:11–22

---

22. Hay, *Glory at the Right Hand*, 34–51, 164–66; Hurtado, *Lord Jesus Christ*, 501–2.

23. Employed here (9:13–14) is the Judean comparsion of lesser to greater (*qal wa-homer*): "how much more the blood of Christ"; see also 10:28–30 ("how much worse the punishment"). Also, in Heb 9:14, "the blood" is a metonymy for both physical death and the life-giving atoning sacrifice of Jesus. On the blood of Christ signifying his "death" that brings "life," see Kuma, *Centrality of Αἷμα (Blood) in Hebrews*. See also Christian and Jewish discussion on (a) supersessionism (i.e., replacement theology), (b) new or renewed covenant, and (c) the Levitical cult, in Bauckham, *Epistle to the Hebrews and Christian Theology*, 151–225. On Jer 31 and Ezek 36 conveying a *new* covenant, not a renewed one, see Leene, *Newness in Old Testament Prophecy*, ch. 3.

2. Amplification of thesis (in 9:11–22) 9:23—10:18

IV. Epilogue (peroration): Summary of arguments 10:19—13:21
   A. First recapitulation of exhortations (also anticipates
      10:32—12:17) (*pistis*) 10:19–32
      1. We have direct access through
         Jesus the high priest (cf. 4:14–16; 6:12) 19–22
      2. Let us hold fast to our confession (cf. 3:6; 4:14, 16) 23
      3. The apocalyptic dangers of apostasy (cf. 6:1–6) 26–31
   B. Encomium of faith in the context of community
      affliction and hortatory applications 10:32—12:17
      1. Prelude to encomium: exhortations to a
         community formerly afflicted 10:32–38
      2. Doctrine: encomium on the virtues
         of those who have faith (*pistei*)[24] 11:1–40
      3. Exhortations derived from encomium on faith 12:1–17
   C. Second recapitulation of exhortations 12:18—13:17
      1. Direct access through Jesus (cf. 4:14–16; 10:19–22) 12:18–24
      2. The apocalyptic dangers of apostasy
         (cf. 6:1–6; 10:26–31); 12:25–29
      3. Service and compassion
         (cf. 6:10; 10:24, 34) 13:1–3, 16
      4. Respect your leaders/teachers (cf. 5:12) 13:7, 17
      5. Do not be misled by human regulations (cf. 9:9–10) 9
      6. We seek a heavenly city (11:10, 16; 12:22) 14
      7. Offer spiritual sacrifices (cf. 10:8–10)[25] 15–16
   D. Ethos: author appeals to his own conscientious and
      honorable behavior 18–19
   E. Prayer and Doxology 20–21
   F. Epistolary Postscript 22–25

---

24. The repeated use of *pistei* ("by faith") introducing 18 exempla in Heb 11:3–17 is a good example of anaphora or "like sentence beginnings" Aune, *Literature and Rhetoric*, 34. See also Rhee, "Chiasm and the Concept of Faith."

25. Given the focus on ritual sacrifice in Hebrews, the phrase "sacrifice of praise" is unusual as is "confession" (*homologein*) being the fruit of our lips, 13:15 (cf. Hos 14:2). The literary device used here is called catachresis (Gk. "misuse, misapplication"), one word changed for another that is *remotely* connected with it (e.g., "drink the pure blood of the grape," Deut 32:14; "death is swallowed up in victory," 1 Cor 15:54; cf. "nations drink of the wine of wrath of her fornication," Rev 14:8; 18:3). See Bullinger, *Figures of Speech*, 674–80; Lanham, *Handlist of Rhetorical Terms*, 31.

Final appeal to listen willingly to this "word of
exhortation" (13:23; cf. 3:13)

The proem introduces readers to Jesus Christ, God's final revelation who is superior (*kreittōn*)[26] both to the angels (intermediaries between God and humanity) and Moses (leader of God's people). Next, readers are introduced to Jesus Christ the high priest (to be discussed in the diegesis and apodeixis). Then readers are exhorted to heed God's word and to seek entry into God's heavenly rest.

The diegesis (narration of the case) first develops the doctrine of Christ's priesthood by an analogy with Aaron (5:4). Numerous exhortations are also presented here (5:12—6:20) that will be repeated later in the book (10:19-39; 12:18—13:17). Finally, statements are made concerning Melchizedek (5: 10; 6:20; cf. Gen 14:18; Ps 110:4), anticipating further discussion (ch. 7). Melchizedek provides a priestly order for Christ superior (*kreittōn*) to the Levitical priesthood. The Qumran Melchizedek Document (11Q13 or 11QMelch, first century BCE), a pesher on OT texts (Lev 25:13; Ps 82:1-2; Isa 52:7), presents Melchizedek as a heavenly redeemer who will appear to atone for the sons of light (11Q13, II.7-11).[27]

The apodeixis displays the proofs concerning Christ's superiority over the Levitical system (7:1—10:18). It is the book's longest doctrinal section. Hebrews 9:11-22 introduces topics expounded in more detail immediately after this pericope (i.e., 9:23—10:18). The so-called supersessionism of Hebrews (cf. 1 Clem., Barn., Ign., Justin) reflects a replacement of the Levitical cult in a post–70 CE reality.[28]

The epilogue consists of recapitulations of earlier exhortations (cf. 10:19-32; 12:18—13:17); an encomium on the virtues of the faithful (ch. 11) in the context of the community's afflictions (10:32-39) and with its

---

26. The Greek *kreittōn* pertains to being of "high status, more prominent, higher in rank, preferable, better." At least 12 of 19 total occurrences in NT are in Hebrews (e.g., 1:4; 6:9; 7:7, 19, 22; 8:6; 9:23; 10:34; 11:16,35, 40; 12:24), BDAG, 566. The heightening effect of this lesser-to-greater inference (Heb. *qal wahomer*), showing that the antitype (Christ) is much greater than the type (Aaron or Moses), is a defining characteristic of typology, see Goppelt, *Typos*, 199, 202; on Hebrews see 161-78.

27. Horton, "Melchizedek," in *NIDB* 4:28-29; Horton, *Melchizedek Tradition*.

28. See Bauckham et al., eds., *Epistle to the Hebrews and Christian Theology*, 151-225; A. C. Mitchell, after examining Heb 7:1-12; 8:7-13; 10:1-10, maintains that the author of Hebrews was not promoting supersessionism, in Mitchell, "'A Sacrifice of Praise': Does Hebrews Promote Supersessionism?"

accompanying exhortations (12:1–17);[29] the author's appeal to his own character as a Christ-follower (12:18–19); and a prayer with a doxology (vv. 20–21). Then, it ends with an epistolary postscript (vv. 22–25).

The special attention given in the epilogue to the exhortations, by means of recapitulation and elaboration, confirms the deliberative function of the book. Hebrews seeks to persuade its readers through doctrinal and scriptural exposition to continue in the faith, and to dissuade them from wavering in their beliefs (e.g., with an encomium of faith), as a result of their doubts, discouragements, and exposure to false teachings.

Ethical and Doctrinal Alignment

An examination of the ethical and doctrinal alignment of Hebrews provides some helpful clues for understanding other questions relating to the book's content, authorship, and addressees. In this section we will look at the following aspects of the thought-world of Hebrews: the author's dependence on the Judean Scriptures in Greek (LXX); possible influences from Alexandrian-Judean writings, Qumran, Gnostic proclivities; and finally, the author's relationship to Greco-Judean messianism.[30]

---

29. Cockerill, *Hebrews*, 515, faults Rhee, "Chiasm and the Concept of Faith," for not interpreting ch. 11 in the broader context of Heb 10–12.

30. The Greek *Ioudaios*, often rendered "Jews," is best translated "Judeans," an ethnic group connected to the land of Judea (Gk., *Ioudaia*), Jerusalem, and its temple (BDAG, 478). It also applies to Judeans of Galilee or those Greco-Judeans of the diaspora ("dispersed" outside of Judea, Josephus, *Apion* 2.38–39). Christ-followers of the first two centuries were either Judean or Gentile followers of Jesus the Messiah. Both groups considered themselves to be Hebrews or members of the Israelite faith (an insider self-designation). Both Philo (*Prob.* 175–91) and Josephus (*War* 2.119, 166; *Ant.* 18.11–12) describe certain subsets of the Judeans (e.g., Essenes, Pharisees) as philosophical groups. Regarding Gk., *Christianismos* ("Christianism") as separate from *Ioudaismos*, Ignatius (ca. 107 CE) begins to make this distinction (*Magn.* 10.1,3; *Phld.* 6.1; *Christianos*, Rom.3.3), whereas Tertullian (ca. 200) advances "Christian" self-definition over against "Judaism" (*Marc.* 4.6,33; 5.4,6). See J. H. Elliott, "Jesus the Israelite Was neither a Jew nor a Christian: On Correcting Misleading Nomenclature"; S. Mason, "Jews, Judaeans, Judaizing, Judaism: Problems of Categorization in Ancient History."

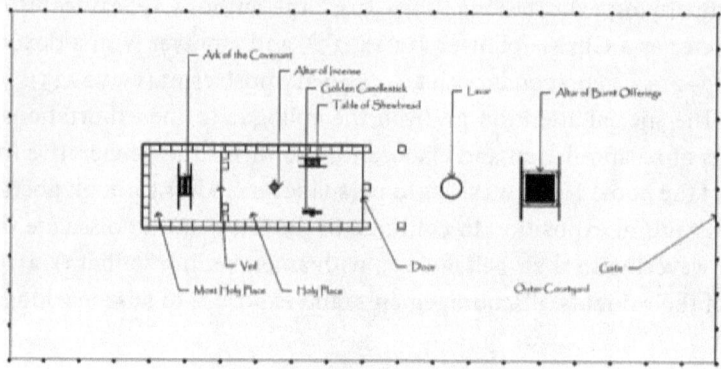

Figure 2: Tabernacle Schematic

The Judean Scriptures

No NT book, aside from Revelation, is so permeated with OT quotations, citations, allusions, and echoes as Hebrews. Along with the many allusions to and echoes of the Judean Scriptures, one study lists twenty quotations from the Pentateuch, 11 from the Prophets division, and 28 from the Writings (26 from the Pss including repetitions of preferred passages).[31] Favorite texts in Hebrews are Psalms 2 (kingship), 8 (crowned with glory) 95 (wilderness testing), 110 (kingship and Melchizedek reference), Proverbs 3 (the discipline of the Lord) and Jeremiah 31:31–34 (new covenant). Although the LXX was the primary text of the author, there are about six textual deviations due to either the author's own free renderings or his use of text versions no longer extant. These textual variants are also found in other NT books. Many of these texts are used elsewhere in the NT and may constitute a testimonia (cf. 4QTest; 4QFlor), an anthology of favorite OT texts circulated by the early church.[32]

According to Hebrews, the Judean Scriptures are replete with meaning and significance for Christ and his church. The OT prophecies ("oracles of the Lord," Heb 2:3) find their fulfillment in the time of Jesus and his people. Israel's life and worship are viewed as preparatory for

---

31. Bratcher, *Old Testament Quotations in the New Testament*, 57–67; for helpful discussion, see Guthrie, "Hebrews." Note: Hebrew Prophets division includes Joshua, Judges, Samuel, and Kings along with the Major and Minor Prophets. See also Moyise, *Later NT Writings and Scripture*, 81–110; Longenecker, *Biblical Exegesis*, 140–66; Guthrie, "Hebrews' Use of the Old Testament." See also my discussion of intertextuality in Revelation (p. 157).

32. Hodgson, "Testimony Hypothesis"; Bergsma, "Testimonia," 456–57; Albl, *And Scripture Cannot Be Broken*.

the coming of Christ. One could even assert that Christ, of whom the Scriptures testify, is viewed here as a resolution to the enigma of Israel's history, ritual, and ideals.[33] This approach is prevalent in the NT and early noncanonical works.

It has been observed that the use of the OT in Hebrews has similarities with rabbinic midrashic interpretation that seeks to penetrate the spirit of the Scriptures and employs rabbinc argumentation (e.g., *qal wahomer*, "lesser to greater") to expound and explicate this view.[34] The midrashic approach is not unlike, sensus plenior, coined by modern Catholic scholars to indicate the deeper (nonliteral) meaning intended by God, but not clearly intended by the human author, e.g., Isaiah, the Psalmist.[35] Two other ancient methods of OT interpretation, possibly used in Hebrews, will also be examined in discussion that follows: the allegorical interpretation of Philo of Alexandria and the pesher exegesis of the Dead Sea Scrolls of Qumran.

Judean Tradition of Alexandria

It has been argued that Hebrews reflects the Alexandrian school of "Judean Platonism" and has its closest parallels with Philo of Alexandria (ca. 20 BCE—50 CE).[36] Plato's dualistic view of the material world as only a shadow of the true realm of ideas was attractive to some Greek-speaking Judeans. Philo, for example, who was convinced that Judean tradition fulfilled all Hellenistic aspirations, interpreted the Scriptures allegorically to support this conviction. This form of interpretation perceived deeper, hidden meanings conveyed in the familiar biblical stories. Examples of this mystical exegesis include: Abraham's journey into unknown Canaan, which became an example of the soul's migration from human bondage (*Migr.*). Melchizedek, the priest of Salem (Gen 14), in Philo refers to reason, which rules with justice over the body and soul (*Alleg. Interp.*

---

33. Westcott, *Epistle to the Hebrews*, 493. For Hebrews, the OT texts are oracles of Christ that also testify of both him and his work (1:2; 2:3), Attridge, *Epistle to the Hebrews*, 23–25.

34. Midrash (from Heb. *darash* "seek, investigate," cf. Ps 119:10; 1 Sam 9:9; Deut 17:4), see Miller, "Midrash"; Longenecker, *Biblical Exegesis*, 18–24; Caird, "Exegetical Method of Hebrews." On *qal wahomer* or a minore ad majus (cf. Matt 7:11; Rom 11:12; Heb 9:13–14), see Soulen and Soulen, *Biblical Criticism*, 7.

35. For sensus plenior, see Soulen and Soulen, *Biblical Criticism*, 192.

36. Moffatt, *Epistle to the Hebrews*, xxx–iv; Spicq, *L'Epitre aux Hébreux*, 1:39–91. Note: Texts of Philo are from the Loeb Classical Library, 1929–53, ten volumes.

3.79-80). Egypt is the place of material bondage (*Agr.* 89). Moses was the perfect hero-king who revealed in himself the unwritten law behind the Torah (*Mos.* 1,2). Judean religion was revealed to Moses as the true mystery religion. The plans for building the wilderness tent were immaterial forms that Moses saw with the eyes of his soul (*Mos.* 2.73-74). All of these allegorical examples reflect Philo's dualistic views from Platonism.

Does not Hebrews reflect somewhat this allegorical interpretation from a Platonist standpoint?[37] Are not the human priest, sanctuary, and sacrifices of ancient Israel merely the "shadowy copy" of the reality manifested in Jesus Christ and his sacrificial death? Are not the author's analogies between shadow and reality (8:5; 10:1), the earthly and the heavenly (8:1-4; 9:23-24), the created and the uncreated (9: 11), the transitory and the enduring (7:23-24; 10:34; 13:14), obvious indicators of Platonic dualism? Do not the invisible heavenly future things (11:1, 16; 12:22; 13:14) constitute the true reality in Hebrews? Do not unusual etymological interpretations (e.g., "Melchizedek," 7:2) and stark metaphorical associations (e.g., "curtain" = "flesh," 10:20; also 3:6; 13:14) signify a form of exegesis like that of Philo? Besides reflecting a similar dualistic worldview and allegorical interpretation, both Hebrews and Philo make use of the LXX and share both common vocabulary (e.g., *athlēsis, dysermēneutos*) and topics (e.g., Melchizedek, wilderness tabernacle, faith, angels, Abraham).

Even though similarities are numerous, the differences are profound. First, the dualism in Hebrews is grounded in a two-ages scheme of redemptive history, i.e., the former age of the old covenant (Israel) and the new age of last days (messianic age). Comparisons between old Levitical worship and the work of Christ must be viewed in this framework. Second, because Hebrews maintains this scheme of salvation history, its exegesis presupposes a typological correspondence of persons and events in history. (For example, the mysterious and preeminent priesthood of Melchizedek is a type of Christ's office. Some correspondence of these two personages in history is presupposed [7:2-3].) Third, Hebrews uses the vocabulary and topics common to Philo in a different and independent manner. For example, Abraham's journey into Canaan is portrayed as a historical example of faith, not as the soul's migration from human bondage, as in Philo. Therefore, even though Hebrews and Philo may share a common heritage of Hellenistic Judean religion,

---

37. See Montefiore, *Hebrews*, 6-11, who favors this view; Williamson, *Philo and the Epistle to the Hebrews*, 11-81, 142-233, however, argues *against* it.

possibly Alexandrian, there are insufficient parallels to establish Hebrews as Philonic or Platonic.³⁸

It must be added, however, that Hebrews shares literary and thematic features with other works that probably originated from Alexandria, the home of Philo. For example, the "famous people of faith" chapter of Heb 11 has numerous parallels with 4 Macc 17 and Sir 44–49. Hebrews also shares features with the Wisdom of Solomon (e.g., wisdom motifs, blend of doctrine and exhortation, eschatology) and the Letter of Barnabas (by a Christ-follower; e.g., polemics against Judean legalism, use of typology, blend of doctrine and exhortation). None of these "Alexandrian" writings, however, is as Platonic in emphasis as Philo's works.

Figure 3: C. B. Puskas at the caves near Khirbet Qumran, where the Dead Sea Scrolls were discovered

The Qumran Community

Because of its apparent polemics against certain forms of Judean speculation and legalism, Hebrews, it has been suggested, was addressed to

---

38. The Greek terms in Heb 8:5; 9:23; 10:1, which sound Platonic (*hypodeigma, skia, antitypos*), can be translated by a number of less Platonic-sounding synonyms, see Hurst "How 'Platonic' Are Heb 8:5 and 9:23f.?" J. W. Thompson concedes that the author of Hebrews demonstrates no specific knowledge of Platonism and maintains a Judean eschatological perspective, but he shows that the author "employs Platonic assumptions" (as Philo had) for his own pastoral purposes, "What Has Middle Platonism to Do with Hebrews?"; the quotation is from 51–52.

former members of the Qumran community (Essene Christ-followers?).[39] Let us look at the following similarities between Hebrews and the Dead Sea Scrolls of Qumran: the method of biblical interpretation and four themes—purification, sacrifice, apostasy, and messianism.

In both its method of interpretation and the texts it employed, Hebrews has remarkable similarities to the Qumran writings. The biblical exegeses in both documents presuppose a life-situation in the last days of the messianic age when the veiled meanings of the OT prophecies would be fully understood. This form of pesher interpretation assumed that the OT prophecies spoke to the contemporary situation in an exclusive manner (e.g., Heb 8:8-13/CD 8.19-20; Heb 10:38-39/1QpHab 8.1-3). Furthermore, the same texts are used by both in this manner: e.g., Deut 29:16; 32; 2 Sam 7:14; Pss 95; 110; Jer 31:31-34; Hab 2:3-4.

Let us look at some of the common themes. Although the ceremonial washings criticized in Hebrews (6:1-2; 9:10) recall the teachings and practices of Qumran (1QS 3.4-6, 8-9; 4.20-21), these Essene "waters of purification" could only benefit those of "an upright and humble spirit." Such qualifications would not be condemned in Hebrews. Since the Qumran community did not participate in the ritual sacrifices of the Jerusalem temple, it advocated the offering of "spiritual sacrifices" to God (Heb 13:15-16/1QS 9.3-5). Just as Hebrews does (6:4-6; 10:26-27), so the Qumran community offered little hope of forgiveness for the apostates (1QS 2.13-14). Finally, the preeminence of Christ as apostle and high priest (Heb 3:1-6) might be viewed as a corrective to the messiahs of Qumran: e.g., the rise of the prophet alongside the messiahs of Israel and Aaron (1QS 9.11).

The similarities with the Qumran scrolls provide a number of insights for understanding Hebrews. They clarify many of the author's interpretations of Scripture texts. They also provide some context for understanding the liturgical motifs, messianic speculations, and polemics against Judeans in the book. However, a clear association of the readers of Hebrews with the Qumran community lacks sufficient proof. If the

---

39. Yadin, "Scrolls and the Epistle to the Hebrews." The Dead Sea Scrolls were found in 11 caves at Qumran, 13 miles east of Jerusalem in the Judean desert, discovered between 1947 and 1956, they comprise some 800 documents but in thousands of fragments, dating from ca. 250 BCE to 68 CE, written in Hebrew, Aramaic, and Greek; they contain biblical and apocryphal works, prayers, legal texts, and the rules and rituals of this Essene sect (also mentioned by Philo, Josephus, and Pliny the Elder). The sources for Qumran writings are Vermes, *Complete Dead Sea Scrolls* (1997); and García Martínez, *Dead Sea Scrolls* (1999).

readers are attracted to a Judean sect, it might be the type of Judean group represented by the Essenes of Qumran but not restricted to this group.[40]

Gnostic Writings

As in John's Gospel, Hebrews uses numerous images and motifs also found in gnostic writings.[41] We will look at the following: the preexistence of the Gnostic Redeemer, his descent to earth through heavenly realms, the common origin of both the Redeemer and the redeemed, pilgrimage to a heavenly home, and gnostic rebuttals. Difficulties with these parallels will also be discussed.

The preexistence of the Redeemer is assumed in both writings (e.g., Heb 1:2-3; 2:10; 9:26 /1 Apoc. Jas 24.21-25; 33.21-24; Treat.Res. 44.33-36) and the Redeemer's descent to earth through the heavenly realms (Heb 2:9, 14-18; 5:7-8; 9:11, 14, 24/Treat. Seth 59.20-25; Paraph.Shem 15.29-36) to destroy the powers of death and darkness (Heb 2:9, 14-15; 9:13-14/Nat. Rulers 97.6-13; 1 Apoc Jas 25.10, 21). The divine origins and descent of the Primal Man is also found in gnostic writings like Poimandres (Hermetic writings 1.12-15). The common origin of both the Redeemer and redeemed is also presupposed in both writings (Heb 2:11; 5:9 / Testim. Truth 34.27—35.24; Ep. Pet. Phil. 136.16-28).

Another major motif is the pilgrimage of believers to their heavenly home (Heb 3:11, 18; 4:1, 3, 5, 10-11). This theme in Hebrews has parallels with the motif of the ascent of the soul to its heavenly home in gnostic writings (Treat. Res. 45.36-39; Seth 58.30-59.11; Paraph. Shem 41.21—43.30; 45.31—46.3; 47.648.9). Accounts of the heavenly journey

---

40. Bruce, "'To the Hebrews' or 'To the Essenes'?," esp. 232; Bruce, *Epistle to the Hebrews*, 8; similarities in exegesis are offset by the differences (O'Brien, *Letter to the Hebrews*, 38-40).

41. Gnostics are widespread mystical, sapiential, and philosophical groups of the first three centuries CE. Most emphasized or assumed the belief that a special revealed knowledge (*gnōsis*) can awaken a spark of the divine within the "enlightened ones" liberating them from ignorance of their true identity and delivering them from bondage in a depraved, material world. Thus they are provided some hope of reunion with the lofty, divine, spiritual realm. Sources for the gnostics are from Robinson, *Nag Hammadi*; Layton, *Gnostic Scriptures*; Acts of Thomas and Pseudo-Clementines in Schneemelcher, *New Testament Apocrypha*, 2:426-541; Odes of Solomon, Hermetic, and Mandean writings in W. Barnstone, *Other Bible*, 267-85, 567-80, 696-704; Rudolph, *Gnosis*.

A classic study of Hebrews and the gnostics is Käsemann, *Wandering People of God*, 87-96. See discussion in C. R. Koester, *Hebrews*, 60-61.

of the soul are also given in the Odes of Solomon (35.5-7; 38.1-3), Poimandres (Hermetic writing 1.24-26), the Acts of Thomas (22-28, 80, 85), and the Pseudo-Clementine Homilies (3.20).

Certain emphases in Hebrews may also be viewed as rebuttals of gnostic teaching. Appeals to the suffering and death of the Redeemer on earth (Heb 2:9-10, 14, 17-18; 4:15; 5:7-8; 9:12-14, 22) might be viewed as attempts to counter gnostic teaching that Christ did not actually suffer and die (1 Apoc. Jas. 31.15-26; Treat. Seth 55.8-56.19; Apoc. Peter 81.3—82.14). Also, Hebrews from the beginning (1:5; 2:18) excludes any mediation of salvation through angelic powers, which might be a reaction to the elaborate cosmologies of syzygies (e.g., Nous-Truth) emanating from the Unbegotten Father (e.g., Valentinian system).[42] Finally, the apocalyptic view of the future in Hebrews (1:2; 2:5; 6:5; 9:26-28; 10:35-37; 13:14; cf. Qumran) may be an attempt to counterbalance the gnostic extreme of realized eschatology (i.e., spiritual resurrection as release of soul from body).[43]

Despite these general similarities of motifs and images, there are some problems in the comparison of Hebrews and gnostic writings. First, the theme of the promised heavenly rest is not the goal of the celestial journey of the soul in Hebrews, but of the wanderings of the historical people of God on earth. (Hebrews, however, may be correcting this gnostic view.) Second, the author of Hebrews places too much emphasis on the Levitical culture and priesthood for it to be merely a defense of the salvific significance of Jesus's death only against gnostic teaching. The readers must have been attracted to some form of Judean legalism. Third, the author's (pesher) interpretation of Scripture has little in common with the more esoteric and mystical explanations of the gnostic writings. Fourth, the late dating of many of our gnostic sources (e.g., Hermetic, Mandaean) continues to raise problems whenever comparisons are made with the NT. It is a difficult enterprise to distinguish the earlier gnostic traditions (e.g., Judean Sethian) from later gnostic redactions. Despite these difficulties, the book of Hebrews contains some motifs and images that would surface in gnostic writings (e.g., dualism, Judean wisdom, angelology), even though they would be used in different contexts for

---

42. Valentinian system according to Hippolytus, *Refut. Haer.* 29-36, or Irenaeus, *Haer.* 1-8. See also in the Nag Hammadi Codices (NHC): identifying here the books by their codex and tractate numbers, e.g., Gos. Truth (NHC I, 3); Treat. Res. (I, 4); Tri. Trac. (I, 5); Gos. Phil. (II,3); Val. Exp. (XI,2); see Dunderberg, "School of Valentinus."

43. Exeg. Soul 134.7-16; Gos. Phil. 73.1-5; Treat. Res. 49.10-17.

different reasons.⁴⁴ As a result, there does not appear to be sufficient proof for postulating Hebrews as a specifically antignostic writing.

Hellenistic Christ-followers

With what movement of early Christ-followers might we classify the book of Hebrews? To formulate a plausible answer, we must look at its internal evidence: its language, style, historical allusions, and its conceptual similarities with other early writings by Christ-followers. This evidence will also provide further information about the author.

The language and style of both Hebrews and Luke-Acts are nearest to literary Koine Greek (e.g., writings of Epictetus, Josephus, Philo). The author of Hebrews employs a rich and diverse vocabulary (e.g., 157 words not used elsewhere in the NT).⁴⁵ The author appears to be acquainted with the classical standards of rhythmic prose (e.g., Heb 1: 1–3; Aristotle, *Rhet.* 3.8.6–7). Like the rhetoricians, he employed assonance or similar sounding words (e.g., *parakaleite . . . kaleitai*, 3:13; *emathen . . . epathen*, 5:8; *kalou . . . kakou*, 5:14), alliteration (*polumerōs kai polutrōpos palai . . . patrasin . . . prophētais*, 1:1; *apator, amētor agenalogētos*, 7:3), and rich sounding compound words (e.g., *misthapodosia*, 2:2; 10:35; *euperistatos*, 12:1). His skillful use of grammar and his complex sentence structure seem to betray some acquaintance with Attic Greek.⁴⁶ Obviously at home in the Hellenistic tradition of the literary Koine, the author of Hebrews does not reveal any knowledge of the classical Hebrew or Aramaic dialects.⁴⁷ Instead, he relies heavily upon the LXX in his biblical quotations.

---

44. Pheme Perkins, in her *Gnosticism and the NT*, 9–26, suggests that certain NT texts and early Judean "Sethian strands" of gnostic writing (e.g., Nat. Rulers, Apoc. Adam; Steles Seth) appear to draw upon a "common lexical tradition" of earlier Judean notions of personified wisdom, semidivine beings, angels, and other mediators from heaven (e.g., Prov 8; Sir 24; Wis 8–9; Dan 7:13–14; 1 Enoch 49:3; 51:3; 4 Ezra 5;10–11; Odes Sol. 41; 2 Bar 48; T. Ab. 7:3–12; 9:17–18; Jos. Asen. 14–17). On the criteria used for reconstructing these early strands, see M. A. Williams, "Sethianism," 50–57.

45. These *hapax legomena* are listed and discussed in Williamson, *Philo and the Epistle to the Hebrews* 11–18.

46. For more information, consult: Moulton et al., *Grammar of New Testament Greek*, 2:24–25; Moffatt, *Hebrews*, lvi–lxiv. On figures of speech (alliteration, metonymy) in Hebrews, see C. R. Koester, *Hebrews*, 92–96; Bateman, *Charts on the Book of Hebrews*, 185–99.

47. Moulton et al., *Grammar of New Testament Greek* 2:24–25; Moffatt, *Hebrews*, lvi–lxiv. There are only six textual deviations from the LXX which could have been due either to the author's own free renderings or Greek text versions no longer extant.

Sparse historical allusions in Hebrews may indicate that the author and his readers belonged to the second generation of Christ-followers (2:3), were acquainted with Timothy the associate of the apostle Paul (13:23), had experienced past persecution (10:32-34, under Nero?), and awaited more persecution (12:4, under Domitian?).

Let us now look at the similarities of Hebrews with other writings by early Christ-followers. Although it is clearly different from Paul's writings in language, style, and theological emphasis,[48] Hebrews contains some general Pauline themes. In Christology, both Hebrews and Pauline writings speak of Christ as the image of God (Heb 1:3; 2 Cor 4:4), his agency over creation (Heb 1:2; Col 1:16), and his obedience (Heb 5:8; Phil 2:8).[49] Both writings discuss the new covenant (Heb 9:15; 2 Cor 3:6) and the administration of the Spirit's gifts (Heb 2:4; 1 Cor 12:11). Discussion of faith, with Abraham as the leading model (Heb 11; Rom 4) and with Hab 2:4 as a major text (Heb 10:3 8; Rom 1:17; Gal 3:11) appears in both Hebrews and Paul. Finally, Israel's disobedience in the wilderness is used as an example of warning (Heb 3:7-4:10; 1 Cor 10:1-11). Although the above themes are employed differently for different reasons, the similarities may reveal that either Hebrews and Pauline tradition shared a common collection of themes (e.g., testimonia), or that the author of Hebrews was familiar with some form of Pauline tradition. In support of the latter possibility, the author and his readers were acquainted with Paul's associate Timothy, who seems to be living at the time of writing (13:23).[50]

The selection of favorite OT texts in Hebrews appears to have been influenced by earlier traditions or testimonia of Christ-followers. Perhaps the christological or messianic interpretation of the OT came with

---

See also Longenecker, *Biblical Exegesis*, 150-51; Westcott, *Epistle to the Hebrews*, 481.

48. Paul could not have written Hebrews; see D. Guthrie, *NT Introduction* 671-74, 682; Moffatt, *Hebrews* xvii-xxi. In Hebrews there is the absence of typical Pauline abruptness, digressions of thought, and emotional pathos. See also O'Brien, *Letter to the Hebrews*, 4-6.

49. For an extensive list of christological titles in Hebrews, Paul, and the Gospels (e.g., Christ, Son of God, Lord, Shepherd), see Bateman, *Charts on Hebrews*, 120-22. For favorite titles ascribed to Christ in Hebrews (e.g., Great Priest, High Priest, Pioneer, Apostle, Forerunner, Mediator), see ibid., 119. Small, *Characterization of Jesus in Hebrews*, 254-56, following the encomiastic topics of ethos, finds seventeen character traits of Jesus, e.g., divinity, humanity, power, dignity, authority, compassion, piety, humility, and endurance. See also Lane, *Hebrews 1-8*, cxxv-cxliv; and Bauckham, "On the Divinity of Christ in the Epistle to the Hebrews."

50. "Timothy" may refer to Paul's associate (Bruce, *Hebrews*, 390; O'Brien, *Letter to the Hebrews*, 6, 539), although a late date (90) could challenge this identity.

the tradition. The earlier testimonia tradition also may have had some of the midrashic or pesher influences, discussed earlier (p. 24).⁵¹

Figure 4: Levitical Priests of the Tabernacle

In distinction from Pauline tradition, the author of Hebrews takes a more radical stance against the "old covenant" tradition. Even though Paul opposed Judean legalism as a precondition for Gentile salvation (e.g., Galatians), the apostle seemed to know some Hebrew as well as Hellenistic Greek and maintained cultural and historical ties with both Jerusalem ("the collection") and Judean traditions (Rom 9:1–4; 2 Cor 11:22). The author of Hebrews would probably agree with Paul's stance against Judean legalism but goes beyond Paul in having no apparent acquaintance with the Hebrew language and maintaining no ties with Jerusalem or contemporary Judean traditions. The author's only apparent understanding of Judean tradition concerns ancient Israel of the Greek OT.

If we interpret correctly the "Hebrews" and "Hellenists" of Acts 6:1 as referring to Hebrew- and Greek-speaking Judean Christ-followers respectively, Hebrews might be classed with the latter group ("Hellenists") and Paul with the more liberal wing of the former ("Hebrews").⁵² Let us

---

51. Longenecker appears to make this conclusion in his *Biblical Exegesis*, 165.

52. For more information, see Brown and Meier, *Antioch and Rome*, 1–9; Hengel,

examine these "Hellenists" in Acts to discern any similarities with the book of Hebrews. According to Acts, the Hellenist movement began at Jerusalem and was associated with Stephen (6:1–5, 8–14). The group was scattered throughout Judea after Stephen's death (8:1), and it spread to Samaria with Philip (8:4–6), onward to Phoenicia, Cyprus, Antioch (11:19–20), and eventually to Ephesus and Rome. This group of Greek-speaking Judean Christ-followers did not converse in Hebrew or Aramaic (6:1). They not only opposed Judean legalism for Gentiles but also saw no abiding significance in the worship at the Jerusalem temple (7:47–51/Isa 66:1–2).

Since Stephen is the main exponent among Hellenistic Christ-followers in Acts, a comparison of Stephen's speech with Hebrews would be instructive.[53] First, even though both regard the tabernacle as built by Moses according to a divine pattern (Gk. *typos*, Acts 7:44/Heb 8:5), it is still an imperfect structure (Acts 7:39–46/Heb 7:18–19; 8:7, 13; 9:11). Second, the patriarchs and their descendants are portrayed in both writings as the wandering people of God (Acts 7:3–4, 6, 29, 34, 36–38, 42/ Heb 3:16–17; 11:8–16, 22, 27, 29, 38; 13:4). Third, both speak of Israel leaving Egypt under Moses and of its rebellion in the wilderness (Acts 7:36,39–40/ Heb 3:16–17). Fourth, both speak of Joshua and the promise of rest (*katapausis*, Acts 7:44–45, 49; Heb 3:7—4:10). Fifth, each one speaks of the call of Abraham (Gen 12) and mentions Abraham's nonpossession of the land (Acts 7:3–5/Heb 11:8–10, 13, 14). Sixth, both the Stephen speech and Hebrews focus on Jesus as the goal of salvation history (Acts 7:55–56/Heb 12:2). Finally, both speak of the angels as ordainers of God's law (Acts 7:53/Heb 2:2) and of God's word as "living" (*zōē*, Acts 7:38/Heb 4:12).[54] Although these topical similarities are interpreted differently, they reflect a more radical stance toward the Judean heritage.[55]

Between Jesus and Paul, 1–29; Hill, *Hellenists and Hebrews*; Puskas and Robbins, *Introduction*, 212–15.

53. Although the speeches of Acts are primarily Lukan creations, they often contain *historical information* that can be corroborated with other writings (e.g., Acts 22:3/Gal 1:14; Acts 13:46/Rom 1:16; Acts 18:26–27/Rom 11:7–8). Furthermore, like most literary men of antiquity, Luke knew that his speeches had to be realistic and appropriate to the different speakers and occasions. On the comparison of Stephen's speech and Heb, see Manson, *Epistle to the Hebrews*, 36, 50, 159–97.

54. See also similar typological use of the LXX (e.g., Gen 12 in Acts 7 and Heb 11; Exod 25 in Acts 7 and Heb 8) and a fondness for the same OT characters as heroes and saints (e.g., Abraham, Joseph, Moses, and the prophets in both Acts 7 and Heb 11).

55. Such a position expressed by Stephen and the Hellenists appears to run counter to Luke's own concern to present Jesus and his followers as faithful Israelites loyal to

Even though Hebrews does not mention the Jerusalem temple, its emphasis on the preeminence of Jesus as great high priest makes it agree by implication with the "anti-temple" motif of Stephen: "the Most High does not dwell in houses made with human hands" (Acts 7:48; cf. Heb 9:11). The Gospel of John more directly agrees with this so-called anti-temple statement, since the body of Jesus is the temple (John 2:19–21; cf. 4:21). The Gospel of Mark's portrait of Jesus advocating big changes in torah observance (Mark 2:15–3:6; 7:1–13) is especially relevant for this type of Christ-following in a Hellenistic context. All these writings advocating major changes in Judean cult and ritual (for the benefit of outsiders) conform to a Hellenistic type of Christ-following, which is appealing to Gentile believers (e.g., Heb 10:10). In the second century, this form of Christ-following will develop in such a way that it reflects an even greater separation of church and synagogue, as seen in the Letter of Barnabas and Letter to Diognetus, which both share stylistic similarities with Hebrews.

The Authorship

We will first look at the external and internal evidence for the authorship of Hebrews. Then I will draw my own conclusions based partly on the previous study of its thought-world. The external evidence will also disclose its reception in the early church.

External Evidence

Despite the fact that Clement of Rome (95 CE) is the first to quote from Hebrews (1 Clem 36:2–5; 17:1) no mention is made of its author. Clement of Alexandria (ca. 200) was the first to ascribe it to Paul. The apostle supposedly wrote it in the Hebrew language and it was translated by Luke into Greek. According to Clement, Paul did not identify himself in the book because he was the apostle to the Gentiles, not to the Hebrews.[56] Origen, Clement's successor in Alexandria, stated that the thoughts were the apostle's but the diction and phraseology belonged to someone else, possibly Clement of Rome. Origen concludes, however: "But who it was

---

the law (e.g., Luke 2:21–24,41–43; Acts 3:1–2; 5:12–13; 18:18; 20:16). Thus the speech in Acts 7 may reflect Stephen's views or is at least in keeping with Luke's technique of composing speeches that were realistic and appropriate to each speaker and situation.

56. Clement of Alexandria according to Eusebius, *Hist. eccl.* 4.14.2–3.

that really wrote the epistle, God only knows."[57] Tertullian (ca. 210) attributed it to Barnabas, the companion of Paul (*On Purity* 20). Martin Luther (1537) separated Hebrews from the Pauline letters and attributed the book to Apollos (cf. Acts 18:24).[58] Other candidates for the authorship of Hebrews have been Silas (1 Pet 5:13), Philip the evangelist (Acts 21:8), and Priscilla (Acts 18:26).[59]

Internal Evidence

The internal evidence for the authorship of Hebrews is sparse. As I noted earlier, the author wrote in polished literary Koine Greek. Although he shares certain themes with Paul (e.g., faith, new covenant), he writes differently, argues differently, and thinks differently than the apostle.[60] The thought forms of Hebrews have some resemblance to Alexandrian Judean religion, but not enough to regard it as a Philonic writing or a book written by Apollos the Alexandrian (Acts 18:24-28; 1 Cor 1-4).[61] Hebrews shares some general motifs with gnostic views (e.g., Redeemer from heaven, journey motif) and some specific differences, but there is insufficient proof to describe it as a polemic against gnostic teaching[62] The polemics of Hebrews, however, address a type of Judean sectarianism like that at Qumran (e.g., Heb 6:1-2; 9:10; *Manual of Discipline* 1QS 3-4).[63]

---

57. Origen, according to Eusebius, *Hist. eccl.* 6.25.11-12; see also Eusebius, *Hist. eccl.* 3.38 (Clement as author of Hebrews).

58. See Martin Luther, *LW* 8:178; Zahn, *Introduction to the New Testament*, 2:364.

59. See Guthrie, *NT Introduction*, 674-82. Cockerill, *Epistle to the Hebrews*, 2n1, questions Priscilla's authorship because of the *masculine* pronouns throughout, especially when describing himself (Heb 11:32, "tell"; Gk. *diēgoumenon*). For a more complete list of possible authors with discussion, see Bateman, *Charts on Hebrews*, 17-34.

60. Guthrie, *NT Introduction*, 671-74, 709-11; Cockerill, *Hebrews*, 6-8.

61. Montefiore, *Hebrews*, 6-11, argues for the Philonic character of Hebrews and Apollos as its author. Williamson, *Philo and the Epistle to the Hebrews*, argues against the Philonic character of Hebrews and weakens the argument for Apollos as its author.

62. O'Brien, *Letter to the Hebrews*, 38. Nevertheless, the emphasis of Hebrews on both the *humanity* and *suffering* of Jesus (2; 4:15; 5:7-8; 9) and its apocalyptic view of the *future* (1:2; 2:5; 6:5) are characteristics of emerging orthodoxy that opposed such "false teachings"; see Puskas and Robbins, *Introduction*, chs. 14-15.

63. The author of Hebrews also appears to share some common themes and exegetical techniques with those at Qumran (e.g., spiritual sacrifices, Melchizedek, apostasy, pesher interpretation of Scripture). From Josephus we learn that Essenes like those at Qumran lived in other areas of Judea, outside of Jerusalem.

The viewpoint of the author is similar to that of Hellenistic Christ-following. He is a representative of a Greek-speaking Christ-following, linguistically and culturally separated from Judean tradition. The author appears to be a second-generation Christ-follower (2:3) and is only casually acquainted with Pauline tradition (despite 13:23). His critique of Israelite tradition has some similarity to that found in Mark, John, or even the Letter of Barnabas or the Letter to Diognetus.

The Place of Composition

The place of composition for the writing might be any urban center of Hellenism, where an influx of Platonic and Near Eastern wisdom, gnostic, and Essene teaching could be found. Candidates for the place of authorship might be Alexandria of Egypt, Antioch of Syria, or Ephesus of Asia. Rome does not appear to be a likely location because of Heb 13:24: "those who are from Italy (*apo Italias*) salute you," which seems to imply that Italians away from Italy (*apo Italias*) are greeting those (perhaps) in Italy or Rome.[64] Palestine does not seem to be a likely location because the author shows little or no acquaintance with Jerusalem or Palestine of his day.[65] His knowledge of Palestine seems to be derived from the LXX. It is noteworthy that one candidate for authorship who arrived in Ephesus (ca. 50) is the Hellenistic Judean Apollos, "a native of Alexandria," "an eloquent man" (Acts 18:24) "instructed in the way of the Lord" (v. 25), instructed further by Priscilla and Aquila (v. 26)—a man who had an active ministry in Corinth (Acts 18:27—19:1; 1 Cor 1:12; 3:4, 21–22; 16:12).[66] Even though the authorship question is unsettled, the urban centers associated with this candidate (esp. Alexandria and Ephesus) are significant for possible places of composition.

The Audience

The title "To the Hebrews" was not supplied by the author. By 200 CE the designation was found in an early Greek manuscript (P[46]). Clement

---

64. The superscripts of some manuscripts ("To the Hebrews from Rome [or Italy]"), however, support the idea that the author (along with the others mentioned) was writing "from Italy," see Cockerill, *Hebrews*, 722; see footnote in *NA*[27], 587.

65. The author's lack of acquaintance with the Palestine of his day may also raise doubts about Antioch of Syria, near Palestine, as the place of origin. See maps on pp. 9, 66 of this book.

66. Reis, "Apollos," 203–4; Cockerill, *Hebrews*, 9–10.

of Alexandria claims that his teacher, Pantaenus (180), knew it by this title, and Tertullian (210) refers to it in this manner.[67] The superscription "to the Hebrews" probably originated from an analysis of the book itself, since it seems to be addressed to Judeans who were lapsing from their faith in Jesus. Some, in disagreement with the traditional title, argue that the book was addressed to Gentiles, not Hebrews.[68] Since the LXX, used in Hebrews, was the Bible of early Christ-followers, both Gentile and Judean believers would have been acquainted with it. The author does not deal with the Judean tradition of his day or any Judean-Gentile controversies, only with canonical Israel. The statements on restoring to repentance after "being enlightened" (Heb 6:4) and falling away from the "living God" (3:12) and the mention of "dead works" (6:1; 9:14) suggest that the author is combating a return to pagan idolatry ("strange teaching," 13:9).[69] Finally, those who stress the gnostic motifs and polemics in Hebrews maintain that the book argues against the gnostic denial of the importance of Jesus's death for salvation, and not against Judean belief and practice.[70]

The reasons for maintaining a Gentile audience for Hebrews, however, are not too convincing. First, the appeal to the Greek OT may not be relevant for Gentile Christ-followers relapsing into paganism. Second, the omission of Judean-Gentile controversies (e.g., circumcision in Galatians) is understandable if the book is addressed to a Judean audience. Third, the imagery of falling away from the "living God" (3:12) can also be interpreted as Israelite disobedience in the wilderness (Ps 95), relevant for Judeans of the first century CE. Hebrews 6:1–2 and 9:13–15 seem to imply the Judean antecedents of the readers. Fourth, the argument that Hebrews concerns gnostic, not Judean, polemics lacks conclusive data. The antignostic view does not account for the many Qumran parallels (e.g., ceremonial washings, purification, pesher interpretation) or also

---

67. Pantaenus is cited by Clement of Alexandria in Eusebius, *Hist. eccl.* 6.14.3-4; Tertullian titles the book *To the Hebrews* in *On Purity* 20.

68. The language of direct access to God through Jesus the high priest (Heb 4:14–16; 10:19–22; 12:18–24) would certainly be important to Gentile Christ-followers who were former "god-fearers" (e.g., Acts 10:1–2) and had been restricted to the southern edge of the temple mount (Josephus, *War* 5.194); on the first-century limestone inscription forbidding a "foreigner" (*allogenēs*) to enter the inner court of the temple area, see Finegan, *Archeology of the New Testament*, 119–20. On god-fearers, see Collins and Harlow, *Early Judaism* (2010), 681–82.

69. On the unique and appealing ontology behind Greco-Roman worship, see Gupta, "'They Are Not Gods!'"

70. H. Koester, *Introduction to the New Testament*, 2:278.

the amount of space devoted to the Israelite wilderness experience (Heb 3:7—4:11), Levitical sacrifice and priesthood (4:14—5:10; 9:2—10:18), and the old and new covenants (9:1–20), which still have significance for the readers (e.g., Heb 7:11).[71]

The audience of Hebrews was probably a group of Judean Christ-followers discouraged in their faith and perhaps attempting to return to their Judean rites and observances. This act of "apostasy" (whatever it involved) may have resulted from both the pressures of Roman persecution (10:32–34) and the uncertainties resulting from the delay of the Lord's return (vv. 35–37). This view would not exclude Gentile Christ-followers who were formerly "god-fearers" (e.g., Acts 10:1-2) from making up some of the intended audience.

Even though the readers are probably Greek-speaking Judeans, they seemed to have been attracted to a type of sectarian Judean tradition similar to that practiced at Qumran (e.g., Heb 6:1–2; 9:10/1QS 3–4). Perhaps there were some converted Judean priests in their midst (cf. Acts 6:7) who had a natural interest in the ritual details that our author criticized. Whatever form of Judean tradition they may have been attracted to, these Judean Christ-followers had concerns similar to those of the original "Hebrews" of the Jerusalem church (Acts 6: 1).[72] This conservative wing of Hebrew Christ-following was also interested in upholding certain Judean practices, like observing the food and purity laws (e.g., Acts 10:9–20; 15:19–20; 21:25). The writer of Hebrews, perhaps representing a more liberal group of Hellenistic Christ-followers (e.g., Acts 7; John) warns his readers against apostasy and argues that the Christ-following (practiced by his group) is the better way.[73]

---

71. For further critique of the theory of a Gentile audience for Hebrews, see Bruce, *Hebrews*, 5–8; Lane, *Hebrews 1–8*, liv. See chart showing a Judean Christ-follower audience as the majority opinion, in Batemann, *Charts on Hebrews*, 39.

72. Despite the harsh statements on "apostasy" by the author of Hebrews, the readers may have only been interested in practicing a more Judean form of Christ-following (cf. Gal), and not forsaking the faith in Christ altogether. On priests of Palestine (ca. 60 CE) who may have been Jesus followers, see Martin, *James*, lxii–lxix.

73. Manson, *Hebrews*, 159–72, unfortunately, expresses this theme in more supersessionist language. Such "*new* covenant" language, deeply rooted in Israelite tradition, reflects a post-temple setting that would have bolstered the obsoleteness of the Levitical cult, see Eisenbraum, "Letter to the Hebrews," *JANT*, 406–26.

The Destination

Various locations for the destination of Hebrews have been postulated.[74] We will examine the two localities: Jerusalem and Rome.

It has been argued by some that Hebrews was addressed to readers in Jerusalem or Palestine. Either location would be a likely place for the readers to be enticed back to Judean traditions. It was in the Jerusalem church that a distinction was first made between "Hebrews'" and "Hellenists" (Acts 6:1), although we do not know how long it lasted. In Acts 8:1–6, the Hellenistic Judean Christ-followers were driven out. Jerusalem remained cosmopolitan with Judeans, Greeks, and Romans, even after the temple's destruction (70 CE). The statements in Hebrews of "serving the saints" and helping the poor or afflicted (6:10; 10:34; 13:16) may be allusions to assisting the poor in Jerusalem (cf. Rom 15:26; 1 Cor 16:1–4). In the rural areas outside Jerusalem, there would have been numerous Essene communities, like Khirbet Qumran, which represented a type of sectarian Judean tradition to which the readers may have been attracted. References to the former sufferings of the readers (Heb 10:32; 12:4) may denote persecution from the Jerusalem Judeans (cf. Acts 4:1–2; 8:16) or the tragedies leading to or resulting from Jerusalem's destruction (Josephus, *War* 6.220—357).

Jerusalem as the destination of Hebrews has problems. First, worship in Jerusalem was dominated by the temple, to which no explicit reference is made. Second, the statements of needing "someone to teach you" (5:12) and remembering "your leaders who spoke to you the word of God" (13:7) seem inappropriate for the earliest Christ-following community, the Jerusalem church. Third, if a post–70 date is maintained for Hebrews, it weakens considerably the likelihood of a Jerusalem destination since the temple was destroyed, and the city no longer was the center for Judean rites and rituals as it had been. Most of these objections are removed if the destination was to somewhere else in or near Palestine (e.g., Caesarea, Samaria, or Syria).

The destination of Hebrews favored by most is Rome. Several reasons can be provided. First, there was an early Judean and Judean Christ-follower presence there (1 Macc 14:24; 15:15–24; Cicero, *Flacc.* 66–69;

---

74. Two examples: first, Colossae or Lycus Valley, because of similar problems of angelic intermediaries addressed (Heb 1–4/Col 2:18) and ritual tendencies (Heb 5–10/Col 2:14–15); and, second, Alexandria, because of parallels with Wisdom, 4 Maccabees and Philo, although these may tell us more about the *author*, than the situation of the addressees.

Josephus, *Ant.* 14.69-79; Acts 2:5, 10; 18:1-2; 28:17-22; Rom 2:17-18; 16:3). Second, it was in Rome that Hebrews was first known (1 Clem 9:4; 12:1; 36:1-2; Shepherd of Hermas 140).[75] Third, the concluding salutation in Heb 13:24 seems more naturally understood as given by Italians away from Italy who are sending greetings home, rather than as given by Italians to folks at some non-Italian destination.[76] Fourth, Timothy (Heb 13:23) was probably known to Roman Christ-followers.[77] Fifth, the persecutions of Heb 10:32-34 and 12:4 could refer to those under Nero. Sixth, the Roman church appears to be composed of both Judean and Gentile believers (cf. Rom 4:1; 11:13) who met in separate house churches (Rom 16:5, 14, 15). Hebrews was probably addressed to a particular house church within the Roman community that was composed of conservative Judean Christ-followers experiencing a crisis of faith (cf. Rom 2:17-29?).[78]

Although I favor a Roman destination for Hebrews, the position also has its shortcomings. First, Clement of Rome was also familiar with letters of Paul that were not addressed to Rome (e.g., 1 Corinthians). Moreover, it is difficult to pinpoint the specific nature of the persecutions in Heb 10:32-35. Finally, the apparent concerns of the Judean Christ-followers deduced from Paul's rhetoric in Romans (e.g., 2; 9-11) are different from those in Hebrews (although a later date for Hebrews might account for the differences).

The Date

The latest possible date for Hebrews would be around 95 CE, the date of 1 Clement, which first cites the work (1 Clem 9:3-4; 10:1-7; 12:1; 17:1,5; 19:2; 27:2; 36:2-6; 43:1; 56:3-4; 64:1). A date prior to 70 CE cannot be inferred either from the silence concerning the catastrophe of 70 CE or references to an imminent crisis (8:13; 10:25). The persecutions that

---

75. The Shepherd of Hermas, from Rome ca. 120-140 CE, betrays some acquaintance with Hebrews in discussing the issue of second repentance after baptism (Herm. Mand. 4.3.1-7; Herm. Vis. 2.2.4-5; Herm. Sim. 9.26.5-6), an issue first mentioned in Hebrews (Heb 6:4-6; 10:26-31; 12:17), see C. R. Koester, *Hebrews*, 23.

76. There are problems with this verse. Do "they of Italy" simply mean "Aquila and Priscilla" (Acts 18:1-2)? Can we be sure it is a specific historical reference?

77. Again, it must be asked if this "Timothy" was the associate of Paul. If Hebrews was written ca. 90, would Paul's associate still be alive?

78. On this identity crisis, see Bruce, *Hebrews*, 9; Manson, *Hebrews* 159-62, 172-89, 187-92.

the community has already experienced (10:32-34, Neronian? Tacitus, *Annals* 15.44.6) and the theological proximity to John's Gospel (e.g., similar high Christology, Hellenistic Christ-followers, Judean conflict and polemics)[79] point to the late first century. The writer and readers are probably second-generation Christ-followers (2:3; 13:7). The new suffering that threatens the readers (12:3-11) may point to the time of Domitian (81-96; Eusebius, *Hist. eccl.* 3.18.4). Therefore, Hebrews was probably written around 90 CE.[80]

Conclusion

In our study of Hebrews, we looked at its literary genre, rhetorical structure, thought-world, authorship, addressees, place of destination, and date. First, we argued that Hebrews was an early sermon put into written form for a distant audience. As do other homilies, it combines doctrine and exhortation to persuade or dissuade its audience. Second, we outlined Hebrews as a form of deliberative persuasion, concerned with future issues of expedience. Hebrews contains a proem (1:1—4:12), a statement of the case (4:13—6:20), a demonstration of evidence (7:1—10:18), an epilogue summarizing the arguments (10:19—13:21), and an epistolary postscript (13:22-25). Third, we noted the author's dependence on the LXX, his common heritage of Hellenism with Alexandrian Judeans, his affinity with both Qumran eschatology and pesher interpretation of Scripture, his utilization of motifs also found in gnostic writings (e.g., heavenly Redeemer, wandering motif), and the similar beliefs that he shares with Hellenistic Christ-followers: e.g., Stephen, Mark, and John.

Fourth, we deduced from the book that the author was skilled in Hellenistic style and diction, and conversant with traditions similar to

---

79. See Heb 1:1-4/John 1:1-5 (with God at creation); Heb 4:14-16/John 14:6 (Jesus provides access to God); Heb 10:11-14/John 11:49-52 (his vicarious suffering & death); Heb 13:20-21/John 10:11,14 (Jesus the shepherd of his sheep); see also Heb 15:7-9/John 17; Heb 2:10-11/John 17:17-19; Heb 6:8/John 15:6; Heb 13:12/John 19:17-18. Both make ample use of the christological titles "Son," "Son of God," and "Lord." Note also the high amount of intertextuality between Hebrews and John in the indexes of O'Brien, *Letter to the Hebrews*, 570; and Michaels, *Gospel of John*, 1086.

80. See the following works for a post-70 date: Kümmel, *Introduction*, 403; Kistemaker, *Hebrews*; Brown, *Introduction*, 696-97; and the following for a pre-70 date: Guthrie, *NT Introduction*, 701-5; Cockerill, *Hebrews*, 38-41. Both Attridge, *Epistle to the Hebrews*; and C. R. Koester, *Hebrews*, assign the dating of Hebrews to the general period of 60-90.

those of the Alexandrian Judeans, gnostic teaching, and the Dead Sea Scrolls. He represents a type of Hellenistic Christ-following that was separate from Judean practices and viewed many of its traditions as obsolete (or irrelevant) for Christ-followers (cf. John's Gospel). It is pure guesswork to assign a name to the author of Hebrews. Fifth, the addressees appear to be Hellenistic Judeans attracted to a form of sectarian tradition similar to that at Qumran. Their concerns also reflect those of the earlier Hebrew Christ-followers of Jerusalem, who sought to retain their Judean traditions. Sixth, both Jerusalem and Rome are the most promising candidates for the place of destination. Rome is favored because Hebrews was first known there, it best accounts for the closing greeting of those "from Italy" (13:24), the Roman church had both Judean and Gentile believers, and a Rome location is less threatened by a post–70 date. Finally, because the book is a product of second-generation Christ-following, it has thematic affinities with John's Gospel, reflects early persecutions with more anticipated, and can be dated no later than 1 Clement: a date of composition for Hebrews around 90 CE is plausible.

The book of Hebrews provides readers with a rich early Christ-following interpretation of the Israelite Scriptures, employing Judean exegesis, Hellenistic rhetoric, and various literary devices. It also presents for its readers a bold and articulate statement about the superiority and finality of Christ the Son of God (as high priest, mediator, pioneer),[81] and it reveals the wide gap already emerging between church and synagogue.[82]

The author's vision of Christ is memorable, as John Calvin (1509–64) states:

> There is, indeed, no book in the Holy Scriptures which speaks so clearly of the priesthood of Christ, so highly exalts the virtue and dignity of that only true sacrifice which he offered by his death, so abundantly treats of the use of ceremonies as well as of their abrogation, and, in a word, so fully explains that Christ is the end of the Law. Let us not therefore suffer the Church of God nor ourselves to be deprived of so great a benefit, but firmly defend the possession of it.[83]

---

81. Hurtado, *Lord Jesus Christ*, 502, writes: "The author's rather robust treatment of the relationship between Jesus and Melchizedek is clearly driven and shaped fundamentally by powerful convictions about Jesus."

82. Eisenbaum, "Letter to the Hebrews," *JANT*, 406–7.

83. Calvin, *Commentary on the Epistle to the Hebrews*, xxvi.

2

The Letter of James

Introduction

JAMES IS THE FIRST NT book of the so-called Catholic or General Epistles (Eusebius, *Hist. eccl.* 2.23.23–25). This category was applied to James, 1 and 2 Peter, 1, 2, and 3 John, plus Jude by the fourth-century church because it was believed that they were epistles addressed to (or received by) "all the churches." There are, however, not a few problems with the label "Catholic" or "General" Epistles. First, with two possible exceptions (Jas 1:1; 2 Pet 1:1), these books are addressed to specific audiences (e.g., 2 and 3 John) and specific regions (1 Pet 1:1). Second, certain books (e.g., James, Jude) were not received by all the churches (see Canonicity Question, pp. 41–42). Third, although most begin like an epistle, only 2 and 3 John have enough characteristics to be confidently labeled "ancient letters."[1] Fourth, this category of seven books seems to reflect the Great Church's attraction for grouping in multiples of seven: fourteen letters of Paul (twice seven) including Hebrews.[2] Furthermore, the books are prob-

---

1. On the distinctions of "letter" (2–3 John, Phlm, papyri) and literary "epistle" (Plutarch, Seneca), see Deissmann, *Light from the Ancient East*; Klauck, *Ancient Letters*, sees these two categories of letter and epistle as insufficient (70–72) and reminds us of a third-century-CE source that lists twenty-one different kinds of letters (197).

2. Lüdemann, *Heretics*, 202–3, 317n690. See also, e.g., the Muratorian Fragment 47–50 where it states that Paul, following the example of John [Rev 2–3] "writes only by name to seven churches." According to this document (second century, or later), the seven letters are addressed to Corinthians, Ephesians, Philippians, Colossians, Galatians, Thessalonians, and Romans, cited in Stevenson, *New Eusebius*, 124.

ably not arranged chronologically and they are difficult to date. Their sequence in the NT, however, may have been derived from the name order in Galatians 2:9: "James, Cephas (Peter), John."[3] We will first examine James, looking at questions of canonicity, authorship, historical setting, literary characteristics, genre, and rhetorical structure.

The Canonicity Question

James[4] was a NT book whose canonical authority was disputed for centuries. Contrasting it with a collection that included John's Gospel, 1 John, Romans, Galatians, Ephesians, and 1 Peter, Martin Luther called James "an epistle full of straw, because it contains nothing evangelical."[5] Even though he observed that it was assembled by a "good, pious man" and admitted that it contains "many excellent passages," Luther denied that it was the work of an apostle and believed that the writer lived "later than St. Peter or Paul."[6] Two difficulties that the German Reformer had with James were" (a) its apparent contradiction with Paul's teaching on justification by faith (e.g., Jas 2:20-21 vs. Rom 4:2-3); and (b) its absence of any reference to the suffering, death, and resurrection of Christ, which were essential to him in apostolic teaching.[7] For the above reasons, Lu-

---

3. The (authoritative) lists of Athanasius and Epiphanius have the Catholic Epistles arranged in this order (James, Peter, John) with Jude concluding the collection probably because of its brief contents (similar to that of 2–3 John). See lists in McDonald and Sanders, *Canon Debate*, 592–93.

4. Commentaries and other studies on James are Davids, *Epistle of James*; Dibelius, *James* (rev. Greeven); Martin, *James*; Painter, *Just James*; McKnight, *Letter of James*; Laws, *Commentary on the Epistle of James*; Marcus, "Evil Inclination in the Epistle of James"; Mayor, *Epistle of James*; Reese, "Exegete as Sage"; Ropes, *Critical and Exegetical Commentary*; Ward, "Works of Abraham," 283–90; Painter and deSilva, *James and Jude*; Heil, *Letter of James*.

5. Luther's "Preface to the New Testament" (September Testament, 1522), in Dillenberger, *Martin Luther*, 19. The metaphor of "straw" may have been derived from 1 Cor 3:12–15, symbolizing perishable building material. See also Luther, *LW* 35: 395–97.

6. Luther's "Preface to the Epistles of St. James and St. Jude," 1522 in *Martin Luther*, 35–37; and Luther, *LW* 35: 395–97. In his writings Luther made favorable use of the following passages to support his arguments or illustrate a theme, James 1:6–8 (*LW* 42:76), 1:13 (*LW* 4:132), 1:18 (WA 41:585–86); 2:19 (*LW* 30:12); 5:16 (*LW* 4:339–40). He took issue, of course, with Jas 2:22 (*LW* 34:317) but also the use of Jas 5:14–16 to support the Catholic Sacrament of Extreme Unction or Last Rites (*LW* 36:11–12).

7. Luther, *LW* 35:396–97; see also Kümmel, *NTHIP*, 24–26.

ther placed James at the end of his translation of the NT with the other books that he also regarded as questionable in content: Hebrews, Jude, and Revelation.

In the fourth century, Eusebius classed James with other NT books that were "disputed" or "spoken in opposition" among the churches, the antilegomena: James, Jude, 2 Peter, 2 and 3 John. Although there are some possible allusions to James in 1 Clement and the Shepherd of Hermas, no reference to it is found in key Western witnesses like the Muratorian Fragment, Irenaeus, Tertullian, and Cyprian. Theodore of Mopsuestia rejected it, but Origen both acknowledged and made use of it. It was chiefly under the influences of Athanasius, Jerome, and Augustine that James was finally recognized as canonical.[8] After Luther's criticisms, most controversies about the book were concerned with theories about its Judean character (e.g., was it a Christ-follower's redaction of a Judean book?) and speculations about its place in the development of early Christ-following (e.g., was it anti-Pauline?).

Authorship

Arguments for Authenticity

Who is this James who introduces himself with the simple designation "servant of God and of the Lord Jesus Christ"? The NT ascribes this name to five men:[9]

(a) James the son of Zebedee (Mark 1:19; 3:17; Acts 12:2)

(b) James the son of Alphaeus (Mark 3:18)

(c) James the brother of Jesus, son of Joseph and Mary (Mark 6:3; 1 Cor 15:7; Gal 1:19; 2:9,12; Acts 12:17; 15:13; 21:18; Jude 1)

(d) James the Younger (Mark 15:40, son of Mary, Mark 16:1)

(e) James the father of the apostle Jude (Luke 6:16; Acts 1:13)

We know next to nothing about individuals (b), (d), and (e). Person (a) is excluded, since he was martyred in 44 CE under Herod Agrippa I, years before the book was probably written. What therefore remains is (c) James the brother of Jesus (Mark 6:3; 1 Cor 15:7).[10] He was the

8. Kümmel, *Introduction*, 405–6.
9. Ibid., 411–12.
10. In church history there has been disagreement on who was the mother of

well-known leader of the Jerusalem church (Gal 1:19; 2:9; Acts 12:17; 15:13; 21:18).

Arguments for James the Just

Further accounts of James are supplied by diverse sources: Josephus, Hegesippus, the Gospel according to the Hebrews, the Pseudo-Clementine writings, and both the First and Second Apocalypses of James. Much scholarly effort has been undertaken to glean historical data from these largely legendary accounts.[11] Some recurring motifs about him are that James the brother of Jesus was also called James the Just, that he was respected by his fellow Judeans because of his reverence for the torah,[12] and that since he was in conflict with certain Judean leaders, they killed him by stoning in Jerusalem after a hasty trial.[13]

The mention of James's reverence for the law is found only in Christ-follower sources. Hegesippus places the death of James in the interval between the death of the Roman procurator Festus and the arrival in Judea of his successor, Albinus (ca. 62 CE). This transition period between procurators would have been an opportune time for the Sanhedrin in Jerusalem to judge and execute its own criminals.[14] The death of James in 62 CE therefore has some historical plausibility. Closely connected with this "historical kernel" was the belief among Christ-followers (i.e., a theological interpretation) that the destruction of Jerusalem was the result of God's punishment on the Judeans for the murder of righteous James.

James "the Lord's brother" (Gal 1:19). Here are three prominent views. Jerome's theory was that James was actually the cousin of Jesus and the son of Mary's sister. Epiphanius believed that James, and Jesus' other brothers, were sons of Joseph by a previous marriage. Helvidius maintained that the "brothers of Jesus including James, were the actual children of Mary and Joseph. For further discussion, see Mayor, *James*, viii–xxxvii; and especially, Ropes, *James*, 53–62.

11. Brown, "Jewish and Gnostic Elements"; Mayor, *James*, xxxvii–xli; Ropes, *James*, 62–74; Schoeps, *Jewish Christianity*, 18–58; see especially Painter, *Just James*, 105–223.

12. Hegesippus (ca. 180) cited in early fourth century, Eusebius, *Hist eccl* 2.23.4–18.

13. Hegesippus; Josephus, *Ant.* 20.197–203; third century, *Second Apocalypse of James* 57.20–24; 50.13—62.15; 63.20, in Robinson, *Nag Hammadi*, 273–76; "The Ascent of James" source in the Pseudo-Clementine *Recognitions* 1.43–44; 53.4–62; 64–71, in *ANF* 8:89–96.

14. Execution by stoning was a recommended punishment in the Mishnah, *Sanhedrin* 6.1–4; 7.4 (a third century source probably referring to a first century practice of Palestine).

Although they may contain an early witness to the martyrdom of James, the Pseudo-Clementine writings (third century) abound with the piety and propaganda of Ebionite Christ-followers. These Judean Christ-follower writings exalted the characters of both James and Peter because of their alleged Judean piety, and denounced Paul because his views, they insisted, challenged the Judean law. They even identified Paul with the villain "Simon Magus" of Acts 8:18–20. Like the gnostic Apocalypses of James, these accounts are embellished with esoteric doctrines and theological speculations.

Origen of Alexandria (250 CE) was probably the first to cite the Letter of James as Scripture and James the Just as its author.[15] Later the fourth-century Councils of Hippo (393) and Carthage (397) supported Origen's views.

Let us consider some internal arguments for the view that James the Just, the brother of Jesus, was the book's author. We will focus on the parallels in the Gospels and Acts, then on the book's Judean character.

Comparisons of the book of James with the speeches of James in Acts have been used to support the view of Jacobean authorship.[16]

TABLE 2.1 James and Acts Parallels

Phrase	James	Acts
Epistolary greeting (*chairein*)	1:1	15:23
"Beloved" (*agapētos*)	1:16,19; 2:5	15:25
"Keep away from the bad" (*tēreō/diatēreō*))	1:27	15:29
"Visit" (*episkeptomai*)	1:27	15:14
"Listen (my) brothers" (*adelphoi akousate*)	2:5	15:13
The name invoked (*epikaleō*)	2:7	15:17
"Purify yourselves" (*hagnizō*)	4:8	21:24
"turn away from/turn to the bad" (*epistrephō*)	5:19–20	15:19

Even though some of these words appear infrequently in Acts and might suggest the use of pre-Lukan material, to some scholars it seems unlikely. These scholars claim that they are actually Lukanisms because they are

---

15. E.g., Origen, *Commentary on John* 19:6; Origen, *Commentary on Epistle to the Romans* 9:24, cited in Mayor, *James*, lxiv–lxv.

16. Mayor, *James*, iii–iv. See also McKnight, *Letter of James*, 24–25.

found in speeches that seem to be mostly Lukan creations.[17] Therefore it would be difficult to derive a "theology of James" from them.

The book's Judean background lends some support for Jacobean authorship. The author made use of the LXX:

TABLE 2.2 James and the Old Testament Parallels

Phrase or Topic	James	OT
The flower falls	Jas 1:10–11	Isa 40:6–7
Love your neighbor as yourself	Jas 2:8	Lev 19:18
No adultery or murder	Jas 2:11	Exod 20:13–14
Abraham offers up Isaac	Jas 2:21	Gen 22:2,9
Abraham believed in God . . .	Jas 2:23	Gen 15:6
Made in God's likeness . . .	Jas 3:9	Gen 1:26
God resists proud, grace to humble	Jas 4:6	Prov 3:34
The Lord of Sabbaoth hears	Jas 5:4	Isa 5:9
The Lord is compassionate, merciful	Jas 5:11	Ps 103:8 (LXX Ps 102:8)

Greek was a second language for most Galilean Israelites.[18] He also used Judean phraseology (e.g., "diaspora," 1:1; "synagogue," 2:2; "Lord of Sabaoth," 5:4) and was concerned with certain Judean legal matters (2:9–11; 4:11–12). The book, however, makes no mention of circumcision, ritual purity, or food laws. Allusions and figures used in the book may even reflect a Palestinian setting: e.g., "the early and late rains" (October and April; Jas 5:7); the rough (Galilean) sea waves driven by the wind (1:6); the hot, withering dryness of a Palestinian sirocco (1:10–11; cf. Job 27:21; Hos 13:15).[19]

This information indicates that the author of James was acquainted with the LXX, Judean phraseology, and legal matters. It also seems to mirror a Palestinian setting. Such a background is not inconsistent with our understanding of James the Just. It is difficult to establish, however,

---

17. See discussion of the speeches of Acts in Pervo, *Acts*, 17, 38–39; and Puskas, *Conclusion of Luke-Acts*, 38–44. Perhaps the author of James was familiar with traditions about James similar to those found in the book of Acts (i.e., a common or similar source).

18. The following work has made a strong case for the prevalence of Hellenistic Greek in first-century Palestine: Hengel, *Judaism and Hellenism*. Galilee was also adjacent to Gentile, Greek-speaking regions.

19. See Davids, "Palestinian Tradition in the Epistle to James."

that the author knew Aramaic or Hebrew because his Semitic style seems dependent on the LXX.[20]

Figure 5: *Sermon on the Mount*; woodcut on vellum by Christian Rohlfs (1849–1938)

James and the Sermon on the Mount

Although the book mentions the name of Christ only twice (1:1; 2:1) and does not refer to Jesus's life, death, and resurrection, the author was familiar with the teaching of Jesus, especially the Sermon on the Mount (and Plain):[21]

---

20. On Semitisms in James, see Moulton et al., *Grammar of New Testament Greek*, 4:116–19. Note, however, the caution expressed in Moule, *Idiom Book of New Testament Greek*, 171–91.

21. For more parallels, see Davids, *Epistle of James*, 47–50; McKnight, *Letter of*

TABLE 2.3 James and the Sermon on the Mount Parallels

Themes	James	Matthew	Luke
Joy in the midst of trials	1:2	5:10–12	6:22–23
Exhortation to perfection	1:4	5:48	
Asking for good gifts	1:5	7:7, 11	(11:9)
Against anger	1:20	5:22	
Hearers and doers of the word	1:22	7:24	6:46–47
Keeping the whole law	2:10	5:19	
The blessings of showing mercy	2:13	5:7	
The blessings of peacemakers	3:18	5:9	
Friendship of world/enmity with God (two masters: God & mammon)	4:4	6:24	(16:13)
(God's) exalting the humble	4:9–10	5:4–5; (23:12)	(14:11)
Against judging others	4:11–12; 5:9	7:1–5	6:37
Moth and rust spoil riches	5:2	6:19–20	(12:33)
The prophets as examples	5:10	5:11–12	6:23
Against oaths, swearing	5:12	5:33–37	

From the above data, proponents of Jacobean authorship might make the following argument. Even though James the Just was not a believer until after the resurrection (1 Cor 15:7), as the brother of Jesus he would have been exposed to his brother's teaching (e.g., the Sermon on the Mount) in Galilee where he lived. It must be underscored, however, that an *eyewitness* interpretation of the parallels with Jesus's teaching is only one of many explanations.[22] Considering the options, it is plausible that the author of James was dependent on one of the following: Matthew's Gospel,[23] Luke's Gospel, both Gospels, Q or a special collection of sayings. Furthermore, some of these alleged parallels may have been

---

James, 25–6. Some sayings might be agrapha of Jesus, not recorded in the four Gospels: e.g., Jas 1:12; 2:5.

22. For an overview, see Davids, "Tradition and Citation in the Epistle of James," 113–26. Some have called James a "sermon on the Sermon of the Mount."

23. Other parallels between James and Matthew are: Jas 1:6/Matt 21:21; Jas 2:8/Matt 22:39 (Lev 19:18); Jas 2:19–20/Matt 7:21; Jas 3:1/Matt 23:8–12; Jas 3:2–3/Matt 12:36–37; Jas 5:9/Matt 24:33; see Shepherd, "Epistle of James and the Gospel of Matthew."

unwritten sayings of Jesus (agrapha) similar to Q but distinctive enough to have circulated independently of the Gospel tradition (e.g., Jas 1:2; 2:5; cf. Acts 20:35). A few of these options will be explored later.

Arguments against Authenticity

A number of difficulties arise in ascribing the book's authorship to James the Just. First, would a Galilean peasant craftsman (carpenter?) have had such an able mastery of literary Koine? Second, if the author was the Lord's brother, why does he not mention it (cf. Jude 1)? Third, would James the Just have spoken of the law in the same manner as we find in the book? Fourth, the apparent dependency of James on other early Christ-follower teaching raises problems about its being an original, eyewitness document. After examining each of these points, we will consider their implications for determining the book's date.

The author writes in a relatively polished Koine.[24] It is confirmed by his skillful use of rhetorical devices (e.g., alliteration, wordplay, simile) and his cultivated vocabulary (e.g., *katēpheia, apokueō, deleazō, chrē*). There are 63 words not found elsewhere in the NT, 45 of which are in the LXX. The author is not verbose, and effectively uses language rich in poetic imagination (e.g., 1:6, 10–12, 15, 17–18). Clear examples of alliteration in James are found in 1:2, *peirasmois peripesēte poikilois* and 1:21, *dio . . . deksasthe . . . dynamenon*. An example of concatenation (i.e., the linking together of clauses and sentences by a key word or its cognate) occurs in Jas 1:2–6 as follows: patience (v. 3), patience (v. 4); nothing lacking (v. 4), if any of you lack (v. 5); let him ask (v. 5), but let him ask (v. 6).

Although the language of James may not measure up to the literary Koine of Philo or (even) Hebrews, its rich vocabulary and ornate style still raise difficulties with Origen's view of Jacobian authorship. As a native of Galilee, James the Just was probably acquainted with Greek as well as his native Aramaic and probably Hebrew.[25] But would a Galilean peasant or artisan have had such mastery of a second language? The author of James wrote as if Greek were his mother tongue. Perhaps an amaneunsis (i.e.,

---

24. See Davids, *Epistle of James*, 58–59; Mayor, *James*, clxxix–ccxxxi, 233–52; Ropes, *James*, 24–27; Dibelius, *James*, 34–38; Turner, *Style* (1976), 4:114–20.

25. Argyle, "Greek among the Jews of Palestine"; Hengel, *"Hellenization" of Judea*, 8.

a scribal secretary) was used, as Paul had employed on occasion (e.g., Tertius in Rom 16:22; cf. Jer 36:4).[26]

Another problem concerns the absence of any mention of the author's supposed relationship to Jesus or his family at Nazareth. Would James the brother of Jesus have omitted such information? Even though the book's images appear to recall agrarian Palestine (e.g., Jas 1:10; 3:11, 18; 4:14; 5:7), they do little to support the claim that this author was a Galilean called James the Just. The alleged parallels of James with the Sermon on the Mount can be interpreted in numerous ways (e.g., dependence on Matthew, Q, or the M source) and need not suggest that the author was an eyewitness.

The characterization of the law as "a perfect law of freedom" (1:25), and a set of ethical commands (2:11; cf. Gal 5:3) does not seem to square up with the view of James in Acts, Galatians, and Hegesippus. In these latter sources, James the Lord's brother has a more Judean legalistic frame of mind and a special concern for cultic and ritual requirements (e.g., Acts 15:29; 21:23–24; Gal 2:9). The book of James makes no mention of such Judean ritual and cultic demands.[27]

The numerous parallels of James with other early writings by Christ-followers raise doubts about its originality if it was the product of an eyewitness of Jesus. We will briefly compare James with Paul (including the so-called deutero-Pauline writings), 1 Peter, and the Shepherd of Hermas.[28]

---

26. This suggestion is often connected with a two-stage theory: the first is a Judean-Christ-followers homily (from James?); the second is the composite of the homily incorporated into a "literary epistle" with more polished Greek (see Davids, *Epistle of James*, 12–13).

27. It is possible, however, that the (final) author of James (writing 70–80?) was a spiritual descendant of the type of Hebrew Christ-following advocated by James. After the destruction of the temple (70 CE) and the rise of a Gentile majority, ethical concerns of the law would became even more prominent than the cultic and ritual aspects. Of course, the Pharisees (and Jesus) already had such an ethical emphasis even before 70. See various factions in Painter, *Just James*, 74–78.

28. For more detailed parallels, see Mayor, *James*, lviii–lxii, xciv–xcvi, xcviii–cii.

TABLE 2.4 James and Paul Parallels

Topic	James	Paul
Trials bring endurance, approval, or maturity	1:3–4	Rom 5:3–4
The goal of perfection	1:4	Eph 4:13–14
Tossed about by the wind	1:6	Eph 4:14
Put away evil	1:21; 3:14	Col 3:8; Eph 4:22
Not hearers of the law but doers are justified	1:22, 25	Rom 2:13
Law is perfect, holy, good	1:25; 2:8,12	Rom 4:1–5, 16–22
Who deceive (*apataō*) themselves	1:26	1 Cor 3:18 Gal 6:3
Keep (*tēreō*) yourself unspotted (*aspilon*) or pure	1:27; 3:8	1 Tim 5:22; 6:14
Choosing the poor of the world	2:5	1 Cor 1:27
Love your neighbor as yourself	2:8	Rom 13:9 Gal 5:14
Abraham justified by works or faith?	2:21–23	Rom 4:1–5, 16–22
Natural (*psychikos*), not from above/the Spirit	3:15	1 Cor 2:14

The author of James seems to be acquainted with the teaching of Paul, especially on the question of justification by works. Paul himself made statements that appear to reconcile faith and works (e.g., "faith working through love," Gal 5:6; cf. 6:2; "obedience of faith," Rom 1:5; "doers of the law" Rom 2:13–15; "holy torah," Rom 7:12; "covenant blessings," Rom 9:4; "love your neighbor," Rom 13:9–10). Martin Luther, however, believed that the two interpretations of *justification* could not be reconciled (cf. his Preface to Revelation).[29] The discussion in Jas 2:21–24 is inconceivable

---

29. That is, one is justified before God by faith *alone*, not works. Luther (1483–1546) did seek to distinguish love directed to one's neighbor and faith in Christ, which *alone* justifies one before God, LW 25:111. The Roman Catholic Council of Trent (1545–63) expressed the view that "our good works preserve our salvation, and . . . sustain the righteousness of faith that we have received" (Session IV, Canons 24, 32). The *Formula of Concord (Solid Declaration)* 1577, Article IV, reacting to Trent and an internal (i.e., Majoristic) controversy further clarifies Luther's distinction by stating that good works to one's neighbor are expected of the Christian who is *already* justified by faith, Kolb and Wengert, *Book of Concord*, 574–81.

without the activity of Paul preceding it in some way. There, of course, were early misconceptions of Paul in his lifetime. Yet the debate no longer appears to have the historical Paul present (e.g., Gal 5:13–14). It appears that James is correcting an image of Paul that has become formalized. He seems to oppose some excessive antinomian trend of a later Pauline theology. Those who consider Colossians, Ephesians, and 1 Timothy to be deutero-Pauline see these parallels lending support to a postapostolic date.

Closely connected with this "historical kernel" was the Christ-follower belief (i.e., a theological interpretation) that the destruction of Jerusalem was the result of God's punishment on the Judeans for the murder of righteous James.[30] If this is the case, it might explain why the author was at odds with an excessive form of Pauline Christ-following practiced in his day (cf. Jas 2:14ff.): e.g., the legacy of James has been vindicated and should be continued.

TABLE 2.5 James and First Peter Parallels

Topic	James	1 Peter
To those of the dispersion (Gk., *diaspora*)	1:1	1:1
Rejoice in manifold trials (*poikilois peirasmois*)	1:2	1:6
The proving (*dokimion*) of your faith	1:3	1:7
The withering grass and falling flower	1:10–11	1:24
Begotten (brought forth) by God's word (word of truth)	1:18	1:3,23
Submit (*hypotassō*) to God	4:7	5:6
Resist the devil (*diabolos*)	4:7	5:8–9
Perishable gold and silver (*chrusos, arguros*)	5:3	1:18
Covers a multitude of sins (*plēthos harmartiōn*)	5:20	4:8

The parallels of James with the so-called deutero-Pauline books (Eph, 1 Tim; Tab 2.4) and 1 Peter raise some questions. Was the book of James influenced by these writings that are considered postapostolic?[31]

---

30. For more discussion on this phase of Christ-followers, see Puskas and Robbins, *Introduction*, 212.

31. See, later in this chapter, arguments for 1 Peter as a postapostolic writing (written after the historical Peter). Postapostolic writings are characterized by a conservative spirit and a moral-legalist trend, not unlike the Hebrew Christ-following of James and Peter; see Puskas and Robbins, *Introduction*, 212, 229.

Even if direct dependency on these books is unlikely, all the above writings share motifs and imagery which are (mostly) characteristic of a later period of Christ-following (ca. 80–90 CE).

TABLE 2.6 James and Shepherd of Hermas Parallels

Topic	James	Hermas Mandates
Double-mindedness (*dipsychos*) and prayer	1:6–8	9.1–6
Double-minded/bad-tempered man is unstable in all his actions	1:8	5.2.7
What is earthly and heavenly	3:15,17	9.9–11; 11.11
The indwelling Spirit of God	4:5	3.1; 5.2.5–7
Resist the devil and he will flee from you	4:7	12.5.2
God, who is able to save and destroy	4:12	12.6.3
Object of prayer: to know God's compassion	5:11	9.2

Again, it is unlikely that James is dependent on the Mandates, even if the parallels derive from an *early* stage of Hermas (ca. 140). It is uncertain that Hermas is dependent on James, although some have favored this interpretation (Laws, Dibelius). It is arguable, though, that the two works share themes common to postapostolic Christ-following.[32]

The Alternate Theories

The difficulties raised with the view of the brother of Jesus as author of James leave several alternate theories for its authorship. First, the book was written by James the Just, but he relied on a skilled amanuensis to write it. The use of scribes or secretaries (Lat. *amanuensis*, "by hand") is typical in ancient letters (e.g., Marcus Tullius Tiro, the secretary of Cicero;

---

32. Sophie Laws sees Hermas as dependent on James and argues for Rome as the place of composition for both in Laws, *Commentary on the Epistle of James*, 22–23. Seitz argues for a common source, in "Relationship of the Shepherd of Hermas to the Epistle of James"; Dibelius sees common traditions, in his *James*, 31–32; Mayor lists many parallels, *James* lviii–lxii; see also Osiek, *Shepherd of Hermas*, 26, 132, 134, 438.

Tertius in Rom 16:22). Second, the book was perhaps written by an unknown James of early Christ-followers. This view has some merit and may lend support to the book's delayed acceptance in the Great Church. Third, the book may have been composed by an unknown teacher of the postapostolic period who wrote *in the name of* James the Just, the great leader of the early Jerusalem church. This position is held by those who assert that a disciple of Paul (not Paul) wrote, e.g., Ephesians, 1 Timothy (the "deutero-Pauline" letters) in the name of the apostle. The practice was not uncommon among disciples or admirers of both the apostles and great leaders among Christ-follower.[33] A fourth view, that the book was originally anonymous and later ascribed to James the Just, avoids the difficulties of intentional pseudonymity (theory 3) but lacks internal textual and external patristic support. The third view seems to be a majority opinion—that the book was written *under the authority of* James the Just, brother of Jesus and original leader of the Jerusalem church, but the first view (that James the Just relied on the scribal skill of an amanuensis) is not without some support.

If the book was written in the name of James the Just, perhaps its real author (a disciple?) adhered to a similar type of conservative Judean Christ-following. Even though the author does not appear to follow the cultic and ritual concerns traditionally ascribed to James (Acts 15; 21), the author was at odds with an excessive form of Paulinism (Jas 2:14ff.) practiced in his day. Like the figure of James portrayed in Acts and Hegesippus, the author of the so-called letter advocates a moderate position between two extremes: e.g., not *either* faith or works, but *both* faith and works.

The Date and Location

If James the Just authored the book, its date would need to be *before* his death in 62 CE,[34] although a disciple could have gathered up his teaching shortly afterwards. The position that James was composed later by a disciple *in the name of* the Lord's brother places the date of the book after

---

33. Painter, *Just James*, 237–40; Collins, *Letters That Paul Did Not Write*, 75–87.

34. On the stoning of James ca. 62, see Josephus, *Ant.* 20.197–203; Eusebius, *Hist. eccl.* 2.1.5; 23.1–2; *2 Apoc Jas* 61; see Painter, *Just James*, 118–42; McKnight, *Letter of James*, 20–23.

62 CE, in the later first century.³⁵ Parallels to 1 Peter and the later caricature of Paul's teaching opposed in James both seem to support this view. A Palestinian setting (e.g., Tiberius, Caesarea) in the late first century seems plausible,³⁶ but a pre–70 date (from Jerusalem) is not unlikely.

The Genre

Epistolary Features

Although it reads like a collection of wisdom sayings and ethical exhortations, James has some features of a literary epistle (but see my note, p. 40n1). It opens like a letter: "James, a servant of God and of the Lord Jesus Christ, to the twelve tribes in the Dispersion: Greetings." The title of the addressees is probably symbolic for Christ-followers or Judean Christ-followers living outside Palestine (cf. 1 Pet 1:1) and perhaps disenfranchised.³⁷ Like some ancient letters, James opens with a blessing or thanksgiving that is doubled (*charan*, 1:2–11, *makarios* 12–27; cf. 1 Macc 10:25–45; 1 Thess 1–2; Phlm 4–7). James also closes with a peroration (5:7–20; cf. 1 John 5:13–21) that contains an eschatological injunction (Jas 5:7–8), an oath formula (v. 12), and the mention of prayer (vv. 13–18; cf. 1 Thess 5:16–18, 25).³⁸ These general correspondences to the ancient letter may indicate that this collection of proverbs and exhortations was combined in an artificial letter form.

---

35. On the date of James, early and late, see Mayor, *James*, cxxi–clxxviii; Moo, *Letter of James*, 9–27; see chart in Davids, *Epistle of James*, 4.

36. Ropes, *James*, 28–33, 49; Painter, *Just James*, 240–41.

37. "Dispersion" (Gk. *diaspora*) originally of those Judeans forced to live outside Judah after the Babylonian captivity, 586 BCE (Jer 28:6; 2 Chr 36:20; John 7:35); used also in 1 Pet 1:1 of Christ-followers outside Jerusalem (perhaps disadvantaged). If the book is late first century (after 70) the addressees were probably Gentile Christ-followers, including perhaps a Judean-Christ-follower minority. If it was written before 70 CE (or 62), one would expect a mostly Judean-Christ-follower audience. Martin, *James*, 10, arguing for a Palestinian destination for James, interprets the phrase in Jas 1:1 symbolically as a condition of (solidarity in) suffering rather than as the place where they have been scattered (cf. Sir 44:23; 45:11; 2 Esd 6:7; 1QM 2:2; 3:14; 3:23—9:17; 1QSa 1:15).

38. Francis, "Form and Function of the Opening and Closing Paragraphs of James and 1 John."

Figure 6: Sculpture bust of Seneca (ca. 4 BCE—65 CE), Roman statesman, philosopher, and dramatist. National Museum of Berlin.

Sapiential and Hortatory Features. These concise wisdom sayings, ethical exhortations, and moral dialogues in James were prevalent forms in Hellenism. They are found in Judean sapiential (i.e., wisdom) literature (e.g., Proverbs, Sirach), homilies that were probably connected with the synagogue (e.g., Tob 4; Wis 1–5), and Stoic ethical writings (e.g., Epictetus, Seneca the Younger). Jacobean themes (e.g., enduring trials, divine wisdom, resisting evil and pursuing good) and familiar images (e.g., decaying wealth, reflections in a mirror, storms and seas) are also found in these hortatory writings.[39]

Because James shares many characteristics with paraenetic works, it has also been compared to Christ-follower works like the Didache and Barnabas (esp. Barn 19–20). Both of these books contain the teaching of the "two ways": the way of life and way of death, which are often ethical directives for new converts. As in Hebrews and 1 Peter, so in James the grammar abounds with imperative verbs (over one hundred: e.g., "know this, be doers, do not speak evil"). Because it prefers wisdom maxims over doctrinal exposition (e.g., it has almost no Christology), James can

---

39. Mayor, *James*, lxxiv–lxxvi (wisdom parallels); Sidebottom, *James*, 4–6; Malherbe, *Moral Exhortation*. On James 4:5 in the context of the Eldad and Modad traditions (LXX Num 11:26–30), see Bauckham et al., *Old Testament Pseudepigrapha*, 1:249–56, 686.

be closely identified with Judean hortatory literature (Prov 1–9; Wis 1–5; 4 Macc; Tobit 4; and T. 12 Patr.).

Rhetorical Devices

Metaphors and Similes

James uses figures of comparison (both metaphor and simile) derived from rural life (1:10–11; 3:11, 18; 4:14; 5:7), the sea and stars (1:6, 17; 3:4), domestic life (1:15, 18, 23; 2:26; 4:4; 5:2) and public life, (1:12; 4:1; 5:4).[40]

Repetition

One noteworthy rhetorical device used in James is the linking of clauses and sentences by the repetition of a catchword or its synonym.[41] It is found in Jas 1:2–8 ("patience," "asking"), 1:12–15 ("temptation," "lust"), 1:19–20 ("wrath"), 1:21–25 ("word," "doer"), 1:26–27 ("worship"), 3:24 ("offend," "body," "turn about"). A variety of other parenetic (hortatory) writings employ this device. We will give examples from Greek, Judean, and early Christ-follower writings with repeated words set in parentheses.

> *Greek*: Pseudo-Isocrates, *To Demonicus* 15–16 ("shameful"); 22 ("trust," "distrust," "oath"); 37 ("evil"); 43 ("danger").
>
> *Judean*: Tobit 4:13 ("arrogance"); 4:16–17 ("bread"); 4:18–19 ("counsel"); 12:6–8 ("works of God," "almsgiving"); Wisdom 6:20–21 ("that you may reign," "kingdom," "kingdom of God").
>
> *New Testament writings*: Matt 6:31–34 ("do not be anxious"); 10:26–31 ("do not fear," "fear not"); 18:6–14 ("one of these little ones"); Mark 9:49–50 ("salt," "salted with fire"); Rom 12:13, 17 ("pursue," "bless,"

---

40. For parallels with other Hellenistic writings, see Mayor, *James*, lxxxi–lxxxiii.

41. Mayor lists them in *James* ccxii–cxxiv, calling them paronomasia to convey the repetition of a like or "nearly like" word. Dibelius, *James*, 94–99 labels this technique concatenation (Lat. "link together") to convey the gradual ascent (anabasis) or climax achieved by this piling up of catchwords. With some qualification James also employs the following literary devices: "anadiplosis" (like sentence endings and begininigs) and "climax" or graduation in Bullinger, *Figures of Speech*, 251–55 (anadiplosis), 256–59 (climax). See also Lanham, *Handlist of Rhetorical Terms*, 10, 36.

"minds," "set mind," "all people"); Gal 6:3–10 ("bear," "reap," "occasion"); Col 3:9–15 ("put on," "give thanks," "be thankful").

When this "piling up" of catchwords achieves a buildup or climax it is called concatenation, anabasis, or gradual ascent. It is also a device used in both ancient and modern fairy tales or folk literature.[42]

Diatribe

As in the teachings of Teles Bion (third century BCE), Epictetus (first century CE), Musonius Rufus (first century CE), Plutarch (first and second centuries CE), and Seneca (first century CE), James employs the dialogical form of diatribe.[43] It probably originated in philosophical schools, where a teacher would try to expose the errors of his students and lead them into a more correct understanding of philosophy and life.

The diatribe includes the following features.[44] (1) It often begins with an apostrophe or indicting address to an imaginary dialogue partner or interlocutor (e.g., "You senseless person!" Jas 2:20; "Adulterers!" 4:4). Usually the interlocutor is a caricature of a proud or pretentious person who is censured by exposing his moral contradictions. (2) Objections to the author's claims or false conclusions drawn from the author's argument are raised by the interlocutor (e.g., "But someone will say, 'you have faith and I have works . . .'" 2:18a). The author's reactions to them are an indicting answer ("show me your faith apart from your works, and I by my works will show you my faith" 2:18b), a maxim or wise saying (2:19), counterquestions (e.g., 2:20–21), an abrupt rejection, supporting examples (e.g., Abraham, Rahab), or an analogy (e.g., body/spirit, faith/works). (3) Throughout the diatribe, a dialogical exchange occurs where the author or the interlocutor leads the questions, but the author guides the discussion to its resolution (2:14–26). In James 2, the author is clearly in control of the dialogue.

---

42. Adapted from Dibelius, *James*, 7–11.

43. See "Diatribe," in Aune, *Literature and Rhetoric*, 127–29. In another NT book, see Stowers, *Diatribe and Paul's Letter to the Romans*; Song, *Reading Romans as a Diatribe*. On the examples of diatribe in Epictetus and Musonius Rufus, see Malherbe, *Moral Exhortation*, 129–34.

44. Davids, *Epistle of James*, 22; on diatribe features, see Stowers, *Diatribe*; and Stowers, "Diatribe," 127–29.

By using the diatribe form of dialogue, the author of James is not so much concerned with polemics against opponents and outsiders. He seems to be interested in leading his readers into a greater commitment to the faith of Christ-followers by exposing false thinking and behavior. Along similar lines, Paul employed the diatribe in Rom 2–4 and 9–11.

The Rhetorical Structure

Basic Features

This rhetorical analysis will attempt to find a unified structure behind the book's diverse themes and literary forms.[45] James contains (prophetic) denouncements of wrongdoers (4:4–5; 4:13—5:6) characteristic of judicial or courtroom rhetoric; but in James these denouncements function more as refutations to the (anticipated) objections of his opponents. The many ethical exhortations also give the book a deliberative function. Deliberative or advisory rhetoric seeks to persuade its listeners or readers to follow acceptable practices and to dissuade them from unacceptable behavior. Therefore, the invectives in James 4–5 would seek to dissuade unacceptable behavior by way of illustration: these real or fictional opponents exemplify behavior that the readers are to avoid.

In deliberative rhetoric,[46] success rests on establishing two persuasive motives for the desired action: (1) honor or virtue (e.g., Jas 1:4, 12, 25, 27; *kalon*, 2:7–8, 19, 21; 3:2, 13, 17–18; 4:10, 16; 5:11, 17–18, 20); and (2) advantage (e.g., 2:14, 16, *ophelos*; 2:20, 22, 24; 5:15, 16, 20). The audience is persuaded by means of "proofs," which are appeals to the character of the speaker (ethos, Jas 1:1), to the emotions of the audience (pathos, e.g., 2:5–7, 14–16, 19–20; 4:1–4, 8–9, 13–14; 5:1–6), and to reason or logos (e.g., protasis "if" and apodosis "then" 1:5; use of *gar* "for, because," in enthymemes 1:6–7, 9–11, 19–21). The structure of a deliberative speech includes: (1) the proem or introduction (1:2–25), (2) the proposition or thesis of the author (embedded in proem, 1:19–25), (3) the proof or ar-

---

45. For a review of other structural outlines of James (e.g., by Bauckham, Davids, Johnson, Martin, Moo), see McKnight, *Letter of James*, 50–55.

46. According to the classical handbooks of Aristotle, *Rhetoric*; Cicero *On the Orator; Topics; Rhetoric to Herenntus*; and Quintilian, *On the Education of the Orator*. Classical examples of deliberative rhetoric are Demosthenes, *Third Philippic* (341 BCE) and lsocrates, *On Peace* (355 BCE). See also "Deliberative rhetoric" in Aune, *Literature and Rhetoric*, 124 ; Puskas, "Apostolic Advice," 202–6.

gumentation (2:1—5:6), and (4) the peroration, or concluding summary (5:7–20).

The Rhetorical Structure of James

I. Epistolary Prescript	1:1
A. Sender and addressees	
1. Ethos of sender as "a servant of God"	1a
2. Goodwill of addressees secured with designation "the twelve tribes of the Dispersion" (cf. 1 Pet 1:1)	1b
B. Salutation: "Greetings"	1c
II. Proem with Topics/Propositions Developed in Proof	1:2–27
A. First series of topics to be developed: testing, wisdom, and wealth	1:2–11
1. Trials (*peirasmoi*) that test your faith	1:2–4
—opening enthymeme on fortitude to be developed in peroration (cf. 5:7–11; cf. 1 Pet 1:6–7; Rom 5:3ff)	4
2. Wisdom that comes from above (to be developed in Proof, 3:13–18, Proposition A)	5–8
a. Advice on praying for wisdom (Prov 2:6; Wis 6–9)	5
b. Opening enthymeme on "praying with faith," to be developed in peroration (cf. 5:13–18)	6
"two-souled" repeated in proof (cf. 4:8)	8
3. The humble and the rich[47] (reversal; anticipates poor/rich topic in Proof, 2:5–7; 4:13—5:6, Proposition B)	9–11
B. Second series of topics to be developed: testing, hearing, doing, and pure worship	1:12–27
1. Those who endure (*hypomenō*) and those who fail the testing (amplifies advice in 1:2–4)	12–15
a. The blessing of the one who endures the testing (cf. Rev 2:10; anticipates topic in 5:11)	12
b. The error of the one who fails the testing	13–16
i) theodicy (implicit in vv. 5–7; cf. Sir 15:11–20)	13
ii) the process of lust (*epithymia*) in *peirazō* anticipating 4:1–12 (cf. 1 John 2:16)	14–16

---

47. Cf. on great reversal, Luke 6:24–25; 13:30; life as withering grass, fading flower, Ps 103:15–16; Isa 40:8.

  c. Assurance for all tests: God is a faithful/generous
    giver who begat us by the word of truth[48] (cf. 1:5)   17–18
2. "Be quick to listen (attentively), slow to speak,
 slow to anger" (v. 19) Proposition C   19–21
  a. Slowness in speech and anger (19) with supporting
    reason (20) anticipates discussion of the tongue,
    3:1–4 (cf. Prov 17:27–28; Sir 5:11–13)   19–20
  b. Concluding advice: put away evil; receive the
    implanted (*emphuton*) word[49] (anticipates 4:7–10)   21
3. "But be doers of the word and not merely hearers"
 (v. 22, Proposition D; cf. "four soils," Matt 13:3–9)   22–25
  a. Thesis statement   22
  b. Supporting illustration (mirror image;
    cf. 1 Cor 13:12; Plutarch, *Mor.* 1.42B)   23–24
  c. Promised blessing for those who focus on the
    "perfect law of liberty," and abide by it in practical
    service, cf. Ps 19:7   25
4. Worthless and pure worship (*thrēskeia*)   26–27
  a. Premise on worthless (*mataios*) worship, leading
    to argument on taming the tongue (1:19; 3:1–12)   26
  b. Identifying pure worship, which illustrates being
    "doers of the word" (1:22–25) and leads to the
    arguments in 2:5–13 and 14–17[50]   27

III. Proof with Refutation of Opposing Views   2:1—5:6
 A. Favoritism (*prosōpolēmpsia*) to rich is worthless worship   2:1–13

---

48. "Gave us birth" (Gk. *apokueō*) by the word of truth (cf. John 1:1–5; LXX Gen 1:26; 1 Pet 1:23; Col 1:15) is the positive counterpart of the negative "desire" that has conceived and "gives birth to" sin (*apokueō*, Jas 1:15).

49. "Lay aside/receive in meekness" (Jas 1:21) recalls Eph 4:23–24 ("put off/put on," cf. Col 3:5, 10–12; Heb 12:1; 1 Pet 2:1; 3:21). For "implanted word," see Jer 31:33 (LXX 38:33): God's new covenant when the law (*nomos*, LXX) is given "to the mind" (*dianoian*, LXX) and "inscribed on the heart," cf. Deut 30:14 LXX; Rom 10:8. See also Barn. 9:9, "the one who placed within us the implanted (*emphuton*) gift (*dōrean*) of his covenant (*diathēkēs*)" (cf. Barn. 1:2). Scot McKnight arranges Jas 1:19–21 in a chiasm (A B B' A') and thus highlights the reception of the implanted word (21b) as a concluding complement or supplement (A') to the threefold command in v. 19 (A), *Letter of James*, 135.

50. It is not enough to "hear" (1:22) and "to believe" (2:19); one must also act (cf. m. 'Abot, 1.17; 3.13), Jas 1:27 specifies the *right* kind of action, Martin and Elliott, *James, I–II Peter/Jude*, 25; cf. Exod 22:22–23; Deut 10:18; Isa 1:17; Jer 22:3; Matt 25:34–36; Jas 2:15–16.

1. Opening statement	1
2. Supporting reasons	2–13
a. Illustrated by hypothetical situation	2–4
b. Expressed by series of rhetorical questions	
(amplifies "poor/rich" topic in Proem, 1:9–11)	5–7
c. "Love your neighbor" (cf., Lev 19:18) in contrasting conditional statements ("if... but if...")	8–11
3. Conclusion, which reiterates motifs of perfect and royal law of liberty (1:25; 2:8)	12–13
B. The disadvantage of faith without works (amplifies topic of being "doers of the word," 1:22–25)	2:14–26
1. Thesis statement (with two appeals to *ophelos*, "good, profit," typical of deliberative rhetoric)	14–17
2. Refutation of opposing view (apostrophe 1; 3:13; 4:4, 13)	18–20
3. Proofs from Scripture (Abraham, Rahab)	21–25
4. Conclusion of argument drawn from analogy of body without spirit	26
C. Taming the tongue (amplification of topics, be "slow to speak," 1:19; & "unbridled tongue," 1:26; cf. Matt 12:36–37)	3:1–12
D. Wisdom that "comes from above" (amplification of topic introduced in Proem, 1:5–8; cf. Gal 5:19–23)	3:13–18
1. Opening address to "the wise and understanding" (apostrophe 2)	13–14
2. Enthymeme on practices contrary to wisdom from above	15–16
3. Conclusion: virtues that manifest wisdom from above	17–18
E. Evil desire (*epithymeō*) is the source of conflicts among people and with God (amplifies topic, *epithymia*, in proem, 1:14–15)	4:1–12
1. Opening question & counter-question on source of conflicts	1
2. Proof: the futile cycle of evil desire	2–3
3. Refutation of opponents ("Adulterers!" apostrophe 3)[51]	4
4. Peroration w/ exhortations & prohibition on slander	7–12
a. Closing exhortations: "submit... to God... resist the devil... lament... humble yourselves"[52]	7–10

---

51. Opening discussion breaks off to address the faithless in a prophetic denouncement, cf. Ezek 23:45; Isa 57:3 (LXX *moichos*).

52. In Jas 4:8, the opponents are called "double-minded" or "two-souled" (*dipsychoi*), used earlier in 1:8, in a similar manner (cf. 1 Clem 11.2; Herm. Vis. 3.4.3; Herm.

  b. Enthymemes on speaking against; judging others
    (cf. Matt 7:1ff)   11–12
 F. The rich (& their clients) will vanish in their undertakings
  (amplification of poor/rich argument in Proem, 1:9–11) 4:13—5:6
   1. Indictment of proud merchants (apostrophe 4)[53] 4:13–17
   2. Prophetic indictment of unjust landowners
    (cf. Amos 8:4–8; apostrophe 5)   5:1–6
    a. Summons to offenders: "you rich people"   1
    b. Calling of witnesses: their corrupt wealth   2–3
    c. Accusations against offenders (fraud, v. 4) with
     resulting judgment (day of slaughter, v. 5)   4–6

IV. Peroration of Topics Discussed   5:7–20
 A. On patient endurance (*makrothymeō*) before the parousia
  (reiterates topic of endurance, *hypomonē*, in Proem, 1:2–4, 12) 7–11
   1. Introduction: "Be patient, therefore"   7a
   2. Supporting agricultural illustration
    (cf. 1 Cor 9:7, 10; 2 Tim 2:6)   7b
   3. Supporting exhortation (v. 8) and enthymeme on
    murmuring (*stenazō*, v. 9; cf., speaking against, 4:11) 8–9
   4. Concluding examples of patient endurance in
    the lives of the prophets (v. 10) and Job
    (v. 11; *hypomonē*, cf. 1:2–4, 12)   10–11
 B. Take no oaths, be pure in speech so that you might not fall
  under judgment (recalls topics on speech and judgment in Proem,
  1:19, and Proof, 2:12; 3:2, 5–10; 4:11–12; cf. Matt 5:34–37; Jer 5:2;
  Zech 5:3b)   12
 C. On prayer (*proseuchē*) and petition (*deēsis*), especially when
  facing adversity (recalls asking in faith when tested, 1:5–8;
  asking wrongly, 4:3; and humbly approaching God, 4:7–10) 13–18
   1. Opening invitations to audience: pray when suffering
    or cheerful   13–14

Mand. 9.5–6; Herm. Sim. 8.7.2). It is the condition of the faithless one who has befriended the world order that is in conflict with God's ways (Jas 4:8). It is the opposite condition of those who are called the "pure ("clean," *katharoi*) in heart," who will "see God" (Matt 5:8).

 53. These self-confident planners of business (4:13–17; cf. Amos 8:4ff) may not be "the rich" but rather are clients of rich patrons, who are busy with their plans to serve them in return for (or because of) their rich benefactions; see Batten, *What are They Saying about the Letter of James?*, 67–70, 99–100.

2. The blessings of the prayer of faith (recalling 1:6-8)
      and of confessing your sins to one another for the prayer of
      the righteous (maxim, recalling right behavior before God,
      3:9-10; 4:8)   15-16
   3. The concluding example of Elijah, who was like us but
      prayed earnestly, and God answered his prayers
      (recalling 1:5-8; 4:3, 7-10)   17-18
D. Deliberative aim of book expressed: to turn the sinner away
from sinning (recalls topics on deception, 1:16, 22, 26; 3:14; infidel-
ity, 4:4, 7-8; and deliberate wrongdoing, 4:17; cf. 1 Pet 4:8)   19-20
   1. Premise: "if anyone wanders from the truth and is
      brought back by another"   19
   2. Conclusion as maxim: "whoever brings back a sinner
      from wandering will save the sinner's soul and . . . cover a
      multitude of sins" (recalling topics in 1:21; 2:14; 4:12; 5:15;
      cf. 1 Tim 4:16; Ps 32:1/31:1 LXX)   20

The Historical Situation

Although the book of James is replete with typical literary forms and stylistic techniques of rhetoric, their selection and inclusion provide some clues for understanding the historical situation of the author and his readers.

The author views himself as a teacher (3:1) and seeks both to persuade his readers to follow an honorable and advantageous course of action (e.g., 1:12, 25; 2:8; 5:11, 15-16) and to dissuade them from falling into error (4:17; 5:19-20). The argument of the book, therefore, coincides well with deliberative rhetoric.

The audience appears to be a community of Christ-followers living outside Palestine (1:1) who are anxiously waiting for the parousia (5:7-11) and seem to be undergoing some kind of oppression or persecution (viewed as a "testing") from wealthy landlords and perhaps rich merchants within their community (1:9-10; 2:1-7; 4:13-17; 5:1-6; cf. 1:2-8, 12-15).[54] The author is concerned about the behavior of his readers in

---

54. Linked to the question of the rich and poor is the topic of patrons and clients, prevalent in the Roman world (Vhysmeister, "Rich Man in James 2"; Kloppenberg, "Patronage Avoidance in James." Eschatology may also function to encourage the poor and threaten the rich (Tiller, "Rich and Poor in James"; see also Carroll, *The Return of Jesus in Early Christianity*, 121-30).

their context of persecution (1:2–8, 12–15). As a result, he emphasizes the importance of good works along with faith (2:14–26). Perhaps the readers were preoccupied with some extreme form of Paulinism (2:23–24) or were merely lax in practicing their faith. The problems facing the community appear to be dividing it (3:14–16; 4:1–3). The quarreling and strife (intensified by persecution?) seem to be related to the selfish ambition of some members (3:14–16; 4:1–3) and their partiality towards the oppressive wealthy in their midst (2:1–7). It is difficult to connect these statements with any specific historical event.[55]

The Author's Response

In response to the problems of division and strife (3:14–16; 4:1–3) the author encourages pure speech (1:26; 3:1–12; 4:11–12; 5:12), godly wisdom (1:5; 3:13, 17–18), patience/fortitude (1:2–4, 12), and praying with faith (1:58; 4:3; 5:13–18). These instructions are expressions of maturity and growth that are expected in both faith and practice. In the midst of their problems, the author encourages his readers to be faithful doers of the word (1:22–25, 27) like their spiritual predecessors (e.g., Abraham, Rahab, Job, and Elijah). As a moderator between two extremes (Judaizers and Paulinists), the author exemplifies a more conservative form of Judean Christ-following, not unlike that of James the Just. The book of James is also a characteristic of emerging orthodoxy among Christ-followers adjusting to life in the world (cf. the Didache).

Conclusions

The canonical authority of James was disputed for centuries. Even though it gained canonical status under the influence of Athanasius and Jerome, Martin Luther challenged it in the sixteenth century. The book appears to be Judean-Christ-follower writing from Palestine, containing some

---

55. Martin, *James*, lxi–lxix, sets the letter after 59 CE, in Syro-Palestine, a life-setting known from, e.g., Josephus, *Ant.* 20.180–81, where aristocratic land-owning high priests (pro-Roman) oppressed the lower-working-class priests who sympathized with the zealots and sicarii to bring about a regime change (contra Rome; cf. Eusebius, *Hist. eccl.* 2.20). James's support for the poor involved the lower priests, some of whom were believers (Acts 6:7; 21:20) against the rich aristocratic high priests. Dibelius, *James*, 45–47 is skeptical about linking the statements in James to any historical event, because of the stereotypical nature of paraenesis in James.

vestiges of early Jesus sayings. Despite the above observations, it seems unlikely that James the Just, brother of Jesus, authored the book. The polished Koine Greek style, the apparently postapostolic features, and the lack of strong supporting evidence all raise problems with James the Just as the book's author. Oral traditions from James may have been written down by a skillful scribe in a two-stage development (tradition and redaction). Because of his prominence among early Christ-followers, the work may have also been ascribed to James by a later admirer or advocate of his conservative type of Christ-following.

The numerous parallels with Judean wisdom, Stoic ethical discourses, and early Christ-follower homilies suggest that James is a collection of wisdom sayings set within the framework of a hortatory book or homily. The rhetorical and stylistic devices (e.g., concatenation, diatribe) are typical of ancient hortatory or homiletical writings (e.g., Wis Sol, Stoics, Paul). The twofold purpose of the author—to persuade his readers to adopt acceptable behavior (1:12, 25; 2:8; 5:11, 15–16) and to prevent future error (4:17; 5:19–20)—coincides well with the function of deliberative rhetoric.

For the Lutheran Dietrich Bonhoeffer, James 2 and related passages had immediate relevance for his pastoral theology:

> Grace and deeds belong together. There is no faith without good work, just as there is no good work without faith. Christians need to do good works for the sake of their salvation.[56]

Bonhoeffer's statements find some support in Martin Luther, who, while maintaining that faith alone saves, wrote:

> O it is a living, busy active thing, this faith. It is impossible for it to not be doing good things incessantly. It does not ask whether good works are to be done, but before the question is asked, it has already done this, and is constantly doing them. Whoever does not do such works is an unbeliever.[57]

---

56. Bonhoeffer, *Discipleship*, 278.
57. Luther, "Preface to Romans, 1546," in *LW* 35:370.

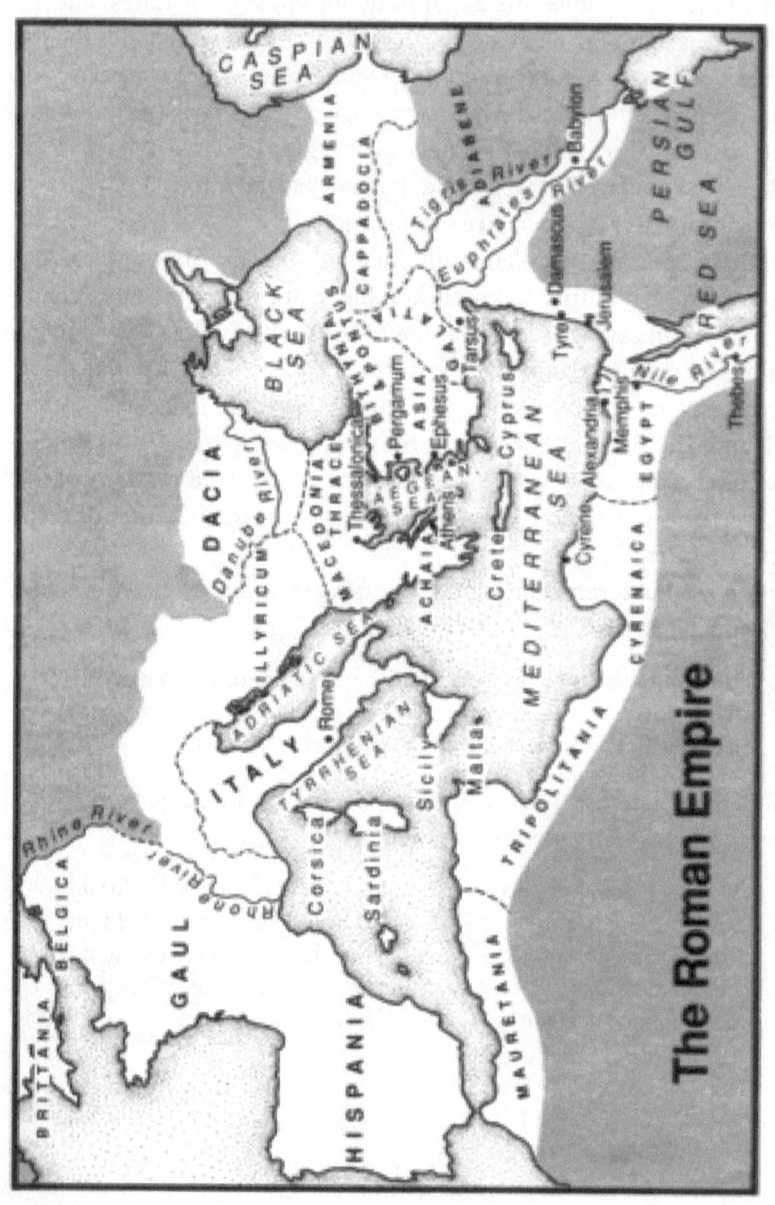

Map B: The Roman Empire in the first century CE

3

The First Letter of Peter

THIS BOOK HAS BEEN described as "a microcosm of Christian faith and duty; the model of a pastoral charge; a gallant and high-hearted exhortation which breathes a spirit of undaunted courage and exhibits as noble a type of piety as can be found in any New Testament writing; one of the most pastorally attractive and vigorously confident documents in the New Testament."[1] Although the distinctiveness of 1 Peter is often underrated because of its apparent dependence on other writings, the book provides us with helpful insights concerning the ethical standards, doctrinal beliefs, and liturgical patterns of an early Christ-follower community in an antagonistic pagan environment (4:3–4, 12–16).[2]

Authorship

Arguments for Authenticity

Both Irenaeus (*Haer.* 4.9.2; 4.16.5; 5.7.2) and Clement of Alexandria (according to Eusebius, *Hist. eccl.* 2.15.2) ascribe Petrine authorship to the

---

1. Elliott, "Rehabilitation," 244; cf. Selwyn, *First Epistle of Peter*, 1, 4.

2. For commentaries and other studies, see Donelson, *I & II Peter and Jude*; Vinson et al., *1 & 2 Peter, Jude*; Jobes, *1 Peter*; Hengel, *Saint Peter*; Senior and Harrington, *1 Peter, Jude and 2 Peter*; Achtemeier, *1 Peter*; Perkins, *First and Second Peters, James, and Jude*; Elliott, *1 Peter*; Elliott, *Home for the Homeless*; Elliott, "Rehabilitation"; Martin and Elliott, *James, I–II Peter/Jude*; Goppelt, *Commentary on 1 Peter*; Best, *1 Peter*; Beare, *First Epistle of Peter*; Cross, *1 Peter*; Dalton, *Christ's Proclamation to the Spirits*; Balch, *Let Wives Be Submissive*; Kelly, *Epistles of Peter and Jude*; Michaels, *I Peter*; Moule, "Nature and Purpose of 1 Peter"; Selwyn, *First Epistle of St. Peter*; Harner, *What Are They Saying about the Catholic Epistles?*

book. Polycarp seems acquainted with it by the first half of the second century (e.g., Polycarp, *Phil.* 1.2; 2.1–2; 8–1). Eusebius, in the fourth century, listed it as an acknowledged authority in the churches (*Hist. eccl.* 3.3.1, 4). Jerome, in his letter to Bishop Nepotian, in 395, quotes from 1 Pet 3:15 and 5:2 (*Ep.* 52.7).

In the book's epistolary prescript the sender is identified: "Peter an apostle of Jesus Christ" (1:1). Attempts have been made to support this claim by comparing 1 Peter with the teachings of Christ in the Gospels and the preaching of Peter in Acts.[3] Let's examine some examples.

"If you are reviled (Gk. *oneidizō*) . . . you are blessed" (1 Pet 4:14) recalls similar statements in the Beatitudes (*oneidizō*, Matt 5:11), and "casting all your anxieties on him" (*merimna*, 1 Pet 5:7) recalls Jesus's admonition "do not be anxious (*merizō*) about tomorrow" (Matt 6:34). The call to "be alert" (*grēgoreō*, 1 Pet 5:8) is reminiscent of Jesus's teaching on end-time expectancy (*grēgoreō*, Matt 24:42–44). The exhortation to "clothe yourselves with humility" (5:5) recalls similar teaching of Jesus to his disciples (Luke 12:35). Even though these (alleged) parallels can be interpreted in numerous ways (e.g., Matt and Luke as possible sources), the author claims to be "a witness to the sufferings of Christ" (1 Pet 5:1).

TABLE 3.1 First Peter and Acts Parallels

Topic	1 Peter	Acts
God's foreknowledge (Gk., *prognōsis*)	1:2	2:23
God is impartial (*aprosōpolēmptēs*)	1:17	10:34
God raised Jesus from the dead	1:21; 3:21–22	2:32–33; 10:40–41
The rejected stone has become the head.	2:6–8	4:10–11
Baptism for the forgiveness of sins	3:21 (cf. 1:22–23)	2:38; 10:43–48
Judge of the living and the dead	4:5	10:42

The following observations can be made regarding the above parallels. The author of 1 Peter could have made use of the Gospels of Matthew and Luke (or a source common to both). Therefore, the parallels do not

---

3. For the words of Christ in 1 Peter, see Gundry, "'Verba Christi' in 1 Peter"; for a comparison of 1 Peter and the Petrine speeches of Acts, see Selwyn, *First Epistle of St. Peter*, 33–36.

necessarily confirm that the author was an eyewitness of Jesus's ministry. The parallels with Acts (Tab. 3.1) are not decisive, because the sermons of Acts are considered by many scholars to be more Lukan than Petrine (or Pauline).[4]

Arguments against Authenticity

The author was at home in the Greek language. The Greek here seems even smoother than Paul's. It is closer to literary Koine (cf. Wisdom; 2 Maccabees; 4 Maccabees) and is influenced by the LXX. Therefore, it seems unlikely that Peter, an unlearned Galilean fisherman (Acts 4:13) who spoke in a provincial Aramaic dialect (Matt 26:73), and who was past middle age and in the midst of busy evangelistic activity, would have learned to write such impressive literary Koine.[5]

The theory that Silvanus the scribe (see 1 Pet 5:12) composed the letter under Peter's direction does not resolve all the problems of polished Koine in 1 Peter. Silvanus is not mentioned as coauthor in the prescript, as in 1 and 2 Thessalonians (cf. 2 Cor 1:19). If the mention of Silvanus in 1 Peter references the same Silvanus mentioned in the Thessalonian letters, even then the alleged parallels between 1 Peter and the Thessalonian correspondence do not conclusively establish an influence by the same Silvanus.[6] The language and style of 1 and 2 Thessalonians are distinctly Pauline (although 1 Peter contains some Pauline parallels). Furthermore, if this scribe was also Silas of Acts (15:22, 27, 32, 40; 16:25; 17:10; 18:5), he was a Judean from Palestine who may have lacked enough proficiency in Greek to qualify him as the author of 1 Peter. Despite the fact that the Silvanus secretarial theory cannot be disproven, it does not resolve all the problems.[7]

---

4. For example, see Fitzmyer, *Acts of the Apostles*, 103-8. Although Fitzmyer concedes that pre-Lukan material may have been incorporated, he concludes that many scholars find it "impossible to ascertain the historicity of the speeches," 106.

5. Hengel makes these observations in his *Saint Peter*, 12-13. Jobes, "Syntax of 1 Peter," however, finds some Aramaisms and less than native proficiency.

6. For comparisons of 1 Peter and 1-2 Thessalonians, see Selwyn, *First Epistle of St. Peter*, 369-84.

7. For the defense of the Silvanus secretarial theory see Selwyn, *First Epistle of St. Peter*, 9-17; and Jobes, *1 Peter*, 5-19. For a critique of this theory, see Beare, *First Epistle of Peter*, 212-16. Note that Goppelt, *Commentary on 1 Peter*, 50; and Kelly, *Epistles of Peter and Jude*, 32, also appropriate the Silvanus hypothesis with some reservations. See also Richards, *Paul and First-Century Letter Writing*.

Figure 7: Arch of Titus, Roman Forum (81 CE), celebrating
victory in the war with the Judeans (66–70 CE)

The trials and conflicts of 1 Peter (1:6–7; 2:12, 15; 4:4, 12, 14–16; 5:8–9) are generic, but if they indicate Roman persecution (e.g., "suffer, tested by fire"), they probably occurred after the time of Peter. According to Eusebius (*Hist. eccl.* 2.25) and Tertullian (*Praescr.* 36), both Peter and Paul were martyred in Rome under Nero (ca. 64–67). There is little evidence, however, that these Neronian persecutions spread to the provinces addressed in 1 Peter (i.e., Pontus, Galatia, Cappadocia, Asia, and Bithynia). Sporadic and localized persecution of Christ-followers occurred in the provinces during the reigns of Domitian (93–96 CE; see Suetonius, *Dom.* 10–17) and Trajan (ca. 112; see Pliny the Younger, *Ep.* 10.96–97). It thus appears that the apostle Peter died before Roman pressure was exerted on Christ-followers in the provinces (cf. 1 Pet 4:14–16). Nevertheless, if the accounts of Paul and associates in conflict with (mostly)

Judeans and certain pagans in Galatia and Asia (e.g., Acts 14:5-6, 11-20; 19:21-41; 2 Cor 11:24-33; Gal 5:11; 6:17) reflect ongoing local trouble with townspeople, it may indicate that early Christ-followers there were involved in disputes that Roman officials often overlooked or considered too minor to prosecute (see, e.g., Acts 18:12-17). Those who professed loyalty to Christ as Lord would have expected to encounter some animosity and hostility from others who honored traditional gods and the imperial cult.[8]

Comparisons with other NT and early Christ-follower works[9] also raise some doubts about the originality of 1 Peter as an eyewitness document.

(1) *1 Peter and Romans:* 1 Pet 1:14 (Rom 12:2); 1:21 (Rom 4:24); 1:22 (Rom 12:9-10); 2:5 (Rom 12:1); 2:6-8 (Rom 9:32-33); 2:13-17 (Rom 13:1-7); 3:8-9, 11 (Rom 12:16-18); 4:7-11 (Rom 12:3-8)

(2) *1 Peter and Ephesians:* 1 Pet 1:3 (Eph 1:3); 1:10-12 (Eph 3:2-6); 1:20 (Eph 1.4); 2:1 (Eph 4:25, 31); 2:2-6 (Eph 2:10-22); 3:1 (Eph 5:22); 3:22 (Eph 1:20-21)

(3) *1 Peter and the Pastorals:* 1:3-5 (Titus 3:4-7); 1:20 (2 Tim 1:10); 2:1, 10 (Titus 3:3); 2:9 (Titus 2:14); 2:13-3:7 (2:8-12; Titus 2:2-10); 4:16 (2 Tim 1:12); 5:1-2 (Titus 1:5-6)

(4) *1 Peter and James:* 1:1 (Jas 1:1); 1:6-7 (Jas 1:2-3); 1:23 (Jas 1:18); 1:24 (Jas 1:10-11); 2:1 (Jas 1:21); 4:8 (Jas 5:20); 5:5-6 (Jas 4:6-7); 5:9-10 (Jas 4:7-10)

(5) *1 Peter and Hebrews:* 1:1 and 2:11 (Heb 11:13); 1:2 (Heb 12:24); 1:19 (Heb 9:14); 2:24 (Heb 10:10); 2:25 and 5:4 (Heb 13:20); 3:9 (Heb 12:17)

---

8. Although he regards it as a Lukan composition, Haenchen is inclined to accept the general truth of the Gallio account (Acts 18:12ff), in his *Acts of the Apostles*, 541. On both official and unofficial local persecutions, see Achtemeier, *1 Peter*, 32-36. Looking at Roman conflict management in first-century Anatolia (Asia Minor), the following study argues for *both* formal and informal, unofficial and official, measures taken against Christ-followers who did not participate in voluntary associations and the worship of the traditional gods and the imperial cult; it shows how general animosity can easily turn into legal accusations (Williams, *Persecution in 1 Peter*, chs. 6-8). Emperor Decius (249-51) was the first to initiate an empire-wide persecution of "Christians."

9. Derived from Kelly, *Epistles of Peter and Jude*, 11-12; see also Selwyn, *First Epistle of St. Peter*, 365-466. Some of the above parallels employ similar Greek words (e.g., *parepidēmos*, Heb 11:13) or phrases, those found in, e.g., 1 Pet and Jas, are extensive.

(6) *1 Peter and the Synoptic tradition:* 1:10–11 (Matt 11:13; 13:17); 1:17 (Matt 6:9); 2:6–8 (Matt 21:42, 44); 2:12 (Matt 5:16; Luke 19:44); 3:9 (Matt 5:44; Luke 6:28); 4:13–14 (Matt 5:10; Luke 6:22–23); 5:7 (Matt 6:25,32; Luke 12:22,30)

(7) *1 Peter and 1 Clement:* 2:9 (1 Clem 59.2); 2:21 (1 Clem 16.17); 4:8 (1 Clem 49.5); 5:5 (1 Clem 30.2; 57.1)

The above parallels can be interpreted in a number of ways.[10] Some may reflect common (perhaps early oral) traditions and lend some credence to Petrine authorship. But advocates against this view conclude that an anonymous author made use of Paul's letter to the Romans and certain Synoptic traditions. The close parallels with the so-called deutero-Pauline writings (e.g., Ephesians, Titus) seem to indicate that the author of 1 Peter was associated with the Pauline school. Similarities with Hebrews, James, and possibly 1 Clement reflect a similar perspective among early Christ-followers near the end of the first century. First Clement (ca. 96 CE) may also have been familiar with 1 Peter.

Conclusions on Authorship

Although 1 Peter is not merely a product of Pauline Christ-following, common Petrine and Pauline use of various liturgical, paraenetic, and doctrinal traditions is evident. Although the case against Petrine authorship is persuasive to many, it is still possible to view 1 Peter as the product of a Petrine school that sought to preserve and propagate traditions associated with the apostle Peter.[11] The theory that Silvanus the scribe (1 Pet 5:12) composed the letter (under Peter's direction?) is still worthy of some consideration.

---

10. See the survey in Elliott, "Rehabilitation," 247–48, 254. Elliott, *1 Peter*, 40, concludes that the Petrine author was not dependent on Paul for his thoughts and formulations.

11. Hengel, *Saint Peter*, 12, suggests that the two (pseudepigraphic) letters of Peter were prepared by those who wanted to do something about the lack of materials when compared to the collected letters of Paul, as well as to strengthen the faithful who were facing increasing oppression during the reigns of Domitian and Trajan. The following article is supportive of Hengel's (pseudepigraphic) position: Ansberry et al., "Pseudepigraphy and the Canon," in Hays and Ansberry, eds., *Evangelical Faith*, esp. 157.

The Audience

The communities to which 1 Peter was addressed were scattered over a large region. Pontus and Bithynia, Galatia, Cappadocia, and Asia (1 Pet 1:1) are the titles of the four provinces of the Roman Empire that during the first two centuries, covered all of Anatolia between the Taurus Mountains and the Black Sea (i.e., most of modern Turkey). With the exceptions of Galatia and Asia, these provinces were not visited by the apostle Paul. They were thoroughly Hellenized regions, although there was a large mixture of races, cultures, and religious traditions.[12] The addressees appear to have been Gentiles because of references to their former pagan practices and traditions (1 Pet 1:14, 18; 2:9; 3:5-6; 4:3). Certainly Hellenistic Judeans resided in these regions (e.g., Saul of Tarsus, Gal 6:12-13; Acts 14:1, 19; 19:8-10, 17) but their presence is not explicit in 1 Peter. The phrase, "exiles of the dispersion" (1:1) originally referred to Judeans living outside Palestine (e.g., Deut 30:3; Neh 1:9; Dan 9:7), but here it is probably a symbolic designation of Gentile Christ-followers *temporarily* residing in a hostile world awaiting the bliss of a heavenly homeland (1 Pet 2:11-12; 4:11-17; cf. Heb 13:14: Jas 1:1; 4:4).

The primarily Gentile audience addressed here appears to be new or recent converts from paganism (2:9). Along with the baptismal language and imagery in 1 Peter (e.g., 1:2, 22-23; 2:1-2; 3:21), there are possible clues of a liturgical rite in progress for them: "now" (*nun*, 1:12; 2:10, 25; 3:21; "just newborn infants" (*artigennēta brephē*, 2:2). The ritual initiation into the community could also be regarded as the realization of certain eschatological privileges (e.g., salvation, an inheritance).[13] The exhortations in 1 Pet 2:3—3:7 may have functioned as a specific address to baptismal candidates. See my discussion of liturgical and baptismal features, later in this chapter for more information.

The audience may have been experiencing or anticipating various kinds of trials or suffering. Perhaps it was persecution, slander, or discrimination for their faith (*peirasmos*, 1 Pet 1:6; *katalaleō*, 2:12; *pathein*, 2:21; *kakos*, *loidoreō*, 3:9, *paschō*, 14, 17; *pyrōsis* 4:12-19; *pathēmatos*, 5:9-10). By 110 CE in Bithynia (1 Pet 1:1; 2:12), locals were (sometimes) arrested for worshiping Christ, though they could be released if

---

12. Hiebert, "Designation of the Readers in 1 Peter 1:1-2." See map on p. 66 of this book.

13. For helpful overview of baptismal imagery in 1 Peter, see Hartman, "Baptism"; and Hartman, *"Into the Name of the Lord Jesus,"* 115-21.

they denounced their faith and invoked the gods. Pliny the Younger, a governor of Bithynia, wrote to Emperor Trajan on this matter, and the emperor supported him; but Trajan cautioned against using any anonymous informants or accusers, which established a bad legal precedent.[14] Earlier, under Domitian (81–96), we have no evidence of any official and empire-wide persecution of Christ-followers.

Figure 8: Denarius of Augustus Caesar wearing a laurel wreath. Adopted sons, Gaius and Lucius, stand facing each other, each one resting a hand on a shield with spear behind.

Nevertheless, any reluctance and hesitation shown by Peter's community regarding the observance of the imperial cult or the local gods so prevalent in Greco-Roman society might have aroused the suspicion of local citizens, who could have interpreted these hesitant actions as disloyalty to Rome or as a threat to the local cult (cf. Acts 19:23–27).

Some pressure might have come also from the local Judean community (as well as "Gentiles," 2:12). These Jesus followers (mostly Gentile) proclaiming Christ as Israel's messiah and quoting freely from the Judean Scriptures might have been viewed as a threat to the Judeans (cf. Acts 18:12–13). The attitudes of these *former* pagans towards the Roman cult might have been more immoderate (or less nuanced) than the view of the local Judeans, thereby making their own adjustment and adaptation under Rome more difficult in this (presumably) post-temple period.

14. See Pliny the Younger, *Letters* 10.96–97 (LCL); later ca. 155 (under Antonius Pius, Hadrian's successor) Justin Martyr reports on the prosecution of certain Christ-followers, *1 Apol.* 4–7; (citing 1 Pet 4:15–16) 1.7.4; for discussion, see McKnight and Modica, *Jesus Is Lord, Caesar Is Not*, chs. 1–2.

Figure 9: A Roman couple holding hands.
Heliograph by Arents after E. Guillame. Iconographic Collections.

If the ethical exhortations in 1 Peter supply any clues about the addressees, then the following data are noteworthy. The audience of 1 Peter appears to be undergoing some test or trial involving something bad for them, perhaps suffering slander or discrimination. It is a diverse community. There seems to be some merchant or upper-class women in the congregations, who could afford fashionable styles (3:1–6).[15] There were

---

15. On financially secure women in the Roman world, breaking with traditional roles, morality, and customs, see, e.g., Sallust, *Bell. Cat.*, 25; Cicero, *Cael.* 32, 35. On the Hellenistic ideal of the modest matron, see a neo-Pythagorean letter ascribed to a woman (Melissa) in Judge, "Woman's Behavior"; and discussion in Pomeroy, *Goddesses, Whores, Wives, and Slaves*, 149–226. The Christ-follower women of Asia Minor with their own kind of "liberated behavior" (e.g., Priscilla, Phoebe, Junia) may have occasioned some stereotypical Hellenistic slander: e.g., "only 'loose women' dressed

also domestic slaves (*oiketēs*, 2:18-19) and young people (5:5). Frequent allusions to baptism and the former life of paganism seem to imply that many were recent converts. The communities were organized under the direction of "elders" (Gk. *presbyteros*, a word that can denote both rank [5:1] and age [5:5]).[16] They are to "tend their flock" willingly, not by compulsion, as examples (*typoi*) to the flock (5:2-3; cf. 2 Sam 5:2; Ezek 34:12). The readers are part of "God's household" (4:17), a "spiritual household" (2:5), a "chosen race, a royal priesthood, a holy nation" (2:9). These communities in need of solidarity and cohesion are primarily Gentile.[17]

The Date

The earliest date for 1 Peter would be during the Neronian persecutions (64-67 CE), and the latest would be the time of Polycarp (140 CE), who appears to quote from it (*Phil* 1.2; 2.1-2; 8-1). If it was not authored by Peter himself (Silvanus?) and seems to reflect a situation after his death (64 CE), a date after Nero is not unreasonable. The advance of Christ-following to Pontus, Cappadocia, and Bithynia probably happened a decade or two after the deaths of Peter and Paul.[18] Since 2 Peter knew of 1 Peter (3:1) as did probably 1 Clement (96 CE), a date in the last years of Domitian's reign, 93-96 CE, has some support. The illuminating information about the Roman prosecution of "troublesome" Christ-followers in the province of Bithynia (ca. 110 CE) in the correspondences of Pliny and Trajan (*Ep.* 10.96 and 97), indicates a situation similar to that which is found in 1 Peter (e.g., "you have had to suffer"; "[your faith] is tested by fire," 1:6-7; cf., 2:12,15; 4:4,12,14-16; 5:8-9).[19]

---

fashionably and spoke in public." Such "liberated behavior" (Gal 3:28) may have prompted the patriarchal injunctions in 1 Pet 3 to dress conservatively and behave with the quiet demeanor of a Greco-Roman matron (Corley, "1 Peter," 352). See also, on this Hellenistic ideal, Balch, *Let Wives Be Submissive*, 98-102. Elliott, *1 Peter*, 594-99 discusses some of the difficulties related to 1 Pet 3:1-7, e.g., submitting to abuse. For helpful survey of discussion, see Cortez, "1 Peter and Postmodern Criticism," esp. 163-66.

16. BDAG, 861-62; Kelly, *Epistles of Peter and Jude*, 3-5. Some important witnesses (P^{72} ℵ[2] A) include *episkopeō* "take oversight, oversee" (1 Pet 5:2), Metzger, *Textual Commentary*, 625.

17. On the need for cohesion among this community of resident aliens living in a hostile world, see Elliott, *1 Peter*, 150-53, 474-79.

18. Elliott, *Conflict, Community, and Honor*, 5.

19. Pliny the Younger, *Letters and Panegyricus* (2 vols.) 2:119-21, 126-7. See also

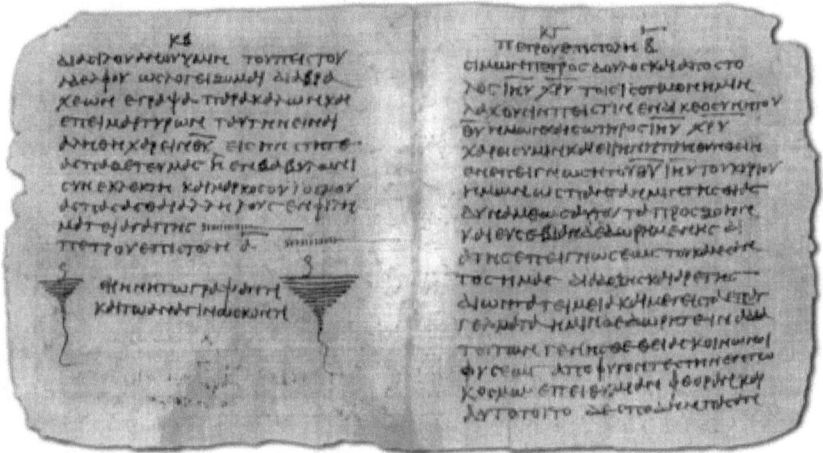

Figure 10: Papyrus 72, of 1 and 2 Peter (third century).

The Place of Composition

First Peter claims to have been written from "Babylon" (5:13). We have no evidence, however, that Christ-followers had settled in the ancient city Babylon near the Euphrates River (in modern-day Iraq) in the first and second centuries.[20] Therefore the name must be symbolic for another location. In numerous sources Babylon is used as a cryptogram for Rome as the persecutor of God's people (Rev 14:8; 16:19; 17; 2 Bar 11:1–2; 67:7–8; 4 Ezra 3:12, 28; Sib. Or. 5.153, 158, second century). This usage probably arose after Rome had destroyed Jerusalem's temple (70 CE), just as the Neo-Babylonians had done previously (in 587 BCE). As I stated earlier (p. 70), there is also a tradition that Peter was martyred in "Rome" (Eusebius, *Hist. eccl.* 2.25; Tertullian, *Praescr.* 36). Furthermore, there are close parallels between 1 Peter and 1 Clement (written from Rome), and the Roman traditions preserved in Hippolytus, *Apostolic Tradition*—all supporting the Roman origin of 1 Peter (see my note on p. 85n36).

Klauck, *Ancient Letters*, 77, 450.

20. The following study mentions monastic communities in Mesopotamia, but in the sixth century CE and later: Siegal, *Early Christian Monastic Literature*.

Use of the Judean Scriptures

For a book of only five chapters, 1 Peter has a surprising amount of OT quotations—at least twenty—and many allusions and echoes—thirty to forty.[21] Almost all follow some version of the Septuagint (LXX). Variations are often due to changes in verb tense, mood, person, or christological application. Our English OT (NRSV) is based on the Masoretic Text (MT).

TABLE 3.2 First Peter and the Old Testament Parallels

Theme	1 Peter	OT
"You shall be holy for I am holy"	1:16	Lev 19:2; cf. 11:44–45; 20:7
"all flesh is like grass . . . word of the Lord endures forever."	1:22–25 (cf. Jas 1:10–11)	LXX Isaiah 40:6–8
"Tasted that the Lord is gracious (*chrēstos*)"	2:3	LXX Ps 33:9 (MT Ps 34:8)
"I lay in Zion . . . a cornerstone elect, precious . . . whoever believes . . . will not be ashamed"	2:6 (Rom 9:33)	LXX Isa 28:16
"The stone . . . rejected has become the very head of the corner"	2:7 (Matt 21:42; Acts 4:11)	LXX Ps 117:22 (MT Ps 118:22)
"a stumbling stone, rock of offense (*skandalos*)"	2:8 (Rom 9:32)	Isa 8:14 (28:16)
"an elect race, a royal priesthood . . . God's own people"	2:9	Exod 19:5–6; Isa 43:20–21
"called you out of darkness into this marvelous light"	2:9b	Isa 9:2
"Once not a people, now a people of God . . . once no mercy, now you received mercy"	2:10 (Rom 9:25)	Hos 1:6, 9; 2:1, 23
"Who did no sin, nor was deceit found in his mouth"	2:22	Isa 53:9

---

21. Carson, "1 Peter," in Beale and Carson, *Commentary of NT Use of OT*, 1015–45; see also Moyise, *Later NT Writings and Scripture*, 42–61.

Theme	1 Peter	OT
"He bore our sins ... by his wounds you were healed ... you were going astray like sheep"	2:24–25	Isa 53:4–6, 12 (Ezek 34:6, 16)
Sarah called Abraham "lord (*kyrios*)"	3:6	Gen 18:12
"those who desire life ... Keep their tongues from evil ... do good ... seek peace ... Lord's eyes on righteous"	3:10–12	LXX Ps 33:13–17 MT Ps 34:12–16
Do not fear their fear ... "Sanctify Christ as Lord"	3:14–15	LXX Isa 8:12–13
Having gone preached to the spirits in prison	3:19 (4:6?)	*1 Enoch* 9:10–11; 10:11–15
"In the days of Noah" Angels, authorities, and powers are subject to him	3:20 (cf. Luke 17:26) 3:22	Gen 6:1–8; *Jub* 4:33—5:5; *1 Enoch* 6–10 LXX Ps 8:7; 110:1–3
"Love covers a multitude of sins"	4:8 (Jas 4:20)	Prov 10:12
"The Spirit of God ... is resting on you"	4:14	LXX Isa 11:2
If righteous are scarcely saved, Where will impious and sinner appear?	4:18	LXX Prov 11:31
"God opposes the proud but gives grace to the humble"	5:5 (cf. James 4:6)	LXX Prov 3:34
"Cast all your care upon, ... for he cares ..."	5:7	LXX Ps 54:23; Wis 12:13 (MT Ps 55:22)

Some noncanonical (1 Enoch, Jubilees) and deuterocanonical writings (Wisdom) were included because they are either presupposed (1 Pet 3:19–20) or complete the thought expressed in the verse (5:7). Quotations are drawn from Torah, Prophets, and Writings, but 1 Peter quotes most from Isaiah, next from the Psalms, and then Proverbs. These sections of biblical exposition have affinities with both rabbinic argumentation[22] and the pesher exegesis of Qumran implied by 1 Peter 1:10–12 (cf. Acts 2:14–21).[23] Many of these texts are used elsewhere in early Christ-follower writings (NT, Justin, Barn.) and may constitute a testimonia (cf. 4QTest; 4QFlor), an anthology of favorite OT texts circulated by the early church.[24] The author interprets many of these texts in light of the death and resurrection of Christ and finds in them a suffering-followed-by-glory theme, which is appropriate for new converts facing or anticipating some kind of suffering.[25]

The Genre

Epistolary Features

The book begins and ends like a Pauline letter (e.g., sender, addressees, greetings, 1:1–2; final greetings and benediction, 5:12–14) and contains numerous literary forms found elsewhere in the NT. For examples, 1 Peter contains:

---

22. E.g., the rabbinic inference from minor to major (*qal wahomer*, "light and heavy") is used in 1 Pet 2:21 servants/Christ; 3:1–6, wives to husbands/Sarah to Abraham; and the catchword linkage of similar words between two texts (*gezeira sheva* "comparison of equals") in 1 Pet 2:6–8 where the texts of Ps 117/118 are christologically linked with Isa 8; 28 by "stone" (*lithos*). These are two examples of the rabbinic middoth ("rules"); the original seven may date back to Hillel (first century BCE), see Bakhos, "Midrash, Midrashim," 944–49.

23. "This is that spoken by the prophet Joel," Acts 2:16; Bruce, *NT Development of OT Themes*, 20–21, 49, 89, 109. Pesher (Heb. "interpretation, commentary," cf. Eccl 8:1) is sometimes called "midrash pesher" (Vermes) to convey the idea of a nonliteral biblical interpretation often focused on present fulfillment—"this is that." See Aune, "Pesharim," in *Literature and Rhetoric*, 347–50; Longenecker, *Biblical Exegesis*, 18–30, prefers a separate treatment of rabbinic midrash and Qumran pesher (although a NT book could employ both).

24. Hodgson "Testimony Hypothesis"; Bergsma, "Testimonia," in *Literature and Rhetoric*, 456–57; Albl, *And Scripture Cannot Be Broken*.

25. Schutter, *Hermeneutics and Composition in 1 Peter*; Moyise, *Later NT Writings and Scripture*, 59–60. Two major NT interpretative approaches that connect the biblical text with the Christ event are: one of "prediction" and fulfillment (e.g., Matt 8:17) and one of biblical type with Christ as antitype (Rom 5:14). See Westermann, ed., *Essays on OT Hermeneutics*; Longenecker, *Biblical Exegesis*, 76–79.

- a prayer of blessing and thanksgiving 1:3-12 (cf. 2 Cor 1:3-7; Eph 1:3-14)[26]

- hymns 1:18-21; 2:21-25; 3:18-19 (cf. Col 1:15-20; 1 Tim 3:16; "ode" Rev 15:3-4)[27]

- catecheses and Christ-follower holiness codes (cf. Lev 17-26) 1 Pet 1:13-22 (1 Thess 4:19) and 1 Pet 2:1-2 (Col 3:8-17; Jas 1:21)

- baptismal formulae 1:22-23; 2:1-2; 3:21 (Rom 6:1-4; Col 2:12)

- biblical catenae 2:5-10; 3:8-12 (Rom 10:18-21; Heb 1:5-13)[28]

- tables of household duties 2:13-3:7 (Eph 5:21-6:9; Col 3:18-41; Titus 2)[29]

- catalogues of vices and virtues 4:3-11 (Gal 5:19-23; Col 3:5-15)

- eschatological admonitions[30] 1:13; 4:1-5, 12-19 (1 Thess 5:5-11; 2 Thess 1:5-12).

---

26. Gk. *eulogētos* (Heb. *beraka*), 1 Pet 1:3; 2 Cor 1:3; Eph 1:3; here a declaration to the worshipping community (not directed to God as in Heb. *baruk 'attah*), Michaels, *1 Peter*, 16. First Peter 1:3-12 (with v. 2) also functions as a musical overture announcing key themes to be developed later in the book, e.g., born anew, hope, mercy, chosen, tested by fire, sufferings of Christ (often as *imitatio Christi*), bring honor or honor (*timē*).

27. Hymns in 1 Peter also include doxologies (4:11; 5:11) as well as acclamations to Christ (1:18-21; 2:21-25; 3:18-19); see Farris, "Hymns, New Testament." These so-called hymns comment on or amplify the teaching of 1 Peter, and *function* in a way similar to the chorus in Classical Greek drama (e.g., Euripides, Aeschylus and Sophocles). Here a group of actors described and commented on the main action of a play with song, dance, or recitation. See my discussion of Revelation and Greek drama (p. 159n49). The *content* of the hymns of acclamation have similarities to the paean (Gk. *paian*) addressed to Apollo, Asclepius, and Zeus, usually at festivals (more sober than the boisterous dithyramb, sung to Dionysus at banquets), see "Paean," in Hornblower and Spawforth, *Oxford Classical Dictionary*, 1090.

28. Many of these texts are used elsewhere in the NT and may constitute a testimonia, an anthology of favorite OT texts circulated by the early church, see Dodd, *According to the Scriptures*; Hodgson, "Testimony Hypothesis."

29. On the debate of whether household codes (Ger. *Haustafeln*) protect Christ-follower identity (J. H. Elliot) or seek to uphold Greco-Roman expectations or ideals (D. L. Balch), see Horrell, "Between Conformity and Resistance"; and Pardee, "Be Holy, for I Am Holy."

30. There about 34 ethical exhortations (imperative mood) in 1 Pet (e.g., "be sober," Gk. *nēphontes*, 1:13; "be holy," 1:15; "love one another," 1:22; "Honor everyone . . . Fear God," 2:17; "glorify God," 4:16). Some (e.g., 1:13; 4:1-5, 12-19) but not all, include this eschatological motive or conclusion.

Liturgical and Baptismal Features

In order to contextualize the liturgical and baptismal imagery in 1 Peter, we will compare the images, themes, and language of 1 Peter with what we know of the practices, images, and language of mystery-cult ceremonies in the Roman world.[31] There are specific differences, but 1 Peter contains concepts of regeneration (1:3-4) also prevalent in many mystery cults. In them is the basic idea that an intensification of vitality through participation in the life of a god and a change of mind through an experience of the sacred. See, for example, the taurobolium in the mystery cult of Attis usually called Cybele (as early as third century BCE) from Asia Minor. In this dramatic ceremony, the high priest in full vestments goes into a trench with a grated covering over it; above him a bull was slaughtered, and the blood poured down through the holes onto the priest's body. The blood contains a vital force (Lev 17:11; Rev 7:14). The bull personifies this vitality, which is transferred to the priest on behalf of others and for him to carry out his work for other members. The priest's bloody garment was kept in a temple until the frightful ceremony is repeated after a certain span of time.[32]

In comparison with the mystery cults, regeneration in 1 Peter is also accomplished through a cultic act: here baptism (3:21 ; see my discussion, pp. 89-90). The vitality or benefit conferred, however, is not limited to a certain span of time; it is "imperishable" (1:4, 23). The Christ-follower's inheritance is "kept in heaven," not in an earthly temple; it is not "a blood-stained garment," but a treasure "undefiled" and "unfading" (1:4).

Although the earliest written sources for the mystery cults are diverse and from the second century CE (and later), their traditions and practices date much earlier. There are also parallels between 1 Peter and the rites of proselyte baptism in Judean tradition, which probably share

---

31. See Perdelwitz, *Mysterien religion und das Problem des 1 Petrus briefes*; Selwyn, *First Epistle of St. Peter*, 305-11; Beare, *First Epistle of Peter*, 35-37, 82-85, 114-17, 120-23, 130-33, 169; Godwin, *Mystery Religions*, 8, 23-24, 58, 111; Klauck, *Religious Context*, 81-152.

32. Taurobolium, is literally the "capturing of a bull with a rope lasso"; later it became the name of the *sacrificial* bull. The source that details this ritual is from the fourth-century Christian Prudentius in his *Peristephanon*, a collection of hymns in honor of martyrs; see Klauck, *Religious Context*, 127-28; Beare, *First Epistle of Peter*, 36; Godwin, *Mystery Religions* 8, 23-24, 58, 111.

a similar environment with the pagan mystery cults. Other similarities between 1 Peter and the mysteries[33] include:

(a) 1:2, *sprinkling with his blood*. This is another image similar to the taurobolium, where the blood of a bull dripped from a grated platform onto the priest below. The sprinkling with blood also has parallels in the ancient Hebrew sacrificial codes (Exod 24:8; 29:20-21; Lev 14:14).

(b) 1:23, *born anew, not of perishable seed but imperishable*. In the Hermetic writings, man's soul in union with the god received the "seed of God," being impregnated by the divinity.

(c) 1:5, *guarded* (Gk. *phroureō*) *by the power of God*. This concept corresponds to the *katochoi* or "prisoners of the god," who were under divine protection in the Serapeum (temple), as novices waiting for their initiation.

(d) 2:2, *like newborn infants, long for the pure, spiritual milk so that by it you may grow into salvation*.[34] The administration of milk and honey was part of the initiation rites of votaries of Cybele (Sallustius, *Concerning the Gods and the World* 4). Milk and honey were also given to newly baptized Christ-followers in the second century (cf. 1 Cor 3:2). The mysteries also referred to "spiritual worship" (*Poimandres* 31). The use of "pure" (*adolon*) in 1 Pet 2:2 may be in deliberate contrast with the "adulterated" milk of the mystery cults.

(e) 2:9, *of him who called you out of darkness into his marvelous light*. This dualistic concept (dear to gnostics) was also prevalent in the mysteries. "Calling" was necessary before the *mystēs* could approach the sanctuary of Isis; and in her ceremonies, as well as in those of Dionysius and Mithras, the votary had to pass through a darkened chamber into a place of wonderful light. In the dark chamber he experienced fear and humiliation, but as he ascended into the light, he was greeted with songs of joy and found festal garment and a crown (wreath) awaiting him (according to Apuleius and Pausanias).

---

33. From Selwyn, *First Epistle of St. Peter*, 305-11; Goppelt, *Commentary on 1 Peter*, 82-83, 129-31; see also Klauck, *Religious Context*, 81-152.

34. Such language conveys the *new* status of the recipients/hearers; see Martin, "Christians as Babies."

Figure 11: Christ-follower painting of a baptism (third century)

On the basis of the above parallels and similarities with early catholic liturgies, it has been argued that 1 Pet 1:3—4:11 was originally a liturgy for Christ-follower neophytes on the occasion of their baptism.[35] Perhaps some of the addressees had belonged previously to a mystery cult.

Liturgical parallels to 1 Peter from emerging orthodox Christ-followers are found in Hippolytus, *Apostolic Tradition* 16-34; Letter to Diognetus 11-12; Didache 7; 9; Irenaeus, *Demonstration of the Apostolic Preaching* 7; Hermas, Sim. 9.16; Justin Martyr, *First Apology*

---

35. The view of 1 Peter as a baptismal liturgy was originally developed in Perdelwitz, *Mysterien religion* (1911) and featured in Windisch, *Die Katholischen Briefe* (3rd ed. rev. by H. Preisker), see discussion in Kelly, *Epistles of Peter and Jude*, 15-20. See also Marie É. Boismard, "Liturgie Baptismale dans la Prima Petri"; Boismard, *Quatres Hymnes Baptismales*; Harner, *What Are They Saying about the Catholic Epistles?*, 36-39. In Cross, *1 Peter*, the suggestion that the baptismal liturgy was also a Christ-follower Passover celebration lacks evidence, but its revising of the liturgical theories of Perdelwitz and Preisker is noteworthy. For criticisms, see Thornton, "1 Peter"; Moule, "Nature and Purpose of 1 Peter"; Martin and Elliott, *James, I–II Peter/Jude*, 58.

61–67; Athanasius, *Easter Letter* 11; and the baptismal instructions of John Chrysostom. Liturgical parallels can also be found in the Mishnah concerning the order of worship in the synagogue (*m. Meg.* 3:5—4:6; *Yoma* 7:1; *Ber.* 1–2) and the purification rites of sprinkling or immersion with "sin-offering water" (*m. Hag.* 2:5–6; *Mik.* 1:1; 5:1; 8:2–5; cf. Num 19:18–19). Early examples of Christ-follower baptisms are found in Acts 8:26–39 (Ethiopian eunuch) and 16:23–32 (household at Philippi).

Along with the baptismal language and imagery in 1 Peter (e.g., 1:22–23; 2:1–2; 3:21) there are possible clues of a liturgical rite in progress: "now" (*nun*, 1:12; 2:10, 25; 3:21); "just now born infants" (*artigennēta brephē*, 2:2). The act of "putting up one's robes, tying them around oneself to get ready for some immediate action" (Gk. *anazōnnumi, osphus*, 1:13, baptism?). The ritual initiation into the community could also be regarded as the realization of certain eschatological privileges (e.g., salvation, an inheritance). The change of tense from 1:21 to 1:22 may indicate the actual baptismal act. The exhortations in 2:3—3:7 may have functioned as a primitive catechesis or holiness code for the three classes present for baptism: slaves, wives, and husbands. The change of setting in 4:12—5:11 (imminent persecution) may be regarded as a general address to the congregation, whose mature Christ-following lifestyle would inevitably bring them into conflict with their pagan neighbors. The celebrant who officiates at the ceremony is a head elder or bishop (2:25; 5:1,4). Let us now view an outline of 1 Peter as a (Roman) baptismal liturgy.[36]

---

36. "Roman" because of 1 Peter's probable origins, and similarities to the Roman traditions preserved in Hippolytus, *Apostolic Tradition* (220 CE). On "Hippolytus, St." (and his authorship of *Apostolic Tradition*) see Cross and Livingstone, *Oxford Dictionary of the Christian Church*, 778–79.

The Structure of 1 Peter[37]

I. Epistolary prescript (added later?)	1:1–2
II. Liturgy for candidates receiving baptism	1:3—4:11
A. Exordium: Opening prayer by presiding bishop[38]	
(*episkopos*, 2:25; 5:2; *presbyter*, 5:1, 5)	1:3–12
B. Bishop's formal charge to candidates before baptizing them	1:13–21
1. Protasis: you are privileged beneficiaries of God's grace (drawn from vv. 2, 3–12)	
2. Apodosis: "Be holy for I (God) am holy" (Lev 19:2)	13–21
a. Exhortations to holiness (cf. Lev 17–26)[39]	13–16
b. Motives for holiness (e.g., judgment, redemption)	17–21

Baptismal act[40]

C. Bishop addresses newly baptized on their initiation into the redeemed community	1:22–25
"Now that you have purified your souls, . . . you have been born anew"	
D. Bishop's invitation to newly baptized as members of the community to partake of the Eucharist	2:1–10
1. "Like newborn infants, long for the pure spiritual milk that by it you may grow up in salvation" (cf. 1:23; Heb 4:12–13)	2
2. "For you have tasted that the Lord is good" (Ps 34:9)	3

---

37. For alternative outlines, see Achtemeier, *1 Peter*, 73–74; Donelson, *I & II Peter and Jude*, 17–19; Perkins, *First and Second Peter, James, and Jude*, 21–22.

38. First Peter 1:3–12 (with v. 2) functions as a musical overture (orchestral introduction) announcing key themes to be developed later in the book, e.g., born anew (1:3,23), hope (1:3, 21; 3:15), mercy (1:3; 2:10), chosen (1:2; 2:4–9), tested by fire (1:6–7; 4:12), sufferings of Christ (1:11; *imitatio Christi*, 2:21, 23; 3:18; 4:1, 13; 5:1), honor/bring honor (*timē*, 1:7; 2:17; 3:7).

39. Selwyn concludes from this emphasis on holiness that the author understands the church as a "neo-Levitical community at once sacerdotal and sacrificial," in his *First Epistle of St. Peter*, 460. Whereas Leviticus is addressed to priest, 1 Pet 1:3—4:11 are addressed to candidate receiving baptism.

40. For the act of baptizing, see Acts 8:38–39; cf. Easton, *Apostolic Tradition of Hippolytus* 21.11–18 (pp. 46–47). Moule, however, finds no liturgy in progress here, "Nature and Purpose of 1 Peter," 4.

3. "Come to him [Christ], to that living stone . . ." (Ps 118; Isa 28)   4
4. "That you may proclaim the mighty acts" (cf. 1 Cor 11:26) "of him who called you out of darkness into his marvelous light" (Isa 9:2)   9
5. "Once you had not received mercy" (cf. Hos 1–2), "but now you have received mercy"   10

*** First Communion of Newly Baptized[41] ***

E. Catechesis for newly baptized: Christ-following Holiness Code   2:11—4:11
  1. Exordium: maintain good conduct as aliens in an evil age   2:11–12
  2. Body of community and household rules   2:13—3:12
    a. Community rule 1: subordinate (Gk. *hypotassō*) to civil authorities[42]   13–17
    b. Household rules (house slaves, wives, husbands)   2:18—3:7
      Hymn on Christ's humiliation (2:21–25)
  3. Community rule 2: Live in harmony and do not be revengeful   3:8–12
  4. Peroration of catechesis   3:13—4:11
    a. Maintain good conduct in an evil age   3:13–17
    b. Hymn on Christ's victory over evil[43]   3:18–22
    c. The share of the baptized in Christ's victory   4:1–6
      Hymn of Christ's suffering (cf. 2:21–25)
    d. Christ-following life in view of the parousia (cf. 2:12) doxology (4:11c-d)   4:7–11

---

41. For examples of the Eucharist ceremony after the baptismal rite, see Easton, *Apostolic Tradition of Hippolytus* ch. 26; Justin Martyr, *First Apology* 65; cf. *Didache* 7–9.

42. Elliott, *1 Peter*, 484–86, labels this section "honorable subordinate conduct." On *hypotassō* and *tassō*, "to bring about an order of things by arranging or putting in their place," see BDAG, 991, 1042.

43. In this context the hymn of Christ's triumph over the cosmic powers of evil (3:18–22) functions as a complement to the hymn of Christ's suffering and humiliation in 2:21–25. A link (death, dead, flood, judgment) between 1 Pet 3:18–19 and 4:6 (*spiritually* dead) is also established in a chiasm (inverted parallelism); see Green, *1 Peter*, 120–21.

F. Bishop addresses the entire community that is facing
(*ginomai*) some fiery trial (*pyrōsis*)⁴⁴   4:12—5:11
    1. "Christian" joy and confidence in a time of testing
       (*imitatio Christi*, cf. 2:21–23)   4:12–19
    2. Exhortation to leaders⁴⁵ and the faithful   5:1–5
 G. Peroration: final exhortations on humility,
    watchfulness, and the grace of God   6–11

III. Epistolary postscript (later addition?)   12–14
 A. Note on Silvanus the scribe   12
 B. Greetings from one who is "in Babylon" and Mark   13
 C. Closing exhortation and benediction   14

The Rhetorical Function

The view that 1 Peter is an adapted form of a baptismal homily finds some support in the book's rhetorical function.⁴⁶ Although the parenetic sections (1:13–21; 2:1–3; 2:11–20; 3:1–17; 4:1—5:11) has an advisory aspect (to dissuade and persuade), it is heavily flavored with the epideictic function of the book: to extol the common virtues and values of following Christ and to intensify adherence to them.⁴⁷ The opening prayer magnifying Christ (1:1–12), extoling Christ and his people (2:4–10, 21–25), the

---

44. The theory of two letters, based on the two different situations of "persecution" presupposed (3:13–17 and 4:12–17), has too many problems, see Moule, "Nature and Purpose of 1 Peter," 9–11. In my view, the possibility (or plausibility) of suffering (*paschō*, optative mood, 3:13–17) is included in the address to recent converts, and the experience (*ginomai*, present ptc.) of some fiery ordeal (*pyrōsis*, 4:12–17) is included in the general address to practicing Christ-followers who are living out their faith as "exiles" in a hostile world. The first instruction concerns the real prospect of suffering as a "Christian" (cf. 4:16), and the second, is a problem (of persecution?) that is testing the community. See also Hill, "On Suffering and Baptism in 1 Peter."

45. Some important witnesses (P⁷², ℵ², A) include *episkopeō* "take oversight, oversee" in 1 Pet 5:2, i.e., the work of a bishop or overseer (Metzger, *Textual Commentary*, 2nd ed., 625).

46. I have argued this same point in Puskas and Reasoner, *Letters*, 174–77—that although Ephesians is structured like a baptismal homily, the advisory aspect (to dissuade and persuade for a given situation) is subordinate to the epideictic function of the book: to extol the common values of Christ-following and intensify adherence to them.

47. D. F. Watson focuses on the hortatory feature and thus sees 1 Peter as deliberative or advisory rhetoric, in his "Epistolary Rhetoric of 1 Peter, 2 Peter, and Jude."

triumph of Christ over the powers (3:18–22), more examples of Christ to emulate with divine favor (4:1, 13; 5:1, 4, 10), and two doxologies (4:11; 5:11) support this encomiastic function. The address in 1 Peter 1:22—2:10 functions as specific exhortations to new converts, 1 Peter 4:12—5:14 can be viewed as general exhortations to the community (including leaders, 5:1-4), and 5:6-11 as closing admonitions. The above exhortations, although influenced by suffering of some kind (1:6; 2:12. 21; 3:9, 14, 17; 4:12ff), are generic enough to have been used in *other* contexts.[48] They tend to be typical paraeneses embedded with Christology, but also containing here baptismal imagery (1:3, 23-24; 2:9-10; 3:20-21). In our discussion of Hebrews, we mentioned the epideictic influence of both hymns and OT imagery on early Christ-follower sermons (p. 14n16).

Christ's Triumph over the Powers

The wording and form of 1 Pet 3:18-22 resemble that of 1 Tim 3:16, but it is difficult to determine if one is an adaptation of the other. One distinctive feature of the so-called Petrine hymn is Christ's proclamation to the spirits. In Judean tradition, these spirits are the rebellious angels of Genesis 6, the cause of Noah's flood, who are subsequently imprisoned, and to whom Enoch announces their final judgment (1 En 12–13; 2 En 7; Jub 10). This context explains the Noah reference in 1 Pet 3:20 and anticipates Christ's subjection of the "angels, authorities, and powers" (3:22).[49] Since by the end of 3:18, Christ's resurrection has already taken place, it follows that the preaching to the imprisoned spirits seems to be performed by the already-risen Christ.[50] Therefore, 1 Pet 3:19 does not refer to "evangelizing the [spiritually] dead" (4:6), nor the "descent

---

48. Selwyn, *First Epistle of St. Peter*, 18, has suggested that 1 Pet reflects a persecution fragment common to 1-2 Thessalonians, Acts, and the Synoptic Gospels that was circulated, but it has been difficult to prove. The parallel charts that he provides, however, do underscore the general usage of these paraeneses in *other* somewhat similar situations (497–61).

49. See Dalton, *Christ's Proclamation to the Spirits*, 177–202. On the difficulties of interpreting this text, see France, "Exegesis in Practice"; Marshall, *New Testament Interpretation*, 264–81. See also Michaels, *1 Peter*, 211; Donelson, *I & II Peter and Jude*, 112 (both commentaries supporting Dalton's view).

50. Martin and Elliott, *James, I-II Peter/Jude*, 95-99; "Christ ascended into heaven and preached to the spirits," (presupposing their supposed location in one of the lower spheres of heaven, cf. 2 Cor 12:2; Rev 12:7-9); Luther, "Commentary on 1 Peter" (1522), in *LW* 30:115 ("Christ ascended to heaven and preached to the spirits").

into hades" (cf. the Apostles' Creed). It rather expresses the early Christ-follower interpretation of Christ's triumph over the cosmic powers of evil (1 Cor 15:24–26; Eph 1:20–22; 4:8–10; Col 2:15). The resurrected Christ announces to these fallen spirits their final defeat, not a second chance to repent.[51] This news of Christ's authority over "the angels, authorities, and powers" (3:22) would be an encouragement to the readers, who feel oppressed by forces outside of their control.

In 1 Peter, water baptism does not appear to be a purification rite, as in Judean and pagan rituals. It involves an appeal or pledge (Gk. *eperōtēma*) to God for a clear conscience.[52] It is not the water itself or alone that effects the saving action. Noah and his sons were saved through the floodwater, not because of it. God, however, was active in the floodwaters of Noah's time and is active in the waters of baptism. In 1 Peter, water is the chosen means of God's saving action, which is rooted in the resurrection of Christ (3:20–21).[53] The readers would be encouraged by such words, for as Martin Luther (later) put it, "I will remember my baptism and remind God of his covenant, and then fulfil the work and purpose of my baptism."[54]

Conclusion

First Peter provides one with helpful insights concerning the ethical standards, doctrinal beliefs, and liturgical patterns of early Christ-followers in a hostile environment. Even though a case for Petrine authorship can be made, the polished literary style, the apparent postapostolic allusions, and the extensive parallels with other early Christ-follower writings raise doubts about it. As a result, 1 Peter may have been written in the late first century (during persecution at the time of Domitian?) to mostly Gentile Christ-followers of pagan background (1:14, 18; 4:3) from various provinces of Asia Minor (1:1). The place of writing, "Babylon," is probably a cryptogram for Rome, the persecutor of God's people (cf. Rev 16–18).

---

51. Luther wrote, "I cannot accept the interpretation that the gospel should be preached to the dead" (*LW* 30:121). For recent discussion in support of the traditional Catholic position (i.e., a triumphal descent into hell), see Pitstick, *Light in Darkness*, 30–60.

52. See BDAG, 164–65(*baptisma*), 362 (*eperōtēma*).

53. For further discussion, see Kelly, *Epistles of Peter and Jude*, 159–63; Goppelt, *Commentary on 1 Peter*, 266–71; Thurén, *Argument and Theology in 1 Peter*, 161–64.

54. Luther, "Holy and Blessed Sacrament of Baptism" (1519), in *LW* 35:42–43.

First Peter begins and ends like a Pauline letter and contains numerous literary forms of early Christ-followers (e.g., hymns, catecheses, ethical lists). Of particular interest is the liturgical and baptismal material. Comparisons with the rituals of mystery cults (e.g., Cybele and Mithra) and parallels with other early Christ-follower liturgies (e.g., *Apostolic Tradition*; Justin Martyr) recommend a reading of 1 Peter as a Roman baptismal service. Along with the baptismal language and imagery are indications of a liturgical rite in progress (1:21 to 1:22 may even indicate the actual baptismal act). The exhortations in 1 Pet 2:3—3:7 may have functioned as a specific address to baptismal candidates, and those in 4:12—5:11 as a general address to the congregation. The epistolary prescript and postscript could have been added when the liturgy was circulated among the churches.

Concerning the interpretation of 1 Pet 3:18–22, some observations were made. Christ's proclamation to the spirits in prison may be an image of the risen Christ's triumph over the powers of evil, and not a descent into hades. Also, it is unlikely that the water of baptism itself or alone accomplishes salvation, but it is the chosen means used to effect salvation through the resurrection of Christ (3:20–21).

It is ironic that James and 1 Peter, the first two books of the General Letters, which share many motifs and images, should be viewed in such a diverse manner through church history. For example, Martin Luther grouped 1 Peter with John's Gospel and Paul's letters, especially Romans, as "the true kernel" of the NT because of the way they present Christ to readers. The book of James, although he quoted select passages, was regarded by Luther as "an epistle full of straw, because it contains nothing evangelical."[55]

---

55. Luther's "Preface to the New Testament" (1546), in *LW* 35:361–62.

4

Jude and 2 Peter

Introduction

The relationship between the two writings called the Letter of Jude and the Second Letter of Peter is so close that I have chosen to discuss them together here, rather than separately in their canonical order (i.e., 1–2 Pet, 1–3 John, Jude).[1] Both contain a large amount of almost identical words and phrases. Both also maintain similar views of the Christ-follower faith and its opponents. Furthermore, both books remained on the disputed list of the NT collection until the fourth century. What type of literary relationship exists between Jude and 2 Peter? What are their similarities and differences? Why was their authenticity questioned for so many centuries? These questions, along with the literary characteristics and structures of 2 Peter and Jude, will be examined in this chapter.

Jude and 2 Peter: The Similarities[2]

TABLE 4.1 Jude and Second Peter Parallels

Topic	Jude	2 Peter
1) Self-description of author and blessing of peace	vv. 1–2	1:1–2
2) Exhortation to remember	v. 5	1:12–13

1. See the explanation in Reese, *2 Peter & Jude*, 13–14.
2. See Hultin, "Literary Relationships among 1 Peter, 2 Peter and Jude." Note that my topics here follow the chronological order of 2 Peter.

Topic	Jude	2 Peter
3) The infiltration of ungodly persons who are to be judged	v. 4	2:1–3
4) The fall and punishment of the angels	v. 6	2:4
5) The judgment upon Sodom and Gomorrah	v. 7	2:6
6) The vices and rebelliousness of those of the flesh	v. 8	2:10
7) The reluctance of angels to blaspheme angelic powers	v. 9	2:11
8) Opponents as wild beasts who blaspheme	v. 10	2:12
9) Metaphors of treachery applied to those "who feast with you"	v. 12a	2:13
10) Followers of greedy Balaam	v. 11	2:15
11) Metaphors from nature illustrate the deceit and fate of the opponent	v. 12b–13	2:17
12) Other vices of speech and practice applied to opponents	v. 16	2:18
13) Remember the words of the apostles of the Lord	v. 17	3:2
14) Scoffers will come in the last days, following their own passions	v. 18–19	3:3
15) The coming day of judgment	v. 14–15	3:10
16) Exhortations for readers to remain faithful	v. 20	3:14
17) To Christ be glory, both now and forever	v. 25	3:18

The Similarities Explained

These correspondences are too close to be coincidental. At least three explanations have been offered: both drew upon a common source, Jude borrowed from 2 Peter, and 2 Peter borrowed from Jude.

The Common-Source Theory

This theory has some validity. Although there are close correspondences, actual verbal agreement is rare (except for 2 Pet 2:17b and Jude 13b). In the polemical sections of both books, we find vague and exaggerated accusations that could have been derived from a common tradition of anti-heretical polemics. For example, the opponents are identified with Cain and Balaam, the typical villains of Judean tradition. One set of parallels also seems to presuppose the independent use of an early Greek myth: the overthrow of the Titans by Zeus (Hesiod, *Theogony* 732–33).[3] Both Jude 6 and 2 Pet 2:4 appear to divide between them the words of the story of the fallen angels, influenced by traditions in 1 Enoch (e.g., Jude: "chains, deepest darkness"; 2 Peter: "deepest darkness [Gk. *tartarus*])."[4]

Despite such observations, there are obstacles to this theory. First, the parallels are not confined to the polemical sections (see topics 1, 2, 16, and 17 in Table 4.1). Second, almost everything in Jude appears in some form in 2 Peter (e.g., 19 of 25 verses in Jude are reiterated in 2 Peter). If there were a common source it would almost be identical with Jude. The common-source theory would therefore make it difficult to resist the conclusions that Jude is merely the slavish imitation of an earlier work and that the source of 2 Peter is basically identical to Jude.

2 Peter as a Source for Jude

Advocates of this theory present the following arguments. First, there is the argument of possible allusions to 2 Peter. The false teachers of Jude are like those "previously written about" in 2 Peter (v. 4; cf. 2 Pet 2:1): "Remember the words previously spoken by the apostles . . . about scoffers in the last days" (Jude 17–18; cf. 2 Pet 3:2–3). Unfortunately, these references in Jude are too vague and generalized to function as probable allusions to 2 Peter. Second, the false teachers that 2 Peter foresaw (using the future tense, 2:1–3) are now experienced in Jude, which uses the present tense (vv. 8, 10) and the past tense (vv. 4, 11). However, 2 Peter may be employing the future tense as a literary device. The author also

---

3. Glasson, *Greek Influence in Jewish Eschatology*, 62–67; Bauckham, *Jude, 2 Peter*, 51–52 sees a common derivation from ancient Near Eastern myth: these "fallen angels" are even called "Titans" in Josephus, *Ant.* 1.73 (cf. Gen 6:4); Jdt 16:6; Sib. Or. 2:231 (Bauckham, *Jude, 2 Peter*, 249).

4. Especially the "Book of the Watchers" (1 Enoch 1–36); see Donelson, *I & II Peter and Jude*, 116–17.

changes from future to present tense at several points (see 2:10, 17–18; 3:5). Third, it seems inexplicable that the apostle Peter would depend on an obscure Christ-follower like Jude; it would seem instead that the lesser (Jude) would be influenced by the greater (Peter). This argument, of course, presupposes the questionable view that 2 Peter was authored by the apostle Peter. Despite the detailed arguments of older commentators,[5] the evidence for the priority of 2 Peter is meager. Again, it would be difficult to avoid the following conclusion: if Jude borrowed from 2 Peter, there would be scarcely anything original in Jude.

Jude as a Source for 2 Peter

Of the three theories mentioned, the dependency of 2 Peter on Jude seems the most plausible. It is easier to conceive of 2 Peter softening the harsh invectives, omitting difficulties, and improving on the style of Jude, rather than vice versa. Let us compare the two books. Second Peter seems to omit several of the sins attributed to the false teachers in Jude (topics 3, 5, 6, 10 in Table 4.1). Second Peter also appears to abbreviate Jude's accounts of the crime and punishment of the angels (topic 4) and the judgment on Sodom and Gomorrah (topic 5). Furthermore, the author of 2 Peter omits the references to Cain and Korah and tones down the exuberant denunciation of Balaam (topic 10).

Regarding Israelite history, Jude ignores chronological order, whereas 2 Peter carefully observes the events listed below as they appear in the sequence of both books:

Table 4.2 Second Peter, Jude, and Israelite History Parallels

2 Peter	Jude
1) *omits*	Israel in the wilderness
2) fallen angels	fallen angels
3) the flood	*omits*
4) Sodom and Gomorrah	Sodom and Gomorrah
5) *omits*	Cain
6) Balaam	Balaam
7) *omits*	Korah

---

5. For example, Luther, *Pastoral Epistles* (1546), 397–98; Zahn, *Introduction*, 2:250–51, 265–67, 285; Bigg, *Epistles of Saint Peter and Saint Jude*, 216–24.

Unlike Jude, which follows its own distinct arrangement, 2 Peter deliberately arranges the biblical events in a chronological scheme, from the fall of the angels to the time of Balaam.

The attitudes of both books to Judean Scriptures also suggests that 2 Peter was a later adaptation of Jude. Whereas Jude freely draws illustrations from 1 Enoch 60:8; 93:3 (Jude 14) and the Assumption/Testament of Moses 5:5; 7:9 (Jude 9, 12–13, 16), 2 Peter seems to maintain a stricter view of Scripture and omits some of these "apocryphal" references at the expense of obscuring the meaning of the passage (e.g., topics 1, 5, 7 in Table 4.2).[6]

It also should be noted that the letter of 2 Peter is struggling to keep its community together in the face of a delayed but inevitable end. Whereas Jude is more concerned that certain community members are being "snatched away" by ungodly ones, who distort God's grace.[7]

The Canonicity Question

Along with 2 and 3 John, Jude and 2 Peter remained on the disputed list of the NT until the fourth century, and even afterwards their authenticity was questioned. Was it the brevity of these books, their meager contents, or their persistent threatening tone that aroused the suspicions about them?[8]

Jude

The book of Jude received earlier recognition than 2 Peter. Both Tertullian of Carthage (ca. 200) and Clement of Alexandria (200) refer to it

---

6. Nevertheless, 2 Pet 2:4 ("Tartarus") may have been informed by apocryphal 1 En. 20:2; Sib. Or. 4:186; as well as LXX Job 41:24; also, 2 Pet 3:3–4 may have been influenced by the apocryphal traditions of Eldad and Modad (LXX Num 11:26–30) also found in 1 Clem 23:3–4; 2 Clem 11:2–4, see Bauckham et al., *Old Testament Pseudepigrapha*, 1:250–56; Bauckham, *Jude and the Relatives of Jesus*, 284–85. For survey of discussion, see Mason, "Biblical and Nonbiblical Traditions in Jude and 2 Peter."

7. Bauckham, *Jude, 2 Peter*, 151–54; Aichele, *Letters of Jude and Second Peter*, 40–63; on a comparison of Jude (with its fear of the ungodly infiltrators) and the 1956 horror film *Invasion of the Body Snatchers*, see Aichele, *Letters of Jude and Second Peter*, 24–39.

8. These and other questions are explored in Grünstäudl and Nicklas, "Searching for Evidence."

by name, and it appears on the list of the Muratorian Fragment (second century or later). Origen of Alexandria (250) was aware of the doubts concerning Jude (and 2 Peter) but cites it and seems to regard it as authoritative.[9] The Bodmer Papyrus of Egypt (P[72], third century) includes both Jude and 2 Peter. If 2 Peter is dependent on Jude, it would be the earliest witness of Jude's authority among early Christ-followers (late first or early second century).

In the Nag Hammadi Library (third and fourth centuries) there are about ten shared phrases or echoes of Jude in various codices (Ap. John, Great Pow., Testim. Truth, Teach. Silv.).[10]

2 Peter

No NT book has had a more difficult struggle to gain acceptance than 2 Peter. In the West it seems to have been unknown or ignored until the mid-fourth century. Jerome (ca. 385) reports that many disregarded it because of differences in style with 1 Peter (*Vir. ill.* 1; *Comm. Eccl.* 1) and suggested the theory that two different amanuenses (secretaries) were used (*Ep.* 120.11). Second Peter was first recognized in the East with its appearance in P[72], the Sahidic Coptic NT, and the Apocalypse of Peter (all mid-second century to third century).[11] Even though Origen (ca. 250) knew of its disputed status, he frequently cited it under the name of Peter. Eusebius of Caesarea (324) also knew the doubts about 2 Peter and classed it among the "disputed" writings (*Hist. eccl.* 3.3.1-4; 25.3). Despite its canonical recognition by Athanasius of Alexandria (367) and the Third Council of Carthage, the Syrian churches disputed the authority of 2 Peter until the sixth century. In the sixteenth century, its authenticity was rejected by Erasmus in the *Annotationes* to his Greek NT, 1516. Luther recognized it as a secondary NT writing along with James, Jude,

---

9. Patristic quotations are cited in Bigg, *Epistles of Saint Peter and Saint Jude*, 305-10. See lists and catalogues in McDonald and Sanders, *Canon Debate*, Appendix D.

10. See Scripture index in Evans, et al., *Nag Hammadi Texts*, 536-37.

11. Nag Hammadi Tri. Trac. I,5, 113.5-11 alludes to or echoes 2 Pet 1:20-21 (prophtets); and Great Pow. VI, 4, 38.34-26 alludes to 2 Pet 2:45 (Noah's preaching). Apoc. Pet. alludes to 2 Pet 2:2,15,21; see Bauckham, *Jude, 2 Peter*, 148-50 (parallels), 162-63 (attestation).

and 2-3 John.[12] Calvin considered 2 Peter as worthy of acceptance, but (for stylistic reasons) attributed it to the work of Peter's disciple.[13]

Jude: The Authorship

Arguments for Authenticity

The author calls himself, "Jude, a servant of Jesus Christ and brother of James" (v. 1). His brother James is probably the well-known brother of Jesus and leader of the Jerusalem church (1 Cor 15:7; Gal 1:19; 2:9; Jas 1:1). Jude is mentioned among the brothers of Jesus in the Gospels (Matt 13:55; Mark 6:3). Near the end of Domitian's reign (ca. 95), Hegesippus reports that two descendants of Jude, the brother of the Lord, were suspected of being descendants of King David. They were examined personally by the emperor but were released as harmless. Later they are reported to have been leaders of the church and to have lived until the time of Trajan (98-117).[14] The name Judas Thomas (the twin) was also recognized as an authority in gnostic circles (e.g., in the Gospel of Thomas) and was later called the twin brother of Jesus (Acts of Thomas 39). If Jude is an antignostic book, perhaps "brother of James" instead of brother of Jesus was preferred for polemical reasons.[15]

---

12. Luther, *LW* 35:362, 391-92.

13. "So then I conclude, that if the Epistle be deemed worthy of credit, it must have proceeded from Peter; not that he himself wrote it, but that some one of his disciples set forth in writing, by his command, those things which the necessity of the times required" (Calvin, *Catholic Epistles* [1551; 1855 trans.; repr., 1979], 363-64). See also Zahn, *Introduction to the New Testament*, 2:283n.1. Aichele, *Letters of Jude and Second Peter*, 43, 69-70, claims that 2 Peter's refinement of Jude's crude polemics helped both books to gain some acceptance in the church.

14. According to Eusebius, *Hist. eccl.* 3.20.1-3.

15. Robinson and Koester, *Trajectories*, 134.

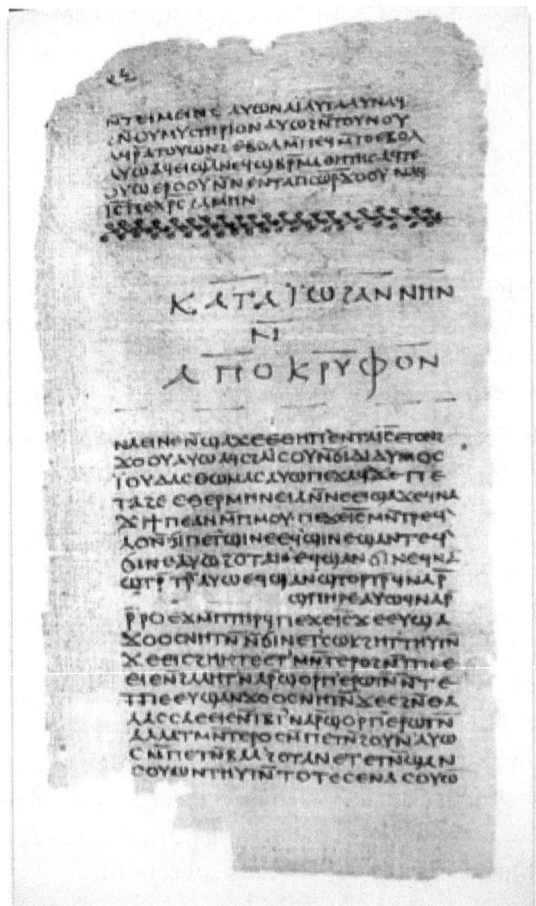

Figure 12: Folio 32 of Nag Hammadi Codex II, with the ending of the Apocryphon of John, and the beginning of the Gospel of Thomas.
Used by permission of the Yale Divinity School Library.

Arguments against Authenticity

Was the book written by Jude, the brother of James and Jesus? The author was acquainted with Judean apocalyptic writings (vv. 9, 11). His interpretation of Judean texts is similar to the pesher interpretation of Qumran (cf. 4QFlor, 11QMelch). But the author speaks of the apostles like a pupil from a time long afterward (Jude 17). He assumes a belief of "a faith once for all delivered to the saints" (3), but in statements against false teachers he cites with equal authority both Judean and early Christ-follower predictions (14, 17). All this suggests that the book of Jude is a writing from a later phase of early Christ-following. The high level of competence in Greek,[16] the wide vocabulary (e.g., 14 *hapax legomena*), and rhetorical skills do not suit well a Galilean villager like the brother of James and Jesus.

An Alternate Theory

The book was probably written near the end of the first or beginning of the second century, perhaps by a follower or admirer of Jude, the brother of Jesus. The identity of the opponents in Jude, although replete with polemical rhetoric,[17] reminds one of the libertine gnostics.[18] The letter, however, assumes that its readers already know who the opponents are, what they believe, and how they live.

The book's use of Pauline words and phrases like "called"; "loved"; "saints"; "grace"; "*psychikoi*, edification"; and "pray in the Holy Spirit" may indicate an influence from Pauline Christ-following. Its similarity in language and thought to the Pastorals (with its use of words like "faith," "remind," "godliness," and "deny") and to certain patristic writings[19] align Jude with emerging orthodoxy. Its view of the end-times, like that in 2 Thessalonians, Mark 13, and Revelation, underscores the resurgence of apocalypticism among Christ-followers in the late first century. The authoritative use of apocryphal texts in Jude reflects a period before the NT Scriptures were more narrowly defined (e.g., before the acceptance of 2 Peter, before the emergence of Marcion's collection).

Jude: The Place of Composition

The possible setting of the book can only be deduced from its contents or early reception in certain localities. A Palestinian setting might be inferred from the following data: its ascription of authorship to Jude from Galilee, use of Judean apocalyptic texts, Aramaic expressions (vv. 14–15),

---

16. Examples of Jude's command of Greek can be found in vv. 3, 7, 9, 10. A flavor for Greek poetry is also detected, with echoes of Moschus, Euripides, and Hesiod (v. 13); see Bauckham, *Jude, 2 Peter*, 6–7, 15–16.

17. Wisse, "Epistle of Jude in the History of Heresiology."

18. On libertine gnostics, see Irenaeus. *Against Heresies* 1.6.2–3; Clement of Alexandria, *Stromateis* 3.2–4; 7.7.17; Epiphanius, *Panarion* 40.2–4. See comparisons in Puskas and Robbins, *Introduction*, 235–37.

19. See 1 Clem. 20.12; 65.2; Barn 2.10; Polycarp, *Phil.* Intro; 3.2. *Mart. Pol.* 21.

and affinities with Qumran exegesis (Judea).[20] However, nearby Syria, Asia Minor, or Achaia (because of antinomian issues addressed), and Egypt (Clement of Alexandria, Origen, "Ethiopic" 1 Enoch) have also been suggested.

2 Peter: The Authorship

Arguments for Authenticity

In contrast to the writers of 1 Peter, James, and Jude, the author of 2 Peter makes great efforts to ascribe apostolic authorship to his work. The author introduces himself ceremoniously as "Symeon Petros, servant and apostle of Jesus Christ" (1:1), refers to the tradition that Jesus had predicted his martyrdom (1:14), emphasizes that he had been a witness of Jesus's transfiguration (1:16–18), presupposes 1 Peter in stating "this is now the second letter I am writing to you" (3:1),[21] and does not fail to mention that Paul is his "beloved brother" (3:15; cf. Gal 2:9).

Arguments against Authenticity

The following arguments, however, make it improbable that the above data are autobiographical allusions of Simon Peter. The reference to the transfiguration (1:16–18) seems to be derived from the Synoptic Gospels (Matt 12:18; 17:5; Luke 9:31–32). The prediction of Peter's death recalls the episode in the later epilogue to John's Gospel (John 21:18–19) and the language of 2 Cor 5:1 ("unfolding of this tent"). The author of 2 Peter equates the writings of his "beloved brother Paul" with "the other scriptures" (2 Pet 3:15–16; cf. 2 Tim 3:16). It is furthermore unlikely that Peter the disciple of Jesus would use Jude as his source.

Finally, the language of 2 Peter has similarities with the written idioms of second-century Christ-followers.[22] It is a thoroughly Hellenized

---

20. Bauckham, *Jude, 2 Peter*, 6–8, 15.

21. 2 Pet begins and ends in a manner reminiscent of 1 Peter (2 Pet 1:21/1 Pet 1:1; 2 Pet 3:16–17/1 Pet 5:12; Jude 24) and shares some similar words with it ("removal," *apothesis*; "conduct," *anastrophē*; "spotless," *aspilos*; "virtue," *aretē*; "brotherly love," *philadelphia*). Apart from these few similarities there are vast differences in language and style that have been noted for centuries (e.g., since Jerome and Luther).

22. H. Koester, *Introduction to the New Testament*, 2:298–300. Linguistic and thematic parallels with the Pastoral Letters, 1 Clement, Ignatius, Justin Martyr, and Melito of Sardis lend some support for an early second-century date, for parallels see Bigg,

literary language, using phrases like "participants in divine nature" (1:4) that seem foreign to earliest Christ-followers.[23] It betrays familiarity with Greek stories (2 Pet 2:4 and the myth of Titans) and Greek proverbs (the sow in the mire, 2 Pet 2:22; Heraclitus). The language of 2 Pet 1:3–11 echoes some of the Hellenistic imperial and civic decrees.[24] Borrowings from Atticistic rhetoric (e.g., Aristides, Plutarch, Philo, Josephus) also distinguish 2 Peter from the Koine Greek of the early Christ-follower writings (e.g., Mark, John, Paul's letters).

The mention of Paul and his letters in 2 Pet 3:15–16 probably reflects a tendency to view these two apostles (Paul and Peter) as primary authorities in the church.[25] In 2 Peter, the apostles are mentioned alongside the prophets as if both were accessible in authoritative writings (3:2). From its allusions and sources, a collection of NT Scriptures can be deduced: Jude, 1 Peter, a collection of Paul's letters (e.g., 1 Thessalonians, Romans, Galatians, 1 and 2 Corinthians), Matthew and (possibly) Luke. Like Dionysius of Corinth (ca. 180), the author of 2 Peter is also concerned about those who twist the Scriptures.[26] Based on the above data, a time of composition shortly after the writing of Jude (late first or early second century) has some likelihood.

2 Peter: The Historical Situation

Although its polemical language is stereotypical, it seems plausible, as in the case of Jude, that gnostics are the opponents in 2 Peter. The author may even have reformulated his thought against specific gnostic interpretations of Genesis.[27] Conscious of a more defined collection of Scrip-

---

Epistles of St. Peter and St. Jude, 205–10.

23. The phrase, however, is found in Plato, Seneca, Philo, Josephus, Clement of Alexandria. Other distinctly Hellenistic phrases in 2 Peter are "divine power" (*theia dynamis*), "glory and excellence (*doxa kai aretē*) "piety" or "godliness" (*eusebeia*) and "eyewitness" (*epoptēs*).

24. Danker, "2 Peter 1: A Solemn Decree." See also Danker, *Benefactor,* 238; Watson and Callan, *First and Second Peter,* 134–35.

25. Ignatius of Antioch (ca. 115) also reflects this tendency (e.g., Ign *Rom* 4.3). The Pastoral Letters, however, only seem concerned with extending and completing the Pauline heritage.

26. Dionysius of Corinth is cited in Eusebius, *Hist. eccl.* 4.23.12.

27. On 2 Pet 2:4–10 and its discussion of Gen 6:1–4, Noah, Sodom and Gomorrah, and Lot, see H. Koester, *Introduction to the New Testament,* 2:299; on gnostic mythological interpretations of Gen 6, see Perkins, *Gnosticism and NT,* 15–18.

tures, the author omits the apocryphal texts in Jude and labels the gnostic speculations (or writings) "cleverly disguised myths" (1:16). In a fashion reminiscent of Greco-Roman theodicies, the author also seems to indict the gnostics for their mockery of a future eschatology which probably results from their own overrealized eschatology.[28] Finally, in distinction from early Christ-follower expectations, 2 Pet 3:5–13 presents a doctrine of the end of the world in a manner palatable for Stoic sensibilities.[29]

Figure 13: Epicurean philosopher Metrodorus (331–278 BCE)

28. It is possible that the gnostic belief in living a spiritual resurrection in the present would also manifest itself in skepticism concerning expectations about a future parousia and speculations about retribution after death; see Talbert, "II Peter and the Delay of the Parousia." The following are theodicies of the Roman period: e.g., Plutarch, *De Sera Numinis Vindicta*; 1 Clem 23. For a comparison of 2 Peter and ancient theodicies, see Neyrey, "Form and Background."

29. For example, compare "'the conflagration of the cosmos" in 2 Pet 3:10, 12 with the Stoic Chrysippus, *Fragment* 625.4–5; Zeno, *Fragment* 98 (both in Barrett, *NT Background* [1987], 66–68); and Seneca, *Ep.* 91.12; see Harrell, "Stoic Physics." For a discussion on the eschatological differences of 2 Peter and early Christ-followers, see Käsemann, "Apologia for Primitive Christian Eschatology"; and Carroll, *Return of Jesus in Early Christianity*, 136–46.

Because Epicureans (cf. Acts 17:18) regard "pleasure" (Gk. *hēdonē*) as the chief human good with an "absence of pain," (contra 2 Pet 2:13–14), and deny both an afterlife as well as divine intervention in earthly life (Diog. Laert. 10.28–39; 2 Pet 3:9), it has also been suggested that Epicureans are the opponents here.[30] Josephus had even labeled the Sadducees as Epicurean (*War* 2.164) and the rabbis regard the scoffers (*apikoros*), the undisciplined, and antinomian, as Epicureans (*m. 'Abot* 2:14; *m. Sanh.* 10:1; *b. Sanh.* 99b). Plutarch's polemics against "the Epicureans" share some similarities with the content in 2 Peter. See, for example, the slowness (*bradutēs*) of the deity to punish the wicked, an Epicurean argument against divine justice (Plutarch, *Sera.* 548C–549B/2 Pet 3:9), or regarding stories of divine justice as myths (*mythoi*; Plutarch, *Def. Orac.* 420B/2 Pet 1:16), and skepticism concerning the authenticity of prophecy (Plutarch, *Def. Orac.* 434B; *Pyth. Orac.* 414E, 418E; *Suav. viv.* 111D-E/2 Pet 1:19–21; 3:10–12). As noted earlier, the "antihedonist" polemic of 2 Pet 2:13–14 may have addressed certain Epicurean abuses.[31]

In conclusion, the "false teachers" (2 Pet 2) may have had a mixture of beliefs. They also may have been a group that was distinct from "the mockers" (2 Pet 3).[32]

Jude: The Genre

What is the literary form of Jude? Is it a letter, homily, or polemical tract?

The Ancient Letter Genre

Jude has a letter opening with sender, addressees, and salutation or blessing (Jude 1–2; cf. 2 Thess 1:1–2; 1 Tim 1:1–2; 2 Tim 1:1–2; Polycarp, *Phil.* intro; *Mart. Pol.* intro). It also has a body opening, stating the occasion and theme of the book (Jude 3–4; cf. 1 Tim 1:3–7; 3 John 5–8; *Mart. Pol.* 1.1–2). Finally, it has a paraenesis (Jude 20–23; cf. 2 Thess 3; 1

---

30. Neyrey, *2 Peter, Jude*, 122–28; Neyrey, "Form and Background"; Davids, *Letters of 2 Peter and Jude*, 133–36; Asmis, "Epicureans." Luther identified the opponents of 2 Peter 3 as Epicureans in his preface to 2 Peter (*LW* 35:392). Interpreters before Luther had already cited passages like Luke 12:19 ("eat, drink, be merry," cf. Eccl. 8:15; Tob 7:10) as Epicurean.

31. Jobes, *Letters to the Church*, 371–72. See also Inwood and Gerson, *Epicurus Reader*, especially the polemic of Plutarch, 68–74.

32. Donelson, *I & II Peter and Jude*, 210.

Tim 6:11-21; Polycarp, *Phil.* 8-10) and a doxology (Jude 24-25; cf. Rom 16:25-27; 2 Clem. 20.5; *Mart. Pol.* 21). It however, lacks many significant NT epistolary features: thanksgiving, closing greetings, mention of travel plans.[33]

The Homily

The body of Jude, is more like a homily in letter form. It consists of a series of expositions from scriptural texts (vv. 5-19), a paraenetic section (vv. 20-23), and a closing doxology, also found in homilies (vv. 24-25; cf. 2 Clem 20.5; *Mart. Pol.* 21).

The exposition of scriptural texts (e.g., Zech 3:1-4; 1 Enoch 1:9; 5:4; 60:8) is similar to the pesher exegesis of Qumran. This form of interpretation viewed the scriptural texts as end-time prophecies that spoke exclusively to the interpreter's situation, which was the time of eschatological fulfillment. Similar to Jude's exposition of Scripture are the commentaries on various texts according to a particular theme, like "apostasy" (e.g., 4QFlor, 11QMelch, 4Q176, 4Q177, 4Q182, 4Q183).[34]

Jude, however, lacks much of the paraenesis characteristic of Judean exhortations and Christ-follower homilies (Jude 20-23; cf. T. 12 Patr.; Hebrews; 1 Peter; 2 Clement). Its content is more concise than these examples (e.g., tract) and it lacks the kerygma of Christ-follower homilies.

A Polemic

What predominates in Jude are the polemics against false teachers. The enumeration of their sins (Jude 4, 8, 10, 12-13, 16) is characteristic of the vice lists found in early Christ-follower letters (e.g., Rom 1:29-31; 1 Cor 6:9-10; Gal 5:19-21; Col 3:5,8; Eph 4:31; 5:3-5; 1 Tim 1:9-10; 2 Tim 3:2-5; 1 Clem 35.5-10) and Cynic-Stoic discourses (e.g., Epictetus, Seneca). Jude's mention of the appearance of the ungodly in the last days

---

33. The ancient letter had diverse forms, however. Klauck, *Ancient Letters*, 197, e.g., cites a third-century-CE source, *Formae epistolicae*, that lists twenty-one *different* kinds of letters (e.g., commendatory, censorious, admonishing, praising, advisory, apologetic).

34. Bauckham, *Jude, 2 Peter*, 5. See my earlier discussion on pesher exegesis, pp. 24, 80, 99). For further identification of these biblical texts from cave 4, etc., see Fitzmyer, *Dead Sea Scrolls*, 33-34. On the prophetic judgment-salvation paradigm in Jude, see Lockett, "Objects of Mercy."

(Jude 14-19; cf. 2 Tim 3:1-5) is also emphasized in apocalyptic literature. In these writings evil opponents face certain judgment (e.g., Rev 2:9-10, 20-25; 21:8; 22:5; 1 Enoch 91:6-8; 1QS 2:5-9, 14-17; 1QM 18-19; 1QpHab). Jude's stark portrait of false teachers and their historical predecessors (e.g., Cain, Balaam, Korah) also establishes a precedent for the attacks of the so-called church heresiologists (e.g., Irenaeus, Hippolytus, Epiphanius).[35]

Jude: The Rhetorical Function and Structure

In order to perceive the rhetorical function of these diverse forms in Jude, we must also analyze the book structurally. Although the polemical aspects reflect a forensic concern for the justice of past wrongdoings, the thesis (vv. 3-4) and closing exhortations (vv. 20-23) underscore the need to intensify present adherence to common values (epideictic rhetoric). This emphasis of demonstrative rhetoric includes both the praise of common virtues and the censure of characteristic vices.[36] Examples of this negative aspect of display rhetoric (i.e., "invective") are Lucian, *Passing of Peregrinus* and *Alexander the False Prophet*. Both satirical biographies by Lucian (ca. 160) heap ridicule on Peregrinus and Alexander in an attempt to destroy any following that the two teachers might have had. Even though they are also found in judicial speeches (e.g., Demosthenes and Lysias), invectives (including those in Jude) can function as the negative counterpart of epideictic rhetoric. Vices of cowardice, dishonor, and discord as well as invectives against opponents are often used in funeral orations and other ceremonial speeches.

The author of Jude, therefore, seeks to intensify adherence to the common faith through praise and censure. He not only exhorts his readers to "contend for the faith" (v. 3) and to adhere to Christ-follower virtues (vv. 20-23), but he calls himself "a servant of Jesus Christ" and identifies his readers as "those who are called, beloved in God ... kept for

---

35. Wisse, "Epistle of Jude in the History of Heresiology." On Jude's "paranoid phobia" regarding the ungodly who are different and perhaps even proto-orthodox, see Aichele, *Letters of Jude and 2 Peter*, 24-39.

36. For ancient rules on virtues and vices in display rhetoric, see Aristotle, *Rhetoric* 1.3.3,12-13,27-28; 1.9.24-37; *Rhetorica ad Herrenium* 3.6.1-2; Quintilian 3.7-23). Watson, *Invention, Arrangement, and Style*, 33 sees Jude as deliberative (advisory) rhetoric which relies heavily on epideictic (demonstrative) rhetoric in its efforts to advise and dissuade.

Jesus Christ" (v. 1). He is eager to write about "our common salvation" (v. 3a) and refers to Jesus as "our only Master and Lord" (v. 4). The attitude of "Michael the archangel" to the celestial ones is contrasted to that of the false teachers (vv. 8-9). Enoch's prophecy of the Lord's coming in judgment with his "holy myriads" and the predictions of "the apostles of our Lord Jesus Christ" concerning the last days, are to bring comfort and hope to the Christ-follower readers. The climactic doxology of praise to God (vv. 24-25) serves as the peroration of Jude's argument. Within this context of praising common values, the author of Jude presents, by contrast, the censure of the opponents, whose crimes are typical of all the enemies of God's people, and whose punishment by God is certain (vv. 4-19). In conclusion, the book of Jude may be categorized as a homiletical tract in epistolary form, which praises the common faith and censures its opponents.

The Rhetorical Structure of Jude[37]

I. Proem/epistolary prescript[38]	1-2
A. Sender and addressees	1
1. Ethos of sender as "Jude, a servant of Jesus Christ and brother of James"	1a
2. Secures goodwill of addressees by calling them "those who are called, beloved in God the Father and kept for Jesus Christ (display rhetoric; cf. vv. 24-25)	1b
B. Salutation (ornamental to set readers in a favorable frame of mind, cf. prescript to Ign., *Pol.*)	2
II. Proposition	3-4
A. Thesis: Exhorting (*parakalōn*) you to contend (*epagōnizomai*) for the faith that was once for all delivered to the saints, i.e., "'our common salvation'" (epideictic rhetoric)	3

---

37. For an alternative rhetorical outline focusing on the deliberative (advisory) aspects of Jude, see Watson, *Invention, Arrangement, and Style*, 77-78. For other, more thematic outlines, see Bauckham, *Jude, 2 Peter*, 5-6; Donelson, *I & II Peter and Jude*, 165; Painter and de Silva, *James and Jude*, 189.

38. Jude is characterized by an economy of expression. Therefore the epistolary prescript also serves as the prologue or proem of the rhetorical structure.

B. Supporting reason: "For certain intruders have stolen among you, people who long ago were designated for this condemnation (*krima*) as ungodly."	4
III. Narration of facts: The ungodly, who are designated for divine judgment (amplification of v. 4)	5–19
A. First three types from the Judean Scripture[39]	5–7
1. Unbelieving Israelites who were destroyed in the wilderness (cf. Num 14:29–37)	5
2. Fallen angels kept in prison until judgment day (1 Enoch 10:6–7; 12:4; 22:1)	6
3. Immoral cities of the plain (cf. Gen 19:4–25) who underwent eternal punishment	7
B. Application of above negative examples and positive example of Michael's rebuking of the devil	8–10
1. In like manner those infiltrators in our midst practice immorality	8
2. Michael rebukes their devil (anticipates "The Demonstration" vv. 20–23)	9
3. The "intruders" do by instinct that for which they will be destroyed	10
C. Three more types from the Judean Scriptures	11
1. Cain's way	
2. Balaam's error	
3. Korah's rebellion	
D. Application of above examples to current situation of infiltrators, with derogatory metaphors from heaven and earth	12–13
E. Prophecy of Enoch and application	14–16
1. "The Lord is coming with ten thousand of his holy ones" (1 Enoch 1:9)	14–15
2. Application to present situation	16
F. Peroration: prophecy of apostles and application	17–19
1. Introduction ("remember, beloved" cf. vv. 3, 5)	17
2. "in the last days there will be scoffers following their own passions"	18
3. Application to present situation	19

---

39. The applications of Scripture texts in Jude are similar to the pesher interpretations of Qumran, especially to thematic pesharim (e.g., 4QFlor, 11QMelch, 4Q176, 4Q177, 4Q182, 4Q183). See discussion in Bauckham, *Jude, 2 Peter*, 5.

IV. Demonstration of proposition 20–23
Exhortations (cf. *parakalōn*, v. 3) and actions expected of those
"who contend for the faith" (v. 3) 20
   A. Series of activities expected of the "beloved" (cf. vv. 3, 17)
   with a closing exhortation 20–21
   B. Series of exhortations to be followed by the "beloved"
   in specified ways 22–23

V. Peroration: Closing Doxology to God (cf. vv. 2–3): 24–25
   A. Who has power to save and keep the "beloved" 24
   B. To whom glory and authority are ascribed 25

The Genre of 2 Peter

Second Peter appears to be a final testament in an epistolary framework. It not only describes itself as a letter (3:1) but has a standard letter opening (1:1-2), an opening proem (1:3-11), an occasion for writing (vv. 12-15), a paraenetic section (3:14-18a), and a closing doxology (v. 18b; cf. Jude 24-25; Rom 16:25-27). Within this epistolary form is the traditional farewell speech or testament (1:12—3:18a).

The testament is a widespread genre in Judean and Christ-follower literature.[40] It often consists of a farewell speech with ethical admonitions of a departing leader (or parent) to his people (children). Most farewell speeches summarize his ethical and doctrinal instructions to be followed in the future. The ethical admonitions are usually connected with eschatological warnings and revelations of the future. These eschatological features in the speech assume the belief that a great individual in the last hours of life is endowed with prophetic insights of the future, and able to predict the destiny of his people (or children). Often his revelation of the last days provides a basis for eschatological exhortations. The final testament is basically a literary creation. It is generally ascribed to the departing leader (or parent) years after his death (Lat., *vaticinium ex eventu*).[41]

---

   40. For farewell speeches, see, e.g., Gen 47:29–49:33; Josh 22–24; Deut 31–33; 1 Chr 29; Tob 14:3–11; T. 12 Patr.; 1 Enoch 91–104; 4 Ezra 14:18–36; 2 Bar 78–86; Jub 10; 20–22; 30–36; Adam and Eve 25–29; Josephus, *Ant.* 4.309-19; Acts 20:17-38; John 13:31–17:26; 2 Tim 3:1–4:8; Acts of John 106-7; Acts of Peter 36-39; Acts of Thomas 159-60; farewell dialogue of Socrates in Plato's *Phaedo*. For further discussion, see Kurz, "Luke 22:14–38."

   41. For more information on the features of the last testament and farewell speech, see Bauckham, *Jude, 2 Peter*, 131-35; Donelson, *I & II Peter and Jude*, 211, focuses on

The ornate style and poetic rhythm of 2 Peter, with its figures of speech and repetition of words and phrases, also has similarities with the Nemrud Dagh Decree, Asia, inscribed on the mausoleum of Antiochus I (86–38 BCE), describing his benefactions and listing regulations for rituals to be observed at his site.[42]

The Rhetorical Structure of 2 Peter[43]

As a testament in epistolary form, 2 Peter (like Jude) is concerned with intensifying adherence to common values (epideictic rhetoric).[44] A farewell speech extolling common virtues is labeled by Menander Rhetor (300 CE) as *ho syntaktikos logos* (*Menander Rhetor* 2.15). Specific examples of this form of demonstrative rhetoric are the farewell address of Jesus in John 13:31—17:26, Paul's farewell speech in Acts 20:17–38, and the farewell address to Origen by Gregory Thaumaturgos in 328 CE (which is not fictional).[45]

The call to remember in 2 Peter (1:12–13,15; 3:1) appears in other farewell speeches (e.g., John 14:26; 2 Tim 1:3, 5) and forms of epideictic rhetoric (e.g., Rom 15:14–15; Jude 17). The censure of opponents (2 Peter), as mentioned in Jude, is the negative counterpart of praising common values. The autobiographical allusions, (1:12–18) typical of farewell addresses (John 13–17; Acts 20; 2 Timothy), also provide narrative background for the thesis (1:12–15).

I. Epistolary prescript	1:1–2
A. Sender and addressees	1
1. Ethos of sender as Peter, servant, apostle	1a

---

2 Peter as a NT letter and is reluctant to classify it as either a last testament or farewell speech.

42. Danker, *Benefactor*, 238; see also Watson and Callan, *First and Second Peter*, 134–35.

43. For alternative outlines, more thematic, see Bauckham, *Jude, 2 Peter*, 135; and Donelson, *I & II Peter and Jude*, 210–11.

44. Watson, *Invention, Arrangement, and Style*, 85–86, sees 2 Peter as deliberative rhetoric but does not deny both the epideictic and judicial aspects of the letter; on the different types of rhetoric, see ibid., 9–13; for his rhetorical outline of 2 Peter as deliberative rhetoric, see ibid., 141–42.

45. Kennedy, *New Testament Interpretation*, 76; Kennedy, *Classical Rhetoric*, 140–41.

JUDE AND 2 PETER

2. Goodwill of addressees secured by the elaborate description of them	1b
B. Salutation (ornamental to set readers in a favorable state of mind)	2
II. Proem	1:3–11
A. Encomium on the divine blessings[46] granted to the elect	3–4
B. Initial exhortation to supplement your faith with seven specific virtues (vv. 5–7) and supporting reasons (vv. 8–9)	5–9
C. Concluding exhortation: make firm your call & election	10–11
III. Proposition	1:12–15
A. Thesis: "Therefore I intend to keep on reminding you of these things, though you know them already and are established in the truth that has come to you."	12
B. Amplification of thesis as a last will and testament by an eyewitness of Christ	13–15
IV. Narration of facts	1:16–21
A. Apostolic eyewitness testimony	
1. Apostolic ethos of author/eyewitness	16
2. Eyewitness testimony (cf. Matt 17:5; Ps 2:7; Isa 42:1) substantiating the author's claims	17–18
3. Author's claim to prophecy, and exhortation to heed the message	19
B. Amplification of "prophecy" topic: the divine origins of prophecy	20–21
V. Digression: The certain judgment of false teachers (a contrast to true prophets, cf. 1:21)	2:1–22
A. Opening statement on false teachers and their certain judgment	1–3
B. Examples of previous judgments stated with conditional premises and conclusion	4–10a
1. Four premises: e.g., "if God did not spare . . . if he rescued Lot" (v. 8, parenthetical statement on Lot)	4–8
2. Conclusion to four premises: then the Lord knows how to rescue the godly and keep the unrighteous under	

---

46. Second Pet 1:3–11 also has noteworthy parallels to Hellenistic imperial and civic decrees, commemorating the many benefactions bestowed on a community by its benefactor; see Danker, "2 Peter 1: A Solemn Decree."

punishment until the Day of Judgment v. 9—amplification
on topic of "the unrighteous"   10a
C. Moral Failings (ethos) of Opponents and Their Punishment—
a series of comparisons and metaphors[47]   10b–22
D. Concluding statements on the deplorable consequences
of apostasy (cf. 2:15; cf. Prov 26:11)   20–22

VI. Proof   3:1–13
  A. Recapitulation of thesis (cf. 1:12–15); found also in
first letter: "remember the words spoken in the past by the holy
prophets" (cf. 1:19ff.) "and the commandment of the Lord and
Savior spoken through your apostles."   1–2
  B. First topic of thesis:
    1. Opening statement: those in the last days who will
scoff at the delayed promise of the Lord's return   3–4
    2. Rebuttal of the scoffers' position   5–7
  C. Second topic of thesis   8–10
    1. Opening statement: "With the Lord one day is like
a thousand years" (and vice versa)   8
    2. First amplification of opening statement: "The Lord is not
slow about his promise . . . but is patient"   9
    3. Second amplification of opening statement: "But the day
of the Lord will come like a thief, and then the heavens
will pass away."   10
  D. Peroration of proof   11–13
    1. Transitional and introductory statement: "Since all
these things will be dissolved," practice holiness and
earnestly desire "the coming of the day of God"   11–12
    2. Concluding statement: But according to his promise
(cf. 1:4) "we wait for new heavens and a new earth, where
righteousness is at home" (cf. Isa 65:17; 66:22)   13

VII. Peroration   3:14–18
  A. Opening enthymeme on Christ-follower ethics resulting
from end-time expectation

---

47. Since epideictic rhetoric includes both praise and censure, the topics on which praise is founded will, by their contraries, serve as the basis of censure *Rhet ad Herren* 3.5.10. Note also the many OT allusions in 2 Peter 2 (omitting Jude's use of 1 En., and As. Mos.): e.g., Num 22:28; 31:16; Deut 23:5; Jer 2:13; Neh 13:2; Prov 21:16; 26:11.

    1. Transitional and introductory statement: "Therefore,
       beloved" (cf. 3:1, 8, 17)   14a
    2. Doctrinal premise: "while you are waiting for these things"
       (cf. 3:12–13)   14b
    3. First hortatory conclusion: "strive to be found by him
       at peace (contra 2:10–12) w/o spot or blemish" (contra 2:13).
    4. Second hortatory conclusion: "and regard the patience
       (*makrothymia*) of our Lord as salvation (cf. 3:9)   15a
  B. Appeal to Paul's letters as support   15b–16
    1. "So also our beloved brother Paul wrote to you..."
       on the Lord's forbearance and eschatological ethics (cf.
       vv. 14–15) "as he does in all his letters"   15b
    2. Amplification of topic on Paul's letters (i.e., they
       are misunderstood and misinterpreted by the ignorant
       and unstable)   v. 16
  C. Recapitulation of thesis   3:17–18
    1. Introduction (recalling 1:12; 3:1): "You therefore,
       beloved, since you are forewarned..."   17a
    2. Negative admonition: "that you are not carried away
       with the error of the lawless (recalls 2:18–19)   17b
    3. Positive exhortation: "grow in grace..." (recalls 1:5–8)   18a
    4. Concluding doxology (*doxa*) to Jesus "our Lord"
       (recalls the laudation of 1:3–4)   18b

Conclusion

In this chapter on Jude and 2 Peter we examined their mutual relationship, canonical recognition, authorship, setting, literary character, and rhetorical structure. We observed that Jude was probably the source for 2 Peter, because the latter seems to omit, abbreviate, and rearrange the former. Jude received canonical recognition sooner than 2 Peter, although the difficulties for the acceptance of Jude may have concerned its use of apocryphal books (i.e., 1 Enoch, Asssumption of Moses). Doubts about the Petrine authorship of 2 Peter, its brevity, and the apparent use of material from Jude are some factors for its slow recognition and continued controversy over it in the church.

Jude may have been written in the late first or early second century and appears to be an example of the resurgence of apocalypticism among

Christ-followers (cf. Mark 13; 2 Thessalonians; Revelation). Second Peter may be a refined pseudepigraphic work (Theory 3, p. 53) with a heightened awareness of a collection of NT Scriptures. The problem of gnostic libertinism in Jude (p. 100n18) had developed into a controversy of misinterpreting texts and scoffing at the doctrine of the parousia and final judgment in 2 Peter. The opponents in Jude seem to be infiltrators, whereas in 2 Peter they appear to be surfacing as a group outside the church.

Although Jude is known for its polemics against false teachers, it seems to be a homily in epistolary form written to promote the common faith and to censure opponents (in the prophetic tradition). The ornate style of 2 Peter seems to signal that it a farewell speech in epistolary form, which, like Jude, extols the values of Christ-followers and denounces its counterfeits. Both writings, containing debate and attack, return in the end to a sense of confidence and celebration with which they both begin: doxology.

5

The Letters of John

Introduction

The history of Christianity includes too many conflicts and schisms.[1] In the Letters of John we find a community torn by such conflict. The two sides of the dispute include those who are loyal to the author of the letters (the elder/presbyter) and those who had left the community (1 John 2:19). How this problem and related issues are addressed here are noteworthy for anyone who has experienced church conflicts. Despite the background issues, these writings include conciliatory themes of divine love, unity, and mutuality, along with exhortations to live righteously and abide in God or Christ the Son.

Of the three so-called Letters of John only 2 and 3 John are undisputedly ancient letters.[2] Second and Third John also have specific audiences, whereas the audience of 1 John is deduced from its contents.

---

1. On "schism," see Cross and Livingstone, *Oxford Dictionary of the Christian Church*, 1473. See also discussion in Thompson, *1–3 John*, 13–18.

2. On a formal analysis of 2 and 3 John, see Klauck, *Ancient Letters*, 27–40. See my discussion on pp. 117, 128–30. For commentaries and other studies on the Johannine letters, see Brown, *Epistles of John*; Brown, *Beloved Disciple*; Bultmann, *Johannine Epistles*; Köstenberger, *Theology of John's Gospel and Letters*; Lieu, *I, II, III John*; Smith, *First, Second, and Third John*.

The Authenticity Question

The earliest clear allusion to the Johannine letters is in Polycarp's *To the Philippians* 7.1 (ca. 140), which alludes to 1 John 4:2-3, and possibly 1 John 3:8 and 2 John 7. In Irenaeus's *Against Heresies* (ca. 180) there are direct citations from 1 and 2 John.[3] Tertullian of Carthage (ca. 200) cites 1 John about forty times and refers to it as the work of the apostle John.[4] Clement of Alexandria (200) not only cites 1 John but speaks of it as "the greater epistle," presupposing knowledge of another epistle (*Miscellanies* 2.15.66; 3.4-32). Although the fourth-century historian Eusebius placed 1 John among the "acknowledged books" and 2 and 3 John among the "disputed" (*Hist. eccl.* 3.24.17; 3.25.2-3), he ascribed to the apostle John the authorship of the Fourth Gospel and those letters in which he calls himself a presbyter (*Demonstration of the Gospel* 3.5.88).

Authorship[5]

Did the same author write all three Johannine letters? A variety of responses have been given to this question.[6] A case can be made, however, for the common authorship of all three letters, although it is less likely that the same author composed the Fourth Gospel.[7] First, I will state my case by comparing 2 and 3 John. Then I compare and contrast the Gospel

---

3. *Against Heresies* 1.16.3 (2 John 11); 3.16.5 (1 John 2:18-22); 3.16.8 (2 John 7-8; 1 John 4:1-2; 5:1).

4. *Against Marcion* 5.16; *Against Praxeas* 28; *Against Gnosticism* 12.

5. Material from this section derived from Brown, *Epistles of John*, 14-35; and Lieu, *I, II, III John*.

6. For example, (1) the author of the Fourth Gospel also wrote 1 John, but "the presbyter" wrote 2 and 3 John, or (2) *each* document (1, 2, 3 John) was written by a *different* author. Trebilco, *Ephesus* (2007), 264-67, argues for all Johannine writings written by John the elder. Von Wahlde, *Gospel and Letters of John*, 1:50-55, also sees the elder as author of all three letters, responding to issues resulting from a literal interpretation of the second edition of John's Gospel.

7. Irenaeus assumes that the author of the Gospel and the Letters was "John the disciple of the Lord" (*Haer.* 3.16.5,8). Eusebius, who mentions that Papias (an associate of Polycarp) made use of 1 John (*Hist. eccl.* 3.39.17), notes, however, that Papias made a distinction between John the apostle and Evangelist, and another John, the presbyter and presumed author of 1 John (*Hist. eccl.* 3.39.3-5). Dodd, "First Epistle of John and the Gospel of John," made this distinction. Marshall, *Epistles of John*, 43, suggested that perhaps Eusebius (or Papias) was wrong, and that John the apostle was also John the elder, as in 1 Pet 1:1 ("apostle"); 5:1 ("copresbyter"). There are also issues with the Petrine authorship of 1 Peter, as noted earlier (see pp. 69-72).

of John and all three Johannine letters. The comparisons and contrasts will also provide the groundwork for determining the sequence in which the Johannine letters were written.

2 and 3 John

Second and Third John are almost identical in length (under 250 Greek words), about the standard size of a sheet of papyrus. They have similar opening and closing formulas (my translation from the Greek):

> Opening: "the presbyter . . . whom I love in the truth . . . I rejoiced greatly" (2 John 1, 4; 3 John 1, 3).

> Closing: "many things . . . to write to you . . . paper and ink" (2 John), "'Ink and pen'" (3 John), "I am hoping to be with (see) you . . . to speak to you mouth to mouth to mouth . . . greet(s) you" (2 John 12-13; 3 John 13-15).

The minor variations in both letters are more understandable if they are from the same writer, who would not have repeated himself with complete consistency (cf. the openings and closings of Paul's undisputed letters). There is also nothing in the style or content of 2 and 3 John that would make common authorship unlikely. Furthermore, why would a forger choose a letter whose author claimed only the modest title "the presbyter" (NRSV "elder")?

1 and 2 John

Did the same author who wrote 2 and 3 John, the "presbyter," write 1 John? A comparison of 1 and 2 John indicates numerous similarities. Both 1 and 2 John deal with those who have left the community, denied Christ's coming in the flesh, and are thereby branded antichrists and deceivers. Both stress the importance of loving one another. And the author of each displays full confidence that his view of Christology and ethics is conformable with what was from the beginning. Even though there are minor differences between 2 and 3 John and 1 John,[8] these can be viewed

---

8. For example, (1) the author of 1 John is unidentified; (2) the audiences of 2 and 3 John are specified; (3) terms and phrases like "elect lady," "the *truth* that abides," and "son of the Father," are found only in 2 John; and (4) the expression "walk in truth" appears only in 2 and 3 John.

as variations of one Johannine style rather than as the work of different authors.

The Letters and the Gospel of John

Was the author of the Johannine letters also the author of the Fourth Gospel? Given the similarities in content and structure between the Gospel of John and the 1 John, some have likened their relationship to the relationships between Luke and Acts, 1 and 2 Thessalonians, Colossians and Ephesians, and 2 Peter and Jude. Extensive lists of parallels[9] of 1 John and the Gospel can also be drawn up:

Table 5.1 First John and the Gospel of John Parallels

Themes	1 John	Gospel of John
Beginning word, life revealed/made flesh	1:1–3	1:1, 2, 4,14
We have seen and testify in the Father's (God's) presence	1:2	3:11
Unity of Father and Son	1:3; 2:24	5:20; 10:30, 38; 14:10
Joy-filled/fulfilled	1:4	15:11; 16:24; 17:13
God is light; I am the light	1:5	8:12; 9:5
Walking (abiding) in darkness/light	1:5–7; 2:9–11	8:12; 11:7–10; 12:35, 46
Know, do, act in truth	1:6; 2:21; 3:19	3:21; 8:32; 18:37
Have no sin	1:8	9:41
Truth being in a person	1:8; 2:4	8:44
Jesus/Holy Spirit as Paraclete[10]	2:1	14:16, 26; 15:26; 16:7

---

9. Some of the following parallels are derived from Brown, *Epistles of John*, 757–58; Painter, *1, 2, and 3 John*, 61–72; Köstenberger, *Theology of John's Gospel and Letters*, 129–35; and Parsenios, *First, Second, and Third John*, 8. Second and Third John also include themes from John's Gospel: e.g., unity of Father and Son (2 John 9), truth (2 John 1; 3 John 3, 8), in the flesh (2 John 7), a new commandment (2 John 5), love one another (2 John 5), fulfilled joy (2 John 12).

10. In John 14:16, Jesus refers to the Holy Spirit as "another Paraclete," but no one else is called a Paraclete in the Gospel, 1 John 2:1, however, refers to Jesus as the Paraclete. Does John's Gospel presuppose 1 John here? See Parsenios, *First, Second, and Third John*, 13.

Themes	1 John	Gospel of John
"Little children" (*teknia*)	2:1, 12, 28; 3:7, 18; 4:4; 5:21	13:33
Keep (God's/Jesus's) commandments	2:3, 4; 3:22, 24; 5:3	14:15, 21; 15:10
Abide in God/Christ[11]	2:6, 27–28; 3:6, 24; 4:15–16	6:56; 15:4, 6–7
A new commandment	2:7–8	13:34
Conquered Evil One (Prince of the World)	2:13, 14	16:17
Love one another	2:27–28; 3:11, 23; 4:7, 11	13:34; 15:12, 17
Born of God	2:29; 3:9	1:13; 3:3–8
Children of God (*tekna theou*)	3:1, 2, 10	1:12; 11:52
Everyone who does sin	3:4, 8–9	8:34
Hated by the world	3:13	15:18–19; 17:14
Passed from death into life	3:14	5:24
Laying down his life for others	3:16	10:11, 15, 17–18; 15:13
Divine indwelling and Spirit	3:24	4:17
Confess Christ	4:2	9:22
Jesus coming in the flesh	4:2	1:14
Spirit of truth	4:6	14:17; 15:26; 16:13
God's love in sending his only Son	4:9–10	3:16–17
We have known and believed	4:16	6:69
Believe Jesus is Messiah/Christ	5:1	20:31
Conquers (*nikaō*) the world	5:4	16:33
Water and blood	5:6–8	19:34–35
The witness (*martyria*) of men	5:9	3:33; 5:34
Purpose of writing	5:13	20:31
To know the true one Jesus Christ	5:20	17:3

11. Of the 118 NT passages in which "abide/remain (Gk. *menō*), 67 occur in the Johannine writings (40 in the Gospel; 24 in 1 John, 3 in 2 John). In the Johannine

Despite the similarities, there are enough noteworthy differences between John's Gospel and 1 John to propose separate authors. First and most obvious are the differences in genre. John's Gospel is a narrative of the life and teaching of Jesus, and 1 John is an exposition of Johannine teaching, probably circulated with the other Johannine letters. Second, there are specific grammatical differences. The grammar of the Gospel is transparent (e.g., John 1; 15) whereas that of 1 John is often opaque (e.g., 1 John 1:1–4; 3:19–20; 5). Also, some grammatical features frequent in John (e.g., "for," *gar*; "therefore," *oun*) rarely occur in 1 John. Fourth, certain key vocabulary in the Gospel almost never occurs in 1 John: e.g., "Lord" (*kyrios*, e.g., John 1:23; 6:68; 9:38; 20:28), "judge/judgment" (*krinō, krisis*, John 3:17–18; 5:22–30; 8:16; except *krisis* in 1 John 4:17), "to seek" (*zēteō*, John 7:18; 13:33; 20:15), "to send" (*apostellō*, John 3:17; 11:42; 17:3, 18–25; except 1 John 4:9–10, 14).

The fifth set of differences between 1 John and John concern their distinct theologies.

(a) First John, for example, refrains from using some christological titles or attributes. In fact, what is often attributed to Christ in the Gospel (Jesus is the light, Jesus's commandments) is ascribed only to God in 1 John.[12] Also, 1 John emphasizes the reality and tranquility of the Son of God who came in the flesh, whereas the Gospel speaks of the Word of God made flesh, who reveals God's glory.

(b) The sacrificial and atoning character of Jesus's death is more explicit in 1 John (1:7; 2:2; 3:16; 4:10) than in the Gospel, where Jesus's death is viewed as a triumph and glorification (12:27–32: 13:1; 14:30–31; 16:10–11, 33; 17:1).

(c) First John gives less attention to the Spirit (2:1; 3:24; 4:1–6,13; 5:6, 8) than John's Gospel does (John 1:33; 3:33; 7:39; 14:17, 26; 15:26; 16:13; 20:22).

---

writings, it denotes an inward, enduring personal communion. So of God in his relation to Christ (John 14:10), of Christ-followers in their relation to Christ (John 6:56; 15:4ac; 1 John 2:6, 24c), of Christ relating to Christ-followers (John 15:4a, 5), of Christ-followers relating to God (1 John 2:24c, 27–28; 3:6, 24a; 4:13), of God relating to Christ-followers (1 John 3:24; 4:12–13, 15), of the word of God (1 John 2:14), of the words of Christ (John 15:7b; cf. 1 John 2:24ab), of the love of God (1 John 3:17), of the seed of God (1 John 3:9), of truth (2 John 2), of the wrath of God (John 3:36), of eternal life (1 John 3:15), of the Spirit of truth (John 14:17), see BDAG, 631.

12. The epithets of Jesus the Christ, the Word with God, the source of Life, the glory of the Son, and Light of the world (John 1:1–2, 4, 14b; 2:11; 8:12; 9:5; 12:41, 46; 20:31) may have been *misinterpreted* in a docetic manner by the opponents of 1 John. This *misinterpretation* may be what 1 John is seeking to correct.

(d) John's Gospel seems to offer some present effects of future expectation, so-called realized eschatology: e.g., "may have eternal life" (John 3:16-19, 35-36; 5:24; 6:26-27, 40, 54); "I am the resurrection" (11:25, 26); "now is the judgment of this world" (12:31; 17:3). First John, on the other hand, envisions a future judgment and final revelation of the Son of God (1 John 2:28; 3:2).[13]

(e) There are no quotations from the Scriptures in 1 John although there are many in John's Gospel. John 13–17, which has the most parallels to 1 John, includes, for example, two quotations (Jn 13:18 /Ps 41:9; 15:25 / Ps 69:4) and several allusions and echoes (e.g., Jn 16:22/Isa 66:4; Jn 16:32/ Zech 13:7; Jn 17:12/Isa 57:4.[14]

The final set of differences between 1 John and John's Gospel concern their life settings.[15] (a) First John lacks the Judean Christ-follower context of John's Gospel (and the Gospel's many quotations of and allusions to the Judean Scriptures). (b) In John's Gospel there are Judean critics, seekers, and followers of Jesus with whom the community has entered into debate, whereas in 1 John the debate is only carried on with insiders who have now left the community (i.e., secessionists). (c) None of the critics or opponents in John's Gospel (e.g., John 5:18) seem to have so high a Christology as those in 1 John (e.g., contra docetism, 1 John 4:2-3; 5:6; cf. 2 John 7).

Conclusions on Authorship

From the above differences, it appears that John's Gospel and 1 John were not written at the same time, to the same audience, or by the same person.[16] However, the similarities of vocabulary and structure strongly

---

13. Of course John's Gospel also includes references to futuristic eschatology (e.g., 5:28-29; 6:39-40, 44; 12:48b), but these seem to be subordinate to his "realized eschatology."

14. See chart of common themes in 1 John and John 13–17, in Smalley, *1, 2, and 3 John*, xxx. Although it has no OT quotations, 1 John is familiar with, e.g., Gen 1:1/1 Jn 1:1; the Cain story, Gen 4:8/1 Jn 3:12ff; and some OT covenant themes (see my note on p. 137n52).

15. Brown, *Epistles of John*, 28–30; On John's worldview and use of the OT, see Köstenberger, *Theology of John's Gospel and Letters*, 275–310.

16. Bauckham argues that all the Johannine writings are the work of the Beloved Disciple. He identifies the Beloved Disciple as John the elder (*not* the son of Zebedee) mentioned by Papias (Eusebius, *Hist. eccl.* 3.39.3ff). Bauckham also links this John the elder to an anonymous disciple called along with Andrew in John 1:35-40. He is thus

suggest that both works are products of a Johannine school. A parallel to this relationship might be found in the links between Colossians and Ephesians. Both seem to be products of a Pauline school, although probably from two different authors.[17] I will therefore refer to the author of 1–3 John as John the elder, not the apostle.

The Johannine Comma

It must be noted that 1 John 5:7–8 (in the KJV) was written by neither the author of 1 John nor a Johannine redactor. The passage is absent from every Greek manuscript except four late ones (from the eleventh through the fifteenth centuries). From a late (sixth-century) edition of the Latin Vulgate the passage appears to have found its way into the Oxford Greek edition of 1520 and was even added by Erasmus to the 1522 edition of his Greek text (subsequent editions known as the "Textus Receptus," the basis of the KJV). The passage makes an awkward break in the original wording (1 John 5:6, 9), and if it *were* original, no good reason can be found for the omission of this rich Trinitarian passage in almost all NT Greek manuscripts.[18]

The Opponents of the Johannine Communities

Some readers of the Johannine letters may have denied that Jesus is the Christ, the Son of God (1 John 2:22–23) and that he came in the flesh (4:2–3; 2 John 7).[19] If their behavior is implied in the following

---

an eyewitness, but he is *not* one of the Twleve; see Bauckham, *Jesus and the Eyewitnesses*, 358–471.

17. For more discussion, see Puskas and Reasoner, *Letters*, 144–49, 206–11. The deutero-Pauline authorship of, e.g., Colossians and 2 Thessalonians, has been challenged by, e.g., D. Guthrie, and T. Zahn.

18. The word "comma" means here part of a book or sentence. See discussion in Metzger, *Textual Commentary*, 2nd ed., 647–49; and Metzger, *Text of the New Testament*, 3rd ed., 101–3; see also Brown, *Epistles of John*, Appendix IV: Johannine Comma, 775–87.

19. This view is called *docetic*, from Gk. *dokeō* "seem," i.e., Christ "seemed" to be human but was not: see the fleshly appearance and form of Jesus in Gos. Philip II, 3.56.29–34; and Gos. Truth I, 3. 31.1–9; see statements against docetism—Ignatius, Eph. 7.1, *Smyrn.* 2.1–3.2; 4.2; 5.2 *Trall.* 10.1; Polycarp, *Phil.* 7.1. Hurtado, *Lord Jesus Christ*, 420–21, cites Judean examples of angels from God having only "the appearance of human form" in Philo, *Abr.* 119–23; Josephus, *Ant.* 1.197; and Tobit 12.6–22—thus indicating Judean resistance to the idea of God or his emissaries appearing as humans.

statements, they are viewed as libertine and antinomian—committing sin, not acknowledging their sin as sin, and failing to keeping the commandments (1 John 1:6, 8, 10; 2:4, 11, 15; 3:8, 15, 17).[20] These opponents are also secessionists who have left the community and are leading others to follow them (2:19, 26).

Diotrephes, who is opposed in 3 John 9–10, does not appear to be a secessionist: he is not accused of their false teaching. He may even be reacting to the secessionist problem in his own particular, even misguided, way (cf. 2 John 10). The behavior of Diotrephes seems to be that of a schismatic: rejecting the authority of John the elder, making false charges against him, and refusing to welcome John's emissaries (3 John 9–10).[21]

Several questions have been raised regarding the identity of the opponents in 1–3 John: What group or groups do they represent? How similar or dissimilar are they to the (docetic, libertine) gnostics of the second and third centuries? Is the group (or groups) to be identified with Cerinthus, who was opposed by Polycarp and John the disciple?[22] How are we to understand the problem of the secessionists (1–2 John) and the issue with Diotrephes (3 John) in the order and context of the Johannine correspondence? What statements actually denote historical referents outside the text?[23] Some of these questions will be addressed in the discussion that follows.

20. On gnostic libertines, see Clement of Alexandria, *Strom.* 3.2.4; 7.7.17; Irenaeus, *Haer.* 1.6.2–3; Epiphanius, *Pan.* 26.4.3–4. For discussion of these oftentimes exaggerated denouncements, see Puskas and Robbins, *Introduction*, 235–37.

21. Diotrephes is not accused of false teaching, as are the secessionists of 1–2 John. The conflict in 3 John is over church authority (contra John the elder), not theology. Olsson, *Commentary on the Letters of John* xiv, 15–17, 40–42, assuming intra-Judean conflict in the letters, sees Diotrephes as a synagogue leader who refuses Christ-believing Judeans at his synagogue. On Diotrephes, see Lieu, *I, II, III John*, 274–78; Fry, "Diotrephes." On the adversaries of 1–3 John, see Brown, *Epistles of John*, 47–68.

22. See the following reports on Cerinthus. Polycarp, bishop of Smyrna, ca. 150, considered to be a disciple of John, related a story about John, the disciple of the Lord, who "going to bathe at Ephesus and seeing Cerinthus within, rushed out of the bathhouse without bathing, saying, 'Let us flee lest the bathhouse fall down because Cerinthus the enemy of the truth is within'" (Irenaeus, *Haer.* 3.3.4; Eusebius, *Hist. eccl*, 3.28.6; 4.16). Irenaeus claimed that Cerinthus believed the world was made by a power other than God (*Haer.* 1.26.1; a gnostic demiurge?), the heavenly Christ descended upon the earthly Jesus at baptism, who empowered Jesus to work miracles and announce the unknown father, but who left him at the crucifixion (1.26.1). Irenaeus holds that the teaching of Cerinthus is similar to that of the Nicolaitans (Rev 2:6, 15) and that John wrote his Gospel against Cerinthus (Haer. 3.1.11). See discussion in Brown, *Epistles of John*, 65–68, and Appendix II: Cerinthus, 766–71.

23. This question concerns the challenge of connecting generic statements about

The Order of Composition

Because of insufficient evidence, positions on the chronological order of the Johannine writings must remain tentative.[24] Nevertheless, a position favoring the traditional sequence can be substantiated. First, we will discuss the sequence of 2 and 3 John, next that of 1 and 2 John, then the order of the Gospel and 1 John.

Although 2 and 3 John are chronologically close, because of their similar epistolary features (opening, closing, similar travel plans), some clues hint at a sequence of 2 John followed by 3 John. First, the actions of Diotrephes (3 John 9-10) suggest a reaction to the secession in 1 and 2 John. Second, it is not implausible that 3 John 9 ("I have written something to the church") may be referring to 2 John. Similar contents with analogous denouncements of similar adversaries (1 John 2:18, 22; 4:1-3; 2 John 7, 9) suggest that 1 and 2 John were written about the same time; however, the opponents are denounced at great length in 1 John and only briefly in 2 John. Perhaps the false teachers had not yet arrived at the community of 2 John, whereas in 1 John they are already present. Some have suggested that the instruction to exclude false teachers in 2 John 10-11 provoked the secession described in 1 John 2:19. It is guess work. These differences may stem from geography rather than from a chronological interval. The danger presented by the secessionist teachers may not have reached the outlying Johannine church addressed in 2 John. The author of 1 John seems to live close to his addressees, whereas in 2 John he appears more distant (e.g., "I hope to come to you and talk with you face to face," 12b).

---

libertinism and antinomianism (in 1-2 John) with specific identifiable adversaries (in history). It is also related to the question of type-casting opponents (whoever they are) in a very negative way, discussed in my chapter on Jude and 2 Peter. See also Wisse, "Epistle of Jude in the History of Heresiology."

24. The order of the Johannine letters in the NT is probably because of their size. Like the Pauline writings, which begin with Romans (the longest) and end with Philemon (the shortest), so also are the Johannine letters arranged: 1 John (the longest); next, 2 John (245 words); then 3 John (219 words). See NT lists of the fourth and fifth centuries which support this assertion, McDonald and Sanders, *Canon Debate*, 592-97.

There are, of course, arguments for an alternative order or sequence. Olsson, *Commentary on the Letters of John*, xv, 251-54, e.g., has the Diotrephes problem in 3 John first; 2 John reflects the situation already caused by Diotrephes (secession due to regression back to nonmessianic Judean tradition); and 1 John (last) reiterates warnings and encourages readers to address unhealed wounds and abiding threats.

If the author of 1 John belongs to the central locale of Johannine churches, and the addressees of 2 and 3 John are in the outlying churches, this situation could substantiate our suggested sequence of 1, 2, and 3 John. Yet it is not unlikely that 2 John served as a circulating cover letter for 1 John, which has no address information. Third John may also have been a cover letter (for 1–2 John), perhaps carried by Demetrius (v. 12). The author of 3 John commends Gaius to receive his missionaries and opposes Diotrephes, who has refused any hospitality (3 John 9–10).[25] Securing support, restoring honor, and dealing with opposition would be urgent concerns if the presbyter was using missionaries to warn the Johannine churches against the secessionists, who may have had their own missionaries (2 John 10–11). It is therefore possible that the presbyter/author did not want the secessionists to have the success in the outlying churches that they already had in the central locale.[26]

Even though 1 John seems to contain more primitive features than John's Gospel (e.g., Jesus's atoning death, focus on final eschatology, and some affinities with the Dead Sea Scrolls), it appears to reflect a later life-situation than the Gospel. First John is concerned no longer with the opposition of the Judeans (cf. John 9:22; 12:42) but with internal struggles stemming from a certain overemphasis on the teachings of John's Gospel (e.g., Christology, death as glorification, the teaching role of the Paraclete). Although 1 John contains no direct quotations from John's Gospel, the numerous parallels that 1 John has with it are best explained as a clarification and amplification of ideas in the Gospel by 1 John.

The Dates

The close relationship between the Gospel of John and 1 John has implications for where and when 1 John was written. If John's Gospel was

---

25. "In III John the Elder puts his honor on the line again to recommend Demetrius and any others he might send to Gaius. In the process he seeks satisfaction for the dishonor he suffered at the hands of Diotrephes. III John is the Elder's culturally required attempt at satisfaction. If he kept quiet about Diotrephes' rejection of his previous recommendation, he would lose his honor. By attempting satisfaction, he retains his honor, but at some cost. The cost in question is the publicity and consequent honor Diotrephes gains by being a discriminating host and patron with power. He becomes a person to be reckoned with" (Malina, "III John and Hospitality," 187).

26. Brown, *Epistles of John* 31-32. Earlier in our authorship section (pp. 121-22) we have favored a common author (John the elder?) who is probably a "tradition-bearer" from the same community, for the composition of the Johannine letters.

written around 90 CE (without redactions),[27] then 1 John would have been written shortly after 95 or 100 CE and before Ignatius's confrontation with a more advanced form of docetism in Asia Minor around 110 CE.[28] The dates of 2 and 3 John probably would be between 100 and 110 CE. It is not inconceivable for all these dates to be a few years earlier.[29]

Figure 14: Library of Tiberius Julius Celsus Polemaeanus
(Roman senator, consul, and governor of Asia),
Ephesus, financed by him and erected by his son, 110 CE.
It stored twelve thousand scrolls.

---

27. Arguments for John's Gospel written in the late first century are: (1) the oldest NT fragment (Papyrus 52), which contains parts of John 18:31–33, 37–38, is early second century; (2) the author of the Fourth Gospel seems familiar with Mark and possibly Luke, although he doesn't follow them closely; (3) some statements (John 2:19–20; 11:48) might assume the destruction of the temple in 70 CE; (4) John seems to respond to the delay of the parousia by reemphasizing many of the future hopes as present realities (3:17–19, 36; 5:24; 6:40; 11:25–26; 12:31); (5) the tension with the Judeans (5:1; 6:4; 7:2; 8:44; 12:37–40) and the fact of disciples excluded from the synagogue (9:22; 12:42; 16:2). See discussion in Puskas and Crump, *Gospels and Acts*, 180.

28. Docetic Christology believed that the divine Christ only "seemed" to be, but was not actually, human (see my discussion on p. 122n19). For further discussion on "docetism" in the NT and among early Christ-followers, see Puskas and Robinson, *Introduction*, 239–42. For primary sources, see Robinson, *Nag Hammadi Library*.

29. See Trebilco, *Ephesus* (2007), 271–73.

The Place of Composition

Both Syria (Syrian Antioch or Syro-Palestine) and Ephesus have been argued as places for the writing of the Johannine letters. Both localities may have had gnosticizing and other schismatic groups at an early date, which these letters addressed: for Syro-Palestine see Gospel of Thomas, Steles Seth; for Ephesus, see Acts 20:29-30 and Ignatius, *Phld.* 2.1-2.[30]

Ignatius was a bishop of Syrian Antioch; his letters to churches in Asia (e.g., Ephesus, Tralles) show some familiarity with the Johannine writings, as do the Odes of Solomon and Gospel of Thomas—both from the region of Syro-Palestine.[31] If John's Gospel originated from Palestine or nearby Syria, and 1 John has close affinities with that book, a Syro-Palestinian origin for 1, 2, and 3 John does not seem unlikely.

Irenaeus relates that John, the disciple of Jesus, resided in Ephesus until the time of Trajan, ca. 98 (*Haer.* 3.3.4), and some internal data (e.g., 1 John 4:2-3 with Polycarp, *Phil.* 7.1; Patmos in Rev 1:9) may suggest an

---

30. Certain NT texts and (Judean) Sethian strands of gnostic teaching (Nat. Rulers; Apoc. Adam; Steles Seth) appear to draw upon a common lexical tradition in (mostly) earlier Judean notions of personified wisdom, semidivine beings, angels, and other mediators from heaven (e.g., Prov 8; Sir 24; Wis 8-9; Dan 7:13-14; 1 Enoch 49:3; 51:3; 4 Ezra 5; Ascen. Isa. 10-11; Odes Sol. 41; 2 Bar 48; T. Abr. 7:3-12; 9:17-18; Jos. Asen. 14-17). On the argument for Judean strands of early Gnosticism, see J. D. Turner, "Sethian Gnosticism"; Perkins, *Gnosticism and NT*, 22-24 (Palestinian traditions), 45-49 (Sethian traditions of Syro-Palestine); Perkins, "Nag Hammadi Texts," 209.

On gnostic teaching surfacing early in Ephesus, see Acts 20:29-30 with Ign. *Phld.* 2.1-2; 1 Tim 4:1-5, 7; 6:20; 1 John 4:2-3 with Polycarp, *Phil.* 7.1; the opponents (possibly) in Jude, 2 Pet 2, and Rev 2; Ign. *Trall.* 10; Ign. *Magn.* 8.1-2; Ign. *Eph.* 7-9; Bauer, *Orthodoxy and Heresy*, 82-88. Early gnostic influence in Ephesus (before 110) is questioned, however, by Trebilco, *Ephesus* (2007), 182-83, 190-95, 228-30, 384. Although Ignatius was bishop of Syrian Antioch, most of his correspondence addressed the churches in Asia on issues as *he* understood them (e.g., in Ephesus, Philadelphia, Tralles).

31. Ignatius of Syrian Antioch (ca. 110) is familiar with several themes from John's Gospel (Incarnation, Ignatius, *Trall.* 10; grace and truth, Ignatius, *Magn.* 8.1; Christ the Word, Ignatius, *Magn.* 8.2). The Odes of Solomon (ca. 200, Syria) shares many themes with John. The Gospel of Thomas (ca. 100, Syro-Palestine) is familiar with John's Gospel (Gos. Thom. 77/John 8:12; Gos. Thom. 108/John 7:38); and there are affinities with certain themes in the Dead Sea Scrolls of Judea (modified dualism, 1QS 3.18—4.1; 1QM 1; unity and community, 1QS 8:5; 9:19-20; CD 6:20—7:2; antitemple bias, 11QT). For primary texts, see Vermes, *Scrolls* (1997); García Martínez, DSS (1999). For discussion on John's Gospel, see Puskas and Crump, *Gospel and Acts*, 179-80.

Ephesian origin.[32] Perhaps this information also reflects a movement of Johannine Christ-followers from Syria to Ephesus. Evidence, however, is not too decisive for either location.

The Genre

With what broad literary categories do we equate the Johannine letters? The writings of 2 and 3 John share most of the characteristics of ancient letters, whereas 1 John does not. Therefore, we will first compare 2 and 3 John to the epistolary form, then investigate the genre question of 1 John.

The Genre of 2 and 3 John

Numerous examples of the letter form exist in OT and other Judean writings (e.g., Jer 29; 2 Sam 11; 2 Macc 1–2; Lachish Letters; the Elephantine Papyri), among Greco-Roman philosophers (e.g., Plato, Epicurus, Seneca), by Roman rulers (e.g., Augustus, Trajan), and from Christ-follower leaders (e.g., apostle Paul, Clement of Rome, Ignatius). In Egypt, thousands of private and business letters have been discovered from the Hellenistic and Roman periods.[33] Most ancient letters contain the following parts: (a) an opening, (b) a thanksgiving or health wish, (c) the body, and (d) a closing. We will examine each part in comparison with 2 and 3 John and other ancient letters.[34]

---

32. Polycarp, bishop of Smyrna (near Ephesus), ca. 150, a disciple of John, is said to have related the encounter of John with Cerinthus the gnostic at a bath in Ephesus, according to Irenaeus and Eusebius (see my discussion on p. 123n22). Bauckham, *Jesus and the Eyewitnesses*, 420–23, 452–58, has argued that this John of Ephesus was an eyewitness of Jesus but not John the son of Zebedee (see my p. 121n16). The close parallel of 1 John 4:2–3 with Polycarp, *Phil.* 7.1, might also suggest an Ephesian origin. On the origin of John's Gospel from Ephesus see the similar antisynagogue motifs in John's Gospel (9:22; 12:42) and Revelation (2:9; 3:9, written by John of Patmos, Asia, 1:9); note also the presence of a John the Baptist sect in Ephesus (John 1:35–51; Acts 19:1–7). On Revelation and John the Baptist traditions, see Ford, *Revelation*, 30–37, 388. On the Johannine letters written from Ephesus, see Trebilco, *Ephesus* (2007), 268–71 (external support).

33. For more discussion on the ancient letter form, see Puskas and Reasoner, *Letters*, 28–43; Klauck, *Ancient Letters*, chs. 1–6. See also my discussion on p. 117.

34. On a formal analysis of 2 and 3 John as ancient letters, see Klauck, *Ancient Letters*, 27–40.

(A) Opening (includes Sender, Addressee, and Greeting)
  (1) Sender: "The elder (presbyter)" (2 John 1; 3 John 1). "Presbyter" was probably a title of honor for a tradition bearer who may have been associated with John, the disciple of Jesus.[35]
  (2) Addressees: "to the beloved Gaius" (3 John 1). This gives 3 John the appearance of a private letter, although "friends" of Gaius are also probably included (v. 15). "To the elect lady and her children" (2 John 1). The contents of the letter confirm that "elect lady" is a *fictio persona* for a local church, the members of which are called "her children."
  (3) Greeting: "'Grace, mercy and peace" (2 John 3). The greeting almost appears to be a statement of existing fact instead of a wish. No such greeting appears in 3 John.

(B) Thanksgiving or health wish
  (1) Wish for health: "'Beloved, I pray that all may go well with you and that you may be in good health; just as it is well with your soul" (3 John 2). Third John is the only NT letter that contains a wish of good health, a typical feature in ancient letters. The mention of "as your soul prospers" (Gk. *kathōs euodoutai sou hē psyche*) adds a spiritual dimension.
  (2) Thanksgiving or expression of joy: Here the sender gives thanks to God or gods for various reasons. (e.g., Rom 1:8–17; 1 Cor 1:4–9; Phil 1:3–11). This feature is not explicit in 2 and 3 John but may be implied in the statements at the opening of the letter's body: "I was overjoyed" (2 John 4; 3 John 3). It is part of the Proem.

(C) Body of Letter
  (1) Body Opening: Some common knowledge is assumed between Sender and Addressee.
  ("I know that . . ."). Concerns are also expressed ("I regret that . . .") as well as requests: "I appeal to you . . ." "I ask you . . ." (2 John 5). "Beloved, you do faithfully whatever you do . . ." (3 John 5). "You do well to send them on" (3 John 6). A petition or request forms a part of the body opening.
  (2) Body Middle 1: In these letters it concerns false teachers (2 John 7) and the opposition of church leader, Diotrephes (3 John 9–10)

---

35. Brown, *Epistles of John*, 651; Klauck, *Ancient Letters*, 29.

(3) Body Middle 2: Both include exhortations to "be on your guard," "abide in the teaching" (2 John 8–9), and "do not imitate what is evil but do what is good" (3 John 11).

(4) Body Closing: In 2 John it concerns denying access to false teachers (vv. 10–11), which amplifies what was written of false teachers (vv. 7–9); and in 3 John we have a recommendation to Demetrius of Gaius, the delegate or letter carrier (v. 12).

(D) Letter Closing

(1) Prospective Visit: In 2 John the sender says, "I have much to write to you . . . I hope to come to you to talk to you face to face so that our joy may be complete" (v. 12). In 3 John, the sender has similar plans "I have much to write . . . I hope to talk to you soon and we will talk together face to face" (vv. 13–14). Included here are greetings, a wish for health, or a benediction.

(2) Final Greetings: "Peace to you" (3 John 15). This closing blessing is characteristic of Judean and Christ-follower letters, e.g., 2 Bar 78:2; 1 Pet 5:14. "The children of your elect sister send you their greetings" (2 John 13). "The friends send you their greetings. Greet the friends there each by name" (3 John 15). In 2 John, the community of the author, which is a "sister church," sends farewell greetings to the addressees (cf. 1 Cor 16:19; 1 Pet 5:13). The farewell greetings in 3 John resemble the Pauline custom of greetings: "each by name" (cf. Rom 16:3–23; 1 Cor 16:19–20; Phil 4:21–22).

The Genre of 1 John

The book of 1 John is more difficult to classify generically. All the epistolary characteristics are lacking. For example, there are none of the following: sender, addressee, opening and farewell greeting, health wish, proposed travel plans, benediction.[36] It has been argued that 1 John is more polemical, like Jude and 2 Peter. Although it contains polemics (against the secessionists), 1 John also has more homiletical exhortations (similar to 1 Peter) but includes none of the epistolary features in Jude and 2 Peter. First John has been compared with a Hermetic tractate such

---

36. Köstenberger, *Theology of John's Gospel and Letters*, 126, still understands 1 John to be a situational letter in *broad* terms appealing to the diversity of Greco-Roman letters (e.g., 41 styles according to Pseudo-Libanius, *Epistolary Styles*, 45, 92; fourth–sixth centuries) and citing as diverse examples: Jer 29:4–13; Acts 15:23–29; Rev 2–3.

as *Hermes Trismegistus: Asclepius* (from the late second century CE), but 1 John does not contain any of its philosophical dialogue or diatribe, and the Hermetic tract lacks the polemics and homiletic exhortations of 1 John. This Johannine book has also been compared to homilies or hortatory addresses like Hebrews, James, and the Didache, but it lacks the extensive exhortation and development of teaching in them. Relying on a specific reconstruction of the Johannine community, it has also been argued that 1 John is a "community rule" similar to the Dead Sea Scroll 1QS of the Qumran community.[37] This view is noteworthy (1QS parallels), but the historical reconstructions have not been too convincing.

Ancient Examples

Raymond E. Brown proposed that 1 John is an exposition of the Fourth Gospel to refute the secessionists, who also revered the book.[38] The *pesharim* of the Dead Sea Scrolls are haggadic, midrashic commentary on Scripture (e.g., on Habbakkuk, 1QpH; on Nahum, 4QpNah; on Isaiah, 1QpIsa). They treat the biblical prophecies as referring to the last days, in which the community finds itself living.[39] Later examples of this genre of exposition are *Daniel* by Hippolytus and *Revelation* by Joachim of Fiore.[40] Except for some *pesharim* (e.g., that mention Kittim or Gentile oppressors, Wicked Priest, Man of Lies) most lack the polemics of 1 John, and an apocalyptic focus is lacking in 1 John. A Valentinian gnostic commentary on John by Heracleon, and the gnostic *Gospel of Truth* may serve as parallels because both seek to update and apply the Fourth Gospel to

---

37. Hills, "Genre for 1 John," builds on Brown's construction of the Johannine community (*Jesus and the Beloved Community*) to argue for 1 John as a "community rule" similar to 1QS of the Qumran community.

38. Brown, *Epistles*, 90–100, makes use of this "commentary genre" so as to make better sense of its contents. Von Wahlde, *Gospel and Letters of John*, 1:53, 552–54, sees the author of 1 John correcting the misinterpretation of the second edition of John's Gospel by his opponents.

39. On this contemporarizing biblical interpretation mostly of nonlegal material and especially biblical prophecy, see "Pesharim," in *Early Judaism* (2010), 1050–56. Longnecker, *Biblical Exegesis* (1999), 18–30, makes a distinction between midrashic (rabbinic) and pesher (Qumran) interpretation; Vermes, *Scrolls* (1997), 17–18.

40. First John and these parallels are all general expositions that treat the Bible as if it were speaking to the present (similar to Qumran's *pesherim*). See, e.g., Reeves, *Joachim of Fiore and the Prophetic Future*.

particular situations,[41] but the author of 1 John is not as speculative or mythological as the gnostic authors. We might also suggest as examples of this type of genre Ephesians, which makes use of Colossians, or even 2 Peter, which utilizes Jude for polemical and hortatory reasons. Both are types of exposition that clarify and update the earlier work for a new generation of readers. It must be noted, however, that Ephesians lacks the polemics, and 2 Peter the homiletical exhortations, of 1 John.

An Application

Now that some possible examples of this "genre of exposition" have been provided, we will examine the internal evidence for such a proposal. We have already noted the extensive list of parallels between 1 John and the Gospel. Even though the differences are sufficient to propose different authors, it can be argued that 1 John is relying on the traditions of John's Gospel. In both the prologue (1 John 1:1–3/John 1:1–14) and ending (1 John 5:13/John 20:31), 1 John appears to imitate the Gospel. Also, in conformity with the Gospel's twofold division (the Book of Signs, 1:19—12:50 and the Book of Glory 13:1—20:31), 1 John can also be divided into two similar sections: Walking in the Light 1:5—3:10 and Loving in Deeds 3:11—5:12. In the first sections of both books, there is tension with adversaries, and in the second sections, affection for the followers of Jesus. In 1 John much of the polemics in the Gospel against outside adversaries are now applied to the secessionists from the community of 1 John. For example, the secessionists are called "those who walk in darkness," "those who belong to the devil," and "those who are blinded." The use of the "we" in 1 John also gives readers the impression that the author

---

41. Brooke, *Fragments of Heracleon*. Heracleon's commentary (ca. 170 CE) is derived from quotations in Origen and Clement of Alexandria. Although he favored allegorical interpretation, Heracleon emphasized ethical behavior and individual salvation rather than speculations on the (gnostic) aeons. Pagels, *Johannine Gospel in Gnostic Exegesis* examines the following texts: John 1:1–14 (prologue), 19–34 (the Baptist); 2:12–21 (temple); 4:7–42, 46–54 (two conversions); 8:31–47 ("generation"); 4:35–38 ("seed"). On similar and distinctive interpretative approaches of 1 John and the Gospel of Truth, see Perkins, *Gnosticism and NT*, 160–63. John's Gospel is quoted or alluded to over 1200 times in the Nag Hammadi codices (ca. third–fourth centuries); see Scripture index in Evans et al., eds., *Nag Hammadi Texts*, 503–16 (e.g., Gos. Phil.; Gos. Thom.; Teach. Silv.; Apoc. John; Disc. Seth; Val. Exp.; Gos. Truth; 1–2 Apoc. Jas.).

is either an eyewitness or a tradition bearer of the eyewitnesses of Jesus (1:1–5),[42] and therefore is assuming the same role as the Evangelist.

In reaction to the position of the Johannine secessionists, who probably substantiated their position from the Gospel, 1 John emphasizes both the human career of Jesus (1 John 4:2–3) and the belief in a final judgment (2:28; 4:17). Both emphases would counter the docetic view of Christ and the gnostic preoccupation with realized eschatology and perfectionism, which also seem to be the beliefs of the secessionists.[43] The Gospel of John, a favorite book of later gnostics, could lend support to the secessionist view of Christ and to their ethics. For example, the glories of the preexistent Word as well as the salvation from sin and eternal life that can be realized in the present are all themes of the Fourth Gospel. In this context, 1 John can be seen as qualifying or correcting the extremist interpretations of the Fourth Gospel by the secessionists.

The Structure of 1 John[44]

This alternative outline highlights the biblical rhetoric of the book.[45] Although some chiasms of the entire book tend to minimize the (non-chiastic) differences within paragraphs and phrases, this macrochiastic

42. If the author of 1 John was not an eyewitness himself, a "tradition bearer" would be one possible conclusion to derive from the "we" statements in 1 John 1:1–5.

43. Docetic Christology held that the divine Christ only "seemed" to be human, (see my discussion on p. 122n19). Certain gnostics advocated a realized eschatology, believing that they could immediately experience the benefits of the final resurrection in their own group (Gos. Thom. 51, 113; Ap. John 19.15–34; Exeg. Soul 134.6–15). On perfection, the "perfect man," see Gos. Phil. 70.5–9; 76.18–20; Gos. Truth 24.25–25.15; Tri. Trac. 123.3–6). According to Perkins, *Gnosticism and NT*, 160–63, the evidence is slim that the secessionists of 1 John are an early gnosticizing sect. Köstenberger, *Theology of John's Gospel and Letters*, 94–97, refrains from identifying the opponents of 1 John with a specific heresy (e.g., Cerinthian, docetic).

44. This chiastic outline is derived from Heil, *1–3 John*, 25, 202–3. The entire book by Heil is a commendable effort to demonstrate through his exegesis the validity of this macrochiastic structure of 1 John. However, Welch, *Chiasmus in Antiquity*, 232–33 is skeptical about organizing 1–3 John into macrochiastic outlines. See also my discussion of chiasm in *Revelation* (pp. 158–60). For other structural proposals for 1–3 John, see Köstenberger, *Theology of John's Gospel and Letters*, 171–74; on Hellenistic rhetoric, see Klauck, "Zur rhetorischen Analyse der Johannesbriefe." Establishing paragraph breaks in the text of 1 John is challenging, but the NA[28] Greek NT is a helpful guide here.

45. This approach examines biblical and Semitic texts from the ancient Near East *as well as* the Greco-Roman writings. See www.retoricabiblicaesemitica.org/.

outline is not too problematic. It also does not present major challenges to the proposal (above) that 1 John is an exposition of the Fourth Gospel to refute the secessionists, who also revered the book.[46] The function of the chiastic center (G, 1 John 3:13–17) is almost always enigmatic and challenges readers to reflect and provide their own answers.[47]

A He will Cleanse Us from All Unrighteousness	1:1–10
B If We Keep His Commandment the Love of God Has Been Perfected	2:1–14
C Do Not Love the Things in the World	2:15–17
D The One Confessing the Son Also Has the Father	2:18–27
E You Know Whoever Does Righteousness Has Been Begotten from the Father	2:28—3:6
F We Should Love One Another	3:7–12
G We Ought To Lay Down Our Lives for the Brothers (and Sisters)	3:13–17
F' We Should Believe and We Should Love One Another	3:18–24
E' In This You Know the Spirit of God	4:1–6
D' God Has Sent His Son so That We Might Live through Him	4:7–12
C' Just as That One is so We Are in This World	4:13—5:2
B' This Is the Love of God that We Keep His Commandments	5:3–12
A' All Unrighteousness Is Sin	5:13–21

---

46. For the use of chiasm in John's Gospel, including its general plot structure—(A) complication (1:19—12:19); B crisis (12:20–26); A' (12:27—20:31) Denouement—see Puskas and Crump, *Gospels and Acts*, 166–70.

47. See Meynet, "Question at the Center," 214.

The Sources of 1 John

Even though the content of 1 John (and the other Johannine writings) is pervaded with the author's vocabulary and style, certain source theories have been proposed for it. The following overview has the added benefit of highlighting some of the formal, thematic, and stylistic features of 1 John.

Antithetical Statement Source?

One position argues for an antithetical-statement source;[48] another argues for sources that parallel certain legal and liturgical forms of Judean tradition and among early Christ-followers.[49] Even though arguments delineating specific written documents in 1 John are somewhat speculative, a survey of these two positions can highlight some of the noteworthy literary forms in 1 John. The most influential advocate of the antithetical-statement source is Rudolf Bultmann.[50] A recent analysis of this position by Raymond Brown has posited three groups of antithetical statements as outlined below, with examples:

Group A (absolute pronouncements in conditional three-line verse)

1:8 If we say we have no sin,
We deceive ourselves,
and the truth is not in us.

1:10 If we say we have not sinned,
We make him a liar,
and his word is not in us.

See also 1:6–7; 2:4–5, 9–11.

---

48. This view is based on the two (related) theories of von Dobschutz, "Joanneisches Studien, I"; and Bultmann, *Johannine Epistles* are outlined in Brown, *Epistles of John*, 36–43, 760–61.

49. The theory of Nauck, *Die Tradition und Character des ernsten Johannesbriefes*, concerns parallels to Hebrew apodictic law (Exod 20; Deut 5), Qumran renewal ceremony (1QS, CD, 1QM), and early Christ-follower baptismal liturgy (Ephesians, 1 Peter); for discussion see Brown, *Epistles of John*, 43–45.

50. Bultmann, *Johannine Epistles*, 2–3, 16, 18, 39, 45, 54, 57, 65, 68, 76; outlined in Brown, *Epistles of John*, 38–43, 760–61.

Group B (absolute pronouncements in antithetical doublets)

3:6 No one who abides in him sins.
No one who sins has either seen him or known him.

3:7–8 Everyone who does right is righteous.
Everyone who commits sin is of the devil.

*Group C (absolute pronouncements,
some antithetical and some complementary doublets)*

2:23 No one denying the Son has the Father.
Everyone who confesses the Son has the Father also.

3:15 Everyone who hates is a murderer
and does not have eternal life.

5:12 Whoever has the Son has life.
Whoever has not the Son of God has not life.

See also 4:7–8.

Later additions to this "antithetical source" were the theme of final eschatology (2:28; 3:2; 4:17), references to Jesus's sacrificial death (1:7; 2:2; 4:10), moral warning (2:15–17), an allusion to baptism (5:7–9), and an appendix (5:14–21).

Although it is difficult to delineate earlier sources from the author's work and posit them as written documents, this source position has highlighted several noteworthy features of 1 John: (1) the presence of statements that can be interpreted as antilibertine or antignostic (e.g., 1:8, 10; 2:4–5; 3:9; 4:7–8); (2) the presence of solemn pronouncements or slogans that are often contrasted antithetically; and (3) the presence of homiletic or hortatory comments on such statements (e.g., 1:9–10; 2:1–2, 15–17; 4:18; 5:10).

Legal and Liturgical Traditions?

Wolfgang Nauck's source theory argues (with examples) for the presence of parallels between 1 John and the following formal liturgical and legal categories:

(1) The absolute demands of Mosaic law:[51]

"You shall not murder" (Exod. 20:13; Decalogue); "Honor your father and your mother so that your days may be long" (Exod. 20:12, Decalogue); "Whoever strikes father or mother shall be put to death" (Exod 21:15).

(2) Covenant-renewal ceremonies of Qumran:[52]

(a) members are challenged to accept the demands of the new covenant: "That they may love all that God has chosen and hate all that He has rejected, that they abstain from all evil and hold fast to good" (1QS 1:3-51; cf. 1 John 1:5-10; 2:29—3:10).

(b) the challenge is followed by demands that stress right behavior, acknowledgment of sin, keeping the commandments, and brotherly love within the community, which are characteristics that distinguish the "sons of light' from the "sons of darkness" (1QS 1:11—3:12; cf. 1 John 2:7-17; 4:7-21).

(3) Motifs from early Christ-follower baptismal ceremonies[53]

(a) purification (e.g., Eph 2:13-17; 1 Pet 1:22; 1 John 1:9; 2:2; 3:3)

(b) belonging to a community (Eph 2:19; 4:4-6; 1 Pet 2:4-5, 9-10; 1 John 1:7; 2:24-25; 3:1-2)

---

51. See similar absolute demands in 1 John 2:15; 3:15; 4:7-8; 5:12. For further information on absolute or apodictic law in ancient Israel, see Alt, "Origins of Israelite Law"; see also "Apodictic Law" in Soulen and Soulen, *Biblical Criticism*, 13.

52. See the following examples of covenant-renewal ceremonies in ancient Israel: Deut 29:1—31:29; Josh 24; 1 Kgs 22-23; Neh 9. For discussion of this ceremony at Qumran (e.g., 1QS, 1QSa, CD, 1QM, 1QpHab), see Cross, *Ancient Library of Qumran*, 95n96a, 234, 236. The Qumran community renewed the covenant annually, apparently on the Feast of Weeks (1QS 1-2), see Neusner and Scott, *DJBP*, 137. For introductory discussion with primary texts, see also Vermes, *Scrolls* (1997), 28, 43-45, 68-69, (text) 98-101.

53. On early Christ-follower baptismal liturgies, see my discussion of the baptismal and liturgical features of 1 Peter see my discussion on pp. 82-88. On Ephesians, see also Puskas and Reasoner, *Letters*, 174-77.

(c) the cleansing blood of Jesus (Eph 1:7; 1 Pet 1:2; 1 John 1:7)

(d) divine begetting(Eph 1:5, 11; 4:30; 1 Pet 1:3, 23; 2:2; 1 Jn 2:29; 3:9; 4:7; 5:1, 4,18)

(e) choice between two ways (of light and darkness) (cf. Rom 6; Eph 4:17—5:20; Col 2:9–13; 1 Pet 1:3—2:10; 1 John 1:5–7; 2:9–11; Hippolytus, *Apostolic Tradition*, ca. 220 CE).

Despite numerous parallels in 1 John to the above legal and liturgical patterns, specific genetic relationships (or even a common source) behind these parallels are difficult to establish. Whatever legal and liturgical traditions were used, they are dominated by the vocabulary and style of the author of 1 John and were combined with hortatory, homiletical, polemical, and expositional genres.

Conclusion

In our study of the Johannine letters, we have examined the following topics: First, we looked at their usage from the mid-second century to the fourth century of church history and noted the popularity of 1 John and the relative obscurity of 2 and 3 John. Second, in answering the question of authorship, we argued that 1, 2, and 3 John had a common author who may have been an eyewitness (John the elder?) but seems to have been a second-generation "tradition bearer" of the Johannine community. Third, we favored the traditional chronological sequence of 1, 2, and 3 John. Fourth, it was argued that 95–110 CE was the approximate date of the writings. Ephesus had some edge over Syria (or Syro-Palestine), as the place of composition, but we cannot be certain. Regarding the genres of 1, 2, and 3 John, we concluded that 2 and 3 John were ancient letters, and that 1 John was similar to a genre of exposition, which comments upon and updates an older writing (i.e. John's Gospel; cf. Ephesians with Colossians, 2 Peter and Jude), although 1 John also includes its own polemical, hortatory, and homiletical features. An alternative, macrochiastic outline of 1 John was also provided, which highlights its biblical rhetoric. The source theories of 1 John are difficult to establish, but the literary forms and patterns detected are noteworthy for understanding the book.

Throughout this chapter, we have alluded to the threat of the secessionists: those Johannine Christ-followers who had left the communities of 1 and 2 John (1 John 2:19). We also noted that they seemed to be "docetic" in their view of Christ (Christ was divine but only had the "appearance" of humanity) and were apparently libertine and elitist in their lifestyle (not unlike some gnostics).[54] It seems likely that the secessionists misinterpreted John's Gospel to support their extreme views (i.e., docetic Christology, realized eschatology), which the author of 1 John sought to qualify and correct in his book.

The Johannine writings contain foundational Christ-follower insights: that Jesus is one with God as well as one with his people, that love and righteousness are necessary for those who seek to walk in the light as God's children, and that unity is a goal for which all Christ-followers should strive.[55]

---

54. For more discussion on the gnostics and the opponents of 1 John, see Puskas and Robbins, *Introduction*, 224–27, 232–42. Perkins and Köstenberger, are less confident that the secessionists are an early gnostic group (see my discussion on p. 133 n.43).

55. Smalley, *1, 2, and 3 John*, 365.

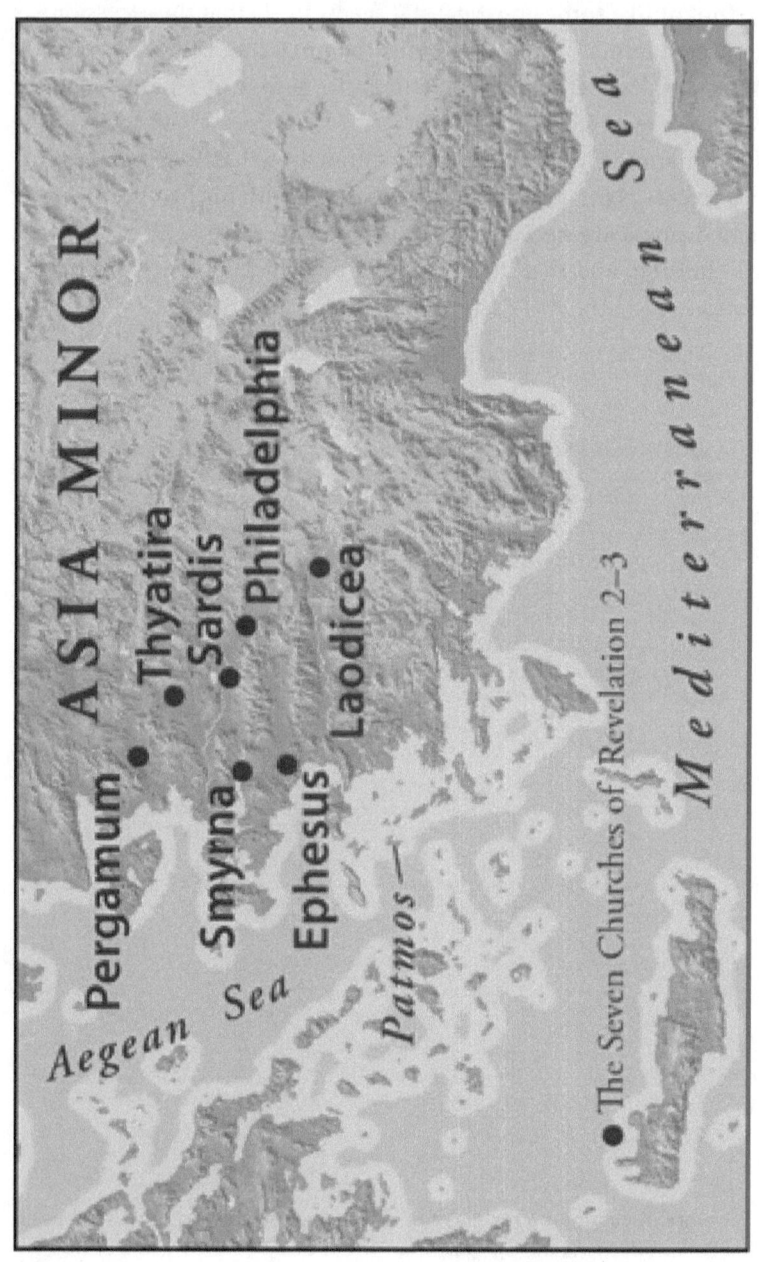

Map C: The cities of the seven churches in the book of Revelation

6

The Book of Revelation

Introduction

The ancient book of Revelation,[1] whose hopeful message is mixed with complex, bizarre, and violent imagery (e.g., a monstrous red dragon, a seven-headed beast, and cosmic warfare), has been and continues to be a source of fascination, perplexity, and inspiration for readers. It held the keen interest of the scientist Sir Isaac Newton, the American theologian Jonathan Edwards, and novelist D. H. Lawrence. It has had a powerful influence on Christian faith, worship, art (e.g., consider Albrecht Dürer and Lucas Cranach the Elder) and music (consider Handel's *Messiah* and the gospel hymn "When the Saints Go Marching In").

From an early period, certain individuals (e.g., Joachim of Fiore in the twelfth century, William Miller in 1844, and Charles T. Russell in 1914) and their followers have regarded Revelation as a codebook that discloses future events. Many futuristic groups share its vision of final

---

1. The book is known in much of the English-speaking world as Revelation: e.g., the book of Revelation, the Revelation of John or St. John (the Divine), and (sometimes) incorrectly as Revelations! Here in this chapter I will call it either Revelation, the book of Revelation, or the Apocalypse. "Apocalypse" is a rough transliteration of the Greek word *apokalypsis*, which suggests *the uncovering of something that was hidden* (like your head when you remove a hat). The Vulgate (Latin translation) of this book of visions begins this way: *Apocalypsis Iesou Christi*, transliterating *apokalypsis* rather than translating from the Greek word; elsewhere the Vulgate gives *revelatio* as a Latin gloss for the word. In most English translations the word is translated with the gloss "revelation." See Puskas and Robbins, *Introduction*, 144.

disaster for human culture. Survivalist groups take literally its teaching on world tribulation by stockpiling food and arming themselves. Space exploration, rapid change through computer technology, terrorism, and the threat of nuclear annihilation might be some external, cultural reasons for the recent fascination with Revelation, whereas feelings of alienation, pessimism, and powerlessness might be some internal, psychological reasons. Whatever the causes might be, the effects of intense interest in apocalyptic books like Revelation are evident today.[2]

What type of literature is the book of Revelation? How do we interpret its bizarre visions and dire warnings? These are two of the complex questions addressed in this chapter.[3] First, I will look at the issue of genres, rhetorical and literary forms, and social-historical context. Next, the structure and arrangement of the book will be examined. Then, I will look at some of the myths and symbols in Revelation.

The Genre and Literary Forms[4]

Most who read Revelation are either impressed or confounded by the book's composite nature. It has many diverse forms found in the Gospels, Acts and early Christ-follower letters. Revelation also shows more dependency on the Scriptures (OT) for its images and phraseology than any other NT book (see Koester, *Revelation*, 123-25).

Like the Gospels and Acts, Revelation contains sayings, dialogues, and other forms of direct discourse within a narrative framework.[5] The

---

2. On the history of interpretation and influence, see C. R. Koester, *Revelation*; and his video lectures with introductory guide: *The Apocalypse: Controversies on Meaning in Western History*. See also Wainwright, *Mysterious Apocalypse*, 21-103, 161-230; Chilton, *Visions of the Apocalypse*.

3. For commentaries, see Aune, *Revelation 1-5*; Aune, *Revelation 6-16*; Aune, *Revelation 17-22*; Beale, *Book of Revelation*; Blount, *Revelation*; Harrington, *Revelation*; Boring, *Revelation*; Beasley-Murray, *Book of Revelation*; Caird, *Commentary on the Revelation of St. John the Divine*; Charles, *Critical and Exegetical Commentary on the Revelation of St. John*; Ford, *Revelation*; Mounce, *Book of Revelation*; Lupieri, *Commentary on the Apocalypse of John*; Malina and Pilch, *Revelation*; C. R. Koester, *Revelation*.

4. In the case of the Apocalypse, the mixture of literary genres and forms has made it one of the most challenging NT books. For different reasons, both the Italian literary critic Benedetto Croce, *Aesthetic* (1909) and the avant-garde Paris journal *Tel Quel* (1962-66) advocated critical theories that transcended all generic boundaries. See Puskas and Robbins, *Introduction*, 104, 144-47. See also my discussion on p. 11n4.

5. Aune, *Literary Environment*, 13, states that each of the four major literary types found in the NT (gospels, acts, letters, apocalypse) "is a 'complex' or 'inclusive' literary

prophetic and apocalyptic materials we find in the Gospels and Acts are especially prevalent in Revelation. Numerous allusions to the Hebrew prophetic writings and to the apocalyptic book of Daniel appear in the Revelation. Revelation shares traits with early Christ-follower letters because it is enveloped by a letter form and contains seven letters to churches. Like the early Christ-follower letters, Revelation includes hymns ("odes," Rev 5:9; 15:3), creeds, catechetical material, ethical exhortation, and both prophetic and apocalyptic material. The composite nature of Revelation has led us to conclude that it is an early Christ-follower prophetic and apocalyptic letter. What components of the book led us to such a conclusion?

The Prophetic Genre

The prophetic character of Revelation can be detected from the book's description of itself and from its literary and thematic parallels with the Hebrew prophetic books. First, Revelation describes its own contents as "prophetic" at the beginning and ending of the book (1:3; 22:7, 10, 18–19). Second, the opening title and motto of Revelation are reminiscent of the prophetic book of Amos (Rev 1:1–3, 7–8; cf. Amos 1:1–2). The messages of both Amos and Revelation are ascribed to obscure individuals (i.e., not to Moses, Adam, or Enoch), and both Amos and Revelation are described as visions or divine disclosures. Third, Revelation has three visions that commission the prophet or seer to do an appointed task. The first, in Rev 1:9–20, is similar to the inaugural vision of Isaiah 6. The second, in Revelation 4–5, is like the commissioning vision in Ezek 1:5–20. The third, in Rev 10:8–11, has parallels to Ezek 2:8—3:3 ("eating the scroll") and functions as the apex of the book's concentric outline (to be discussed under the structure of Revelation). Fourth, the denouncements upon the churches for misbehavior (Rev 2:1—3:22, excluding the constructive directives) are similar to the prophetic judgment speeches in Amos (1:3—2:8; 4:1–2). Fifth, the following literary forms in Revelation also have parallels in the prophetic books: vision reports (e.g., Rev 4:1–11; 6:1–18; 7:1–8; 14:1–5; cf. Amos 7:1–9; 8:1–3), woe oracles (e.g., Rev 8:13; 12:12; cf. Amos 5:18–20; 6:1–7; Isa 3:9–12; 5:8–23; 28:1; 30:1; Ezek 24:6–14; Micah 2:1–4), and a funeral dirge (e.g., Rev 18; cf. Amos

---

genre used to frame a variety of shorter literary forms."

5:1–3; Ezek 26–27; Lam 1). The above are only some of the prophetic features found in Revelation.[6]

The Apocalyptic Genre

The book of Revelation is also apocalyptic in outlook and style.[7] The title of the book, Revelation (1:1), comes from the Greek *apokalypsis*, which means "secret unveilings of the end of the age." Revelation has a prophetic character, but its conceptual outlook is closer to apocalyptic. On the one hand, most of the Hebrew prophetic literature awaited a future political ruler in the real politics of plain history. On the other hand, Revelation does not entertain such nationalistic hopes. Like other apocalyptic writings, Revelation sees the future political scene as hopeless and the human world dominated by angels and demons. According to this perspective, a radical transformation of the world, with cosmic catastrophes and a final punishment of the wicked, is needed to vindicate the faithful righteous.[8] Examples of apocalyptic literature are the book of Daniel, 1 Enoch, 2 Esdras, 2 Baruch, Testament/Assumption of Moses, the War Scroll of

---

6. See Aune, *Prophecy in Early Christianity*; and Aune, "Prophetic Circle of John"; Beasley-Murray, *Revelation*, 19–29; C. R. Koester, *Revelation*, 107–9, 123–25; Gitay, *Prophecy and Prophets*; Moyise, "Prophets in the New Testament"; for a classic depiction of prophets and prophecy, see A. Heschel, *Prophets*, 3–31.

7. For studies, see Hanson, "Jewish Apocalyptic against Its Near Eastern Environment"; Hanson, *Dawn of Apocalyptic*; Koch, *Rediscovery of Apocalyptic*; Schmithals, *Apocalyptic Movement*; Collins, *Apocalypse*; and Collins, *Apocalyptic Imagination*; Barr, *Reading the Book of Revelation*; Bauckham, *Climax of Prophecy*; Flusser, *Qumran and Apocalypticism*; DiTommaso, "Apocalypses and Apocalyticism in Antiquity, Part 1"; DiTommaso, "Apocalypses and Apocalyticism in Antiquity, Part 2"; Collins, ed., *Encyclopedia of Apocalypticism*, vol. 1; Aune, *Literary Environment*, 226–52; García Martínez, *Wisdom and Apocalypticism*; García Martínez, *Qumran and Apocalyptic*; A. Y. Collins, *Cosmology and Eschatology*; and A. Y. Collins, *Combat Myth*; Parry and Tov, *Dead Sea Scrolls Reader* (6 vols); Clifford, ed., "Special Issue on Apocalyptic Literature," *CBQ* 39/3 (1977); Hellholm "Problem of Apocalyptic Genre and the Apocalypse of John"; Wainwright, *Mysterious Apocalypse*; Malina, *On the Genre and Message of Revelation*; Puskas and Robbins, *Introduction*, 44–7, 144–58. See list of Judean and Christ-follower apocalypses in Wilson, *Charts on the Book of Revelation*, 19.

8. For an articulate statement of the unique features of apocalyptic eschatology over against prophetic eschatology see Reddish, *Apocalyptic Literature*, 20: "Hope was shifted from this world and this age to another world and another age. God would not employ ordinary means but supernatural forces to bring about the divine plan."

Qumran (1QM), the Psalms of Thanksgiving (1QH), and the commentary of Habakkuk (1QpHab).[9]

Apocalyptic literature is characterized by the following literary and thematic features: First, there are discourse cycles or visions between a seer and a heavenly being, revealing the secrets of human destiny (e.g., Dan 10; 2 Esd 11–12; 2 Bar 1–4; Rev 4–5; 17).[10] Second, the visions often contain mythical images rich in symbolism: a four-headed leopard with four wings (Dan 7:6), an eagle with twelve wings and three heads (2 Esd 11:1), and a beast with ten horns and seven heads (Rev 13:1). Third, the theme of cosmic catastrophe preceding the end is mentioned: war, fire, earthquake, famine (2 Bar 25–27; 2 Esd 5:1–13; War Scroll; 1QM 1; Rev 6:1—9:21). Fourth, the events of history are regarded as predetermined in fixed periods of time (Dan 9:24; 2 Esd 4:36–37; 2 Bar 25; Rev 4:1; 6:11; 10:7). Fifth, there is to be an end of the present evil order (of the Seleucids or, later, the Romans) and the beginning of a new age inaugurated by a royal mediator or son of man (Dan 7:1–14; 2 Esd 13; 1 Enoch 69:27–29; Rev 19:11–21). Sixth, there is to be a final judgment of the wicked (2 Esd 7:32–38; T Mos/As. Mos. 10; War Scroll, 1QM 18–19; Isa 11; Dan 12; Rev 20) and a vindication of the righteous to a state of eternal bliss in paradise (Sib. Or. 3:783–95; 1 Enoch 32:3; 48–51; 2 Esd 7:36; 8:52; 1QH 16; 1QS 8; 1QM 19; 2 Cor 12:4; Rev 2:7; 21–22).[11]

The Epistolary Genre

Both the epistolary framework and the letters section of Revelation compose our final generic category to examine.[12] After the superscription or title (1:1–3), Revelation reminds us of the opening of an early Christ-follower letter. A salutation identifies the recipients as the churches of Asia

---

9. For primary sources, see Charlesworth, *OTP*, vol. 1; Bauckham, et al., *Old Testament Pseudepigrapha*, vol. 1; Vermes, *Scrolls* (1997); García Martínez, *DSS* (1999); Charlesworth, *Dead Sea Scrolls*.

10. On Greco-Roman seers and oracles, see Flower, *Seer in Ancient Greece*; Potter, "Oracles," 1071–72; and Sourvinou-Inwood, "Delphic Oracle," 445–46 in Hornblower and Spawforth, *Oxford Classical Dictionary*. On sky visions of seers in altered states of consciousness, see Malina and Pilch, *Revelation*, 6–8, 69–72.

11. For studies underscoring the diversity of Judean and Christ-follower interpretations regarding paradise, see Luttikhuizen, *Paradise Interpreted*; Bockmuehl and Stroumsa, *Paradise in Antiquity*.

12. See Klauck, *Ancient Letters*, 349–53; Deissmann, *Light from the Ancient East*, 244–45, 374–75; Puskas and Reasoner, *Letters*, 28–48.

and the sender as John (1:4a). There is also a blessing: "grace and peace" (1:4b-5a) and a doxology: "to him be glory" (1:5b-6). Then the book ends with a concluding greeting, like an early Christ-follower letter: "the grace of the Lord Jesus Christ be with all" (22:21).[13] In fact, Rev 22:18–21 has parallels to 1 Cor 16:22-4. Both have a conditional formula, "if anyone" (1 Cor 16:22: Rev 22:19), followed by an anathema or curse on the disobedient, and the emotive prayer "Come, Lord Jesus" or *maranatha* (1 Cor 16:22; Rev 22:20).[14] The epistolary framework concludes with the wish of grace for all (1 Cor 16:23; with unspecified *pantōn*, 2 Thess 3:18; Rev 22:21). The epistolary beginning and ending of Revelation brackets 1:4—22:21 as a complete unit.

In addition to the epistolary framework, there are seven letters to seven churches in the first section of the book (1:4—3:22). The seven letters are similar to 2 and 3 John, which contain: an opening address, praise or warning, threats and rewards, promise of a future visit, and a final greetings. Upon close examination, the seven letters in Revelation have five sections: (1) an address and commission to write (2:1, 8, 12, 18; 3:1, 7, 14); (2) a messenger formula ("these things says the One who . . .") similar to the pronouncement of the Hebrew prophets ("thus says the Lord") and followed by a description of the heavenly Christ in the inaugural vision (same verses as above); (3) an exhortation introduced by "I know," which includes some or all of the following:

a) a description of the situation, with "I know that . . ." (2:2-3, 13, 19; 3:1, 8, 15),

b) censure, with the formula "but I hold it against you" (2:4, 14, 20) and without this formula (3:2, 16–17),

c) a call to repentance (2:5, 16, 21; 3:3, 19c),

d) revelatory saying introduced by "see" or "behold" (*idou*, 2:10,22; 3:8, 9, 20)

---

13. The translation of Rev 22:21 above is based on an "almost certain reading {B}" of *meta pantōn* ("with all") alone (without specifying "saints" *hagiōn*), according to Metzger, *Textual Commentary*, 2nd ed., 691. See discussion in Blount, *Revelation*, 416–17; and C. R. Koester, *Revelation*, 858–59.

14. Although the readers live in the "not yet," for those who share in the hope of his coming, the present becomes less empty and more complete because the present Lord of the church is the coming Lord of the universe (Thompson, *Revelation*, 190).

e) announcement of the Lord's coming (to judge and save, 2:5, 16, 25; 3:3, 11),[15]

f) exhortation to hold fast (2:10c, 25; 3:2–3, 11).

(4) a call to hear the message directed to all: "let him who has ears to hear . . ." (2:7, 11, 17, 29; 3:6, 13, 22), and (5) an end-time promise: "to the victor I will give . . ." or "he who overcomes will be . . . (2:7,10c, 17b, 26: 3:5, 12, 21).

The seven letters are addressed to seven specific churches that were once located in the ancient province of Asia, which is now the western part of Turkey. Although they are an integral part of the book's structure, these letters mirror the problems of early Christ-followers at a particular place and time. Therefore, in order to understand the original readers and the book itself, it is necessary for us to know the setting, date, and authorship of Revelation.

Figure 15: Model of Pergamum (second century). Roman theater with temple of Dionysus to the (lower) left of theater stoa, and famous altar of Zeus to the right, acropolis area, temple of Trajan above left, and temple of Athena, above center.

---

15. In Rev 2:5, 16; 3:3, the Lord will come to judge. In Rev 2:25 and 3:11 (and Rev 22:20–21), the Lord comes to save and bless, perhaps after the purgation of judgment (cf. Rev 20).

The Place, Destination, and Date

The internal evidence for the setting of the book is explicit. The author is writing from the island of Patmos near Miletus (1:9) and about sixty-five miles from Ephesus. According to Pliny the Elder, the island is eight miles long and five wide (*Nat. Hist.* 4.12.69). The author is addressing seven churches in the province of Asia (1:4, 11). These churches are located in the Asian cities of Ephesus, Smyrna, Pergamum, Thyatira, Sardis, Philadelphia, and Laodicea.[16] The description of the cultural and worship settings of these churches reflects late first-century Asia. The "throne of Satan" in Pergamum (2:13), for example, may refer to either the great altar of Zeus Sōtēr[17] or the cult Asklepios (Mart. *Epig.* 9.16), both prominent in the city, as was the emperor cult.[18] The patristic evidence concurs with the internal data (e.g., Eusebius, *Hist. eccl.* 3.17–18). According to Irenaeus (*Haer.* 5.30.3), Revelation was written towards the end of Domitian's reign (81–96). The internal data of the book, with some external confirmation, support this date.[19]

The Social and Historical Context

The attempt to reconstruct the social-historical environment of Revelation has its challenges. It may have been one of local persecution of Jesus followers who refused to participate in the imperial cult (1:9; 2:13; 13:15–16). The phrase "partners in affliction" (NRSV; Gk. *thlipsis*), however, might also be associated with poverty (2:9–10), suffering in collaboration with "Jezebel" (2:22), or the "great ordeal" (famine, slavery, or political upheaval) endured by those "before the throne" (7:13–14).[20] It is

---

16. For local first-century context, see Hemer, *Letters to the Seven Churches*; Ramsay, *Letters to the Seven Churches*. See map on p. 140 of this book.

17. Deissmann, *Light from the Ancient East*, 281n3. See altar of Zeus, Figure 15 on p. 147 of this book.

18. Ibid., 347. See also Friesen, *Imperial Cults*, chs. 2–3, 8–9; Klauck, *Religious Context*, 255. C. R. Koester thinks "Satan's throne" alludes to the murder there of the Christ-follower, Antipas, "where Satan lives" (Rev 2:13), rather than to a specific structure ("Pergamum," 446–47; C. R. Koester, *Revelation*, 286–87).

19. After extensive study of local conditions in the area, Hemer, *Letters to the Seven Churches*, 2–12, claims that the cumulative effects of his study confirm a date during the reign of Domitian.

20. Thompson, *Revelation*, 55, 109–10. On diversity of meanings for Gk. *thlipsis*, see BDAG, 457.

uncertain if "the affliction" has already been experienced (1:9) or is to be expected in the near future (Rev 2:10; cf. 3:10; 7:13–14; 11:7–9, 14; 12:11; 16:6; 17:6; 18:24; 19:2; 20:4–6). The situation for Judeans and Christ-followers in Asia was not always troublesome. The author of Revelation may have been indicting his readers for their complacency and compromise in readily adjusting to life in the empire (Rev. 2:4–6; 2:20–25; 3:14–21). Some have strayed away from the leadership of John the seer by embracing "false" teaching and practices (Rev 2:6, 14–15, 20).[21]

Figure 16: Denarius of Emperor Domitian (81–96)

Rome is viewed (indirectly) as a prominent threat. It is cryptically portrayed as two beasts inspired by the satanic dragon (Rev 13) and also with the image of Babylon, the mother of prostitutes (ch. 17; cf. the goddess Roma). By the end of the first century, Asia was home to several imperial shrines that had considerable influence on the communities. Local cities competed for the honor of hosting festivals and shrines to the

---

21. For example, there has been some patristic speculation on the Nicolaitans (Rev 2:6, 15). Were they a "gnostic" heresy related to Cerinthus, the opponent of both Polycarp and "John the disciple of the Lord"? See Irenaeus, *Haer.* 3.11.1; Eusebius, *Hist. eccl.* 3.28; 4.14. There are many echoes of or allusions to Revelation in the Nag Hammadi codices; see Evans et al., *Nag Hammadi Texts*, 537–41. Whoever the Nicolaitans were, they were viewed as a threat to John the seer and to the churches of Ephesus and Pergamum. For survey of discussion, see Trebilco, *Ephesus* (2007), 307–35.

goddess Roma, the emperor Augustus, and the imperial deities.[22] Under the Flavians, especially Domitian, the imperial cult was also represented. Domitian was acclaimed "Lord and God" (Martial, *Epig.* 5.8; Suetonius, *Dom.* 13.2) and the worship of his genius was encouraged (locally) in the region.[23] In Thyatira, the emperor was declared to be the incarnation of Apollo and the son of Zeus. Judeans and Christ-followers who did not participate were often persecuted by the locals and may have been prosecuted for dishonoring the the recognized cults (Dio Cassius 67.14). Imperial temples housed assemblies, banks, and marketplaces, making it difficult to buy or sell without the "mark of the beast" (Rev 13:17). Most economic, social, and political functions were related to the imperial cult.[24] However one might interpret *thlipsis* in Revelation (i.e., persecution or affliction due to poverty and exploitation), Rome and the imperial cult was probably involved (directly or indirectly).

Although the tradition that Domitian is the first persecutor of Christ-followers after Nero (Eusebius, *His. eccl.* 4.26.9) is questionable,[25] any local celebrations of his rule, and the related worship of Greco-Roman deities,[26] would *not* have been popular among Judeans and Christ-followers.[27] In addition, there are negative historical allusions in

22. Carey, "Book of Revelation as Counter-Imperial Script," 163. See also Friesen, *Imperial Cults*; and Howard-Brook and Gwyther, *Unveiling Empire*, 102–5.

23. Schüssler Fiorenza, *Book of Revelation*, 193; Klauck, *Religious Context*, 310, cautious about demonizing Domitian, states that during his reign (81–96 CE), an imperial temple in Ephesus (near the Gate of Magnesia entrance) was dedicated to the Flavian dynasty, which included Domitian. Aune, *Revelation 1–5*, lvi–lxx, finds Roman imperial worship in Asia from the time of Augustus to well after Trajan but does not find any *special* emphasis on emperor worship under Domitian (ibid., lxx).

24. See the various ethical and cultic (especially imperial) ties to most associations, clubs, and guilds of Asia Minor, in Ascough et al., *Associations in the Greco-Roman World*, 67–132.

25. We have no evidence of an official and empire-wide persecution of Christ-followers under Domitian (81–96 CE), see Slater, *Christ and Community*, 26–42; Henize, *Johannesapokalypse*, 228–39. Thompson, *Book of Revelation*, chs. 7 and 10, suggests that Christ-followers in Asia were so adapted to life under Domitian that the author is challenging their complacency.

26. See, e.g., Xenophon, *Anabasis* 5.3.7–13; Hesiod, *Theogony* 1–34; Tacitus, *Annals* 4.56.1; For a survey of temple sites (including that of Artemis) near Ephesus, see Trebilco, *Ephesus*, 15–37. For Roman imperial cults in the east, see Klauck, *Religious Context*, 288–330.

27. Their reluctance and hesitation would have aroused the suspicion of local citizens, who may have interpreted their actions as disloyal to Rome. Resistance of any kind would have brought conflict, persecution, and arrest. See Pliny the Younger,

Revelation that seem to signify Domitian. The author speaks of a series of rulers and identifies his own time as that of the "sixth" (17:9-11). Domitian was not the sixth emperor, but he was the sixth to be declared divine by the senate. Allusions to the beast in Revelation 13 and 17 also reflect the late first-century belief that the tyrant Nero (Suetonius, *Nero* 49) had returned from the dead (i.e., Nero redivivus, Sib. Or. 4.119-20, 138-39; 5:93-97, 363ff; 8:153-57; Ascen. Isa. 4:2-14). The controversial reign of Domitian (because of ongoing conflicts with the senate) was also compared to that of Nero: Domitian's reign was, so to speak, "Nero redux."

By 110 CE in Bithynia (1 Pet 1:1; 2:12; Rev 1:13), locals were sometimes arrested for worshiping Christ; they could be released if they denounced their faith and invoked the gods. Pliny the Younger, a governor of Bithynia, wrote to Emperor Trajan on this matter, and the emperor supported him; but Trajan cautioned against using any anonymous accusers, because it would set a bad legal precedent.[28] The document does not presuppose active prosecution of Christ-followers; Pliny regarded them as members of a superstitious sect. His concern was with maintaining loyalty to the emperor and forbidding political associations that were viewed as a threat to the empire.

Again, it is uncertain if the problems encountered in the province of Asia (around 95 CE) were a result of local persecution or some other kind of affliction (e.g., poverty, famine, political unrest). It is unclear also if these problems were actually experienced by the author and readers of Revelation, or if they were perceived to be threats about to happen. Nevertheless, Revelation expects much trouble when the faithful resist the power of the two beasts and the enticements of Babylon. He therefore exhorts his readers to overcome as faithful witnesses, because the Lamb and its allies will be victorious (Rev 2:7, 10, 17, 26; 3:5, 12, 21; 14:1; 19:7; 21:22; 22:12-17).[29]

Letters 10.96-97 (110 CE); and McKnight and Modica, *Jesus Is Lord, Caesar Is Not*, esp. chs. 1-2, 10.

28. Pliny the Younger, *Letters* 10.96-97. In 250, Emperor Decius gave an edict that all inhabitants of the empire make sacrifices for the emperor, causing a reaction among the "Christians," which prompted an empire-wide persecution, that resulted in the deaths of many Christians, including Fabian, bishop of Rome.

29. Carey, "Revelation as Counter-Imperial Script," 164.

Authorship

The author of the book calls himself John (1:1, 4, 9; 22:8), and since he seems closely acquainted with the situation of the churches in Asia, he was probably from that province. His extensive allusions to the Judean Scriptures (LXX); his interest in the priesthood (1:6; 5:10; 20:6), in the twelve tribes of Israel (ch. 7), in the Holy City and temple (11:1–2; 21:1—22:5); and his strict adherence to Judean dietary (*kashrut*) and sexual purity laws (2:14, 20; 12:17; 14:4; 22:14) suggest that he is a Judean follower of Jesus.[30] He uses no specific title in addressing his audience, other than "servant" (1:1) or "brother ... and copartner" (1:9). Furthermore he was probably not the apostle John, the son of Zebedee, since he seems to distinguish himself from the apostles (18:20; 21:14). Although Justin Martyr (*Dial.* 81.4), Clement of Alexandria, and Origen (in Eusebuis, *Hist. eccl.* 6.25) all regarded the apostle John as the author, Dionysius of Alexandria (ca. 250) and Papias ("John the elder" in Eusebius, *Hist. eccl.* 3.39) rejected this view. Eusebius himself is ambivalent on apostolic authorship because some rejected the book as genuine (*Hist. eccl.* 3.25).[31] Regardless of which John wrote it (elder or apostle), the author identifies himself as a prophet (1:1–3, 10–19; 4:1–2; 17:1–3; 21:9–10; 22:6–7), and perhaps he identified with a school of itinerant Christ-follower prophets.[32] John

---

30. Frankfurter, "Revelation." The mention of "synagogue of Satan" may apply to Gentile god-fearers *claiming* an affiliation with Judean tradition as a basis for Christ's salvation (cf. Rom 2:17–24, 28–29) but *disregarding* the meal and purity laws (Rev 2:14, 20; cf. 2 Macc 6:18–19; 4 Macc 5:2, 17–20; Acts 15:20; 1 Cor 8:4–13), ibid., 469. C. R. Koester, *Revelation*, 276, 286, maintains that "synagogue of Satan," an intra-Judean charge (cf. 1QH 10:22; 1QM 15:9), refers to those Judeans that denounce Judean followers of Jesus (i.e., "Israel's remnant") and place them in danger of imprisonment or death (Rev 2:9–10; 3:9).

31. Bauckham, *Jesus and Eyewitnesses*, 424, suggests that Eusebius supported the view of Papias that Revelation was written by John the presbyter, *not* the son of Zebedee (Eusebius, *Hist. eccl.* 3.39.5–7), because Eusebius did *not* regard Revelation as apostolic or canonical (see also my p. 121n16). On the ambivalence of Eusebius regarding the status of Revelation, see Kalin, "New Testament Canon of Eusebius," 399–400.

As noted earlier (p. 149n21), there are many echoes of or allusions to Revelation in the Nag Hammadi codices (e.g., Apoc. John, Gos. Thom., Apoc. Adam, Teach. Silv.), see Evans et al., *Nag Hammadi Texts*, 537–41. Perhaps the gnostic "use" of Revelation in the third and fourth centuries aroused suspicions in some churches regarding the book.

32. Aune, "Prophetic Circle of John"; Beale, *Revelation*, 34–36. See Aune, *Revelation 1–5*, on various source-critical theories (cx–cxx) and a proposed three-stage theory of composition (cxx–cxxxiv).

is often called a seer because many of his visions and prophecies concern "what is to take place after this" (1:19; 4:1; cf. 22:6).[33]

Figure 17: Papyrus 24, Rev. 5:5–8; 6:5–8 (fourth century)

Textual Evidence[34]

The earliest manuscript containing Rev 1:13–20 is the second-century P[98] (Cairo). P[47] (Chester Beatty III) includes Rev 9:10—17:2 (from the late third century), with about eighty singular (distinctive) readings. The fourth-century P[24] (Andover-Newton) contains Rev 5:5–8 and 6:5–8. The fourth-century Codex Sinaiticus probably preserves the original text of Revelation. Two more important witnesses are the fifth-century Codex Alexandrinus (A), containing the complete text of Revelation, and the fifth-century Codex C (*Ephraemi Syri Rescriptus*, Paris), containing most of the text. They constitute, with the thirteenth-century minuscule MS 2053, a reliable textual witness to Revelation.

Literary and rhetorical devices

Let us now discuss the literary and structural features of the Revelation. An analysis of the structure of the book will show that the author arranged material, not in a linear and chronological manner, but in a more

---

33. See Flower, *Seer in Ancient Greece*; Malina and Pilch, *Revelation*, 1–11. Prophetic utterances were more concerned with forth-telling (e.g., "thus says the Lord") than foretelling ("days are coming"); but when such predictions were made, they were based on present occurrences, e.g., impending disaster because of present disobedience; see "Prophecy," in Soulen and Soulen, *Biblical Criticism*, 160–63.

34. Aune provides a helpful overview: *Revelation 1–5*, cxxxvi-clx; on textual variants, see Metzger, *Textual Commentary*, 2nd ed., 662–91.

literary and topical way. This observation finds some support in the numerous repetitions, interruptions of thought, and interludes that occur in the book.[35] Many of these literary and rhetorical devices will be noted in our outline of Revelation.

Intercalation

The author employs the method of inclusion or intercalation throughout the book. This technique of framing or bracketing material (A B A') is employed in the four Gospels, especially Mark.[36] The author frames small segments, large sections, and the entire book by this device. In the prophetic introduction, we have the superscription (1:1–3, A) and a motto (1:7–8, A') that bracket the epistolary prescript (1:4–6, B). In Revelation 8, the announcement (v. 2, A) and description (vv. 6ff., A') of the seven angels with seven trumpets brackets a heavenly liturgy (vv. 3–5, B). Readers are therefore required to view these elements as part of an indivisible whole. In larger sections the technique of intercalation is also employed. Between the Babylon visions in 17:1—19:10 (A) and the Jerusalem visions in 21:9—22:5 (A') is inserted in the parousia-judgment series in 19:11—21:9 (B). Finally, as I mentioned earlier, the entire book (B) is bracketed by an epistolary prescript (1:4–6, A) and conclusion (22:21, A').

Interludes

Closely connected to the technique of intercalation are interludes. These seem to interrupt the progression of the narrative with visions and hymns of end-time salvation (7:1–17; 11:14–19; 12:10; 14:15; 15:24; 19:1–8; 20:4–6). Combined with intercalations, the interludes become part of a double intercalation. For example: Rev 10:1—11:14 is clearly marked as an interlude inserted into the cycle of seven trumpets (8:6—9:21, A; 10:1—11:14 B; 11:15–19, A'). At the same time, however, Rev 10:1—11:14

---

35. For other symbols, images, and figures of speech, see Wilson, *Charts on the Book of Revelation*, 44–57; and Thompson, *Book of Revelation*, 40–52; C. R. Koester, *Revelation*, 141–44. For reference, see Lanham, *Handlist of Rhetorical Terms*.

36. For example, in Mark 2:1—3:6, the controversy dialogues with Jesus's critics are framed by two miracle stories (2:1–12; 3:1–6). See "Intercalation," in Aune, *Literature and Rhetoric*, 230–32; Puskas and Crump, *Gospels and Acts*, 74.

serves as an introduction to the following section of Rev 12–14, since it refers to the same period of persecution by the beast (11:7ff.; 13; 17).

The vision of the small scroll is also held together by the pattern A (10:1—11:14), B (11:15–19), A' (12–14), and is tied to the trumpet septet of the seven-sealed scroll by the same pattern. By the method of intercalation it is tied at the other end to the bowl septet. The introduction to the bowl septet (15:18) is patterned analogously to that of the trumpet septet: appearance of the seven angels—15:1 (A), heavenly liturgy—15:5–8 (B) and the execution of the plagues—16:1ff. (A'). In this sequence 15:2–4 is an interlude that at the same time represents an intercalation (Rev 14, A; 15:1, B; 15:2–4, A'). The vision of the small prophetic scroll thus reaches a climax in 15:2–4, which at the same time ties it to the bowl septet of the seven-sealed scroll.

The examples provided above show that the author does not divide the text into separate sections, but interlocks material from one section to the next. Thus the author joins sections together by interweaving and interlacing them through this method of intercalation.

Numerical Arrangements

Another technique used to achieve this interwoven texture of the book is that of numbers and numerical structures. The book has two scroll visions (Rev 5; 10) and four septets or cycles of seven (seven letters, 2:1—3:22; seven seals, 4:1—8:1, seven trumpets, 8:2—9:21; 11:15–19; seven bowls, 15:1 with 15:5—16:21). The three plague septets are related to each other as prelude, crescendo, and climax, whereas the letter septet points forward to the visions of eschatological salvation.

Gematria

Gematria is the assignment to each letter of the alphabet (of any desired language) a numerical quantity, so that names or words can be referred to as numbers. See, for example, "one who has 50 as an initial will be commander" (Sib. Or. 5:28, Nero?; cf. 3:24–30, Jesus?). The most familiar example of this is 666 in the Apocalypse, and since the early 1800s it has been suspected that this number referred to (Caesar) Nero.[37] Transliter-

---

37. See Rev 13:8; cf. 15:2. Irenaeus (*Haer.* 5.19–30) and Hippolytus (*Treatise on Christ and the Antichrist*, which also include 1 John and 2 Thess) were the first to

ating this name from Greek into Hebrew letters and using the numbers of the Hebrew alphabet for the calculation gives you the number 666; transliterating from Latin into Hebrew will give you the number 616 (a textual variant of 666).

The world of gematria is mysterious,[38] and to enter into it is to immediately find that there are several other dimensions of meaning to words and especially to numbers as the numbers pick up additional related mathematical characteristics traceable to Pythagoreanism and "geometric" forms.[39]

Pre-announcements

Pre-announcements occur when promises to the victor (in chs. 2–3) are repeated in chapters 21–22, and when the announcement of final judgment in 14:6–20 is developed in chapters 17–20. Pre-announcements have a similar function as foreshadowings do in Greek tragedy: that is, both are veiled predictions or forewarnings that become increasingly specific as the action of the work unfolds.

Cross-references and Repetition with Variation

Cross-references are evident, for example, when the characterizations of Christ in the inaugural vision (1:9–20) recur in Rev 2–3, 14:14ff., and 19:11–16. This device enables the reader to readily identify the character in the narrative. Such repetitions occur quite frequently in this book, at times with slight variations, and at times with numerical significance. In the third century, Victorinus, bishop of Poetovio (modern Slovenia), first noticed these repetitions and recurring patterns (*In Apocalypsin)*, which also influenced Jerome's interpretation.[40]

---

identify this figure as an individual tyrant. On the textual variant of the number 616, see Metzger, *Textual Commentary*, 2nd ed., 676.

38. Even the derivation of the word is a bit of a mystery. Some trace it to a Hebrew word, others to a Greek word. Some feel it was a Hebrew word built up from a combination of words from other languages. It was a common practice in antiquity.

39. See Bauckham, *Climax of Prophecy*, ch. 11, "Nero and the Beast" (384–452) for a generous sampling of the process, the theory, and the unusual trails down which such speculation leads. See also Boring et al., *Hellenistic Commentary*, 576–77.

40. For introduction and selected primary texts, see http://www.bombaxo.com/victapoc.html. Bauckham, *Climax of Prophecy*, 22–29 explores some of these repeated

Allusion and echo

Allusion is an elusive term, but what is meant is that the author uses subtle means to inform and contextualize his prophecy using texts and traditions. The seer has made more allusions to the sacred texts of the Judeans than has any other NT author.[41] Other words are sometimes used to describe this: *echo, intertextuality, mimesis,* and so forth. This observation is no longer considered to be just a footnote in studies of the Apocalypse. The range of possible allusions mentioned in this previous note (n41) discloses a datum itself, namely, that this is a highly subjective discourse. How much would a skilled first-century reader of a text have processed? How much did the author intend? Does it even matter what the author intended? In biblical studies, the focus on allusion, intertextuality, and the like has been growing in importance.[42] Much of this interest was ignited with the Dead Sea Scrolls (1947).

Contrasts

Contrasts occur between the beast and the Lamb, and between the great harlot and the woman of chapter 12.[43] Contrasts effectively distinguish the identity and role of each character, and the nature and function of each object or image. Consider for example what Bauckham calls the "satanic trinity":[44] the Dragon (12:13–17), Beast #1 (13:1–10), and Beast #2 (13:11–18). Or even more interesting is the tripartite formulaic title given to the beast in 17:8, "the beast that you saw *was and is not and is about to*

---

references. Mealy, *After the Thousand Years,* 13, refers to "the extensive network of cross-references and allusions which affect the interpretation of virtually every passage in Revelation."

41. The Apocalypse rarely quotes directly from the OT, but allusions abound. Some count as many as one thousand (e.g., van der Waal, *Openbaring van Jezuz Christus*; Nestle-Aland (NA[28]) text index cites 635; Aland, ed., *Greek NT* (4th ed) text index has 394; Swete (*Apocalypse*) cites 278; Charles, *Revelation,* cites 226; Bratcher, *Old Testament Quotations,* lists only 11 OT citations. See Beale, "Revelation"; Beale, *Revelation,* 76–99; and Moyise, *Old Testament in the Book of Revelation.* The range of opinion is due to different *criteria for inclusion* of OT material; nevertheless, the book is full of allusions to the OT, almost all from some version of the Greek Septuagint (LXX).

42. For example in OT studies: Fishbane, *Biblical Interpretation*; and in NT studies: Hays, *Echoes of Scripture in the Letters of Paul.*

43. On the interpretation of such imagery, see Rossing, *Choice between Two Cities*; and Johns, *Lamb Christology of the Apocalypse.*

44. Bauckham, *Climax of Prophecy,* 32.

come," in parody of the divine name. The mark of the beast parodies the seal of God (13:16; cf. 7:3; 9:4).

Symbolism

A common stock of symbols and images is employed throughout the book. For example, readers should see the image of the throne in connection with other expressions and symbols of kingship in order to grasp its full-impact symbolic colors (e.g., purple as royalty or luxury, black as death, white as joy or victory, red as slaughter or war, gold as divine splendor). Symbolic numerals are also part of the common stock: seven for perfection or completeness (cf. Gen 2:1–3; 7:2–4), twelve for the twelve tribes of Israel or the people of God (cf. Gen 35:22–26), and three and a half years as an interval of persecution. Two is a number for witnesses, olive trees, or lampstands. These colors and numbers are basically used the same throughout the book.[45] Finally, the notion of end-time war is intensified and enhanced by a variety of terms and symbols of war.[46]

Chiasm

A further method of composition by which the author seems to have arranged the entire book is inverted parallelism, or chiasm, (A B C D C' B' A').[47] It is similar to, but usually has more components than, the intercalation framing device (A B A') and often highlights (in some way) the central section by means of a gradual buildup (A B C **D** C' B' A'). Both the introduction (1:1–8, A) and closing of Revelation (22:10–21, A') contain a letter form, prophetic statements, and a blessing. The inaugural vision and letter septet (1:9—3:22, B) correspond to the visions of final

---

45. See also Beale, *Revelation*, 58–64; Frankfurter, "Revelation," 475.

46. See discussion, e.g., on Harmageddon (Heb. *Har-Meggido*), Rev 16:16, as a symbol (not a location) for "the last resistance of anti-god forces before the Kingdom of Christ" (Beasley-Murray, *Book of Revelation*, 245–46); see also Blount, *Revelation*, 306–7, reflecting similar views; and C. R. Koester, *Revelation*, 660–61, who examines the many etymological interpretations of "Harmageddon" and the difficulties of identifying a specific location.

47. See "Chiasmus," in Aune, *Literature and Rhetoric*, 93–96. On Revelation, see Lund, *Chiasmus in the New Testament*, 323–411; and Welch, *Chiasmus in Antiquity*, 242–48. See also my discussion of chiasm in 1 John, pp. 133–34.

salvation (19:11—22:9, B'): (a) in a manner similar to the inaugural vision of Rev 1:9-20, which introduces "the community under judgment" (Rev 1:9—3:22, B), Rev 19:11-16 introduces "the final judgment and salvation" scene (Rev 19:11—22:9, B'); and (b) the promise to the victorious in Rev 2-3 finds its fulfillment in 19:11—22:9. The vision of seven bowls (15:1, 5 to 19:10, C') is clearly a continuation of the vision of the seven seals and seven trumpets (4:1—9:21; 11:15-19, C), both of which bracket the central section (10:1—15:4, D) of the small prophetic scroll.

This concentric pattern was widely employed in antiquity. In Greek tragedy the play unfolds by means of a complication (A), crisis (B), and denouement (A').[48] Revelation shares other similarities with Greek tragedy.[49] Roman architecture was often characterized by this pattern. Even the seven-branched lampstand in Judean liturgy, the menorah, follows the A B C D C' B' A' pattern.

The Structure

Following the above observations on the compositional techniques of Revelation, we provide the following parallel outlines, highlighting both a chiastic structure and thematic development:

---

48. See Aristotle's *Poetics* 6.12-18; 18.1-3 (fourth century BCE); Puskas and Robbins, *Introduction*, 123-33.

49. On Revelation and Greek tragedy, see Bowman, *First Christian Drama*; Bowman, "Revelation of John"; Bowman, "Revelation," 58-70; Brewer, "Influence of Greek Drama on the Apocalypse of John"; Palmer, *Drama of the Apocalypse*; Blevins, "Genre of Revelation," 393-408. Blevins points out that six of the seven cities of Asia Minor addressed in Revelation had Greek theaters. Ephesus had the largest with a seven-windowed stage. Greek plays also had prologues and epilogues, a number of choruses, interludes, and hymns similar to those in Revelation (4:8; 5:3-12). For example, the hymns or "odes" (Rev 4:8; 5:9-13; 15:3-4) function in a similar way to the chorus in Classical Greek drama (e.g., Euripides, Aeschylus, and Sophocles). Here a group of actors described and commented on the main *action* of a play with song, dance, or recitation. On the Gospels (Mark, John) and Greek tragedy, see Puskas and Robbins, *Introduction*, 123-33.

A	Prologue and epistolary frame 1:1–7	Title 1:1–3 Greeting 1:4–6 Motto 1:7–8
B	The community under judgment 1:9—3:22	Author and situation 1:9–10 Inaugural vision 1:11–20 (1) Censure and encouragement 2:1—3:22 (7 messengers)
C	God's and Christ's reign 4:1—9:21; 11:14–19	Heavenly court 4:1—5:14 (2) Seven seals 6:1—8:1 (3) Seven trumpets 8:2—9:21; 11:14–19
D	The community under oppression 10:1—11:13; 12:1—15:5	Prophetic commissioning 10:1—11:13 Enemies of the community 12:1—14:5 End-time harvest and liberation 14:6–20; 15:2–4
C'	Divine Judgement of Babylon 15:1, 5—19:10	(4) seven bowls 15:1, 5—16:21 Rome and its power 17:1–18 Judgment of Rome 18:1—19:10
B'	Final judgment and salvation 19:11—22.9	Parousia and judgment 19:11—20:15 The new word of God 21:1–8 The new city of God 21:9—22:9
A'	Epilogue and epistolary frame 22:10–21	Revelatory sayings 22:10–17 Epistolary conclusion 22:18–21

In the above outlines, major units forming the chiasm are thematically labeled on the left, and subsections indicating literary relationships (e.g., four septets) are on the right. The book is framed as a letter (A 1:4–5; A' 22:20–21). The outline also highlights the significance of the central section (D).[50] Inserted between the visions of the trumpets and bowls (where God and the Lamb are vindicated, C, C'), the central section of Rev 10:1—15:4 (D) serves as a prophetic word that may interpret (in some way) the situation of the Jesus loyalists in the end-time. God's faithful

---

50. Outline derived from Schüssler Fiorenza, "Composition and Structure of the Revelation of John"; Schüssler Fiorenza, *Book of Revelation*, 175–76. For alternative chiastic outlines, see Lund, *Chiasmus in the New Testament*, 325–27; and Welch, *Chiasmus in Antiquity*, 244–45. For another thematic outline see Harrington, *Revelation*, 22–23. See also four different book outlines in Wilson, *Charts on the Book of Revelation*, 31.

who resist "the inhabitants of earth" (11:10), deceived by the beasts (ch. 13), and consorting with Babylon (14:8; all empowered by the dragon, ch. 12) will face much affliction, but victory belongs to the Lamb and its allies (11:15-18; 12:10-12; 15:3-4).

Figure 18: *Whore of Babylon* (woodcut by Albrecht Dürer [1471-1528]).

Despite the words of comfort and hope for the faithful, Revelation does not refrain from using the vengeful language (19:20-21; 20:10, 15; 21:8) and some misogynist stereotyping (2:20-23; 17:15-17) typical of the very imperial order it opposes.[51] Much of the language condemning spiritual adultery as idolatry, however, is borrowed from Israel's prophetic tradition (Isa 57:3-13; Jer 3:6-25; 13:26-27; Ezek 16:32-42; 23:10-11, 25-29).

51. Carey, "Symptoms of Resistance"; Pippin, "Revelation"; and Pippin, "Revelation/Apocalypse, of John." See also Pippin, *Apocalyptic Bodies*, with illustrations and discussion.

The vengeful language is also nuanced, because the symbol of the conquering Lion is replaced by the Lamb who was slain (Rev 5:5-6; 17:14).[52] Finally, the language of misogyny is balanced (somewhat) by more positive female imagery: The woman (cf., daughter of Zion, Zeph 3:14), despite the dragon's opposition, gives birth (Jer 4:31) to the messiah (Rev 12:5; cf. Ps 2:7), and both woman and child are under God's protective care (Rev 12:13-17; cf. Exod 16:4; 19:4). In contrast to Babylon, mother of prostitutes (17:1-6), the New Jerusalem is presented as a bride clothed in the fine linen of righteous deeds (19:7-8; 21:9; cf. Isa 54:5; 61:10; 62:5; Ezek 16:9-14; Eph 5:25-27).[53]

Symbolic and Mythical Language

Because Revelation is apocalyptic in outlook and style, it employs much mythical and symbolic language. With other ancient writings, Revelation assumes the ancient worldview of a three-storied universe (heaven, earth, hades) inhabited by angels and demons. Like other apocalyptic writings, it visualizes a radical transformation of the world through cosmic catastrophe. Revelation also makes use of well-known mythologies of antiquity. The story of the queen of heaven with the eternal child, in chapter 12, is one example. The elements of myth here are the woman, the child, his birth and ascension, an eagle rising from the sea, and the dragon.[54] This myth is international and found in Egypt (with the figures of Isis, Horus, Seth), in Babylon (with the relationships between Demkina, Marduk,

---

52. See discussion in support of this transformation in C. R. Koester, *Revelation*, 387-88; and Tuckett, *Christology and the New Testament*, 183-85.

53. Mainstream feminist readings focus on reclaiming or recovering the text for women readers, interpreting the women characters as symbols. For example, Jezebel represents errant theology, and the whore of Babylon represents Roma or Roman colonialism (Pippin, "Revelation/Apocalypse," 628-29).

54. The illuminating appearance of "the queen of heaven" (like Ceres, Venus, or Proserpine) described with images of the moon, stars, and flaming fire, Apueleius, *Metam.* 11.2-4. On the mother (Rhea) and child (Zeus) threatened (by Titan), see Sib. Or. 3:132-41. On an eagle rising from the sea with twelve wings and three heads, symbolizing Rome, see 2 Esdr 11; on a man rising from the sea, who, with the clouds of heaven, defeats his enemies with a stream of fire from his mouth, see 2 Esdr 13. See also van Henten, "Dragon Myth and Imperial Ideology," 181-203. C. R. Koester, *Revelation*, 529-30, includes more images from the Judean context: e.g., divine appearances (Ps 104:2), sun, moon, and stars as God's people (Gen 37:9; *T. Ab.* 7:1-7; *T. Naph.* 5:2-4), and the woman's birth pangs (Isa 26:17; Jer 4:31; 1QH 11:7-11), as well as allusions from Sib. Or. and 2 Esdr (cited above).

and Tiamat), in the Greco-Roman world (with the characters of Athena, Artemis, Letho, Apollo, and Python), and in Judea (with the relationships of Israel, the Messiah, and Satan or Leviathan). Other examples of popular mythologies are the heavenly council portrayed as the assembly of the gods (chs. 4–5), the holy wars of the archangel against the serpent (12:7–12), and the god of heaven who defeats the monster of chaos and death to bring forth a new creation (19:11—22:5).[55] See the proposal that the imagery, sequence, and meaning in Revelation are rooted in reading the constellations and other heavenly phenomena in the sky.[56]

Our use of myth is not to be understood in a negative but in a positive and functional sense. Myths are stories about the "world beyond" (divine reality), told in language of "this world" (human reality). Myths are expressed in symbolic language because the realities they convey (e.g., the nature of evil and ultimate hope) are too profound or complex to be rationally explained. Myths are important in human culture because they (a) order human experience with a foundational vision of reality, (b) inform humanity about its identity and destiny, (c) express a saving power in human life, and (d) provide patterns for human actions.[57]

---

55. See C. R. Koester, *Revelation*, for a survey of views on the symbolism of the seven stars, Hades, Rev 1:16 (pp. 246–48), the twenty-four elders of Rev 4:4 (360–62), the four living creatures of Rev 4:6–8 (351–53), a great sign in heaven, Rev 12:1 (541–42), and the stones of the New Jerusalem, Rev 21:19–20 (818–19).

56. Malina, *On the Genre and Message of Revelation*; Malina and Pilch, *Revelation*, 1–5 (citing as support, for this sky perspective in antiquity, e.g., Philo, *Spec. Leg.* I, 13–20, on p. 3, as well as 1 Enoch on pp. 65, 163–66). In whatever way the author of Revelation made use of this imagery, he adapted it for his own message and purpose.

57. Myth has acquired a wide array of meanings: ancient folk tales, superstitions, magicoreligious beliefs, literary images and symbols. In light of these diverse understandings, it is necessary to define myth in a way that is *appropriate to* the materials to be studied, and to employ it *consistently*. Levenson's working definition of myth (*Sinai and Zion*, 103) is a "cast of mind that views certain symbols in terms of an act of unlimited scope and import that occurred, in Brevard Child's words, 'in a timeless age of the past.'" Levinson writes of mythical time which transcends the historicity of the moment. What occurred/occurs/will occur can thus be spoken of as occurring "in that time" (Mircea Eliade) as either protological ("beginning of things") or eschatological ("end of things"). The continuing relevance of protological events can be imputed to any moment. Thus a function of myth is transcending time and reveals quite well its power for theological meaning. Mythic symbols are more 'real' than the flux and change of history" (Ibid., 103). On the pictorial, evocative, tensive (not static), and polyvalent language of Revelation, see also Boring, *Revelation*, 53–59; Beale, *Revelation*, 50–69, prefers the image of "symbolic parable"; for a helpful overview of language and style, see C. R. Koester, *Revelation*, 138–44.

Conclusion

In our discussion of the book of Revelation, we examined genres and literary forms in the book; its setting, date, and authorship; rhetorical and literary devices present in the book; and the overall structure, symbolism, and mythology in Revelation. We discovered that Revelation was a prophetic and apocalyptic letter, written in Asia Minor in the late first century (95 CE) by a Judean Christ-follower prophet named John. The affliction faced or anticipated by the author and his readers might have been local persecution, poverty, famine, or political unrest. Whatever the situation, the author is certain that compromise with Rome's imperial culture is not to be tolerated. Despite the great trouble that resistance to Rome will bring, the faithful will overcome, because the Lamb and its allies will be victorious. The literary techniques we detected in the book include intercalations, interludes, numerical structures, and chiasm. Following the above compositional techniques, we outlined the book in an inverted arrangement: A B C D C' B' A'. The literary techniques and the literary structure of Revelation also have similarities with Greek drama (e.g., the chiastic pattern of complication, crisis, denouement). In our discussion of symbol and myth, we mentioned the ancient worldview of a three-storied universe; the use of international myths such as the story of the queen of heaven and her eternal child (Rev 12); and the use of colors, image clusters, and symbol associations. We also interpreted the term *myth* in a positive and functional manner as transcending time and providing powerful images for theological reflection.

The book of Revelation has a noteworthy ending: "The grace of the Lord Jesus be with all" (*pantōn*, 22:21; cf. 2 Thess 3:18). Even though the words to the churches in Rev 2–3 include sharp warnings, and even though the book itself contains some horrific visions of monsters and catastrophe, its message is given that the reader might be blessed (Rev 1:3). It is appropriate, therefore, that a final word of grace (*charis*, echoing 1:4) is extended to "all" who read the book.[58]

---

58. My translation of Rev 22:21 above follows the Greek text of NA[28] (p. 789). See also C. R. Koester, *Revelation*, 858–59; Metzger, *Breaking the Code*, 106.

Glossary

allegory: Gk. "saying something different from what one means," figurative (non-literal) or metaphorical language used in speech, story, and interpretation of texts (e.g., **Scriptures**). See also **Philo**.

amanuensis: Lat. "by hand," a scribal secretary, writing under the author's direction (e.g., Tertius, Rom 16:22), on behalf of the author, or in the author's name.

anabasis: Gk. "a going up," ascent or march, used in rhetoric to show progression toward a climax in a certain word arrangement. See also **concatenation.**

anadiplosis: Gk. "doubling, folding up," the repetition of the last word of a preceding clause. The word is often used at the end of a sentence and then used again at the beginning of the next sentence.

antinomian: Gk. "against the law"; although the term originated in 16th century debates on law and grace, it is used here of anyone who seeks to transcend or trivialize moral law in the life of faith, see also **libertine**.

apodeixis: Gk. "showing forth" or demonstrating by argument; a proof.

apodosis: The conclusion of a premise or **protasis** in a conditional statement.

authenticity (for ancient documents): Relates to questions of the authorship and authority of a document; specifically, its recognition as authentic and authoritative by Christ-following communities of the second century and later. See also **canon**.

GLOSSARY

canon: Gk. "rule"; a standard list of **NT** (and **OT**) writings recognized by most churches, taking definitive shape in the third and fourth centuries CE. See also **authenticity**.

catachresis: Gk. "misuse, misapplication," used in rhetoric as an implied or even extravagant metaphor where one word is exchanged for another that is only remotely related to it.

catechesis: Gk. "hold fast"; faith instruction, often in preparation for a sacred rite like baptism or communion.

catholic: Gk. "according to the whole"; this category was applied to James, 1 and 2 Peter, 1, 2, and 3 John, plus Jude by the fourth-century church because it was believed that they were letters addressed to "all the churches."

Cerinthus: A controversial **Christ-follower** from Egypt who later resided in Ephesus (ca. 100). His views about Christ are distinctive. He distinguished the man, Jesus of Nazareth, from the divine Christ who descended on Jesus at his baptism and empowered him to perform miracles and proclaim the "unknown Father." On the cross, the divine Christ left the human Jesus to suffer and die alone. The divine Christ, a spiritual being, was immune from all sin and human suffering (**Irenaeus**, *Adv. Haer.* I.26; 1 John 2:22). See also **docetic teaching**.

chiasm: Gk. "crossing", inverted or introverted parallelism, A B C B' A' pattern, drawing attention to the center. See also **intercalation**.

Christ-follower: One who believes that Jesus of Nazareth is the Messiah, a disciple of Christ in the first two centuries CE; the designation of "Christian" was more commonly used in the 3rd and 4th centuries (e.g., Tertullian, *Against Marcion* 4–5). See articles by Elliott and Mason on p.19n30 of this book (concerning "Judaism" & "Christianity").

church: A community of **Christ-followers** gathered for worship and service, meeting in homes (Rom 16:5; Acts 12:12) until the third century CE (e.g., house **church** at Dura-Europos, Syria). See also **Great Church**.

concatenation: Linking of words together in a series, often building to a climax, also called **anabasis** or gradual ascent.

Dead Sea Scrolls: Found in 11 caves at Qumran, 13 miles east of Jerusalem in the Judean desert, discovered between 1947 and 1956, they comprise some 800 documents but in thousands of fragments, dating from c. 250 BCE to 68 CE, written in Hebrew, Aramaic, and Greek; they contain biblical and apocryphal works, prayers, legal texts, and the rules and rituals of this Essene sect (also mentioned by **Philo**, **Josephus**, and Pliny the Elder).

deliberative: In rhetoric, an advisory form of persuasion that seeks to exhort or dissuade, as in e.g., legislative assemblies. See also **paraenesis** and **protreptic**.

deuterocanonical: Gk. "secondary canon" used by Roman Catholics since the Council of Trent (1545–63) to designate books not found in the Hebrew Bible (i.e., protocanonical) but present in the Greek Septuagint. See also **Old Testament**.

deutero-Pauline writings: Letters of Paul whose authorship is disputed mostly because of differences in vocabulary and style, e.g., Ephesians, 1–2 Timothy, Titus, some also include 2 Thessalonians and Colossians.

diatribe: Used by teachers in Hellenistic philosophical schools to expose the errors of his students and lead them into truth, often adddressing a fictitious dialogue partner or objector.

diegesis: Gk. "telling, narration," in rhetoric the narrative description of the case to be presented.

docetic: The teaching that the divine Christ only had the "appearance" of human flesh which was believed to be inherently sinful. See also **Cerinthus**, **gnostic**.

doxology: Gk. "word of praise"; often concluding a prayer or ritual.

encomium: Lat. "eulogy"; praise of a person or thing by extolling inherent qualities. See also **epideictic** and **laudation**.

enthymeme: Gk. "thought" or "piece of reasoning"; often an abridged syllogism where a part is omitted as understood, or a rhetorical syllogism where the premise is only generally true.

epideictic: Gk. "display, demonstration" of common virtues and values; often used in funeral orations, political speeches, or addresses at festivals or civic games. See also **encomium**, and **laudation**.

GLOSSARY

Eusebius Pamphilus: Bishop of Caesarea, ca. 314 CE, known for his *Ecclesiastical History*, which helped to define **Christ-follower** beliefs and practices as a legitimate religion under emperor Constantine (Edict of Milan, 313 CE). See also **Great Church**.

exordium: Lat. "beginning" of a classical oration, introduction (Gk., *prooemium*).

gentiles: Non-**Judean**, Greco-Romans.

gnostics: Widespread mystical, sapiential, and philosophical groups of the first three centuries CE. Most emphasized or assumed the belief that a special revealed knowledge (*gnōsis*) can awaken a spark of the divine within the "enlightened ones" liberating them from ignorance of their true identity and delivering them from bondage in a flawed, material world. Thus they are provided some hope of reunion with the remote, divine, spiritual realm. See also **docetic**, **Nag Hammadi codices** and **Valentinus**.

Great Church: Emerging orthodoxy of the third and fourth centuries, recognized as a legitimate religion by Emperor Constantine, Edict of Milan, 313 CE. See also **Eusebius**.

Greco-Judean: Hellenistic (i.e., Greek-speaking) **Judeans** of the first and early second centuries.

haggadah: Heb. "telling" of stories, as distinct from legal discussions in the **Mishnah** and Talmud; e.g., the Exodus story of the Jewish Passover seder (i.e., order of service).

halakah: Heb. "walk, live," legal portions of the **Mishnah** (200 CE) and Talmud (600 CE) to guide in life's "walk."

hapax legomenon: Gk. "something said only once," in this book, it concerns Greek words used only once in the **NT**, e.g., there are 62 hapax legomena (plural) in 1 Peter.

Haustafeln: Ger. "household rules," outlining the duties of husbands, wives, parents, children, masters,servants, e.g., 1 Pet 2:13—3:7; Eph 5:22—6:9.

heresiologist: One who investigates and catalogues heresies, the distinct opinions of certain sects or factions which often caused a schism within the established religious order that regards them as unorthodox (e.g.,

GLOSSARY

Irenaeus, Hippolytus, and Epiphanius wrote against "heresies"). See also **Great Church**.

Hermetic: Relating to the mythological messenger god Hermes Trimegistos (thrice great), several writings of the third-century **Nag Hammadi codices** are associated with this mythical figure.

homily: Sermonic discourse or moral address, often expounding scriptural texts, associated with exhortation or **paraenesis**. See also **paraenesis** and **protreptic**.

hortatory: Characterized by moral exhortation, often with verbs in the imperative mood. See also **homily, paraenesis** and **protreptic**.

intercalation: Lat. "insertion, interposition," also called a "sandwich technique" (A- B- A') that occurs when a scene serves as "a filler" (B) between "two slices" of the same narrative which "sandwich in" or bracket the inserted scene (A, A'). See also **chiasm**.

invective: Denouncement of opponents or opposing views, also found in prophetic judgment speeches, and courtroom rhetoric.

Irenaeus: Bishop of Lyon (Lungdunum, Gaul, ca. 180 CE) who wrote against **gnostic** teaching and other perceived threats, helping to establish the emerging orthodoxy of the **Great Church** in the late second and early third centuries CE.

Israel, Israelite: The preferred self-designation from one **Judean** to another, also referring to each other as a Hebrew. The sacred writings are called Israel's **Scriptures** (insider designation).

Josephus, Flavius: First century CE, Judean historian, from Judea, who had played a leading role in the early part of Jewish war with Rome (66–70), after brief imprisonment, he won the favor of the Flavian emperors, Vespasian, Titus, and Domitian. He wrote the *Jewish Wars* and later, the *Antiquities of the Jews* (covering much of the **OT**).

Judean: Of the region of Judah, connected to Jerusalem and the temple, the common designation for all Jews of the first two centuries. See my discussion on p. 19n30.

Judean Scriptures: The outsider designation for the sacred writings, used by the **Judeans** and **Christ-followers** containing the **Torah**, Prophets, and Writings (cf. Sir. Prol. 1–2; Luke 24:44), although the collection was not closed until after 70 CE. The **Scriptures** of Israel or (Hebrew) Bible are an insider designation.

kerygma: Gk. "proclamation," NT preaching of the life, death, resurrection, and **parousia** of Christ.

laudation: Lat. "praise, acclaim"; see also **encomium**.

libertine: A lifestyle that seeks to transcend conventional morality, associated with certain gnostics who saw themselves liberated from the material world, criticized as licentious or antinomian by emerging "orthodoxy" (e.g., **Irenaeus**, Hippolytus). See also **heresiologist**.

liturgy: Gk. "worship, service," comprised of prayers, hymns, **Scriptures**, a sacred meal, and sermonic exhortations.

midrash: From the Hebrew "to seek, search," a rabbinic method of scriptural interpretation sometimes employed by **NT** writers.

Mishnah: A rabbinic legal document of the third century CE (including earlier traditions) that addresses issues raised by the **Torah**; it helped to define and establish Judaism. See also **halakah**.

mystery cults: Included secret initiations and public ceremonies; offered hope of life after death and personal communion with a deity. Many reenact the myth of a dying and rising deity; a blend Hellenism and eastern Mediterranean worship, e.g., Eleusinian mysteries, Isis-Sarapis cult of Egypt, Persian Mithra cult, Cybele cult of Phrygia (Asia Minor).

Nag Hammadi codices: Twelve leather-bound papyri manuscripts in book form, found at Nag Hammadi, Egypt, 1945, containing 52 mostly gnostic treatises, dating from the third to fourth centuries, but containing earlier traditions. See also **gnostic** and **Valentinus**.

New Testament (NT): The collection of 27 books from Matthew to Revelation, that received canonical status in the 4th century (although the authority of some were disputed for centuries (2 Pet, Jas, Rev). The name **NT** was ascribed to the collection in the early 3rd century (Tertullian) based on new covenant teaching found in the Prophets (Jer, Ezek) and developed in certain **NT** books (Luke, 1–2 Cor, Heb).

Old Testament (OT): Christian designation for the Jewish Law, Prophets, and Writings (or Tanak), which varies in size among Protestants (39 books following the Hebrew Bible), Greek Orthodox (53 following the Greek **Septuagint**) and Roman Catholics (50 following the Latin Vulgate via the **Septuagint**).

orthodoxy: Gk. "right belief" opposed to "false teaching," a defining characteristic of fourth-century Christianity. See also **Great Church** and **heresiologist**.

paraenesis: Gk. "exhortation, advice"; warnings and moral instruction for students and disciples. See also **protreptic**.

paronomasia: Gk. "beside naming, name differently," playing on the sound or meaning of similar words, see also **concatenation** which often links words together by means of similar wordplay.

parousia: Gk. "arrival, coming, presence"; usually of the return of Christ at the end of the age. See also **kerygma**.

peroration: Lat. "conclusion, epilogue"; often an empassioned summary or review of previous arguments.

pesher: Heb. "interpretation, commentary"; sometimes called "**midrash pesher**" perhaps to convey the idea of a nonliteral biblical interpretation; it generally assumed that the scriptural prophecies spoke to the contemporary situation in an exclusive manner; prominent in several books of the **Dead Sea Scrolls** (e.g., Pesher Nahum; Pesher Habakkuk). See also **midrash**.

Philo of Alexandria: First century CE Judean author (of over 40 titles) who sought to make the Judean way of life relevant to his Greco-Judean contemporaries in Egypt and elsewhere. He favored an allegorical (figurative, non-literal) interpretation of the **Scriptures** (LXX), Stoic ethical ideas, and a Platonic view of the world. See also **allegory** and **Septuagint**.

prolepsis: Gk. "taking beforehand" or "anticipation"; a statement which anticipates some objection or precedes further clarification or amplification.

protasis: The premise ("if" clause) of a conclusion or **apodosis** in a conditional statement.

protreptic: Gk. "urge, compel"; related to moral exhortation and deliberative rhetoric in promoting a particular course of action. See also **paraenesis**.

GLOSSARY

pseudepigraphic: Gk. "false epigrams or names"; ascribed to ancient writings to give credibility to the work (e.g., Testament of Abraham, Treatise of Seth); in addition to forgeries, there are, e.g., works written in honor of a departed leader, those by a disciple on behalf of his teacher, and books by an amanuensis or secretary delegated by the author. See also **authenticity**.

sapiential: Lat. "prudence, wisdom," in this book that which relates to or is characteristic of the wisdom literature of the Greek OT (e.g., Job, Prov, Eccl, Wis, Sir). See also **Septuagint**.

Scriptures: Israel's **Scriptures** are the insider designation for the sacred writings (Law, Prophets, Writings); Judean **Scriptures** are the outsider designation. See also **Judean Scriptures, Old Testament** (**OT**).

Septuagint: (Latin, "seventy" or LXX) Greek translation of the Law, Prophets, and Writings (**OT**), 3rd–2nd centuries BCE, Alexandria. It was the **Scriptures** of the Hellenistic Judeans and **NT** authors, containing books in the Protestant **OT** or Hebrew Bible, and additional writings (e.g., 1–2 Esd, 1–2 Macc, Sir, Tob, Wis) most of which are found in the the Bibles of the Greek Orthodox and Roman Catholic Bibles.

Sethian (Judeo-Sethian): A Judean strand of **gnostic** writings (see **Nag Hammadi codices**), with no apparent **NT** influence, that may reflect a first-century context (e.g., Nat. Rulers, Apoc. Adam, Steles Seth).

testimonia: Collection of **OT** texts used in the **NT** to show that aspects of the life and ministry of Jesus were prophetically anticipated; a collection of biblical quotations was also used at Qumran to support its beliefs and practices (e.g. 4QTestimonia, 4QFlorilegium).

Torah: Heb. "instruction, teaching"; primarily the first five books of the **OT**, but also oral torah eventually incorporated into the **Mishnah** (200 CE) and Talmud (sixth century).

Valentinus: A **gnostic** theologian from Egypt (second century CE), and a contemporary of the **gnostic**, Basilides, also from Egypt; he was a candidate for the bishop of Rome, where Heracleon became one of his followers; the Gospel of Truth from **Nag Hammadi** is a Valentinian treatise; his radical dualistic view of the world and his elaborate scheme of paired angelic beings (dyads, aeons) were sharply criticized by **Irenaeus of Lyons** (ca. 180) and Epiphanius of Salamis (Cyprus, fourth century).

Bibliography

Abbreviations for journals (*JBL*, *NTS*), periodicals (BA), major reference works (*NIDB*), and series (LCL, NIGTC) follow those of B. J. Collins, project director, *The SBL Handbook of Style: For Biblical Studies and Related Disciplines* (2nd ed., Atlanta: SBL, 2014), and also *The Chicago Manual of Style* (15th ed., Chicago: University of Chicago Press, 2003). In my bibliography, the category of *Reference Works* (below) includes primary sources and documents, grammars, dictionaries, lexical aids, handbooks, guides, and works so indicated, including some websites. The *Commentaries of the NT* section focuses on those works that I have cited in my *Introduction* that seek to interpret the books by chapter, verse, or pericope, in a literary, sociohistorical , or theological manner. I have also included here handbooks of the Greek NT and some commentaries (e.g., Letters of Ignatius, Shepherd of Hermas) that are pertinent to NT studies, but are not "NT" commentaries. Category 3, on *Essays, Monographs and Related Works*, includes the following title combination, e.g., studies of the NT and other related writings of antiquity, history, hermeneutics, NT ethics and theology, NT and literary criticism, semiotics, archaeology, mythology, classical studies and linguistics, some in French, German, and others online, all of them are important for NT introduction and interpretation.

Reference Works

Abrams, M. H., and Geoffrey Galt Harpham. *A Glossary of Literary Terms*. 8th ed. Boston: Thomson/Wadsworth, 2005.
Ackroyd, Peter R. et al., eds. *The Cambridge History of the Bible*. 3 vols. in 1. Cambridge: Cambridge University Press: 1976.

BIBLIOGRAPHY

Aharoni, Yohannan, and Michael Avi-Yonah. *The Macmillan Bible Atlas*. New York: Macmillan, 1977.

Aland, Barbara et al., eds. *Novum Testamentum Graece with Dictionary*. Nestle-Aland. 28th rev. ed. Stuttgart: Deutsche Biblelgesellschaft, 2012.

Aland, Kurt, and Eberhard Nestle. *Novum Testamentum Graece with Dictionary*. Nestle-Aland. 27th ed. Stuttgart: Deutsche Biblelgesellschaft, 2001.

Aland, Kurt et al., eds. *The Greek New Testament*. 4th rev. ed. Stuttgart: Bibelgesellschaft, 1998.

Anderson, R. Dean, Jr., *Glossary of Greek Rhetorical Terms Connected to Methods of Argumentation, Figures and Tropes from the Anximenes to Quintilian*. CBET 24. Leuven: Peters, 2000.

Archer, Gleason L., and Gregory Chirichigno. *Old Testament Quotations in the New Testament: A Complete Survey*. 1983. Reprinted, Eugene, OR: Wipf & Stock, 2005.

Ascough, Richard S. et al. *Associations in the Greco-Roman World: A Sourcebook*. Waco, TX: Baylor University Press, 2012.

Aune, David E. *The New Testament in Its Literary Environment*. LEC 8. Philadelphia: Westminster, 1987.

———. *The Westminster Dictionary of New Testament and Early Christian Literature and Rhetoric*. Louisville: Westminster John Knox, 2003.

Barnstone, Willis, ed. *The Other Bible: Jewish Pseudepigrapha, Christian Apocrypha, Gnostic Scriptures, Kabbalah, Dead Sea Scrolls*. San Francisco: Harper & Row, 1984.

Barrett, C. K., ed. *The New Testament Background: Selected Documents*. New York: Harper & Row, 1961. Rev. ed. London: SPCK, 1987.

Bauckham, Richard et al., eds. *Old Testament Pseudepigrapha: More Noncanonical Scriptures*. Vol 1. Grand Rapids: Eerdmans, 2013.

Bauer, Walter et al., eds. *A Greek-English Lexicon of the New Testament and Other Early Christian Literature*. Rev. and ed. by W. F. Danker. 3rd ed. Chicago: University of Chicago Press, 2000.

Bettenson, Henry, ed. *Documents of the Christian Church*. 2nd ed. London: Oxford University Press, 1963. 4th ed. revised by Chris Maunder, 2011.

Bible Works for Windows. Hermeneutika Software. http://www.bibleworks.com/.

Blackman, Philip. *Mishnayoth: Pointed Hebrew Text, English Translation, Introductions, Notes, Supplement*. 7 Vols. New York: Judaica Press, 1964.

Blass, Friedrich W., and Albert Debrunner. *A Greek Grammar of the New Testament and Other Early Christian Literature*. Translated and revised by Robert. W. Funk with suppl. notes of A. Debrunner. Chicago: University of Chicago Press, 1961.

Boda, Mark J., and J. Gordon McConville. *Dictionary of the Old Testament: Prophets*. Downers Grove, IL: IVP Academic, 2012.

Bratcher, Robert G., ed. *Old Testament Quotations in the New Testament*. Helps for Translators 3. London: United Bible Societies, 1961.

Braund, David C. *Augustus to Nero: A Sourcebook on Roman History, 31 BC—A.D. 68*. Totowa, NJ: Barnes & Noble, 1985.

Brooke, A. E. *The Fragments of Heracleon*. Texts & Studies: Contributions to Biblical and Patristic Literature 1.4. 1891. Reprinted, Eugene, OR: Wipf & Stock, 2004.

Brown, Raymond E. et al., eds. *The New Jerome Biblical Commentary*. Englewood Cliffs, NJ: Prentice Hall, 1990.

BIBLIOGRAPHY

Bruce, F. F. *Jesus and Christian Origins Outside the New Testament*. Grand Rapids: Eerdmans, 1974.

Bullinger, E. W. *Figures of Speech Used in the Bible: Explained and Illustrated*. 1898. Reprinted, Grand Rapids: Baker, 1984.

Buttrick, George Arthur, gen. ed. *The Interpreter's Dictionary of the Bible*. 4 vols. New York: Abingdon, 1962.

Caragounis, Chrys C. *The Development of Greek and the New Testament: Morphology, Syntax, Phonology, and Textual Transmission*. WUNT 167. Tübingen: Mohr/Siebeck, 2004.

Cartlidge, David R., and David L. Dungan, eds. *Documents for the Study of the Gospels*. Rev. ed. Minneapolis: Fortress, 1994.

Champion, Craig Brian. *Roman Imperialism: Readings and Sources*. Malden, MA: Blackwell, 2003.

Charlesworth, James H., ed. *The Dead Sea Scrolls: Hebrew, Aramaic, and Greek Texts with English Translations*. 7 vols. Tübingen: Mohr/Siebeck, 1994.

———, ed. *The Old Testament Pseudepigrapha*. 2 vols. Garden City, NY: Doubleday, 1983-1985.

Coggins, R. J., and J. L. Houlden, eds. *Dictionary of Biblical Interpretation*. London: SCM, 1990.

Collins, John J., and Daniel C. Harlow, eds. *The Eerdmans Dictionary of Early Judaism*. Grand Rapids: Eerdmans, 2010.

Collins, John J. ed., *The Origins of Apocalypticism in Judaism and Christianity*. Vol 1 of *Encyclopedia of Apocalypticism*. New York: Bloomsbury Academic, 1998.

Comfort, Philip W., and David P. Barrett, eds. *The Text of Earliest New Testament Greek Manuscripts*. Wheaton, IL: Tyndale, 2001.

Cook, S. A. et al., eds. *The Cambridge Ancient History*. Vols. 7-12. Cambridge: Cambridge University Press, 1928-39.

Crim, K., ed. *The Interpreter's Dictionary of the Bible: Supplementary Volume*. Nashville: Abingdon, 1976.

Cross, F. L., and E. A. Livingstone, eds. *The Oxford Dictionary of the Christian Church*. 3rd rev. ed. Oxford: Oxford University Press, 2005.

Danby, Herbert. *The Mishnah: Translated from the Hebrew with Introduction and Brief Explanatory Notes*. Oxford: Oxford University Press, 1933.

Danker, Frederick W. *Benefactor: Epigraphic Study of a Graeco-Roman and New Testament Semantic Field*. St. Louis: Clayton, 1982.

———. *Multipurpose Tools for Bible Study*. Rev. ed. with CD-ROM. Minneapolis: Fortress, 2003.

Deissmann, Adolf. *Light from the Ancient East: The New Testament Illustrated by Recently Discovered Texts of the Graeco-Romans World*. Rev. ed. Translated by Lionel R. M. Strachan. 1927. Reprinted, Eugene, OR: Wipf & Stock, 2004.

Dickey, Eleanor. *Ancient Greek Scholarship: A Guide to Finding, Reading, and Understanding Scholia,Commentaries, Lexica, and Grammatical Treatises. From Their Beginning to the Byzantine Period*. American Philological Association Classical Resources Series 7. Oxford: Oxford University Press, 2006.

Dines, Jennifer. *The Septuagint*. Understanding the Bible and Its World. New York: T & T Clark, 2004.

BIBLIOGRAPHY

Di Tomasso, Lorenzo. *A Bibliography of Pseudepigrapha Research 1850-1999*. Journal for the Study of the Pseudepigrapha Supplements 39. Sheffield: Sheffield Academic, 2001.

Doenges, N. A. *The Letters of Themistocles*. Monographs in Classical Studies. New York: Arno, 1981.

Easton, Burton Scott, trans. *The Apostolic Tradition of Hippolytus*. Cambridge: Cambridge University Press, 1934.

Eder, Walter, and Johannes Renger, eds. *Brill's Chronologies of the Ancient World: Names, Dates and Dynasties*. Translated and edited by Wouter F. M. Henkelman. Brill's New Pauly Supplements 1. Leiden: Brill, 2006.

Ehrenberg, Victor, and A. H. M. Jones, eds. *Documents Illustrating the Reigns of Augustus and Tiberius*. 2nd ed. Oxford: Oxford University Press, 1970.

Evans, Craig A., ed. *Ancient Texts for New Testament Studies: A Guide to Background Literature*. Peabody, MA: Hendrickson, 2005.

Evans, Craig A. et al., eds. *Nag Hammadi Texts and the Bible: A Synopsis and Index*. New Testament Tools and Studies 18. Leiden: Brill, 1993.

Ferguson, John, ed. *Greek and Roman Religion A Source Book*. Noyes Classical Studies. Park Ridge, NJ: Noyes, 1980.

Finegan, Jack. *The Archeology of the New Testament*. Vol. 1, *The Life of Jesus and the Beginning of the Early Church*. Princeton: Princeton University Press, 1969. Rev. ed., 1992.

Fitzmyer, Joseph A. *The Dead Sea Scrolls: Major Publications and Tools for Study*. Sources for Biblical Study 8. Missoula, MT: Scholars, 1975. Rev. ed. RBS 20, 1990.

———. *A Guide to the Dead Sea Scrolls and Related Literature*. Rev. and Exp. Studies in the Dead Sea Scrolls and Related Literature. Grand Rapids: Eerdmans, 2008.

———. *An Introductory Bibliography for the Study of Scripture*. Subsidia Biblica 3. 3rd ed. Rome: Editrice Pontificio Istituto Biblico, 1990.

Foerster, Werner, comp. *Gnosis: A Selection of Gnostic Texts*. 2 vols. Translated by R. McL. Wilson. Oxford: Clarendon, 1972.

Freedman, David Noel, ed. *The Anchor Yale Bible Dictionary*. 6 vols. New Haven: Yale University Press, 1992.

García Martínez, Florentino, ed. *The Dead Sea Scrolls Translated: The Qumran Texts in English*. Translated by Wilfred G. E. Watson. 2nd ed. Leiden: Brill, 1996.

García Martínez, Florentino, and Eibert J. C. Tigchelaar, eds. *The Dead Sea Scrolls: Study Edition*. 2nd ed. 2 vols. Translated by Wilfred G. E. Watson. Leiden: Brill, 1997. Grand Rapids: Eerdmans, 1999.

Gergel, Tania, and Michael Wood, eds. *Alexander the Great: The Brief Life and Towering Exploits of History's Greatest Conqueror as Told by His Original Biographers*. New York: Penguin, 2004.

Gramcord for Windows/Bible Companion. Gramcord Institute/White Harvest, http://www.gramcord.org/.

Grenfell, Bernard P., and Arthur S. Hunt, eds. *New Classical Fragments and Other Greek and Latin Papyri*. London: Oxford University Press, 1897.

Guggenheimer, Heinrich W., ed. *The Jerusalem Talmud*. First Order: Zeraim Tractate Berakhot. Studia Judaica 18. Berlin: de Gruyter, 2000.

Guirard, Felix, ed. *New Larousse Encyclopedia of Mythology*. New ed. Translated by D. Ames and R. Aldington. London: Hamlyn, 1968.

Hanson, K. C. Homepage. http://www.kchanson.com.

BIBLIOGRAPHY

Harmless, William, SJ, comp. Bibliographies for the Study of the New Testament, http://moses.creighton.edu/harmless/bibliographies_for_theology/.

Hayes, John H., ed. *New Testament, History of Interpretation: Excerpted from the Dictionary of Biblical Interpretation*. Nashville: Abingdon, 2004.

Heckel, Waldemar, and H. C. Yardley, eds. *Alexander the Great: Historical Sources in Translation*. London: Blackwell, 2003.

Hercher, Rudolphus, ed. *Epistolographi graeci: recensuit, recognovit, adnotatione critica et indicibus Instruxit*. Scriptorum Graecorum Bibliotheca 57. 1873. Amsterdam: Hakkert, 1965.

Hewett, James Allen. *New Testament Greek: A Beginning and Intermediate Grammar*. Revised and enlarged by C. Michael Robbins and Steven R. Johnson. Rev. ed. with CD. Peabody, MA: Hendrickson, 2009.

Holmes, Michael W., ed. *The Apostolic Fathers: Greek Texts and English Translations*. 3rd ed. Grand Rapids: Baker, 2007.

Hornblower, Simon, and Anthony Spawforth, eds. *The Oxford Classical Dictionary*. 3rd ed. New York: Oxford University Press, 1996. 4th ed., 2012.

Horsley, G. H. R. et al., eds. *New Documents Illustrating Early Christianity*. Vols. 1–9. *A Review of the Greek Inscriptions an Papyri Published in 1976–87* (in separate vols.). Ancient History Documentary Research Centre of Macquarie University, North Ryde, NSW, Australia, 1981–2002. Grand Rapids: Eerdmans, 1998–2002.

———. *New Documents Illustrating Early Christianity: A Review of the Greek Inscriptions and Papyri Published in 1976*. North Ryde, NSW: Ancient History Documentary Research Centre, Macquarie University, 1981.

———. *New Documents Illustrating Early Christianity: A Review of the Greek Inscriptions and Papyri Published in 1977*. North Ryde, NSW: Ancient History Documentary Research Centre, Macquarie University, 1982.

———. *New Documents Illustrating Early Christianity: A Review of the Greek Inscriptions and Papyri Published in 1978*. North Ryde, NSW: Ancient History Documentary Research Centre, Macquarie University, 1983.

———. *New Documents Illustrating Early Christianity: A Review of the Greek Inscriptions and Papyri Published in 1979*. North Ryde, NSW: Ancient History Documentary Research Centre, Macquarie University, 1987.

———. *New Documents Illustrating Early Christianity: Linguistic Essays*. North Ryde, NSW: Ancient History Documentary Research Centre, Macquarie University,

Hunt, Arthur S., and C. C. Edgar. *Select Papyri*. 2 vols. LCL. Cambridge: Harvard University Press, 1932.

Inwood, Brad, and L. P. Gerson, trans. and ed. *The Epicurus Reader: Selected Writings and Testimonia*. Indianapolis: Hackett, 1994.

Jewish Encyclopedia.com. http://www.jewishencyclopedia.com/.

Jobes, Karen, and Moises Silva. *Invitation to the Septuagint*. Grand Rapids: Baker Academic, 2005.

Kee, Howard Clark. *The New Testament in Context: Sources and Documents*. Englewood Cliffs, NJ: Prentice Hall, 1984.

Kennedy, George A., trans. and ed. *Progymnasmata: Greek Textbooks of Prose Composition and Rhetoric*. Writings from the Greco-Roman World 10. Atlanta: Society of Biblical Literature, 2003.

Kittel, Gerhard, and Gerhard Friedrich, eds. *Theological Dictionary of the New Testament*. Translated by Geoffrey W. Bromiley. 10 vols. Grand Rapids: Eerdmans, 1969–76.

Kittel, Rudolf, et al., eds., Revised by Hans Peter Ruger et al. *Torah, Neviim u-Khetuvim. Biblia Hebraica Stuttgartensia*. 5th ed. Stuttgart: Deutsche Bibelstiftung, 1997.

Klauck, Hans-Josef. *Ancient Letters and the New Testament: A Guide to Context and Exegesis*. Translated and edited by Daniel P. Bailey. Waco: Baylor University Press, 2006.

———. *The Religious Context of Early Christianity: A Guide to Graeco-Roman Religions*. Translated by Brian McNeil. Minneapolis: Fortress, 2003.

Kolb, Robert, and Timothy J. Wengert, eds. *The Book of Concord: The Confessions of the Evangelical Lutheran Church*. Translated by Charles Arand et al. Minneapolis: Fortress, 2000.

Lampe, G. W. H. *A Patristic Greek Lexicon*. New York: Oxford University Press, 1969.

Lanham, Richard A. *A Handlist of Rhetorical Terms*. 2nd ed. Berkeley: University of California Press, 1991.

Layton, Bentley, trans. *The Gnostic Scriptures: A New Translation with Annotations and Introductions*. Garden City, NY: Doubleday, 1987.

Lee, John A. L. *A History of New Testament Lexicography*. Studies in Biblical Greek 8. Berlin: Lang, 2003.

Lefkowitz, Mary R., and Maureen B. Fant. *Women's Life in Greece and Rome: A Source Book in Translation*. 3rd ed. Baltimore: John Hopkins University Press, 2005.

Levine, Amy-Jill, and Marc Zvi Brettler, eds. *The Jewish Annotated New Testament*. New York: Oxford University Press, 2011.

Lewis, Naphtali. *Papyrus in Classical Antiquity*. New York: Oxford University Press, 1974.

Llewelyn, S. R. *New Documents Illustrating Early Christianity: A Review of the Greek Inscriptions and Papyri Published in 1984–85*. North Hyde, NSW: Ancient History Documentary Research Centre of Macquarie University, 1998.

———. *New Documents Illustrating Early Christianity: A Review of the Greek Inscriptions and Papyri Published in 1986–87*. North Hyde, NSW: Ancient History Documentary Research Centre of Macquarie University, 2002.

Llewelyn, S. R., and R. A. Kearnsley. *New Documents Illustrating Early Christianity: A Review of the Greek Inscriptions and Papyri Published in 1980–81*. North Hyde, NSW: Ancient History Documentary Research Centre of Macquarie University, 1992.

———. *New Documents Illustrating Early Christianity: A Review of the Greek Inscriptions and Papyri Published in 1982–83*. North Hyde, NSW: Ancient History Documentary Research Centre of Macquire University, 1994.

Logos Research Systems. Logos Bible Study Software, http://www.logos.com.

Marcos, Natalio Fernandez. *The Septuagint in Context: Introduction to the Greek Version of the Bible*. Translated by Wilfred G. E. Watson. Leiden: Brill, 2000.

Marlowe, Michael D., ed. *Bible Research Internet Resources for Students of Scripture*. http://www.bible-researcher.com/.

Martin, Ralph P., and David H. Edwards, eds. *Dictionary of the Later New Testament & Its Developments*. Downers Grove, IL: InterVarsity, 1997.

McKim, Donald K., ed. *Dictionary of Major Biblical Interpreters*. 2nd ed. Downers Grove, IL: IVP Academic, 2007.

BIBLIOGRAPHY

McLay, R. Timothy. *The Use of the Septuagint in New Testament Research*. Grand Rapids: Eerdmans, 2003.

Meltzer, Edmund S., ed. *Letters from Ancient Egypt*. Writings from the Ancient World 1. Translated by E. F. Wente. Atlanta: Scholars, 1990.

Menander Rhetor. Edited and translated with commentary by D. A. Russell and N. G. Wilson (London: Oxford University Press, 1981).

Metzger, Bruce M. *A Textual Commentary on the Greek New Testament*. 2nd ed. Stuttgart: Deutsche Bibelgesellschaft/United Bible Societies, 1998.

Meyer, Marvin, ed. *The Nag Hammadi Scriptures: The International Edition*. New York: HarperOne, 2007.

Moule, C. F. D. *An Idiom Book of New Testament Greek*. 2nd ed. Cambridge: Cambridge University Press, 1959.

Moulton, James Hope. *A Grammar of New Testament Greek*. 4 vols. Edinburgh: T. & T. Clark, 1908–1976: Vol. 1 (1908) *Prolegomena*, by J. H. Moulton. 1st ed. (1906); 3rd ed. (1908); Vol. 2 (1929) *Accidence and Word Formation*, by Wilbert Francis Howard; Vol. 3 (1963) *Syntax*, by Nigel Turner; Vol. 4 (1976) *Style*, by N. Turner.

Moulton, Harold K., and George Milligan. *The Vocabulary of the Greek Testament*. 1930. Reprinted, Grand Rapids: Eerdmans, 1980.

Moulton, Harold K., and A. S. Geden eds. *A Concordance to the Greek New Testament*. 6th rev. ed. by I. Howard Marshall. T. & T. Clark Biblical Languages. Edinburgh: T. & T. Clark, 2004.

Neusner, Jacob et al., eds., *The Encyclopedia of Judaism*. 4 vols. 2nd ed. Leiden: Brill, 2005.

Neusner, Jacob, and William Scott, eds. *Dictionary of Judaism in the Biblical Period: 450 B.C.E to 600 C.E.* 1996. Reprinted, Peabody, MA: Hendrickson, 1999.

Palmer, Michael. A Comprehensive Bibliography of Hellenistic Greek Linguistics, http://www.greek-language.com/Palmer-bibiography.html/.

Parry, Donald W., and Emanuel Tov, eds. *The Dead Sea Scrolls Reader*. 6 vols. Leiden: Brill, 2004–2005.

Pilch, John J. *The Cultural Dictionary of the Bible*. Collegeville, MN: Liturgical, 1999.

Pietersma, Albert, and Benjamin G. Wright, eds. *A New English Translation of the Septuagint*. New York: Oxford University Press, 2007.

Pliny, the Younger. *Letters and Panegyricus*. Vol. 2, *Letters, Books 8–10; and Panegyricus*. Translated by B. Radice. LCL 59. Cambridge: Harvard University Press, 1975.

Rahlfs, Alfred, ed. *Septuaginta: Id est vetus testamentum graece juxta LXX interpretes*. Stuttgart:Würtemberg Bible Society, 1935. Rev. ed. by Robert Hanhart. 2 vols. in one. Stuttgart: DeutscheBibelgesellschaft, 2006.

Porter, Stanley E., ed *Dictionary of Biblical Criticism and Interpretation*. London: Routledge, 2006.

Reddish, Mitchell G., ed. *Apocalyptic Literature: A Reader*. Peabody, MA: Hendrickson, 1995.

Rice, David G., and John E. Stambaugh. *Sources for the Study of Greek Religion*. Corr. ed. SBLSBS 14. Atlanta: Scholars, 2009.

Robinson, James M., ed. *The Nag Hammadi Library in English*. Rev. ed. New York: HarperCollins, 1990. 4th ed., Leiden: Brill, 1996.

Sakenfeld, Katharine Doob, gen. ed. *The New Interpreter's Dictionary of the Bible*. 5 vols. Nashville: Abingdon, 2006–2009.

Schaps, David. *Handbook for Classical Research*. New York: Routledge, 2009.

Schiffman, Lawrence H. *Texts and Traditions. A Source Reader for the Study of Second Temple and Rabbinic Judaism.* Hoboken, NJ: Ktav, 1998.

Schneemelcher, Wilhelm, ed. *New Testament Apocrypha.* Translated by R. McL Wilson. 2 vols. Louisville: Westminster John Knox, 1992.

———. *New Testament Apocrypha.* Rev. ed. Translated by R. McL. Wilson. Louisville: Westminster John Knox, 2003.

Scholer, David M. *A Basic Bibliographic Guide for New Testament Exegesis.* 2nd ed. Grand Rapids: Eerdmans, 1973.

Seland, Torrey. Online Biblical Studies Resources. http://www.torreys.org/bible/biblia02.html/.

Society for the Study of Biblical and Semitic Rhetoric. Edited by Roland Meynet, SJ. http://www.retoricabiblicaesemitica.org/.

Soulen, Richard N., and R. Kendall Soulen. *Handbook of Biblical Criticism* 4th ed. Louisville: Westminster John Knox, 2011.

Spicq, Ceslas, ed. *Theological Lexicon of the New Testament.* 3 vols. Translated and edited by James D. Ernest. Peabody, MA: Hendrickson, 1994.

Stanton, Elizabeth Cady. *The Woman's Bible: A Classic Feminist Perspective.* Mineola, NY: Dover, 2002.

Stevenson, J., ed. *A New Eusebius: Documents Illustrating the History of the Church to AD 337.* Revised by W. H. C. Frend. London: SPCK, 1987. 3rd ed. Grand Rapids: Baker Academic, 2013.

Stoneman, Richard, and Richard Wallace, eds. *Classical Wall Maps.* New York: Routledge, 1989–1991.

Strack, Hermann L., and Paul Billerbeck. *Kommentar zum Neuen Testament aus Talmud und Midrasch.* 6 vols. Munich: Beck, 1924.

Talbert, Richard J. A., ed. *The Barrington Atlas of the Greek and Roman World.* Princeton: Princeton University Press, 2000.

Tel Quel. French Literary Journal. Edited by Philippe Sollers and Jean-Edem Hallier. Paris: Seuil, 1960–66.

Taylor, Bernard A. et al., eds. *Analytical Lexicon to the Septuagint.* Exp. ed. Peabody, MA: Hendrickson, 2009.

Thayer, Joseph Henry. *A Greek-English Lexicon of the New Testament.* 1889. Reprinted, *Thayer's Greek-English Lexicon of the New Testament.* Peabody, MA: Hendrickson, 1996.

Thesaurus Linguae Graecae: A Digital Library of Greek Literature. University of California, Irvine. http://www.tlg.uci.edu.

Thesaurus Linguae Latinae. Bayerische Akademie. Manfred Flieger, Sec. http://www.thesaurus.badw.de/english/index.htm/.

University of Albany, University Libraries. Guide to Resources in Rabbinic Literature. State University of New York at Albany. http://library.albany.edu/subject/guides/Guide_to_Resources_in_Rabbinic_Literature.html/.

Vermes, Geza. *The Complete Dead Sea Scrolls: Qumran in Perspective.* Rev. ed. Philadelphia: Fortress, 1981.

Vermes, Geza, trans. and ed. *The Complete Dead Sea Scrolls in English.* New York: Allen Lane/Penguin, 1997.

Watson, Duane F. *The Rhetoric of the New Testament: A Bibliographic Survey.* Tools for Biblical Study 8. Blandford Forum, UK: Deo, 2006.

Ziefle, Helmut W., ed. *Modern Theological German: A Reader and Dictionary*. Grand Rapids: Baker, 1997.

Commentaries of the New Testament

Achtemeier, Paul J. *1 Peter: A Commentary on First Peter*. Hermeneia. Minneapolis: Fortress, 1996.
Adam, A. K. M. *James: A Handbook of the Greek Text*. BHGNT. Waco, TX: Baylor University Press, 2013.
Aune, David E. *Revelation 1–5*. WBC 52A. Grand Rapids: Zondervan, 1997.
———. *Revelation 6–16*. WBC 52B. Grand Rapids: Zondervan, 1998.
———. *Revelation 17–22*. WBC 52C. Grand Rapids: Zondervan, 1998.
Attridge, Harold W. *The Epistle to the Hebrews: A Commentary on the Epistle to the Hebrews*. Hermeneia. Philadelphia: Fortress, 1989.
Bauckham, Richard. *Jude, 2 Peter*. WBC 50. Waco, TX: Word, 1983.
Beale, G. K. *The Book of Revelation*. NIGTC. Grand Rapids: Eerdmans, 1999.
Beale, G. K., and D. A. Carson. *Commentary on the New Testament Use of the Old Testament*. Grand Rapids: Baker Academic, 2007.
Beare, F. W. *The First Epistle of Peter*. 3rd ed. Oxford: Blackwell, 1970.
Beasley-Murray, G. R., ed. *The Book of Revelation*. NCB. Rev. ed. Grand Rapids: Eerdmans, 1981.
Best, Ernest. *1 Peter*. NCBC. London: Marshall, Morgan & Scott, 1971. Grand Rapids: Eerdmans, 1982.
Betz, Hans Dieter. *Galatians: A Commentary on Paul's Letter to the Churches in Galatia*. Hermeneia. Philadelphia: Fortress, 1975.
Bigg, Charles A. *A Critical and Exegetical Commentary on the Epistles of St. Peter and St. Jude*. 2nd ed. ICC. Edinburgh: T. & T. Clark, 1902.
Blount, Brian. *Revelation: A Commentary*. NTL. Louisville: Westminster John Knox, 2009.
Boring, M. Eugene. *1 Peter*. ANTC. Nashville: Abingdon, 1999.
———. *Revelation*. Interpretation. Louisville: John Knox, 1989
Boring, M. Eugene et al., eds. *Hellenistic Commentary to the New Testament*. Nashville: Abingdon, 1995.
Brown, Raymond E. *The Epistles of John*. AB 30. Garden City, NY: Doubleday, 1982.
Brown, Raymond E. et al., eds. *The New Jerome Biblical Commentary*. Englewood Cliffs, NJ: Prentice Hall, 1990.
Bruce, F. F. *The Epistle to the Hebrews*. NICNT. Grand Rapids: Eerdmans, 1990.
Buchanan, George Wesley. *To the Hebrews*. AB 36. Garden City, NY: Doubleday, 1972.
Bultmann, Rudolf. *The Johannine Epistles: A Commentary on the Johannine Epistles*. Translated by R. P. O'Hara et al. Hermeneia. Philadelphia: Fortress, 1973.
Caird, G. B. *A Commentary on the Revelation of St. John the Divine*. HNTC. New York: Harper & Row, 1966.
Calvin, John. *Commentaries on the Catholic Epistles*. Edited and translated by J. Owen, 1855. Calvin's Commentaries 22. Grand Rapids: Baker, 1979.
———. *Commentary on the Epistle to the Hebrews*. Edited and translated by J. Owen. 1853. Reprinted, Bellingham, WA: Logos Bible Software, 2010.

Chance, J. Bradley. *Acts*. Smyth & Helwys Bible Commentary. Macon, GA: Smyth & Helwys, 2007.
Charles, R. H. *A Critical and Exegetical Commentary on the Revelation of St. John*. 2 vols. ICC. Edinburgh: T. & T. Clark, 1920.
Cockerill, Gareth Lee. *The Epistle to the Hebrews*. NICNT. Grand Rapids: Eerdmans, 2012.
Collins, Adela Yarbro. *The Apocalypse*. NTM 22. Wilmington, DE: Glazier, 1979.
Culy, Martin M. *I, II, III John: A Handbook of the Greek Text*. BHGNT. Waco, TX: Baylor University Press, 2004.
Davids, Peter H. *The Epistle of James: A Commentary on the Greek Text*. NIGTC. Grand Rapids: Eerdmans, 1982.
———. *The Letters of 2 Peter and Jude*. PNTC. Grand Rapids: Eerdmans, 2006.
DeSilva, David A. *Perseverance in Gratitude: A Socio-Rhetorical Commentary on the Epistle "to the Hebrews."* Grand Rapids: Eerdmans, 2000.
Dibelius, Martin. *James: A Commentary on the Epistle of James*. Revised by Heinrich Greeven. Translated by Michael A. Williams. Hermeneia. Philadelphia: Fortress, 1976.
Donelson, Lewis R. *I & II Peter and Jude: A Commentary*. NTL. Louisville: Westminster John Knox, 2010.
Dubus, Mark. *1 Peter: A Handbook of the Greek Text*. BHGNT. Waco, TX: Baylor University Press, 2010.
Elliott, John H. *1 Peter*. AYB 37B. New York: Doubleday, 2000. Repr., New Haven: Yale University Press, 2001.
Fee, Gordon D. *Revelation*. New Covenant Commentary Series 18. Eugene, OR: Cascade Books, 2011.
Fitzmyer, Joseph A. *Acts of the Apostles*. AB 31. New York: Doubleday, 1998.
Ford, J. Massyngberde. *Revelation*. AB 38. Garden City, NY: Doubleday, 1975.
Goppelt, Leonhard. *A Commentary on 1 Peter*. Edited by Ferdinand Hahn. Translated by John E. Alsup. Grand Rapids: Eerdmans, 1993.
Green, Joel. *1 Peter*. Two Horizons New Testament Commentary. Grand Rapids: Eerdmans, 2007.
Haenchen, Ernst. *The Acts of the Apostles*. Translated by Bernard Noble et al. Philadelphia: Westminster, 1971.
Hagner, Donald A. *Hebrews*. Peabody, MA: Hendrickson, 1990.
Harrington, Wilfrid J. *Revelation*. SP 16. Collegeville, MN: Liturgical, 1993.
Hartin, Patrick J. *James*. SP 14. Collegeville, MN: Liturgical, 2004.
Heil, John Paul. *The Book of Revelation: Worship for Life in the Spirit of Prophecy*. Eugene, OR: Cascade Books, 2014.
———. *The Letter of James: Worship to Live By*. Eugene, OR: Cascade Books, 2012.
———. *1 Peter, 2 Peter, and Jude: Worship Matters*. Eugene, OR: Cascade Books, 2013.
———. *1–3 John: Worship by Loving God and One Another to Live Eternally*. Eugene, OR: Cascade Books, 2015.
———. *Worship in the Letter to the Hebrews*. Eugene, OR: Cascade Books, 2011.
Henize, André. *Johannesapokalypse*. BWANT 142. Stuttgart: Kohlhammer, 1998.
Jobes, Karen H. *1 Peter*. BECNT. Grand Rapids: Baker Academic, 2005.
Johnson, Luke Timothy. *Hebrews: A Commentary*. NTL. Louisville: Westminster John Knox, 2006.

———. *The Letter of James*. AYB 37A. New York: Doubleday, 1995. Repr., New Haven: Yale University Press, 2005.
Keener, Craig S. *The Gospel of John: A Commentary*. 2 vols. Grand Rapids: Baker Academic, 2003.
———. *Revelation*. The NIV Application Commentary. Grand Rapids: Zondervan, 2000.
Kelly, J. N. D. *A Commentary on the Epistles of Peter and Jude*. HNTC. New York: Harper & Row, 1969. Repr., Peabody, MA: Hendrickson, 1999.
Kistemaker, Simon *Exposition of the Epistle to the Hebrews*. New Testament Commentary. Grand Rapids: Baker, 1984.
Koester, Craig R. *Hebrews*. AYB 36. New York: Doubleday, 2001. Repr., New Haven: Yale University Press, 2008.
———. *Revelation*. AYB 38A. New Haven: Yale University Press, 2014.
Kovac, Judith, and Christopher Rowland. *Revelation: The Apocalypse of Jesus Christ*. Blackwell Bible Commentaries. Oxford: Blackwell, 2004.
Kraftchick, Steven J. *Jude, 2 Peter*. ANTC. Nashville: Abingdon, 2002.
Kruse, Colin G. *The Letters of John*. PNTC. Grand Rapids: Eerdmans, 2000.
Lane, William L. *Hebrews 1–8*. WBC 47A. Grand Rapids: Zondervan, 1991.
———. *Hebrews 9–13*. WBC 47B. Grand Rapids: Zondervan, 2000.
Laws, Sophie A. *A Commentary on the Epistle of James*. HNTC New York: Harper & Row, 1980.
Lieu, Judith M. *I, II, III John: A Commentary*. NTL. Louisville: Westminster John Knox, 2008.
Lupieri, Edmondo F. *A Commentary on the Apocalypse of John*. Italian Texts and Studies on Religion and Society. Grand Rapids: Eerdmans, 2006.
Malina, Bruce J., and John J. Pilch. *Social-Science Commentary on the Book of Revelation*. Minneapolis: Fortress, 2000.
Marshall, I. Howard. *The Epistles of John*. NICNT. Grand Rapids: Eerdmans, 1978.
Martin, R. A., and John H. Elliott, *James, I–II Peter, Jude*. ACNT. Minneapolis: Augsburg, 1982.
Martin, Ralph P. *James*. WBC 48. Grand Rapids: Zondervan, 1988.
Mayor, J. B. *The Epistle of James*. 2nd ed. London: Macmillan, 1897.
McKnight, Edgar V., and Christopher Church. *Hebrews–James*. Smyth & Helwys Bible Commentary. Macon, GA: Smyth & Helwys, 2004.
McKnight, Scot. *The Letter of James*. NICNT. Grand Rapids: Eerdmans, 2011.
Michaels, J. Ramsey. *The Gospel of John*. NICNT. Grand Rapids: Eerdmans, 2010.
———. *1 Peter*. WBC 49. Waco, TX: Word, 1988.
———. *1 Peter*. 1988. Grand Rapids: Zondervan, 2015.
Moffatt, James. *A Critical and Exegetical Commentary on the Epistle to the Hebrews*. ICC. Edinburgh: T. & T. Clark, 1924.
Montefiore, Hugh. *A Commentary on the Epistle to the Hebrews*. BNTC. London: Black, 1964.
Moo, Douglas J. *The Letter of James*. PNTC. Grand Rapids: Eerdmans, 2000.
Mounce, Robert H. *The Book of Revelation*. NICNT. Grand Rapids: Eerdmans, 1977.
Neyrey, Jerome H. *2 Peter, Jude: A New Translation with Introduction and Commentary*. AB 37C. New York: Doubleday, 1993.
O'Brien, Peter T. *The Letter to the Hebrews*. PNTC. Grand Rapids: Eerdmans, 2010.

BIBLIOGRAPHY

Olsson, Birger. *A Commentary on the Letters of John: An Intra-Jewish Approach.* Translated by Richard J. Erickson. Eugene, OR: Pickwick Publications, 2013.

Osiek, Carolyn. *The Shepherd of Hermas: A Commentary.* Hermeneia. Minneapolis: Fortress, 1999.

Painter, John. *1, 2, and 3 John.* SP 18. Collegeville, MN: Liturgical, 2002.

Painter, John, and David A. deSilva. *James and Jude.* Paidea. Grand Rapids: Baker Academic, 2012.

Parsenios, George L. *First, Second, and Third John.* Paidea. Grand Rapids: Baker Academic, 2014.

Perkins, Pheme. *First and Second Peter, James, and Jude.* Interpretation. Louisville: John Knox, 1995.

———. *The Book of Revelation.* Collegeville Bible Commentary 11. Collegeville, MN: Liturgical, 1983.

———. *The Johannine Epistles.* NTM 21. Wilmington, DE: Glazier, 1979.

Peterson, David G. *The Acts of the Apostles.* PNTC. Grand Rapids: Eerdmans, 2009.

Pervo, Richard I. *Acts: A Commentary.* Hermeneia. Minneapolis: Fortress, 2008.

Reese, Ruth Ann. *2 Peter and Jude.* Two Horizons New Testament Commentary. Grand Rapids: Eerdmans, 2007.

Richard, Earl J. *Reading 1 Peter, Jude, and 2 Peter: A Literary and Theological Commentary.* Reading the New Testament Series. Macon, GA: Smyth and Helwys, 2000.

Ropes, James Hardy. *A Critical and Exegetical Commentary on the Epistle of St. James.* ICC. Edinburgh: T. & T. Clark, 1916.

Schnackenburg, Rudolf. *The Gospel according to St. John.* Vol. 1, *Introduction and Commentary on Chapters 1–4.* Translated by Kevin Smyth. Edited by J. Massyngberde Ford and Kevin Smyth. Herder's Theological Commentary on the New Testament. 3 vols. New York: Herder & Herder, 1968.

———. *The Gospel according to John.* Vol. 2, *Commentary on Chapters 5–12.* Translated by Cecily Hastings et al. Edited by Kevin Smyth. 3 vols. New York: Seabury, 1980.

———. *The Gospel according to John.* Vol. 3, *Commentary on Chapters 13–21.* New York: Crossroad, 1982.

Schoedel, William R. *Ignatius of Antioch: A Commentary on the Letters of Ignatius of Antioch.* Hermeneia. Philadelphia: Fortress, 1985.

Selwyn, E. G. *The First Epistle of St. Peter: The Greek Text with Introduction, Notes, and Essays.* 2nd ed. 1947. Reprinted, Grand Rapids: Baker, 1981.

Senior, Donald P., and Daniel J. Harrington *1 Peter, Jude and 2 Peter.* SP 15. Collegeville, MN: Liturgical, 2008.

Sidebottom, E. M., ed. *James, Jude and 2 Peter.* NCB. London: Nelson, 1967.

Smalley, Stephen S. *1, 2, and 3 John.* Rev. ed. WBC 51. Grand Rapids: Zondervan, 2008.

Smith, D. Moody. *First, Second, and Third John.* Interpretation. Louisville: John Knox, 1991.

Smith, Robert H. *Hebrews.* ANTC. Minneapolis: Augsburg, 1984.

Spicq, Ceslas. *L'Épître aux Hébreux.* 2 vols. EB. Paris: Gabalda, 1952–1953.

Swete, H. B. *The Apocalypse of St. John.* 3rd ed. 1909. Reprinted, Eugene, OR: Wipf & Stock, 1999.

Talbert, Charles H. *The Apocalypse: A Reading of the Revelation of John.* Louisville: Westminster John Knox, 1994.

Thompson, Leonard L. *Revelation.* ANTC. Nashville: Abingdon, 1998.

Thompson, Marianne Meye. *1–3 John*. IVP New Testament Commentary Series. Downers Grove, IL: InterVarsity, 1992.
Vanhoye, Albert. *A Different Priest: The Epistle to the Hebrews*. Translated by Leo Arnold SJ. Studies Rhetorica Semitica. Miami: Convivium, 2011.
Vinson, Richard B. et al. *1 & 2 Peter, Jude*. Smyth & Helwys Bible Commentary. Macon, GA: Smyth & Helwys, 2010.
Von Wahlde, Urban C. *The Gospel and Letters of John*. 3 vols. Grand Rapids: Eerdmans, 2010.
Watson, Duane F., and Terrance Callan. *First and Second Peter*. Paidea. Grand Rapids: Baker Academic, 2012.
Westcott, B. F. *The Epistle to the Hebrews: The Greek Text with Notes and Essays*. London: Macmillan, 1889.
Windisch, Hans. *Die Katholischen Briefe*. 3rd ed. Rev. by H. Preisker. HNT. Tübingen: Mohr Siebeck, 1951.
Witherington, Ben, III. *Letters and Homilies for Jewish Christians: A Socio-Rhetorical Commentary on Hebrews, James and Jude*. Downers Grove, IL: IVP Academic, 2007.

Essays, Monographs, and Related Works

Adam, A. K. M., ed. *Postmodern Interpretations of the Bible: A Reader*. St. Louis: Chalice, 2001.
———. *What Is Postmodern Biblical Criticism?* GBS New Testament Series. Minneapolis: Fortress, 1995.
Adrados, Francisco Rodriguez. *A History of the Greek Language: From Its Origins to the Present*. Translated by Francisca Rojas del Canto. Leiden: Brill, 2005.
Aichele, George. *The Letters of Jude and Second Peter: Paranoia and the Slaves of Christ*. Phoenix Guides to the New Testament 19. Sheffield: Sheffield Phoenix, 2012.
Aland, Kurt, and Barabara Aland. *The Text of the New Testament: An Introduction to the Critical Editions and to the Theory and Practice of Modern Textual Criticism*. Translated by E. F. Rhodes. Grand Rapids: Eerdmans, 1989.
Albl, Martin C. *"And Scripture Cannot Be Broken": The Form and Function of the Early Christian Testimonies*. NovTSup 96. Leiden: Brill, 1999.
Algra, Keimpe, et al., eds. *Cambridge History of Hellenistic Philosophy*. Cambridge: Cambridge University Press, 1999.
Alt, Albrecht. "The Origins of Israelite Law." In *Essays in Old Testament History and Religion*, 101–71. Translated by R. A. Wilson. Garden City, NY: Doubleday, 1967.
Arnold, Clinton E. *The Colossian Syncretism: The Interface between Christianity and Folk Belief at Colossae*. WUNT 2/77. Tübingen: Mohr/Siebeck, 1995.
Argyle, A. W. "Greek among the Jews of Palestine in New Testament Times." *NTS* 20 (1973–74) 87–89.
Asmis, Elizabeth. "Epicureans." In *AYBD* 2:259–61.
Aune, David E. "The Apocalypse of John and the Problem of Genre." *Semeia* 36 (1986) 65–96.
———. *Apocalypticism, Prophecy, and Magic in Early Christianity: Collected Essays*. Grand Rapids: Baker Academic, 2008.

———, ed. *Greco-Roman Literature and the New Testament*. SBLSBS 21. Atlanta: Scholars, 1988.

———. *Prophecy in Early Christianity and in the Ancient Mediterranean World*. 1983. Reprinted, Eugene, OR: Wipf & Stock, 2003.

———. "The Prophetic Circle of John of Patmos and the Exegesis of Revelation 22.16." *JSNT* 37 (1989) 103–16.

Austin, Michael M. *The Hellenistic World from Alexander to the Roman Conquest: A Selection of Ancient Sources in Translation*. 2nd ed. Cambridge: Cambridge University Press, 2006.

Bailey, James L., and Lyle D. Vander Broek. *Literary Forms in the New Testament: A Handbook*. Louisville: Westminster John Knox, 1992.

Baird, William. *History of New Testament Research*. Vol. 1, *From Deism to Tübingen*. Minneapolis: Fortress, 1992.

———. *History of New Testament Research*. Vol. 2, *From Jonathan Edwards to Rudolf Bultmann*. Minneapolis: Fortress, 2002.

Bakhos, Carol. "Midrash, Midrashim." In *The Eerdmans Dictionary of Early Judaism*, edited by John J. Collins and Daniel C. Harlow, 944–49. Grand Rapids: Eerdmans, 2010.

Balch, David L. *Let Wives Be Submissive: The Domestic Code in 1 Peter*. SBLMS 26. Chico, CA: Scholars, 1981.

Balch, David L., and Carolyn Osiek eds. *Early Christian Families in Context: An Interdisciplinary Dialogue*. Religion, Marriage, and Family. Grand Rapids: Eerdmans, 2005.

Bar-Kochva, Bezalel. *The Image of the Jews in Greek Literature: The Hellenistic Period*. The S. Mark Taper Foundation Imprint in Jewish Studies. Hellenistic Culture and Society 51. Berkley: University of California Press, 2009.

Barr, David L. "The Apocalypse of John in the Light of Modern Narrative Theory." In *1900th Anniversary of St. John's Apocalypse: Proceedings of the International and Interdisciplinary Symposium*, edited by Panagiotis N. Doukellis, 259–71. Athens: Holy Monastery of St. John, 1999.

———. *Tales of the End: A Narrative Commentary on the Book of Revelation*. Storytellers Bible 1. Santa Rosa, CA: Polebridge, 1998.

Bartlett, John R. *Jews in the Hellenistic World*. Cambridge Commentaries on Writings of the Jewish Christian World 1. Cambridge: Cambridge University Press, 1985.

Barton, John. *The Oracles of God: Perceptions of Ancient Prophecy in Israel after the Exile*. New ed. Oxford: Oxford University Press, 2007.

Bateman, Herbert W., IV. *Charts on the Book of Hebrews*. Kregel Charts of the Bible. Grand Rapids: Kregel Academic, 2012.

———. *Early Jewish Hermeneutic and Hebrews 1:5–13: The Impact of Early Jewish Exegesis on the Interpretation of a Siginificant New Testament Passage*. American University Studies. Series 7: Theology and Religion 193. New York: Lang, 1997.

———. *Interpreting the General Letters: An Exegetical Handbook*. Handbooks for New Testament Exegesis. Grand Rapids: Kregel Academic, 2013.

Batten, Alicia J. *What Are They Saying about the Letter of James?* WATSA. New York: Paulist, 2009.

Bauckham, Richard *The Climax of Prophecy. Studies on the Book of Revelation*. Edinburgh: T. & T. Clark, 1993.

———. "James and the Jerusalem Community." In *Jewish Believers in Jesus: The Early Centuries*, edited by Oskar Skarsaune and Reidar Hvalvik, 55–95 Peabody, MA: Hendrickson, 2007.

———. *Jesus and the Eyewitnesses: The Gospels as Eyewitness Testimony*. Grand Rapids: Eerdmans, 2006.

———. *Jude and the Relatives of Jesus in the Early Church*. Edinburgh: T. & T. Clark, 1990.

———. "On the Divinity of Christ in the Epistle to the Hebrews." In *The Epistle to the Hebrews and Christian Theology*, edited by Richard Buackham et al., 15–36. Grand Rapids: Eerdmans, 2009.

———. *The Testimony of the Beloved Disciple: Narrative, History, and Theology in the Gospel of John*. Grand Rapids: Baker Academic, 2007.

———. *The Theology of the Book of Revelation*. New Testament Theology Cambridge: Cambridge University Press, 1993.

Bauckham, Richard et al., eds. *A Cloud of Witnesses: The Theology of Hebrews in Its Ancient Contexts*. LNTS 387. London: T & T Clark, 2008.

———, eds. *The Epistle to the Hebrews and Christian Theology*. Grand Rapids: Eerdmans, 2009.

Bauer, Walter. *Orthodoxy and Heresy in Earliest Christianity*. Translated by a team from the Philadelphia Seminar on Christian Origins. Edited by Robert A. Kraft and Gerhard Krodel. Philadelphia: Fortress, 1971.

———. *Rechtgläubigkeit and Ketzerei im ältesten Christentum*. Tübingen: Mohr/Siebeck, 1934.

Baur, Ferdinand Christian. *The Church History of the First Three Centuries*. 2 vols. Translated by Allan Menzies. 3rd ed. Theological Translation Fund Library 16, 20. Edinburgh: Williams & Norgate, 1875–76.

Beale, G. K. "The Influence of Daniel upon the Structure and Theology of John's Apocalypse." *JETS* 27 (1984) 413–23.

———. "Revelation." In *It Is Written—Scripture Citing Scripture: Essays in Honor of Barnabas Lindars SSF*, edited by D. A. Carson and H. G. M. Williamson, 318–36. Cambridge: Cambridge University Press, 1988.

———. *The Use of Daniel in Jewish Apocalyptic and in the Revelation of St. John*. Lanham, MD: University Press of America, 1984.

Beasley-Murray, G. R. *Baptism in the New Testament*. 1962. Reprinted, Grand Rapids: Eerdmans, 1973.

Bell, Albert. *A Guide to the New Testament World*. Scottdale, PA: Herald, 1994.

Berger, Klaus. "Hellenistische Gattungen im Neuen Testament." *ANRW* II.25/2 (1984) 1231–45.

Berger, Peter L., and Thomas Luckmann. *The Social Construction of Reality*. Garden City, NY: Doubleday, 1966.

Bergsma, John S. "Testimonia." In *The Westminster Dictionary of New Testament and Early Christian Literature and Rhetoric*, edited by David E. Aune, 456–57. Louisville: Westminster John Knox, 2003.

Bevan, E. "Hellenistic Popular Philosophy." In *The Hellenistic Age: Aspects of Hellenistic Civilization*, by J. B. Bury et al., 79–107. Cambridge: Cambridge University Press, 1925.

Bickerman, E. J. *The God of the Maccabees: Studies on the Meaning and Origin of the Maccabean Revolt*. SJLA 32. Leiden: Brill, 1979.

BIBLIOGRAPHY

Bilezikian, Gilbert G. "The Gospel of Mark and Greek Tragedy." *Gordon Review* 5 (1959) 79–86.

———. *The Liberated Gospel: A Comparison of the Gospel of Mark and Greek Tragedy.* Baker Biblical Monographs. Grand Rapids: Baker, 1977.

Black, C. Clifton, and Duane F. Watson, eds. *Words Well Spoken: George Kennedy's Rhetoric of the New Testament.* Studies in Rhetoric and Religion 8. Waco, TX: Baylor University Press, 2008.

Black, David Alan. *New Testament Textual Criticism: A Concise Guide.* Grand Rapids: Baker, 1994.

Blevins, James L. "The Genre of Revelation." *Review & Expositor* 77 (1980) 393–408.

Bockmuehl, Markus. *Jewish Law in the Gentile Churches: Halakha and the Beginning of Christian Public Ethics.* Edinburgh: T & T Clark, 2000.

Bockmuehl, Markus, and Guy G. Stroumsa, eds. *Paradise in Antiquity: Jewish and Christian Views.* Cambridge: Cambridge University Press, 2010.

Boismard, Marie Émile. "Une Litrugie Baptismale dans la Prima Petri." *RB* 63 (1956) 182–208.

———. *Quatres Hymnes Baptismales dans la Première Epître de Pierre.* Lectio divina 30. Paris: Cerf, 1961.

Bonhoeffer, Dietrich. *Discipleship.* Translated by B. Green and R. Krause. Dietrich Bonhoeffer Works 4. Edited by G. B. Kelley and J. D. Godsey. Minneapolis: Fortress, 2003.

Bovon, François. *New Testament Traditions and Apocryphal Narratives.* Translated by Jane Haapiseva-Hunter. Princeton Theological Monograph Series 36. Allison Park, PA: Pickwick Publications, 1995.

———. *Studies in Early Christianity.* WUNT 161. Tübingen: Mohr/Siebeck, 2003. 1st pb ed. with English translations of chs. 3, 8–9. Grand Rapids: Baker, 2005.

Bowman, John Wick. *The First Christian Drama: The Book of Revelation.* Philadelphia: Westminster, 1968.

———. "Revelation." In *IDB* 4:58–70.

———. "The Revelation of John: Its Dramatic Structure and Message." *Int* 9 (1955) 436–53.

Brakke, David. "Canon Formation and Social Conflict in Fourth-Century Egypt: Athanasius of Alexander's Thirty-Ninth *Festal Letter.*" *HTR* 87 (1994) 395–419.

Brant, Jo-Ann. *Dialogue and Drama: Elements of Greek Tragedy in the Fourth Gospel.* Peabody, MA: Hendrickson, 2004.

Breck, John. *The Shape of Biblical Language: Chiasmus in the Scriptures and Beyond.* Crestwood, NY: St. Vladimir's Seminary Press, 1994.

Brewer, Raymond R. "The Influence of Greek Drama on the Apocalypse of John." *ATR* 18 (1936) 74–92.

Brown, Schuyler K. "Jewish and Gnostic Elements in the Second Apocalypse of James." *NovT* 17(1975) 225–37

Brown, Raymond E., and John P. Meier. *Antioch and Rome: New Testament Cradles of Catholic Christianity.* New York: Paulist, 1983.

Brown, Raymond E. *The Community of the Beloved Disciple.* New York: Paulist, 1979.

———. *An Introduction to the New Testament.* ABRL. New York: Doubleday, 1997.

———. "Not Jewish Christianity and Gentile Christianity but Types of Jewish/Gentile Christianity." *CBQ* 45 (1983) 74–79.

Bruce, F. F. *The Canon of Scripture.* Downers Grove, IL: InterVarsity, 1988.

———. *The New Testament Development of Old Testament Themes*. Grand Rapids: Eerdmans, 1968.
———. *Peter, Stephen, James and John: Studies in Non-Pauline Christianity*. Grand Rapids: Eerdmans, 1979.
———. "'To the Hebrews' or 'To the Essenes'?" *NTS* 9 (1963) 217–32.
———. "Transmission and Translation of the Bible." In *The Expositor's Bible Commentary*, edited by Frank E. Gaebelein et al., 1:39–57. 12 vols. Grand Rapids: Zondervan, 1979.
Bultmann, Rudolf. *Primitive Christianity in Its Contemporary Setting*. Translated by R. H. Fuller. Cleveland: World, 1956.
Burns, Jasper. *Great Women of Imperial Rome: Mothers and Wives of the Caesars*. London: Routledge, 2006.
Burridge, Richard A. *Imitating Jesus: An Inclusive Approach to New Testament Ethics*. Grand Rapids: Eerdmans, 2007.
Burtchaell, James Tunstead. *From Synagogue to Church: Public Services and Offices of the Earliest Christian Communities*. Cambridge: Cambridge University Press, 1992.
Buss, Martin J. *Biblical Form Criticism in Its Context*. JSOTSup 274. Sheffield: Sheffield Academic, 1999.
Caird, G. B. *The Language and Imagery of the Bible*. Philadelphia: Westminster, 1980.
———. "Exegetical Method of Hebrews." *CJT* 5 (1959) 44–51.
Campbell, Constantine. *Basics of Verbal Aspect in Biblical Greek*. Grand Rapids: Zondervan, 2008.
Campenhausen, Hans von. *The Formation of the Christian Bible*. Translated by J. A. Baker. Philadelphia: Fortress, 1972.
Carey, Greg. "The Book of Revelation as Counter-Imperial Script." In *In the Shadow of Empire: Reclaiming the Bible as a History of Faithful Resistance*, edited by Richard A. Horsley, 157–76. Louisville: Westminster John Knox, 2008.
———. "Symptoms of Resistance in the Book of Revelation." In *The Reality of Apocalypse: Rhetoric and Politics in the Book of Revelation*, edited by David L. Barr, 169–80. SBLSymS 39. Atlanta: SBL, 2006.
Carroll, John T., ed. *The Return of Jesus in Early Christianity*. Peabody, MA: Hendrickson, 2000.
Casson, Lionel. *Everyday Life in Ancient Rome*. Rev. ed. Baltimore: John Hopkins University Press, 1999.
Charlesworth, James H. "A History of Pseudepigrapha Research: The Re-Emerging Importance of the Pseudepigrapha." *ANRW* II.19.1 (1979) 54–88.
———, ed. *The Messiah: Developments in Earliest Judaism and Christianity*. Minneapolis: Fortress, 1992.
Charlesworth, James H. et al., eds. *Qumran Messianism: Studies in the Messianic Expectations in the Dead Sea Scrolls*. Tübingen: Mohr/Siebeck, 1998.
Chilton, Bruce. *Visions of the Apocalypse: Receptions of John's Revelation in Western Imagination*. Waco, TX: Baylor University Press, 2013.
Christidis, A.-F., ed. *A History of Ancient Greek: From the Beginnings to Late Antiquity*. Cambridge: Cambridge University Press, 2007.
Cohen, Shaye J. D. *From the Maccabees to the Mishnah*. LEC 7. Louisville: Westminster John Knox, 1988.

———. "The Significance of Yavneh: Pharisees, Rabbis, and the End of Jewish Sectarianism." *Hebrew Union College Annual* 55 (1984) 27–53.
Clark, Gordon H., ed. *Selections from Hellenistic Philosophy*. New York: Appleton-Century-Crofts, 1940.
Clifford, Richard J., ed. "Special Issue on Apocalyptic Literature." CBQ 39/3 (July 1977) 307–409
Cohick, Lynn H. *Women in the World of the Earliest Christians: Illuminating Ancient Ways of Life*. Grand Rapids: Baker Academic, 2009.
Collins, Adela Yarbro. *The Combat Myth in the Book of Revelation*. Harvard Dissertations in Religion 9. Missoula, MT: Scholars, 1976.
———. *Cosmology and Eschatology in Jewish and Christian Apocalypticism*. JSJSup 50. Leiden: Brill, 1996.
———. *Crisis and Cartharsis: The Power of the Apocalypse*. Philadelphia: Westminster, 1984.
———. "Numerical Symbolism in Jewish and Early Christian Apocalyptic Literature." ANRW II.21.2 (1984) 1221–87.
Collins, John J. *The Apocalyptic Imagination: An Introduction to the Jewish Matrix of Christianity.* New York: Crossroad, 1989.
———. *Beyond the Qumran Community: The Sectarian Movement of the Dead Sea Scrolls*. Grand Rapids: Eerdmans, 2010.
———. *Jewish Cult and Hellenistic Culture: Essays on the Jewish Encounter with Hellenism and Roman Rule*. JSJSup 100. Leiden: Brill, 2005.
———, ed. *Apocalypse: The Morphology of a Genre*. Semeia 14. Missoula, MT: Scholars, 1979.
Collins, Raymond F. *Letters That Paul Did Not Write: The Epistle to the Hebrews and the Pauline Pseudepigrapha*. GNS 28. Wilmington, DE: Glazier, 1988.
Comfort, Philip. *Encountering the Manuscripts: An Introduction to New Testament Paleography & Textual Criticism*. Nashville: Broadman & Holman, 2005.
Comfort, Philip W., and David P. Barrett, eds. *The Complete Text of the Earliest New Testament Manuscripts*. Grand Rapids: Baker, 1999.
Consdale, Lena. *Qumran and the Essenes: A Re-evaluation of the Evidence*. Texte und Studien zum antiken Judentum 60. Tübingen: Mohr/Siebeck, 1997.
Corley, Kathleen E. "1 Peter." In *Searching the Scriptures*. Vol. 2, *A Feminist Commentary*, edited by Elisabeth Schüssler Fiorenza, 349–60. New York: Crossroad, 1994.
Cortez, F. H. "1 Peter and Postmodern Criticism." In *Reading 1–2 Peter and Jude: A Resource for Students*, edited by Eric F. Mason and Troy W. Martin, 151–66. RBS 77. Atlanta: Society of Biblical Literature, 2014.
Court, John M. *Revelation*. NTG. Sheffield: JSOT Press, 1994.
Cox, Roger L. "Tragedy and the Gospel Narratives." In *The Bible in its Literary Milieu: Contemporary Essays*, edited by Vincent L. Tollers and John Maier, 298–317. Grand Rapids: Eerdmans,1979.
Croce, Benedetto. *Aesthetic as Science of Expression and General Linguistic*. Translated by Douglas Ainslie. London: Macmillan, 1909.
Crook, Zeba A. *Reconceptualising Conversion: Patronage, Loyalty, and Conversion in the Religions of the Ancient Mediterranean*. Beihefte zur Zeitschrift für die neutestamentliche Wissenschaft 130. Berlin: de Gruyter, 2004.
Cross, F. L. *1 Peter: A Paschal Liturgy*. London: Mowbray, 1954.

BIBLIOGRAPHY

Cross, Frank M. *The Ancient Library of Qumrân & Modern Biblical Studies.* Rev. ed. Haskell Lectures 1956-57. Grand Rapids Baker, 1980. 3rd ed., Minneapolis: Fortress, 1995.

Culpepper, R. Alan. *The Anatomy of the Fourth Gospel: A Study in Literary Design.* Foundations and Facets: New Testament. Philadelphia: Fortress, 1983.

———. *The Johannine School: An Examination of the Johannine-School 5 Based on the Investigation of the Nature of Ancient Schools.* SBLDS 26. Missoula, MT: Scholars, 1975.

Dahl, Nils. "The Concept of Baptism in Ephesians." In *Studies in Ephesians: Introduction Questions, Text- & Edition-Critical Issues, Interpretation of Texts and Themes,* edited by David Hellholm et al., 413-39. WUNT 1/131. Tübingen: Mohr/Siebeck, 2000.

Dalton, W. J. *Christ's Proclamation to the Spirits: A Study of 1 Peter 3:18-4:6.* AnBib 23. Rome: Pontifical Biblical Institute, 1965.

Daniélou, Jean. *The Theology of Jewish Christianity.* History of Early Christian Doctrine before the Council of Nicaea 1. Translated and edited John Baker. Philadelphia: Westminster, 1977.

———. *Origins of Latin Christianity.* Translated by David Smith and John Austin Baker. Edited by John Austin Baker. History of Early Christian Doctrine before the Council of Nicea 3. Philadelphia: Westminster, 1977.

Danker, Frederick W. "2 Peter 1: A Solemn Decree." *CBQ* 40 (1978) 64-82.

Daube, David. *Ancient Jewish Law: Three Inaugural Lectures.* Leiden: Brill, 1981.

———. *The New Testament and Rabbinic Judaism.* 1956. Reprint ed. Peabody, MA: Hendrickson, 1994.

Davids, Peter H. "Palestinian Tradition in the Epistle to James." In *James the Just and Christian Origins,* edited by Bruce Chilton and Craig A. Evans, 33-57. NovTSup 115. Leiden: Brill, 2005.

———. "Tradition and Citation in the Epistle of James." In *Scripture, Tradition, and Interpretation,* edited by W. Ward Gasque and William Sanford LaSor, 113-26. Grand Rapids: Eerdmans, 1978.

Davies, W. D. *Introduction to Pharasism.* Facet Books: Biblical Series 16. Philadelphia: Fortress, 1967.

De La Torre, Miguel A. *Reading the Bible from the Margins.* Maryknoll, NY: Orbis, 2002.

De Regt, L. J. "Bible Translation Theory." In *NIDB* 1 (2006) 452-53.

deSilva, David A. *Despising Shame: Honor Discourse and Community Maintenance in the Epistle to the Hebrews.* SBLDS 152. Atlanta: Scholars, 1995.

Desjardins, M. "The Portrayal of the Dissidents in 2 Peter and Jude: Does It Tell Us More about the 'Godly' than the 'Ungodly'?" *JSNT* 30 (1987) 89-102.

Dillenberger, John, ed. *Martin Luther: Selections from His Writings.* New York: Random House, 1962.

Dillon, John. *The Middle Platonists, 80 BC to AD 220.* Ithaca, NY: Cornell University Press, 1977.

DiTommaso, Lorenzo. "Apocalypses and Apocalypticism in Antiquity (Part I)." *CBR* 5 (2007) 235-86.

———. "Apocalypses and Apocalypticism in Antinquity (Part II)." *CBR* 5 (2007) 367-432.

Dobschutz, Ernst von. "Joanneisches Studien, I." *ZNW* 8 (1907) 1-8.

Dochhorn, Jan. "Paulus und die polyglotte Schriftgelehrsamkeit seiner Zeit." *ZNW* 98 (2007) 189–212.
Dodd, C. H. *According to the Scriptures: The Substructure of New Testament Theology*. 1953. Reprinted, New York: Harper & Row, 1967.
———. *The Apostolic Preaching and Its Developments*. 1951. Reprinted, New York: Harper & Row, 1964.
———. "First Epistle of John and the Gospel of John." *BJRL* 21 (1937) 129–56.
Dodds, E. R. *The Greeks and the Irrational*. Berkeley: University of California Press, 1951.
———. *Pagan and Christian in an Age of Anxiety*. Wiles Lectures 1963. Cambridge: Cambridge University Press, 1965.
Donelson, Lewis R. *From Hebrews to Revelation: A Theological Introduction*. Louisville: Westminster John Knox, 2001.
———. *Pseudepigraphy and Ethical Argument in the Pastoral Epistles*. HUT 22. Tübingen: Mohr/Siebeck, 1986.
Donfried, Karl P., ed. "Chronology." In *AYBD* 1:1012–16.
Dowd, Sharyn. "Faith That Works: James 2:14–26." *Review & Expositor* 97 (2000) 195–205.
Dunderberg, Ismo. "The School of Valentinus." In *A Companion to Second-Century Christian "Heretics,"* edited by Antti Marjanen and Petri Luomanen, 64–97. Leiden: Brill, 2008.
Dunn, James D. G. *Beginning from Jerusalem*. Christianity in the Making 2. Grand Rapids: Eerdmans, 2009.
———. *Jesus Remembered*. Christianity in the Making 1. Grand Rapids: Eerdmans, 2003.
———. *Jews and Christians: The Parting of the Ways, AD 70 to 135*. WUNT 66. 1992. Reprinted, Grand Rapids: Eerdmans, 1999.
———. *Unity and Diversity in the New Testament*. 2nd ed. Philadelphia: Westminster, 1992.
Dupont-Sommer, A. *The Essene Writings from Qumran*. New York: World, 1962.
Ehrman, Bart D. *The Orthodox Corruption of Scripture: The Effect of Early Christological Controversies on the Text of the New Testament*. New York: Oxford University Press, 1993.
Ehrman, Bart D., and Michael W. Holmes, eds. *The Text of the New Testament in Contemporary Research: Essays on the Status Quaestionis*. SD 46. 1995. Reprinted, Eugene, OR: Wipf & Stock, 2001. 2nd ed., Leiden: Brill, 2013.
Eisenbraun, Pamela. "The Letter to the Hebrews." In *The Jewish Annotated New Testament*, edited by Amy-Jill Levine and Marc Zvi Brettler, 406–26. Oxford: Oxford University Press, 2011.
Elliott, John H. "A Catholic Gospel: Reflections on 'Early Catholicism' in the New Testament." *CBQ* 31 (1969) 213–23.
———. *Conflict, Community, and Honor: 1 Peter in Social-Scientific Perspective*. Cascade Companions 2. Eugene, OR: Cascade Books, 2007.
———. *A Home for the Homeless: A Sociological Exegesis of 1 Peter, Its Situation and Strategy: With a New Introduction*. 1990. Reprinted, Eugene, OR: Wipf & Stock, 2005.
———. "Jesus the Israelite Was neither a Jew nor a Christian: On Correcting Misleading Nomenclature." *Journal for the Study of the Historical Jesus* 5 (2007) 119–54.

———. "The Rehabilitation of an Exegetical Stepchild: 1 Peter in Recent Research." *JBL* 95 (1976) 243–54. Reprinted in *Perspectives on First Peter*, edited by C. H. Talbert, 3–16. NABPR Special Studies Series 9. Macon, GA: Mercer University Press, 1986.

———. *What Is Social-Scientific Criticism?* GBS New Testament Series. Minneapolis: Fortress, 1993.

Elliott, Keith, and Ian Moir. *Manuscripts and the Text of the New Testament: An Introduction for English Readers.* Edinburgh: T. & T. Clark, 1995.

Elliott, Neil. *The Arrogance of Nations: Reading Romans in the Shadow of Empire.* Paul in Critical Contexts. Minneapolis: Fortress, 2008.

Elliott, Neil, and Mark Reasoner, eds. *Documents and Images for the Study of Paul.* Minneapolis: Fortress, 2011.

Ellis, E. Earle. *The Old Testament in Early Christianity: Canon and Interpretation in the Light of Modern Research.* WUNT 54. Tübingen: Mohr/Siebeck, 1991.

———. *The Old Testament in Early Christianity: Canon and Interpretation in the Light of Modern Research.* Grand Rapids: Baker, 1992.

———. *Paul's Use of the Old Testament.* 1957. Grand Rapids: Baker, 1981.

Elwell, Walter A., and Robert W. Yarbrough. *Readings from the First-Century World: Primary Sources for New Testament Study.* Encountering Biblical Studies. Grand Rapids: Baker, 1998.

Eriksson, Anders, et al., eds. *Rhetorical Argumentation in Biblical Texts: Essays from the Lund 2000 Conference.* Emory Studies in Early Christianity 8. Harrisburg, PA: Trinity, 2002.

Esler, Philip F., ed. *Modelling Early Christianity: Social-Scientific Studies of the New Testament in Its Context.* London: Routledge, 1995.

Farmer, William R. *Maccabees, Zealots and Josephus: An Inquiry into Jewish Nationalism in the Greco-Roman Period.* New York: Columbia University Press, 1956.

Farris, S. "Hymns, New Testament." In *NIDB* 2:923.

Felder, Cain Hope, ed. *Stony the Road We Trod: African American Biblical Interpretation.* Minneapolis: Fortress, 1991.

Feldman, Louis H. "Diaspora Synagogues." In *Sacred Realm: The Emergence of the Synagogue in the Ancient World*, edited by Steven Fine, 48–66. New York: Oxford University Press, 1996.

Ferguson, Everett. *Backgrounds of Early Christianity.* 3rd ed. Grand Rapids: Eerdmans, 2003.

———. *Baptism in the Early Church: History, Theology, and Liturgy in the First Five Centuries.* Grand Rapids: Eerdmans, 2009.

Ferguson, John. *The Religions of the Roman Empire.* Aspects of Greek and Roman Life. Ithaca, NY: Cornell University Press, 1970.

Finegan, Jack. *Handbook of Biblical Chronology: Principles of Time Reckoning in the Ancient World and Problems of Chronology in the Bible.* 2nd ed. Peabody, MA: Hendrickson, 1998.

Finkelstein, Louis. *The Pharisees: The Sociological Background of Their Faith.* 2 vols. 3rd ed. Morris Loeb Series. Philadelphia: Jewish Publication Society, 1962.

Fishbane, Michael A. *Biblical Interpretation in Ancient Israel.* Oxford: Clarendon, 1985.

Fitzmyer, Joseph A. "The Languages of Palestine in the First Century AD." *CBQ* 32 (1970) 501–31.

———. *A Wandering Aramean: Collected Aramaic Essays.* SBLMS 25. Missoula, MT: Scholars, 1979.

Flower, Michael Attayah. *The Seer in Ancient Greece*. Berkeley: University of California Press, 2008.
Flusser, David. *Judaism of the Second Temple Period*. Vol. 1, *Qumran and Apocalyptism*. Translated by Azzan Yadin. Grand Rapids: Eerdmans, 2007.
———. *Judaism of the Second Temple Period*. Vol. 2, *The Jewish Sages and Their Literature*. Translated by Azzan Yadin. Grand Rapids: Eerdmans, 2009.
———. *Qumran and Apocalypticism*. Judaism in the Second Temple Period 1. Grand Rapids: Eerdmans, 2007.
France, R. T. "Exegesis in Practice: Two Samples." In *New Testament Interpretation: Essays on Principles and Methods*, edited by I. Howard Marshall, 252–81. Rev. ed. Carlisle, UK: Paternoster, 1979. http://www.biblicalstudies.org.uk/book_nt-interpretation.html/.
Francis, Fred O. "The Form and Function of the Opening and Closing Paragraphs of James and 1 John." *ZNW* 61 (1970) 110–26.
Frankfurter, David. "Revelation." In T*he Jewish Annotated New Testament*, edited by Amy-Jill Levine and Mark Zvi Brettler, 463–98. Oxford: Oxford University Press, 2011.
Frede, Dorothea, and Brad Inwood, eds. *Language and Learning: Philosophy of Language in the Hellenistic Age*. Cambridge: Cambridge University Press, 2005.
Friesen, Steven J. *Imperial Cults and the Apocalypse of John: Reading Revelation in the Ruins*. Oxford: Oxford University Press, 2001.
Frey, Jörg, Jens Herzer, Martina Janßen, und Clare K. Rothschild. *Pseudepigraphie und Verfassserfiktion in frühchristlichen Briefen (Pseudepigraphy and Author Fiction in Early ChristianLetters)*. Tübingen: Mohr/Siebeck, 2009.
Fry, V. R. L. "Diotrephes." *AYBD* 2:204.
Furnish, Victor Paul. *The Love Command in the New Testament*. NTL. Nashville: Abingdon, 1972.
Gamble, Harry Y. *Books and Readers in the Early Church: A History of Early Christian Texts*. New Haven: Yale University Press, 1995.
———. *The New Testament Canon: Its Making and Meaning*. 1985. Reprinted, Eugene, OR: Wipf & Stock, 2002.
García Martínez, Florentino. *Qumran and Apocalyptic: Studies on the Aramaic Texts from Qumran*. Studies in the Texts of the Desert of Judah 9. Leiden: Brill, 1992.
———, ed. *Wisdom and Apocalypticism in the Dead Sea Scrolls and in the Biblical Tradition*. Bibliotheca Ephemeridum theologicarum Lovaniensium 168. Leuven: Peeters, 2003.
Gerhardsson, Birger. *Memory and Manuscript: Oral Tradition and Written Transmission in Rabbinic Judaism and Early Christianity*. Translated by Eric J. Sharpe. 2nd ed. Biblical Resources Series. Grand Rapids: Eerdmans, 1998.
Gitay, Yehoshua, ed. *Prophecy and Prophets: The Diversity of Contemporary Issues in Scholarship*. Semeia Studies. Atlanta: Scholars, 1997.
Glasson, T. Francis. *Greek Influence in Jewish Eschatology*. Biblical Monographs 1. London: SPCK 1961.
Godwin, Joscelyn. *Mystery Religions in the Ancient World*. San Francisco: Harper & Row, 1981.
Goodman, Martin. *The Roman World 44 BC—AD 180*. London: Routledge, 1997.
———. *The Ruling Class of Judaea, AD 66–70: The Origins of the Jewish Revolt against Rome*. Cambridge: Cambridge University Press, 1987.

BIBLIOGRAPHY

Goppelt, Leonhard. *Typos: The Typological Interpretation of the Old Testament in the New*. Translated by Donald H. Madvig. 1982. Eugene, OR: Wipf & Stock, 2002.

Grant, Frederick C. *Ancient Roman Religion*. New York: Macmillan, 1957.

Green, Joel B., ed. *Hearing the New Testament: Strategies for Interpretation*. 2nd ed. Grand Rapids: Eerdmans, 2010.

Greenlee, J. Harold. *Introduction to New Testament Textual Criticism*. Rev. ed. Peabody, MA: Hendrickson, 1995.

———. *The Text of the New Testament: From Manuscript to Modern Edition*. Peabody, MA: Hendrickson, 2008.

Grünstäudl, Wolfgang, and Tobias Nicklas. "Searching for Evidence: The History of the Reception of the Epistles of Jude and 2 Peter." In *Reading 1–2 Peter and Jude: A Resource for Students*, edited by Eric F. Mason and Troy W. Martin, 215–28. RBS 77. Atlanta: Society of Biblical Literature, 2014.

Gundry, Robert H. "'Verba Christi' in 1 Peter: Their Implications concerning the Authorship of 1 Peter and the Authenticity of the Gospel Tradition." *NTS* 13 (1966–67) 336–50.

Gunkel, Hermann. *Creation and Chaos in the Primeval Era and the Eschaton: A Religio-historical Study of Genesis 1 and Revelation 12*. Translated by K. William Whitney Jr. Grand Rapids: Eerdmans, 2006.

Gupta, Nijay K. "'They Are not Gods!' Jewish and Christian Idol Polemic and Greco-Roman Use of Cult Statues." *CBQ* 76 (2014) 704–19.

Guthrie, Donald. *New Testament Introduction*. 4th ed. Master Reference Collection. Downers Grove, IL: InterVarsity, 1990.

Guthrie, George H. "Hebrews." In *Commentary on the New Testament Use of the Old Testament*, edited by G. K. Beale and D. A. Carson, 919–95. Grand Rapids: Baker Academic, 2007.

———. "Hebrews' Use of the Old Testament: Recent Trends in Research." *CBR* 1 (2003) 271–94.

Hahneman, G. M. T. *The Muratorian Fragment and the Development of the Canon*. Oxford Theological Monographs. Oxford: Clarendon, 1992.

———. "The Muratorian Fragment and the Origins of the New Testament Canon." In *The Canon Debate*, edited by Lee Martin McDonald and James A. Sanders, 405–15. Peabody, MA: Hendrickson, 2002.

Häkkinen, Sakari. "Ebionites." In *A Companion to Second-Century Christian "Heretics."* edited by Antti Marjanen and Petri Luomanen, 247–78. Leiden: Brill, 2008.

Hanson, Paul D. "Jewish Apocalyptic against Its Near Eastern Environment." *Revue biblique* 78 (1971) 31–58.

———. *Dawn of Apocalyptic: The Sociological and Historical Roots of Jewish Apocalyptic Eschatology*. Rev. ed. Philadelphia: Fortress, 1979.

Harnack, Karl Gustav Adolf von. *History of Dogma*. 7 vols. Translated by Neil Buchanan. 1897–1910. Reprinted, Eugene, OR: Wipf & Stock, 1997.

———. *The Mission and Expansion of Christianity in the First Three Centuries*. Translated by James Moffatt. Vol. 1. Theological Translation Library 20. 1908. Reprinted, Eugene, OR: Wipf & Stock, 1997. http://www.ccel.org/ccel/harnack/mission.i.html/.

Harner, Philip B. *What Are They Saying about the Catholic Epistles?* WATSA. New York: Paulist, 2004.

———. "Baptism." In *AYBD*, 1:583–94.

———. *"Into the Name of the Lord Jesus": Baptism in the Early Church*. Studies of the New Testament and Its World. Edinburgh: T. & T. Clark, 1997.
Harrill, J. Albert. "Stoic Physics, Universal Conflagration, and the Eschatological Destruction of the 'Ignorant and Unstable' in 2 Peter." In *Stoicism in Early Christianity*, edited by Tuomas Rasimus et al., 115–40. Peabody, MA: Hendrickson, 2010.
Harrison, R. K. et al., eds. *Biblical Criticism: Historical Literary, and Textual*. Contemporary Evangelical Perspectives. Grand Rapids: Zondervan, 1978.
Hartman, Lars. "Baptism." In *AYBD* 1:591–92.
———. *"Into the Name of the Lord Jesus": Baptism in the Early Church*. Studies of the New Testament and Its World. Edinburgh: T. & T. Clark, 1997.
Hay, David M. *Glory at the Right Hand: Psalm 110 in Early Christianity*. SBLMS 18. SBLMS 18. Nashville: Abingdon, 1973.
Hays, Christopher M., and Christopher B. Ansberry, eds. *Evangelical Faith and the Challenge of Historical Criticism*. Grand Rapids: Baker Academic, 2013.
Hays, Richard B. *The Conversion of the Imagination: Paul as Interpreter of Israel's Scripture*. Grand Rapids: Eerdmans, 2005.
———. *Echoes of Scripture in the Letters of Paul*. New Haven: Yale University Press, 1989.
Hedrick, Charles W., Jr. *Ancient History: Monuments and Documents*. Blackwell Introductions to the Classical World. Malden, MA: Blackwell, 2006.
Hedrick, Charles W., and Robert Hodgson Jr., eds. *Nag Hammadi, Gnosticism & Early Christianity*. 1986. Reprinted, Eugene, OR: Wipf & Stock, 2005.
Hellholm, David. "The Problem of Apocalyptic Genre and the Apocalypse of John." In *Early Christian Apocalyptic: Genre and Social Setting*, edited by Adela Yarbro Collins, 13–64. Semeia 36. Decatur, GA: Society of Biblical Literature, 1986.
Hemer, Colin J. *The Letters to the Seven Churches of Asia in Their Local Setting*. The Biblical Resource Series. 1986. New ed. with foreward by David E. Aune. Grand Rapids: Eerdmans, 2001.
———. "Towards a New Moulton and Milligan." *NovT* 24 (1982) 97–123.
Hengel, Martin. *Acts and the History of Earliest Christianity*. Translated by John Bowden. 1979. Reprinted, Eugene, OR: Wipf & Stock, 2003.
———. *Between Jesus and Paul: Studies in the Earliest History of Christianity*. Translated by John Bowden. 1983. Reprinted, Eugene, OR: Wipf & Stock, 2003.
———. *The "Hellenization" of Judaea in the First Century after Christ*. 1989. Reprinted, Eugene, OR: Wipf & Stock, 2003.
———. *Judaism and Hellenism: Studies in Their Encounter in Palestine during the Early Hellenistic Period*. Translated by John Bowden. 1974. Reprinted, Eugene, OR: Wipf & Stock, 2003.
———. *Saint Peter: The Underestimated Apostle*. Translated by Thomas H. Trapp. Grand Rapids: Eerdmans, 2010.
———. *The Septuagint as Christian Scripture: Its Prehistory and the Problem of Its Canon*. Translated by Mark E. Biddle. Grand Rapids: Baker Academic, 2004.
———. *The Zealots: Investigations into the Jewish Freedmen Movement in the Period from Herod I until 70 AD*. Translated by David Smith. Edinburgh: T. & T. Clark, 1989.
Hens-Piazza, Gina. *The New Historicism*. GBS: Old Testament Series. Minneapolis: Fortress, 2002.

BIBLIOGRAPHY

Henten, J. W. van. "Dragon Myth and Imperial Ideology." In *The Reality of Apocalypse: Rhetoric and Politics in the Book of Revelation*, edited by David L. Barr, 181–203. Society of Biblical Literature Symposium Series 39. Atlanta: Society of Biblical Literature, 2006.
Heschel, Abraham J. *The Prophets*. New York: Harper & Row, 1962.
Hicks, Robert D. *Stoic and Epicurean*. New York: Russell & Russell, 1962.
Hiebert, D. E. "Designation of the Readers in 1 Peter 1:1–2." *Bibliotheca Sacra* 137 (1980) 64–75.
Hill, C. E. "The Debate over the Muratorian Fragment and the Development of the Canon." *Westminster Theological Journal* 57 (1995) 437–52.
Hill, Craig C. *Hellenists and Hebrews: Reappraising Division within the Earliest Church*. Minneapolis: Fortress, 1992.
Hill, David. "On the Evidence of the Creative Role of Christian Prophets." *NTS* 20 (1973–74) 261–74.
———. "On Suffering and Baptism in 1 Peter." *NovT* 18 (1976) 181–89.
———. "Prophecy and Prophets in the Revelation of St. John." *NTS* 18 (1971–72) 401–18.
Hills, Julian V. "A Genre for 1 John." In *The Future of Early Christianity*, edited by Birger A. Pearson et al., 367–77. Minneapolis: Fortress, 1991.
Hodgson, Robert. "The Testimony Hypothesis." *JBL* 98 (1979) 361–78.
Hogeterp, Albert L. A. *Expectations of the End: A Comparative Traditio-Historical Study of Eschatological, Apocalytic and Messianic Ideas in the Dead Sea Scrolls and the New Testament*. Studies in the Texts of the Desert of Judah 83. Leiden: Brill, 2009.
Holman, Charles L. *Till Jesus Comes: Origins of Christian Apocalyptic Expectation*. Peabody, MA: Hendrickson, 1996.
Holmen, Tom, and Stanley E. Porter, eds. *Handbook for the Study of the Historical Jesus*. 4 vols. Leiden: Brill, 2010.
Horrell, David G. "Between Conformity and Resistance: Beyond the Balch-Elliott Debate towards a Postcolonial Reading of 1 Peter." In *Reading First Peter with New Eyes: Methodological Reassessments of the Letter of First Peter*, edited by Robert L. Webb and Betsy Bauman-Martin, 111–43. LNTS 364. London: T & T Clark, 2007.
Horrocks, Geoffrey. *Greek: A History of the Language and its Speakers*. Longman Linguistics Library. London: Longmans, 1997.
Horsley, G. H. R. "The Fiction of Jewish Greek." In *New Documents Illustrating Early Christianity Volume 5: Linguistic Essays*. Macquarie University, 1989.
Horsley, G. H. R., and John A. L. Lee. "A Lexicon of the New Testament with Documentary Parallels: Some Interim Entries, 1." *Filologia Neotestamentaria* 10 (1997) 55–84.
———. "A Lexicon of the New Testament with Documentary Parallels: Some Interim Entries, 2." *Filologia Neotestamentaria* 11 (1998) 57–84.
Horsley, Richard A., ed. *In the Shadow of Empire: Reclaiming the Bible as a History of Faithful Resistance*. Louisville: Westminster John Knox, 2008.
———. *Scribes, Visionaries, and the Politics of Second Temple Judea*. Louisville: Westminster John Knox, 2007.
Horsley, Richard, and Patrick A. Tiller. *After Apocalyptic and Wisdom: Rethinking Texts and Contexts*. Eugene, OR: Cascade Books, 2012.

Horton, Frederick L. *The Melchizedek Tradition: A Critical Examination of the Sources to the Fifth Century A. D. and in the Epistle to the Hebrews*. SNTSMS 30. Cambridge: Cambridge University Press, 1976.

Howard-Brook, Wes, and Anthony Gwyther. *Unveiling Empire: Reading Revelation Then and Now*. The Bible & Liberation Series. Maryknoll, NY: Oribs, 1999.

Hultin, Jeremy F. "Literary Relationships among 1 Peter, 2 Peter and Jude." In *Reading 1–2 Peter and Jude: A Resource for Students*, edited by Eric F. Mason and Troy W. Martin, 27–46. RBS 77. Atlanta: SBL, 2014.

Hurst, L. "How 'Platonic' Are Heb 8:5 and 9:23f.?" *Journal of Theological Studies* 34 (1983) 156–68.

Hurtado, Larry W. *The Earliest Christian Artifacts: Manuscripts and Christian Origins*. Grand Rapids: Eerdmans, 2006.

―――――. "Interactive Diversity: A Proposed Model of Christian Origins." *JTS*. New Series. Volume 64, Part 2 (October 2013) 445–62.

―――――. *Lord Jesus Christ: Devotion to Jesus in Earliest Christianity*. Grand Rapids: Eerdmans, 2003.

Jagersma, Henk. *A History of Israel from Alexander the Great to Bar Kochba*. Translated by John Bowden. Philadelphia: Fortress, 1986.

Jobes, Karen H. *Letters to the Church: A Survey of Hebrews and the General Epistles*. Grand Rapids: Zondervan, 2011.

―――――. "The Syntax of 1 Peter: Just How Good Is the Greek?" *BBR* 13 (2003) 159–73.

Johns, Loren L. *The Lamb Christology of the Apocalypse of John: An Investigation into Its Origins and Rhetorical Force*. WUNT 2/167. Tübingen: Mohr/Siebeck, 2003.

Johnson, Luke Timothy. *Among the Gentiles: Greco-Roman Religion and Christianity*. AYBRL. New Haven: Yale University Press, 2009.

―――――. "The Use of Leviticus 19 in the Letter of James." *JBL* 101 (1982) 391–401.

Jonas, Hans. *The Gnostic Religion: The Message of the Alien God and the Beginnings of Christianity*. 2nd ed. Boston: Beacon, 1963.

Jones, Brian W. *The Emperor Domitian*. London: Routledge, 1992.

Judge, E. A. *Social Distinctives of the Christians in the First Century: Pivotal Essays*. Edited by David M. Scholer. Peabody, MA: Hendrickson, 2007.

―――――. "A Woman's Behavior." In *New Documents Illustrating Early Christianity: Linguistic Essays*, 18–23. North Ryde, NSW: Ancient History Documentary Research Centre, Macquarie University, 1992.

Kalin, Everett. "Re-Examining the New Testament Canon History: 1. The Canon of Origen." *Currents in Theology and Mission* 17 (1990) 274–82.

―――――. "The New Testament Canon of Eusebius." In *The Canon Debate*, edited by Lee Martin McDonald and James A. Sanders, 386–404. Peabody, MA: Hendrickson, 2002.

Kaminsky, Joel S. *Yet I Loved Jacob: Reclaiming the Biblical Concept of Election*. Nashville: Abingdon, 2007.

Kamm, Antony. *The Romans: An Introduction*. 2nd ed. London: Routledge, 2008.

Kampen, John. *Hasideans and the Origin of Pharisaism*. Septuagint and Cognate Studies 24. Atlanta: Scholars, 1988.

Käsemann, Ernst. "An Apologia for Primitive Christian Eschatology." In *Essays on New Testament Themes*, 169–95. 1964. Reprinted, Philadelphia: Fortress, 1982.

———. "New Testament Canon and the Unity of the Church." In *Essays on New Testament Themes*, 103–7. Translated by W. J. Montague. 1964. Reprinted, Philadelphia: Fortress, 1982.

———. "Paul and Early Catholicism." In *New Testament Questions Today*, 236–51. Translated by W. J. Montague. Philadelphia: Fortress, 1979.

———. *The Wandering People of God: An Investigation of the Letter to the Hebrews*. Translated by Roy A. Harrisville and Irving L. Sandberg. Minneapolis: Augsburg, 1984.

Kee, Howard Clark. *Medicine, Miracle, and Magic in New Testament Times*. SNTSMS 55. Cambridge: Cambridge University Press, 1986.

———. *Miracle in the Early Christian World: A Study in Sociohistorical Method*. New Haven: Yale University Press, 1983.

Kennedy, George A. *Classical Rhetoric and Its Christian and Secular Traditions from Ancient to Modern Times*. Chapel Hill: University of North Carolina Press, 1980.

———. *New Testament Interpretation through Rhetorical Criticism*. Studies in Religion. Chapel Hill: University of North Carolina Press, 1984.

Klauck, Hans-Josef. "Zur rhetorischen Analyse der Johannesbriefe." *ZNW* 81 (1990) 205–24.

Kloppenberg, John S. "Patronage Avoidance in James." *Hervormde Teologiese Studies* 55 (1999) 755–94.

Koch, Klaus. *The Rediscovery of Apocalyptic*. SBT 2/22. Naperville, IL: Allenson, 1972.

Koester, Craig R. *The Apocalypse: Controversies on Meaning in Western History*. Chantilly, VA: The Teaching Company, 2011.

———. *The Dwelling of God: The Tabernacle in the Old Testament, Intertestamental Jewish Literature, and the New Testament*. Catholic Biblical Quarterly Monograph Series 22. Washington, DC: Catholic Biblical Association of America, 1989.

———. "Hebrews, Rhetoric, and the Future of Humanity." In *Reading the Epistle to the Hebrews: A Resource for Students*, edited by Eric F. Mason and Kevin B. McCruden, 99–120. RBS 66. Atlanta: Society of Biblical Literature, 2011.

———. "The Message to Laodicea and the Problem of Its Local Context: A Study in the Imagery in Rev 3.14–22." *NTS* 49 (2003) 407–24.

———. "Pergamum." In *NIDB* 4:446–47.

———. *Revelation and the End of All Things*. Grand Rapids: Eerdmans, 2001.

———. "Roman Slave Trade and the Critique of Babylon in Revelation 18." *CBQ* 70 (2008) 766–86.

Koester, Helmut, ed. *Ephesos, Metropolis of Asia: An Interdisciplinary Approach to Its Archaeology, Religion, and Culture*. Valley Forge, PA: Trinity, 1995.

———. *Introduction to the New Testament*. Vol. 1, *History, Literature, and Religion of the Hellenistic Age*. 2nd ed. New York: de Gruyter, 2002.

———. *Introduction to the New Testament*. Vol. 2, *History and Literature of Early Christianity*. 2nd ed. New York: Walter de Gruyter, 2000.

———. *Pergamon, Citadel of the Gods: Archaeological Record, Literary Description, and Religious Development*. Harvard Theological Studies 46. Harrisburg, PA: Trinity, 1998.

Kokkinos, Nikos. *The Herodian Dynasty: Origins, Role in Society, and Eclipse*. JSPSup 30. Sheffield: Sheffield Academic, 1998.

Köstenberger, Andreas J. *A Theology of John's Gospel and Letters: The Word, the Christ, the Son of God*. Biblical Theology of the New Testament. Grand Rapids: Zondervan, 2009.

Kraft, Robert. "The Development of the Concept of 'Orthodoxy' in Early Christianity." In *Current Issues in Biblical and Patristic Interpretation*, edited by Gerald Hawthorne, 47–59. Grand Rapids: Eerdmans, 1975.

Kuma, Hermann V. A. *The Centrality of Αἷμα (Blood) in the Theology of the Epistle to the Hebrews: An Exegetical and Philological Study*. Lewiston, NY: Mellen, 2012.

Kümmel, Werner Georg. *Introduction to the New Testament*. Rev. ed. Translated by Howard Clark Kee. Nashville: Abingdon, 1975.

———. *The New Testament: The History of the Investigation of Its Problems*. Translated by S. McLean Gilmour and Howard Clark Kee. Nashville: Abingdon, 1972.

Kurz, William S. "Luke 22:14–38 and Greco-Roman and Biblical Farewell Addresses." *JBL* 104 (1985) 251–68.

Lampe, G. W. H. "The Evidence in the New Testament for Early Creeds, Catechisms and Liturgy." *ExpT* 71 (1960) 359–63.

Lampe, Peter. *From Paul to Valentinus: Christians at Rome in the First Two Centuries*. Translated by Michael Steinhauser. Edited by Marshall D. Johnson. Minneapolis: Fortress, 2003.

Leene, Henk. *Newness in Old Testament Prophecy: An Intertextual Study*. Oudtestamentishce Studiën 64. Leiden: Brill, 2014.

Levenson, Jon D. *The Death and Resurrection of the Beloved Son: The Transformation of Child Sacrifice in Judaism and Christianity*. New Haven: Yale University Press, 1993.

———. *Resurrection and the Restoration of Israel: The Ultimate Victory of the God of Life*. New Haven: Yale University Press, 2006.

———. *Sinai and Zion: An Entry into the Jewish Bible*. New Voices in Biblical Studies. San Francisco: Harper & Row, 1985.

Levick, Barbara. *Claudius*. Roman Imperial Biographies. New York: Routledge, 2015.

———. *Tiberius the Politician*. London: Routledge, 1999.

Levine, Lee I. *The Ancient Synagogue: The First Thousand Years*. New Haven: Yale University Press, 2000.

Lewis, Jack P. "What Do We Mean By Jabneh?" *JBR* 32 (1964) 125–32.

Lockett, Darian. "Objects of Mercy in Jude: The Prophetic Background of Jude 22–23." *CBQ* 77 (2015) 322–36.

Longenecker, Richard N. *Biblical Exegesis in the Apostolic Period*. 2nd ed. Grand Rapids: Eerdmans, 1999.

———, ed. *Contours of Christology in the New Testament*. McMaster New Testament Studies. Grand Rapids: Eerdmans, 2005.

Longenecker, Richard N., and Merrill C. Tenney, eds. *New Dimensions in New Testament Study*. Grand Rapids: Zondervan, 1974.

Lüdemann, Gerd. *Heretics: The Other Side of Early Christianity*. Translated by John Bowden. Louisville: Westminster John Knox, 1996.

Lund, Nils Wilhelm. *Chiasmus in the New Testament: A Study in Formgeschichte*. Chapel Hill: University of North Carolina Press, 1942.

———. *Chiasmus in the New Testament: A Study in the Form and Function of Chiastic Structures*. Peabody, MA: Hendrickson, 1992.

Luther, Martin. *Luther's Works*. Vol. 8, *Lectures on Genesis, Chapters 45–50*. Edited by Jaroslav Pelikan. St. Louis: Concordia, 1966.

———. *Luther's Works*. Vol. 30, *The Catholic Epistles*. Edited by Jaroslav Pelikan and Walter Hansen. St. Louis: Concordia, 1967.

———. *Luther's Works*. Vol. 35, *Word and Sacrament I*. Edited by Jaroslav Pelikan et al. Philadelphia: Fortress, 1960.

Luttikhuizen, Gerald P., ed. *Paradise Interpreted: Representations of Biblical Paradise in Judaism and Christianity*. Themes in Biblical Narrative 2. Leiden: Brill, 1999.

MacDonald, Dennis R. *Does the New Testament Imitate Homer? Four Cases from the Acts of the Apostles*. New Haven: Yale UniversityPress, 2003.

———, ed. *Mimesis and Intertextuality in Antiquity and Christianity*. Studies in Antiquity and Christianity. Harrisburg, PA: Trinity, 2001.

Malbon, Elizabeth Struthers, and Edgar V. McKnight, eds. *The New Literary Criticism and the New Testament*. JSNTSup 109. Sheffield: Sheffield Academic, 1994.

Malherbe, Abraham J., ed. *The Cynic Epistles: A Study Edition*. Sources for Biblical Studies 12. Missoula, MT: Scholars, 1977.

———. *Moral Exhortation: A Greco-Roman Sourcebook*. LEC 4. Philadelphia: Westminster, 1986.

Malina, Bruce J. *On the Genre and Message of Revelation: Star Visions and Sky Journeys*. Peabody, MA: Hendrickson, 1995.

———. "The Received View and What It Cannot Do: III John and Hospitality." In *Social-Scientific Criticism of the New Testament and Its Social World*, edited by John H. Elliott, 171–94 Semeia 35. Decatur, GA: Scholars, 1986.

Manson, William. *The Epistle to the Hebrews: An Historical and Theological Reconsideration*. The Baird Lecture 1949. London: Hodder & Stoughton, 1951.

Marcus, Joel. "The Evil Inclination in the Epistle of James." *CBQ* 44 (1982) 606–21.

Marjanen, Antti, and Petri Luomanen, eds. *A Companion to Second-Century Christian "Heretics."* Leiden: Brill, 2008.

Marshall, I. Howard. "'Early Catholicism' in the New Testament." In *New Dimensions in New Testament Study*, edited by Richard N. Longnecker and Merrill C. Tenney, 217–31. Grand Rapids: Zondervan, 1974.

Martin, Troy W. "Christians as Babies: Metaphorical Reality in 1 Peter." In *Reading 1–2 Peter and Jude: A Resource for Students*, edited by Eric F. Mason and Troy W. Martin, 99–112. RBS 77. Atlanta: Society of Biblical Literature, 2014.

Mason, Eric F. "Biblical and Nonbiblical Traditions in Jude and 2 Peter." In *Reading 1–2 Peter and Jude*, edited by Eric F. Mason and Troy W. Martin, 181–200. RBS 77. Atlanta: Society of Biblical Literature, 2014.

Mason, Eric F., and Troy W. Martin, eds. *Reading 1–2 Peter and Jude: A Resource for Students*. RBS 77. Atlanta: Society of Biblical Literature, 2014.

Mason, Eric F., and Kevin B. McCruden. *Reading the Epistle to the Hebrews: A Resource for Students*. RBS 66. Atlanta: Society of Biblical Literature, 2011.

Mason, Steve. *Flavius Josephus on the Pharisees: A Composition-Critical Study*. Studia Post-Biblica 39. Leiden: Brill, 1991.

———. "Jews, Judaeans, Judaizing, Judaism: Problems of Categorization in Ancient History." *Journal for the Study of Judaism* 38 (2007) 457–512.

———. *Josephus and the New Testament*. Peabody, MA: Hendrickson, 1992.

McDonald, Lee Martin. "Canon of the New Testament." In *NIDB* 1:536–47.

McDonald, Lee Martin, and James A. Sanders, eds. *The Canon Debate*. Peabody, MA: Hendrickson, 2002.

McKnight, Edgar V., and Elizabeth S. Malbon, eds. *The New Literary Criticism and the New Testament*. Valley Forge, PA: Trinity, 1994.

McKnight, Scot, and Joseph B. Modica. *Jesus Is Lord, Caesar Is Not: Evaluating Empire in New Testament Studies*. Downers Grove, IL: InterVarsity, 2013.

McKnight, Scot, and Grant R. Osborne, eds. *The Face of New Testament Studies: A Survey of Recent Research*. Grand Rapids: Baker Academic, 2004.

Mealy, J. W. *After the Thousand Years: Resurrection and Judgment in Revelation 20*. JSNTSup 70. Sheffield: JSOT Press, 1992.

Meeks, Wayne A. *The First Urban Christians: The Social World of the Apostle Paul*. 2nd ed. New Haven: Yale University Press, 2003.

Merlan, Philip. *From Platonism to Neoplatonism*. 2nd ed. The Hague: Nijhoff, 1960.

Metzger, Bruce M. *The Bible in Translation: Ancient and English Versions*. Grand Rapids: Baker Academic, 2001.

———. *Breaking the Code: Understanding the Book of Revelation*. Nashville: Abingdon Press, 1993.

———. *The Canon of the New Testament: Its Origins, Development, and Significance*. Oxford: Clarendon, 1987.

———. "Literary Forgeries and Canonical Pseudepigrapha." *JBL* 91 (1972) 3–24.

———. *The Text of the New Testament: Its Transmission, Corruption, and Restoration*. 3rd ed. New York: Oxford University Press, 1992.

Metzger, Bruce M., and Bart D. Ehrman, *The Text of the New Testament: Its Transmission, Corruption, and Restoration*. 4th ed. New York: Oxford University Press, 2005.

Meynet, Roland. "The Question at the Center: A Specific Device of Rhetorical Argumentation in Scripture." In *Rhetorical Argumentation in Biblical Texts: Essays from the Lund 2000 Conference*, edited by Anders Eriksson et al., 200–214 Emory Studies in Early Christianity 8. Harrisburg, PA: Trinity, 2002.

———. *Rhetorical Analysis: An Introduction to Biblical Rhetoric*. Translated by Luc Racaut. Rev. ed. JSOTSup 256. Sheffield: Sheffield Academic, 1998.

Michaels, J. Ramsey. *Interpreting the Book of Revelation*. Guides to New Testament Exegesis 7. Grand Rapids: Baker, 1992.

Miller, M. P. "Midrash." In *IDBSup*, 593–97.

Mitchell, Alan C. "'A Sacrifice of Praise': Does Hebrews Promote Supersessionism?" In *Reading the Epistle to the Hebrews: A Resource for Students*, edited by Eric F. Mason and Kevin B. McCruden, 251–68. RBS 66. Atlanta: Society of Biblical Literature, 2011.

Moore, Stephen D. *Poststructuralism and the New Testament: Derrida and Foucault at the Foot of the Cross*. Minneapolis: Fortress, 1994.

Morris, Leon. *The Atonement: Its Meaning and Significance*. Downers Grove, IL: InterVarsity, 1983.

———. *Testaments of Love: A Study of Love in the Bible*. Grand Rapids: Eerdmans, 1981.

Moule, C. F. D. "The Nature and Purpose of 1 Peter." *NTS* 3 (1956–57) 1–11.

Mousourakis, George. *A Legal History of Rome*. London: Routledge, 2007.

Moyise, Steve. *The Later New Testament Writings and Scripture: The Old Testament in Acts, Hebrews, the Catholic Epistles and Revelation*. Grand Rapids: Baker Academic, 2012.

———. *The Old Testament in the Book of Revelation*. JSNTSup 115. Sheffield: Sheffield Academic, 1995.

BIBLIOGRAPHY

———. "Prophets in the New Testament." In *Dictionary of the Old Testament: Prophets*, edited by Mark J. Boda and Gordon McConville, 160–67. Downers Grove, IL: InterVarsity Academic, 2012.

Murphy-O'Connor, Jerome. *Paul the Letter-Writer: His World, His Options, His Skills*. Good News Studies 41. A Michael Glazier Book. Collegeville, MN: Liturgical, 1995.

Mussies, Gerard. "The Use of Hebrew and Aramaic in the Greek New Testament." *NTS* 30 (1984) 416–32.

Nagy, Gregory. *The Best of the Achaeans: Concepts of the Hero in Archaic Greek Poetry*. Baltimore: Johns Hopkins University Press, 1979.

Nauck, Wolfgang. *Die Tradition und Charakter des ernsten Johannesbriefes*. WUNT 3. Tübingen: Mohr/Siebeck, 1957.

Neusner, Jacob. *Early Rabbinic Judaism: Historical Studies in Religion, Literature, and Art*. Studies in Judiasm in Late Antiquity 13. Leiden: Brill, 1975.

———."The Formation of Rabbinic Judaism: Yavneh (Jamnia) from A.D. 70–100." *ANRW* II.19.2 (1979) 3–42.

———. *Introduction to Rabbinic Literature*. ABRL. New York: Doubleday, 1994.

———. *Method and Meaning in Ancient Judaism*. Brown Judaic Studies 10. Missoula, MT: Scholars, 1979.

———. *Rabbinic Judaism: The Documentary History of Its Formative Age, 70–600 C.E.* Bethesda, MD: CDL, 1994.

———. *Rabbinic Literature: An Essential Guide*. Nashville: Abingdon, 2005.

———. *The Rabbinic Traditions about the Pharisees before 70*. 3 vols. 1971. Reprinted, Eugene, OR: Wipf & Stock, 2005.

Neyrey, Jerome H. "The Form and Background of the Polemic 2 Peter." *JBL* 99 (1980) 407–31.

Nicklesburg, George W. E. *Ancient Judaism and Christian Origins: Diversity, Continuity, and Transformation*. Minneapolis: Fortress, 2003.

———. *Jewish Literature between the Bible and the Mishnah: A Historical and Literary Introduction*. 2nd ed. Minneapolis: Fortress, 2005.

Ong, Walter J. "A Dialectic of Aural and Objective Correlatives." In *20th Century Literary Criticism: A Reader*, edited by David Lodge, 498–508. London: Longman, 1972.

———. "A Writer's Audience Is Always a Fiction." In *Interfaces of the Word: Studies in the Evolution of Consciousness and Culture*, 53–81. Ithaca, NY: Cornell University Press, 1977.

Osiek, Carolyn, and David L. Balch. *Families in the New Testament World: Household and House Churches*. The Family, Religion, and Culture. Louisville: John Knox, 1997.

Pagels, Elaine H. *The Johannine Gospel in Gnostic Exegesis*. 1973. SBLMS 17. Atlanta: Scholars, 1989.

Paget, James Carleton. "The Definition of the Terms *Jewish Christian* and *Jewish Christianity* in the History of Research." In *Jewish Believers in Jesus: The Early Centuries*, edited by Oskar Skarsaune and Reidar Hvalvik, 22–52. Peabody, MA: Hendrickson, 2007.

Painter, John. *Just James: The Brother of Jesus in History and Tradition*. Studies in Personalities of the New Testament. Minneapolis: Fortress, 1999.

Palmer, Frederick. *The Drama of the Apocalypse: In Relation to the Literary and Political Circumstances of Its Time*. New York: Macmillan, 1903.

Palmer, Leonard R. *The Greek Language*. 1980. Norman: University of Oklahoma Press, 1996.
Pardee, Nancy. "Be Holy, for I Am Holy: Paraenesis in 1 Peter." In *Reading 1–2 Peter and Jude: A Resource for Students*, edited by Eric F. Mason and Troy W. Martin, 113–34. RBS 77. Atlanta: SBL, 2014.
Pearson, Birger. "Basilides the Gnostic." In *A Companion to Second-Century Christian "Heretics,"* edited by Antti Marjanen and Petri Luomanen, 1–31. Leiden: Brill, 2008.
Perdelwitz, Richard. *Die Mysterien religion und das Problem des 1 Petrus Briefes: Ein literarische und religionsgeschichtlicher Versuch*. Religionsgescheichtliche Verusuche und Vor-arbeiten 9/3. Giessen: Töpelmann, 1911.
Perkins, Pheme. "Gnosticism." In *NIDB* 2:581–84.
———. *Gnosticism and the New Testament*. Minneapolis: Fortress, 1993.
———. *Love Commands in the New Testament*. New York: Paulist, 1982.
———. "Nag Hammadi Texts." In *NIDB* 4:209.
———. *Peter: Apostle for the Whole Church*. Studies on Personalities of the New Testament. Minneapolis: Fortress, 2000.
Pervo, Richard I. *Dating Acts: Between the Evangelists and the Apologists*. Santa Rosa, CA: Polebridge, 2006.
Pilch, John J. *Healing in the New Testament: Insights from Medical and Mediterranean Anthropology*. Minneapolis: Fortress, 2000.
———, ed. *Social-Scientific Models: Models for Interpreting the Bible: Essays by the Context Group, in Honor of Bruce J. Malina*. Biblical Interpretation Series 53. Leiden: Brill, 2001.
Pippin, Tina. *Apocalyptic Bodies: The Biblical End of the World in Text and Image*. London: Routledge, 1999.
———. "Revelation." In *Searching the Scriptures*. Vol. 2, *A Feminist Commentary*, edited by Elisabeth Schüssler Fiorenza, 109–30. New York: Crossroad, 1994.
———. "Revelation/Apocalypse of John." In *The Women's Bible Commentary*, edited by Carol A. Newsom et al., 627–32. Rev. ed. Louisville: Westminster John Knox, 2012.
Pitstick, Alyssa Lyra. *Light in Darkness: Hans Urs von Balthasar and the Catholic Doctrine of Christ's Descent into Hell*. Grand Rapids: Eerdmans, 2007.
Pitt-Rivers, Julian. "Honour and Social Status." In *Honour and Shame: The Values of Mediterranean Society*, edited by J. G. Peristiany 19–77. The Nature of Human Society Series. Chicago: University of Chicago Press, 1966.
Pomeroy, Sarah B. *Goddesses, Whores, Wives, and Slaves: Women in Classical Antiquity*. New York: Schocken, 1975.
Porter, Stanley E., ed. *Handbook to Exegesis of the New Testament*. NTTS 25. Leiden/New York: Brill, 1997.
———, ed. *Hearing the Old Testament in the New Testament*. McMaster New Testament Studies. Grand Rapids: Eerdmans, 2006.
———, ed. *The Language of the New Testament: Classic Essays*. JSNTSup 60. Sheffield: Sheffield Academic, 1991.
Porter, Stanley E., and Dennis L. Stamps, eds. *Rhetorical Criticism and the Bible*. JSNTSup 195. Sheffield: Sheffield Academic, 2002.
Puskas, Charles B. "Apostolic Advice: 1 Corinthians 7 as Deliberative Rhetoric." In *Children of the Calling: Essays in Honor of Stanley M. Burgess and Ruth V. Burgess*,

edited by Eric Nelson Newberg and Lois E. Olena. 199–214. Eugene, OR: Pickwick Publications, 2014.

———. *The Conclusion of Luke-Acts: The Significance of Acts 28:16–31*. Eugene, OR: Pickwick Publications, 2009.

Puskas, Charles B., and David Crump. *An Introduction to the Gospels and Acts*. Grand Rapids: Eerdmans, 2008.

Puskas, Charles B., and C. Michael Robbins. *An Introduction to the New Testament*. 2nd ed. Eugene, OR: Cascade Books, 2011.

Puskas, Charles B., and Mark Reasoner. *The Letters of Paul: An Introduction*. 2nd ed. Collegeville, MN: Liturgical, 2013.

Ramsay, W. M. *The Letters to the Seven Churches of Asia and Their Place in the Plan of the Apocalypse*. London: Hodder & Stoughton, 1904.

Raquel, Sylvie T. "Authors or Preservers? Scribal Culture and the Theology of Scriptures." In *The Reliability of the New Testament: Bart D. Ehrman & Daniel B. Wallace in Dialogue*, edited by Robert B. Stewart, 173–86. Minneapolis: Fortress, 2011.

———. "Canon, New Testament." In *The Lexham Bible Dictionary*, edited by J. D. Barry et al. Logos Bible Software. Bellingham, WA: Lexham, 2014.

Reese, James M. "The Exegete as Sage: Hearing the Message of James." *BTB* 12 (1982) 82–85.

Reeves, Marjorie. *Joachim of Fiore and the Prophetic Future*. New York: Harper & Row, 1977.

Reinhold, Gotthard G. G., ed. *The Number Seven in the Ancient Near East: Studies on the Numerical Symbolism in the Bible and Its Ancient Near Eastern Environment*. Frankfurt: Lang, 2008 (in German, with three contributions in English).

Reis, D. M. "Apollos." In *NIDB* 1:203–4.

Rhee, Victor (Sung-Yul). "Chiasm and the Concept of Faith in Hebrews 11." *BSac* 155 (1998) 327–45.

Richards, E. Randolph. *Paul and First-Century Letter Writing: Secretaries, Composition, and Collection*. Downers Grove, IL: InterVarsity, 2004.

Richards, W. L. *The Classification of the Greek Manuscripts of the Johannine Epistles*. SBLDS 35. Missoula, MT: Scholars, 1977.

Richmond, L. "The Temples of Apollo and Divus Augustus on Roman Coins." In *Essays and Studies Presented to William Ridgeway*, edited by E. C. Quiggin, 198–212. Cambridge: Cambridge University Press, 1913.

Rist, J. M. *Stoic Philosophy*. Cambridge: Cambridge University Press, 1969.

Rist, Martin. "Pseudepigraphy and the Early Christians." In *Studies in New Testament and Early Christian Literature*, edited by David Aune, 75–91. NovTSup 33. Leiden: Brill 1972.

Robbins, Vernon K. *Exploring the Texture of Texts: A Guide to Socio-Rhetorical Interpretation*. Valley Forge, PA: Trinity, 1996.

Robinson, James M., and Helmut Koester. *Trajectories through Early Christianity*. 1971. Reprinted, Eugene, OR: Wipf & Stock, 2006.

Robinson, T. A. *The Bauer Thesis Examined: The Geography of Heresy in the Early Christian Church*. Studies in the Bible and Early Christianity 11. Lewiston, NY: Mellen, 1988.

Rogers, Robert. *The Double in Literature*. Detroit: Wayne State University Press, 1970.

Rossing, Barbara R. *The Choice between Two Cities: Whore, Babylon, and Empire in the Apocalypse*. HTS 48. Harrisburg, PA: Trinity, 1999.

Royse, James R. "Scribal Tendencies in the Transmission of the Text of the New Testament." In *The Text of the New Testament in Contemporary Research: Essays on the Status Quaestionis*, edited by Bart D. Ehrman and Michael W. Holmes, 239-52. SD 46. 1995. Reprinted, Eugene, OR: Wipf & Stock, 2001. 2nd ed., Leiden: Brill, 2013.

Rudolph, Kurt. *Gnosis: The Nature and History of Gnosticism*. Translated by R. McL Wilson. San Francisco: Harper & Row, 1987.

Sanders, E. P. *Jewish Law from Jesus to the Mishnah: Five Studies*. London: SCM, 1990.

———. *Paul and Palestinian Judaism: A Comparison of Patterns of Religions*. Philadelphia: Fortress, 1977.

Sanders, James A. *From Sacred Story to Sacred Text: Canon as Paradigm*. 1987. Reprinted, Eugene, OR: Wipf & Stock, 2000.

Sandmel, Samuel. *Judaism and Christian Beginnings*. New York: Oxford University Press, 1978.

Schiffman, Lawrence H. *From Text to Tradition: A History of Second Temple and Rabbinic Judaism*. Hoboken, NJ: Ktav, 1991.

———. *Reclaiming the Dead Sea Scrolls*. Philadelphia: Jewish Publication Society, 1994.

Schmithals, Walter. *The Apocalyptic Movement, Introduction & Interpretation*. Translated by John E. Steely. Nashville: Abingdon, 1975.

———. *The Theology of the First Christians*. Translated by O. C. Dean. Louisville: Westminster John Knox, 1997.

Schnelle, Udo. *Theology of the New Testament*. Translated by M. Eugene Boring. Grand Rapids: Baker, 2009.

Schoeps, Hans Joachim. *Jewish Christianity: Factional Disputes in the Early Church*. Translated by Douglas R. A. Hare. Philadelphia: Fortress, 1969.

Scholer, J. M. *Proleptic Priests: Priesthood in the Epistle to the Hebrews*. JSNTSup 49. Sheffield: Sheffield Academic, 1991.

Schüssler Fiorenza, Elisabeth. "*Apokalypsis* and *Propheteia*: The Book of Revelation in the Context of Early Christian Prophecy." In *L'Apocalypse johannique et l' Apocalyptic dans le Nouveau Testament*, edited by Jan Lambrecht et al., 106-28. Bibliotheca Ephemeridum theologicarum Lovaniensium 53. Leuven: Leuven University Press, 1980.

———. *The Book of Revelation: Justice and Judgment*. Philadelphia: Fortress, 1985.

———. "Composition and Structure of the Book of Revelation." CBQ 39 (1977) 358-66.

———. "The Followers of the Lamb: Visionary Rhetoric and Social-Political Situation." *Semeia* 36 (1986) 123-46.

———, ed. *Searching the Scriptures*. Vol. 2, *A Feminist Commentary*. New York: Crossroad, 1994.

Schutter, William L. *Hermeneutic and Composition in 1 Peter*. WUNT 2/30. Tübingen: Mohr/Siebeck, 1989.

Scullard, H. H. *From the Gracchi to Nero: A History of Rome 133 BC to AD 68*. 5th ed. New York: Routledge, 1982.

Seitz, O. J. F. "The Relationship of the Shepherd of Hermas to the Epistle of James." *JBL* 63 (1944) 131-40.

Shanks, Hershel, ed. *Christianity and Rabbinic Judaism: A Parallel History of Their Origins and Early Development*. Washington, DC: Biblical Archaeology Society, 1992.

Shepherd, M. H. "The Epistle of James and the Gospel of Matthew." *JBL* 75 (1956) 40-51.

BIBLIOGRAPHY

Sherwin-White, A. N. *Roman Society and Roman Law in the New Testament.* 1963. Reprinted, Grand Rapids: Baker, 1978.

Sherk, R. K. *The Roman Empire: Augustus to Hadrian.* Cambridge: University of Cambridge, 1988.

Shorey, Paul. *Platonism, Ancient and Modern.* Berkeley University of California Press, 1938.

Shotter, David. *Augustas Caesar.* 2nd ed. Lancaster Pamphlets in Ancient History. New York: Routledge, 2005.

———. *Nero.* 2nd ed. Lancaster Pamphlets in Ancient History. New York: Routledge, 2005.

Siegal, Michal Bar-Asher. *Early Christian Monastic Literature and the Babylonian Talmud.* Cambridge: Cambridge University Press, 2013.

Silva, Moises. *Biblical Words and Their Meaning.* Rev. ed. Grand Rapids: Zondervan, 1994.

Skarsaune, Oskar, and Reidar Hvalvik, eds. *Jewish Believers in Jesus: The Early Centuries.* Peabody, MA: Hendrickson, 2007.

Slater, Thomas B. *Christ and Community: A Socio-historical Study of Christology of Revelation.* JSNTSup 178. Sheffield: Sheffield Academic, 1999.

Small, Brian C. *The Characterization of Jesus in the Book of Hebrews.* Biblical Interpretation Series 128. Leiden: Brill, 2014.

Song, Changwon. *Reading Romans as a Diatribe.* Studies in Biblical Literature 59. New York: Lang, 2004.

Stark, Rodney. *The Rise of Christianity: A Sociologist Reconsiders History.* Princeton: Princeton University Press, 1996.

Stegemann, Hartmut, ed. *The Library of Qumran: On the Essenes, Qumran, John the Baptist, and Jesus.* Grand Rapids: Eerdmans, 1998.

Stegner, William R. "The Ancient Jewish Synagogue Homily." In *Greco-Roman Literature and the New Testament,* edited by David E. Aune, 51–69. Atlanta: Scholars, 1988.

———. "Rom 9:6–29—Midrash." *JSNT* 22 (1984) 37–52.

Sterling, Gregory E. *Historiography and Self-Definition. Josephus, Luke-Acts and Apologetic Historiography.* NovTSup 64. Leiden: Brill, 1992.

Sternberg, Meir. *The Poetics of Biblical Narrative: Ideological Literature and the Drama of Reading.* Bloomington: Indiana University Press, 1987.

Stowers, Stanley K. "Diatribe." In *The Westminster Dictionary of New Testament and Early Christian Literature and Rhetoric,* edited by David E. Aune, 127–29. Louisville: Westminster John Knox, 2003.

———. *The Diatribe and Paul's Letter to the Romans.* SBLDS 57. Chico, CA: Scholars, 1981.

———. *Letter Writing in Greco-Roman Antiquity.* LEC 5. Philadelphia: Westminster, 1986.

Strack, Hermann L., and Günter Stemberger. *Introduction to the Talmud and Midrash.* Translated by Markus Bockmuehl. Minneapolis: Fortress, 1992. 2nd ed., Edinburgh: T & T Clark, 1996.

Strelka, Joseph, ed. *Theories of Literary Genre.* University Park: Pennsylvania State University Press, 1978.

Stuckenbruck, Loren. "An Approach to the New Testament through Aramaic Sources: The Recent Methodological Debate." *JSP* 8 (1991) 3–29.

Sweeney, Marvin A., and Ehud Ben Zvi, eds. *The Changing Face of Form Criticism for the Twenty-First Century.* Grand Rapids: Eerdmans, 2003.

Talbert, Charles H. "II Peter and the Delay of the Parousia." *VC* 20 (1966) 137–45.
———. "The Concept of Immortals in Mediterranean Antiquity." *JBL* 94 (1975) 419–36.
———. *Reading the Sermon on the Mount: Character Formation and Decision Making in Matthew 5–7.* 2004. Reprinted, Grand Rapids: Baker, 2006.
Tate, W. Randolph. *Interpreting the Bible: A Handbook of Terms and Methods.* Peabody, MA: Hendrickson, 2006.
Taylor, Bernard A., John A. L. Lee, Peter R. Burton, and Richard E. Whitaker, eds., *Biblical Greek Language and Lexicography: Essays in Honor of Frederick W. Danker.* Grand Rapids: Eerdmans, 2004.
Theissen, Gerd. *The Miracles of the Early Christian Tradition.* Translated by Francis McDonagh. Philadelphia: Fortress, 1983.
———. *The Religion of the Earliest Churches: Creating a Symbolic World.* Translated by John Bowden. Minneapolis: Fortress, 1999.
Thompson, James W. "What Has Middle Platonism to Do with Hebrews?" In *Reading the Epistle to the Hebrews: A Resource for Students*, edited by Eric F. Mason and Kevin B. McCruden, 31–52. RBS 66. Atlanta: Society Biblical Literature 2011.
Thompson, Leonard L. *The Book of Revelation: Apocalypse and Empire.* Oxford: Oxford University Press, 1990.
———. "A Sociological Analysis of Tribulation in the Apocalypse of John." *Semeia* 36 (1986) 147–174.
Thornton, T. C. G. "I Peter, A Paschal Liturgy?" *JTS* 12 (1961) 14–23.
Thurén, Lauri. *Argument and Theology in 1 Peter: The Origins of Christian Paraenesis.* JSNTS 114. Sheffield: Sheffield Academic, 1995.
Tiller, P. A. "The Rich and Poor in James: An Apocalyptic Proclamation." *SBL 1998 Seminar Papers* 37 (1998) 909–20
Todorov, Tzvetan, *The Fantastic: A Structural Approach to a Literary Genre.* Translated by Richard Howard. Cleveland: Case Western Reserve University Press, 1973.
Tolbert, Mary Ann, ed. *The Bible and Feminist Hermeneutics. Semeia* 28. Chico, CA: Scholars, 1983.
Torrey, Charles Cutler. *Documents of the Primitive Church.* New York: Harper, 1941.
Trebilco, Paul. *The Early Christians in Ephesus from Paul to Ignatius.* Grand Rapids: Eerdmans, 2007.
Trobisch, David. *Die Enstehung der Paulusbriefsammlung: Studien zu den Augfängen christ-licher Publizistik.* NTOA 10. Göttingen: Vandenhoeck & Ruprecht, 1989.
———. *The First Edition of the New Testament.* Oxford: Oxford University Press, 2000.
———. *Paul's Letter Collection: Tracing the Origins.* Minneapolis: Fortress Press, 1994.
Trocmé, Etienne. *The Childhood of Christianity.* Translated by John Bowden. London: SCM, 1997.
Troeltsch, Ernest. *The Social Teaching of the Christian Churches.* Translated by Olive Wyon. 2 vols. 1933. Louisville: Westminster John Knox, 1992.
Tuckett, Christopher M. *Christology and the New Testament: Jesus and His Earliest Followers.* Louisville: Westminster John Knox, 2001.
Turner, John D. "Sethian Gnosticism: A Literary History," In *Nag Hammadi, Gnosticism & Early Christianity*, edited by Charles W. Hedrick and Robert Hodgson Jr., 55–86. Peabody, MA: Hendrickson, 1986.
Twelftree, Graham H. *In the Name of Jesus: Exorcism among Early Christians.* Grand Rapids: Baker, 2007.

Vaganay, Leon and Christian-Bernard Amphoux. *An Introduction to New Testament Textual Criticism*. 2nd ed. Translated by Jenny Heimerdinger. Cambridge: Cambridge University Press, 1991.
VanderKam, James C. *The Dead Sea Scrolls Today*. 2nd ed. Grand Rapids: Eerdmans, 2010.
van der Waal, C. *Openbaring van Jezus Christus: Inleiding en vertaling*. Groningen: De Vuurbaak, 1971.
Verner, David C. *The Household of God: The Social World of the Pastoral Epistles* SBLDS 71. Chico, CA: Scholars, 1983.
Vhysmeister, N. "The Rich Man in James 2: Does Ancient Patronage Illumine the Text? *AUSS* 33 (1995) 265–83.
Voelz, James. "The Language of the New Testament." *ANRW* II, 25/2, 893–977.
Wachob, Wesley Hiram, and Luke Timothy Johnson. "The Sayings of Jesus in the Letter of James." In *Authenticating the Words of Jesus*, edited by Bruce D. Chilton and Craig A. Evans, 431–50. NTTS 28/1. Leiden: Brill, 1999.
Wainwright, Arthur W. *Mysterious Apocalypse: Interpreting the Book of Revelation*. Nashville: Abingdon, 1993.
Ward, R. B. "The Works of Abraham: James 2:14–16." *HTR* 61 (1968) 283–90.
Wassertein, Abraham, and David Wassertein. *The Legend of the Septuagint: From Classical Antiquity to Today*. Cambridge: Cambridge University Press, 2006.
Watson, Duane F. "The Epistolary Rhetoric of 1 Peter, 2 Peter, and Jude." In *Reading 1–2 Peter and Jude: A Resource for Students*, edited by Eric F. Mason and Troy W. Martin, 49–55. RBS 77. Atlanta: Society of Biblical Literature, 2014.
———. *Invention, Arrangement, and Style: Rhetorical Criticism of Jude and 2 Peter*. SBLDS 104. Atlanta: Scholars, 1988.
Webb, Robert L., and Betsy Bauman-Martin, eds. *Reading First Peter with New Eyes: Methodological Reassessments of the Letter of First Peter*. LNTS 364. London: T. & T. Clark, 2007.
Webster, John. "One Who Is Son: Theological Reflections on the Exordium to the Epistle to the Hebrews." In *The Epistle to the Hebrews and Christian Theology*, edited by Richard Bauckham et al., 69–94. Grand Rapids: Eerdmans, 2009.
Wedderburn, A. J. M. *A History of the First Christians*. London: T & T Clark, 2005.
Weima, J. A. D. *Neglected Endings: The Significance of the Pauline Letter Closings*. Sheffield: JSOT Press, 1994.
Welch, John W., ed. *Chiasmus in Antiquity: Structures, Analysis, Exegesis*. Salt Lake City, UT: Neal A. Maxwell Institute for Religious Scholarship, 1998.
Westermann, Claus, ed. *Essays on Old Testament Hermeneutics*. Translated by James Luther Mays. Atlanta: John Knox, 1963.
White, John L. *The Form and Function of the Body of the Greek Letter: A Study of the Letter-Body in the Non-Literary Papyri and in Paul the Apostle*. 2nd ed. SBLDS 2. Missoula, MT: Society of Biblical Literature, 1972.
White, L. Michael. *From Jesus to Christianity: How Four Generations of Visionaries and Storytellers Created the New Testament and Christian Faith*. New York: HarperCollins, 2004.
Wiedemann, Thomas. *Greek and Roman Slavery*. 1981. Reprinted, New York: Routledge, 1989.
Wilkinson, Sam. *Caligula*. Lancaster Pamphlets in Ancient History New York: Routledge, 2004.

Williams, Bernard. *Shame and Necessity*. Sather Classical Lectures 57. Berkeley: University of California Press, 1993.
Williams, Michael Allen. *Rethinking Gnosticism: An Argument for Dismantling a Dubious Category*. Princeton: Princeton University Press, 1996.
———. "Sethianism." In *A Companion to Second-Century Christian "Heretics,"* edited by Antti Marjanen and Petri Luomanen, 32–63. Leiden: Brill, 2008.
Williams, T. B. *Persecution in 1 Peter: Differentiating and Contextualizing Early Christian Suffering*. NovTSup 145. Leiden: Brill, 2012.
Williamson, Ronald. *Philo and the Epistle to the Hebrews*. Arbeiten zur Literatur und Geschichte des hellenistischen Judentums 4. Leiden: Brill, 1970.
Wilson, Mark. *Charts on the Book of Revelation*. Kregel Charts of the Bible and Theology. Grand Rapids: Kregel Academic, 2007.
Wilson, Marvin R. *Our Father Abraham: Jewish Roots of the Christian Faith*. Grand Rapids: Eerdmans, 1989.
Winter, Bruce W., and Andrew D. Clark, eds. *The Book of Acts in Its Ancient Literary Setting*. BAFCS 1. Grand Rapids: Eerdmans, 1993.
Wisse, Frederick. "The Epistle of Jude in the History of Heresiology." In *Essays on the Nag Hammadi Texts in Honor of Alexander Böhlig*, edited by Martin Krause, 133–43. NHS 3. Leiden: Brill, 1972.
Witherington, Ben III. *New Testament Rhetoric: An Introductory Guide to the Art of Persuasion in and of the New Testament*. Eugene, OR: Cascade Books, 2009.
Wright, N. T. *The New Testament and the People of God*. Christian Origins and the Question of God 1. Minneapolis: Fortress, 1992.
Yadin, Yigael. "The Scrolls and The Epistle to the Hebrews." In *Aspects of the Dead Sea Scrolls*, eds. Chaim Rabin and Yigael Yadin, 36–55. Jerusalem: Magnes, 1958.
Yeo, Khiok-khng, *What Has Jerusalem to Do with Beijing? Biblical Interpretation from a Chinese Perspective*. Harrisburg, PA: Trinity, 1998.
Ysebaert, J. *Greek Baptismal Terminology: Its Origins and Early Development*. Græcitas Christianorum primæva 1. Nijmegen: Dekker & Van de Vegt, 1962.
Zahn, Theodor. *Introduction to the New Testament*. 3 vols. Translated by J. Trout. Grand Rapids: Kregel, 1953.
Zoch, Paul A. *Ancient Rome: An Introductory History*. Norman: University of Oklahoma Press, 1998.
Zuntz, Gunther. *The Text of the Epistles: A Disquisition upon the Corpus Paulinum*. Schweich Lectures of the British Academy 1946. Oxford: Oxford University Press, 1953.

Index

Page numbers for definitions are in **boldface**

abide/remain, 60, 118, **119n11**, 130, 136
Abraham
    believed God, 45 Tab. 2.2
    call of, 30
    faith of, 28, 32n54
    journey to Canaan, 21
    justified, 50 Tab. 2.4
    offered up Isaac, 45 Tab. 2.2
    and Rahab, 57, 61
    and Sarah, 79, 80n22
Achaia, 9 Map A, 66 Map B, 101. *See also* Greco-Roman; Hellenistic; Greek, Koine
Achtemeier, Paul, 67n2, 71n8, 85n37
Acts of the Apostles, 3–7, 11–13, 30–37, 42–45, 48–49, 53, 54, 68–69, 71, 73, 78, 88n48, 104, 110, 118, 127–28, 130n36, 142, 152n30, 166
Acts of (NT Apocrypha). *See also* apocrypha; canon; gnostic
    John, 109n40
    Peter, 109n40
    Thomas, 25–26, 98, 109n40
Aeschylus, 159n49. *See also* Greek drama
agrapha, 47n21, **48**. *See also* words, of Christ
Alexandria, 9 Map A, 66 Map B
    Judeans of, 21–23, 33, 36n74, 39. *See also* Philo; Plato, Platonism
allegory, allegorical interpretation, 21–22, 132n41, **165**. *See* Philo; Plato, Platonism
allusion/echo, 2, 5, 7, 12, 20, 27–28, 36, 42, 45, 76, 78, 90, 94, 97, 101–2, 110, 112, 116, 121, 132, 136, 143, 148–49, 150–52, **157**. *See also* commentary; exposition; figures of speech; intertextuality; Scriptures
amanuensis, 48–49, 52–53, 69, **165**
anabasis, 56n41, **165**. *See also* concatenation
anadiplosis, 56n41, **165**. *See also* concatenation; paranomasia
angels. *See* power(s), angelic
antichrist, 117, 155n37. *See also* false teachers/teaching; opponents; secessionists
antilegomena, **42**. *See also* canon
antinomian, 51, 101, 104, 122–23, **165**. *See* gnostic(s); libertine
Antioch of Syria. *See* Syria, Antioch of
Apocalypse of (gnostic). *See also* canon; gnostic; Nag Hammadi Library
    Adam, 27n44, 127n30, 152n31, **172**. *See also* gnostic; Seth, Sethian

INDEX

Apocalypse of (gnostic) *(continued)*
    1 and 2 James, 25–26, 43–44, 53n34, 312n41
    John, 132n41, 152n31
    Peter, 26, 97
apocalyptic, apocalypse, 6–7, 17, 26, 32n62, 99–100, 106, 113, 121, 131, 133, 141n1, **144**, 145, 155, 157, 159, 161–62, 164. *See also* eschatology; Revelation, Book of
apocrypha, apocryphal, 5, 24n39, 96n6, 100, 103, 113, **167**
Apocryphon of John, 99 Fig. 12. *See also* gnostic; Nag Hammadi Library
apodeixis, 16, **165**
apodictic. *See* law, apodictic
apodosis, 58, 86, **165**. *See* protasis
Apollos, 32–33. *See also* Hebrews, authorship
apostasy, 6, 16–17, 24, 32n63, 34–35, 72, 105, 112
apostle(s), 24, 28–29, 31–33, 41–42, 53, 68, 70, 72–73, 93–95, 99, 101–2, 107–8, 110, 112, 116, 128, 152. *See also* disciple(s), elder(s), servant(s), of God
apostolic teaching, 41, 111, 152n31. *See also* kerygma
    postapostolic, 51–53, 65, 90. *See also* Paul, deutero-Pauline; tradition-bearers
Aramaic, 24n39, 27, 30, 46, 48, 69, 100, 167. *See also* Hebrew language
Aristotle, 58n46, 107n36, 159n48. *See also* philosophical; rhetoric
Armaggedon. *See* Harmageddon
associations, Greco-Roman, 71n8, 150–51. *See also* church; Greco-Roman; synagogue
Assumption/Testament of Moses, 5, 96, 113, 144–45
Athanasisus of Alexandria, 41–42, 64, 84, 97
atonement. *See* sacrifices, atoning

Attic Greek. *See* Greek
Attridge, Harold W., 10n2, 14n16, 21n33, 38n80
Augustus, Emperor, 74 Fig. 8. *See also* Caesar
Aune, David E., 11n7, 13n11, 15n19, 17n24, 57n43, 58n46, 80n23, 142n5, 144nn6–7, 150n23, 152–54, 158n47
authenticity, 4, 42, 48, 67, 69, 92, 96–99, 101, 104, 116, **165**–66, 171. *See* canon, canonical; James, authorship and authenticity, etc.

Babylon. *See* Rome, symbolized as Babylon
Balch, David L., 67n2, 76n15, 81n29
baptism, 3, 37, 68, 73, 76, 81–85, 89–91, 123, 166
    for the forgiveness of sins, salvation, 3, 68 Tab. 3.1, 82, 89–91. *See also* Sacraments
    of Jesus, 123n22, 166. *See also* Cerinthus; life, of Jesus
    and 1 John, 136–38
    and mystery cult of Cybele, 82–83. *See also* mystery cults
    and 1 Peter, 3, 73, 82–88
Barnabas, Letter of, 23, 31–33, 55
Barrett, C. K., 103n29. *See also* Stoics; Peter, Second Letter of
Batemann, Hebert W., IV, 27n46, 28n49, 32n59, 35n71
Bauckham, Richard, 11n5, 16n23, 18n28, 121n16, 128n32, 152n31, 156nn39–40, 157
BDAG. *See* Danker, Frederick W.
Beale, G. K., 142n3, 152n32, 157n41, 158n45, 163n57
    and D. A. Carson, 78n21
Beloved Disciple, 121n16
better. *See* superior, better
birth, 3, 8, 60n48, 162. *See also* new birth, new born

INDEX

begat, beget, begotten, 51 Tab. 2.5, 60, 134, 138
bishop, overseer (*episkopos*), 85–86, 88, 127, 156. *See also* elder(s)
bless, 56, 147n15
   blessed, 68, 164
   blessing(s), 2, 4, 47, 54, 59, 60, 63, 81, 92, 104, 111, 130, 146, 158
blood, 25n17, 82–83, 119
   of Jesus Christ, 2, 16n23, 138
Bonhoeffer, Dietrich, 65
Brown, Raymond E., 38n80, 115n2, 116n5, 118n9, 121n15, 122n18, 123nn21–22, 125n26, 129n35, 131nn37–38, 135nn48–50
   and John P. Meier, 10n1, 29n52
Bruce, F. F., 25n40, 28n50, 35n71, 37n78

Caesar, 74, 150n27, 155. *See also* Augustus; Domitian; Nero
Caesarea, 9 Map A, 36, 54, 97, 168
call (*kaleō*), calling
   of Abraham, 30
   be alert, hear, remember, repent, 5, 68, 110, 146–47. *See also* ethics, ethical
   confirm calling, 4, 111
   God called, 4, 100, 106–7, 121n16 (Christ)
   out of darkness into light, 78 Tab. 3.2, 83, 86
   of witnesses, 62
Calvin, John, 39, 98n13
canon, canonical, xxi, 4, 8, 34, 41–42, 64, 92, 97, 113, 115, 124, 152, **166**
   canonicity, 40–41, 96. *See also* authenticity
   deuterocanonical, 79, **167**
   noncanonical, 21, 79. *See also* antilegomena
catachresis, 17n25, **166**
catastrophe, cosmic, 144–45, 162, 164. *See also* apocalyptic

catechesis, 85, 87. *See* creeds; doctrine; teach, teaching
catholic, 2, 6, 40, 166. *See also* church, catholic; Roman Catholic
Catholic or General Letters, **40–41**, 67n2, 84n35, 98n13
censure, 4–5, 57, 106–7, 110, 112n47, 114, 146, 159
Cerinthus, 123n22, 128n32, 149n21, **166**
chiasm, 8, 15n20, 19n29, 60n49, 133–34, 158–60, **166**
Christ, Christology, 11n5, 20–22, 28, 38n79, 39n81, 55, 68n3, 78, 80, 87–90, 119–23, 125, 133, 139, 146, 157–59, 161n52. *See also* Gospels; kerygma; life, of Jesus
   imitation of, 81n26, 85n38, 87. *See also* Christ-followers; disciple
   resurrection of, 41, 80, 89–91
   sacrificial death, 16, 79 Tab. 3.2. *See also* salvation; sin
   titles of, 15–16, 28n49, 38n79, 42, 54, 68, 106–7, 120, 127n31, 145–46
   triumph/victory over the powers, 3, 87–91, 156, 158n46, 159–60, 164
   worship. praise, give honor to, 4, 14, 81n27, 73, 88, 93, 151. *See also* worship, of Christ
Christ-followers (Jesus loyalists), 3–4, **19n30**, 27, 35, 71, etc., 150, 160, **166**. *See also* Disciples
Christian (post 200 CE), 19n30, 50n29, 65, 67, 71, 82n32, 87, 115, 144, 151n28, **166**
church, churches, 1–2, 5–8, 20, 42, 68, 86n39, 90, 98, 102, 113–14, 124, 127, 129, 152, **166**
   catholic, 2, 6, 40, 53, 166. *See* catholic

INDEX

church, churches *(continued)*
    community of the redeemed, 86. *See also* chosen race; saints; holy ones
    early church (Jesus assemblies), 3, 20, 31, 80, 81
    house church, 37, 166. *See also* associations; synagogue
    Johannine, 6, 124–25, 129
    seven churches, 7, 40n2, 140
        Map C, 143, 145–49, 164
church fathers. *See* patristics
Cicero, Marcus Tullius, 58n46, 75n15
citation. *See* allusion/echo; intertextuality
citizens. *See* Rome, local citizens
cleanse, cleansing, 134, 138. *See also* holy; pure; sanctify, sanctifying; saints
Clement of Alexandria, 31, 34n67, 67, 116, 123n20, 152
Clement of Rome (1 Clement), 31, 37, 39, 42, 61n52, 72, 116
Cockerill, Gareth Lee, 19n29, 32nn59–60, 33, 38n80
Collins,
    Adela Yarbro, 144n7
    John J., 34n68, 144n7
    Raymond, F., 53n33
Comma, Johannine, **122**. *See also* Erasmus
commentary, ancient, 6, 13n14, 44n15, 80n23, 131–32, 145, 170. *See also* exposition of sacred texts; pesher interpretation
concatenation, 48, 56n41, 57, 65, **166**. *See* paronomasia
confess, confession, 15, **17n25**, 63, 119, 134, 136
conquer, overcome (*nikaō*), 119 Tab. 5.1, 147, 151, 164. *See also* Christ, triumph over the powers
context. *See* life, situation
contrasts, 157. *See also* literary and rhetorical devices

controversy, 1, 34, 42, 50n29, 166
Coptic, Sahidic, 97, 99 Fig. 12
covenant (*diathēkē*), 2, 50, 90
    new, 1, 16, 20, 28, 32, 35, **60n49**, 170. *See* new
    old, 1, 22, 29, 35, 137
    renewed, renewal, 16n23, 135, 137
creeds, 7, 90, 143. *See* catechesis; doctrine; teach, teaching.
crisis,
    of faith, 37,
    identity, 37n78
    imminent, 37
    plot structure, 7, 134n46, 159, 164. *See also* denouement; plot
cross-references and repetition, 156. *See also* literary and rhetorical devices
Cynics, 15, 57, 105. *See* diatribe; Stoics

Daniel, book of, 7, 131, 143–44. *See also* apocalyptic
Danker, Frederick W., 102n24, 110n42, 111n46
    BDAG, 12n9, 18n26, 19n30, 76n16, 87n42, 89n52, 120n11, 148n20
Davids, Peter H., 41n4, 45n19, 46n21, 48–49, 54, 57–58. *See also* James, Letter of
Dead Sea Scrolls, 18, 23–24, 32n63, 80, 100–101, 106, 131, 137, 145, 157, **166–67**. *See also* Qumran; Essenes; Vermes, Geza.
    4QFlorilegium, 20, 80, 99, 105, 108n39, 172
    War Scroll (1QM), 54n37, 106, 127n31, 135n49, 137n52, 145, 152n30.
death, 87, 109, 137, 158
    of Christ-followers, 151–52
    eternal, 103, 119, 163. *See* life, eternal

of James, 43, 53
of Jesus Christ, 34, 38n79, 41, 46, 80, 120, 125, 136, 170. *See* life, of Jesus Christ
of Peter and Paul, 76, 101
deceive, deception, deceit, 50 Tab. 2.4, 57, 63, 78 Tab. 3.2, 93 Tab. 4.1, 117, 135, 160. *See also* false teachers/teaching; antichrist
Decius, Emperor, 4, 71n8, 151n28. *See also* persecution, empire-wide
Decree, Nemrud Dagh, **110**. *See also* Peter, Second Letter of
Demetrius, 6, 125, 130. *See also* John, Letters of
denouement, 8, 134n46, 159, 164. *See also* crisis, plot structure; plot
denouncements, 4–5, 44, 58, 61, 74, 114, 123–24, 143, 151–52, 169. *See also* invectives
deuterocanonical, 79, **167**. *See also* canon
Deuteronomy, 13, 17, 21, 24, 60nn49–50, 73, 109n40, 112n47, 135n49, 137n52. *See also* law
deutero-Pauline, *See* Paul, deutero-Pauline
devil (*diabolos*), 51 Tab. 2.5, 52 Tab. 2.6, 61, 108. *See also* Satan
belong to, 132, 136
Evil One, 119 Tab 5.1. *See also* evil, powers
diaspora (dispersed), 19n30, 45, 51, **54**
diatribe, 57–58, **167**
Didache, 55, 64, 84, 87n41, 131
diet, dietary. *See* food laws
Dio Cassius (Lucius Cassius Dio), 150
Dio Chrysostom, 15. *See also* Cynics
Diognetus, Letter to, 12, 31, 33, 84
Diotrephes, 5, 123–25, 129, 133–34. *See also* John, Letters of

disciple(s), 53, 68, 98,101, 116n7, 123, 126–29, 149n21, 166. *See* Christ-followers
dithyramb, 81n27. *See* hymns, odes
docetic, Docetism, 26, 121, 122n19, 123, 126, 133n43, 138–39, **167**
doctrine, 12, 15–19, 23, 44, 103, 114. *See also* apostolic teaching; catechesis; creeds
doctrinal beliefs, 19, 38, 67, 90, 104, 133, 163
Domitian, Emperor, 4, 8, 38, 74, 148–51. *See also* persecution, Roman; Revelation, social and historical context
double-minded, two-souled (*dipsychos*), 52 Tab. 2.6, 59, **61n52**
doxology, 11, 105, 107, 109, 114, **167**
drama, Greco-Roman, 7, 81. *See also* Greek, drama
dualism, 2, **21–22**, 26, 83, 127, 172. *See* gnostic(s), Plato, Platonic dualism; Valentinus

edict, imperial, 151n28, 168. *See also* Rome, empire of
elder(s), presbyter(s), 116nn6–7, 122, 125, 138, 152. *See also* bishop
elect (*eklekton*), election, 4, 111. *See also* call, calling
chosenness, 3, 137 (what God has chosen)
Lady, sister, 117n8, 129–30
race, chosen race, 76, 78 Tab.3.2, 85n38. *See also* church, community of redeemed
Elliott, John H., **19n30**, 67nn1–2, 72n10, 76nn15–18, 81n29, 87n42, 166.
R. A. Martin and Elliott, 60n50, 67n2, 84n35, 89n50. *See also* Peter, First Letter of

INDEX

Elliott, Neal, and Mark Reasoner, 12n10, 15n18. *See also* protreptic
encomium, **167**. *See also* values, virtues
　of divine blessings, 111. *See also* doxology; laudation; praise
　of Israel's faithful, 2, 14, 17–18. *See also* praise of virtues; rhetoric, demonstrative
endure, endured, 59, 78, 148
Enoch, First, 5, 79, 94n4, 107, 110n40, 145. *See also* apocalyptic; pseudepigraphic writing
enthymemes, 58–59, 62, 113, **167**
Ephesus, 66 Map B, 126–28, 138, 140 Map C, 148–50. *See also* Trebilco, Paul
Epictetus the Stoic, 12n10, 14, 27, 55, 57, 105. *See also* Stoics
Epicurus, Epicureans, 13, **104**, 128
epilogue, 8, 17–19, 38, 101, 159n49, 160, 170. *See also* peroration.
Epiphanius of Salamis, 41n3, 43n10, 123n20. *See also* patristics; Great Church
epistolary form (letters), 11, 15n18, 40, 54, 69n7, 80–81 104–5, 115n2, 117, **128**–30, 145–47
Erasmus, Desiderius, 97, 122. *See also* Comma, Johannine
eschatology, 22n37, 23, 54, 73, 81, 85, 100, 103, 164. *See also* apocalyptic; judgment, final
　realized, 26, 103, 113, **121**, 133n43, 139
　two-age scheme, 22
　visions of the end time, 1, 7, 121, 141–46, 152, 154–60, 164. *See also* prophets, seers
Esdras, Second, 144–45
Essenes, 19n30, 25, 32n63. *See also* Dead Sea Scrolls, Qumran.
ethics, ethical, 3, 7, 15, 19, 49, 54–55, 58, 65, 67, 75, 81n30, 90, 109, 112–13, 117, 132– 33, 143, 150n24. *See also* exhortation; household rules
ethos, 28n48, 58, 108. *See also* rhetoric
Eucharist, 86, 87n41, 170 (sacred meal)
Euripides, 100n16, 159n49. *See also* Greek drama, tragedy
Eusebius Pamphilus, 10n2, 13n15, 32n57, 34n67, 38, 40n2, 42–43, 53n34, 67–68, 70, 77, 97–98, 102n26, 116, 121n16, 123n22, 128n32, 148, 152, **168**. *See also* patristic; Great Church
Evans, Craig A., 97n10, 132n41, 149n21, 152n31
evil (*kakos*), 56, 163. *See also* sin, sins
　age, 86–7, 145. *See also* apocalyptic; eschatology
　Christ's triumph/victory over, 87n43, 89–90. *See also* Christ, triumph/victory
　desire, intentions (*epithymia*), 56, 59, 61
　do not speak, 55 Tab. 3.2, 79
　powers, 3, 87
　put away, resist, 50 Tab. 2.4, 55, 60, 130, 137. *See also* ethics; exhortation; repent
exhortation, hortatory, **11–12**, 14, 55, 58, 88, 105, 110. *See also* homily; paraenesis
exordium, 85–86, **168**. *See also* proem; prologue; rhetoric.
exposition of sacred texts, 15, 19, 55, 80, 105, 120, 131–32, 134, 138. *See also* commentary, ancient
eyewitness(es), 47–49, 68–69, 71, 101–2, 111, 122n16, 128, 133, 138. *See also* tradition, bearer(s)
Ezekiel, 8, 16, 61, 76, 79, 143–44, 161–62, 170. *See also* Prophets

INDEX

faith (*pistis*), 2–4, 10, 14–**17**, 19, 22–23, 32, 35, 37, 50–51, 58, 65, 73–74, 92, 99, 100, 106, 109, 111, 141, 151. *See also* obey
  common, 106–7, 114. *See also* creeds, doctrinal beliefs
  faithful, 8, 14–15, 18, 28, 30, 60, 64, 72n11, 87, 93, 144, 146, 151, 153, 160
  faithless, 56, 60, 61n51, 62n52. *See also* obey, disobedience; sin; unrighteousness
  in Jesus Christ, 34–35, 50. *See also* confess; Christ
  justification by, 41, 50. *See also* justification; righteousness
  living, practicing, 64, 87n44, 105, 165
  and prayer, 59, 63–64. *See also* prayer
  test of, 51 Tab 2.5, 59, 62, 76
  and works, 50, 53, 57, 61, 64–65
false teachers/teaching, 5–6, 19, 32n62, 57–58, 94–95, 104–7, 111, 114, 123–24, 129–30, 133, 149, 170. *See also* antichrist; opponents; secessionists
farewell address (final testament), 4–5, **109**, 114
figures of speech, 17n25, 27n46, 45, 56–57, 110, 153n35. *See also* literary and rhetorical devices
Fitzmyer, Joseph A., 69n4, 105n34
food laws (*kashrut*), 35, 45, **152**. *See also* law, Judean (purity)
foreshadowing. *See* pre-announcments, foreshadowing

Gaius, 6, 125, 129–30. *See also* John, Letters of
Galilee, Galilean, 45, 47–8, 100
Gallio, 71n8. *See also* Rome, empire of

García Martínez, Florentino, 24n39, 127n31, 144n7. *See also* Dead Sea Scrolls
gematria, 155–56. *See also* Metzger, Bruce M.
General Letters. *See* Catholic or General Letters
genre, 7–8, **11**, 13–14, 38, 41, 54, 80, 104, 109, 120, 128, 130–31, 138, 142–45, 159n49, 163n56. *See also* Hebrews, genre; James, genre; etc.
gezeira sheva, 13n13, 80n22. *See also* midrash
gnostic(s), 25–26, 100n18, 103n28, 114, 132–33, 139n54, 149n21, 152n31, **168**. *See also* Heracleon; Nag Hammadi Library; Valentinus; false teaching; teaching, gnostic
  antinomian, 51, 101, 104, 122–23, **165**, 169
  Gnostic Redeemer, 18, **25**–26, 32, 38
  libertine, 100, 122–23, 136, 139, 165, **170**
God, gods. *See* law, of God; mystery cults; praise, of God; power(s); word; worship; etc.
Gospels, the (NT division), 1, 7, 44, 47–48, 68, 98, 101, 142–43, 154, 159n49. *See also* John, the Gospel of; Matthew, the Gospel of
Gospel of (NT Apocrypha). *See also* apocrypha; canon; gnostic; Nag Hammadi Library
  Philip, 26, 122n19, 132n41, 133n43
  Thomas, 98–99, 127n31, 132–33, 152n31
  Truth, 6, 26n42, 122n19, 131–33, **172**
grace, 45, 65, 79, 86–87, 96, 100, 113, 127, 164, 165. *See also* bless, blessing(s)
  and peace, 129, 146

217

INDEX

Great Church, 40, 53, **168**. *See also* patristics, church fathers; Eusebius Pamphilus

Greco-Roman, 3–4, 34n69, 74, 76n15, 81n29, 103, 128, 130n36, 133n45, 145n10, 150, 162, **168**. *See also* Hellenistic; Greek, Koine

Greek. *See also* Septuagint; Scriptures, NT
  Attic, 27, 102
  drama, tragedy, 7, 81n27, 156, **159n49**, 164
  Koine, 14 Fig. 1, **27**, 29, 32, 48–49, 65, 69, 77 Fig. 10, 102, 153 Fig. 17. *See also* Hellenistic
  language, 11–12, 18n26, 19n30, 22n38, 29, 33, 45, 48–49, 71n9, 97, 100, 117, 141n1, 144, 155–56
  manuscripts (papyrus), 14 Fig. 1, 33, 77 Fig. 10, 97, 122, 153 Fig. 17, 157
  poetry, 100n16

haggadah, haggadic, 131, **168**. *See also* midrash

hapax legomena, 27n45, 100, **168**

Harmageddon, 158n46. *See also* apocalyptic; eschatology; Christ, triumph/victory over

Haustafeln, 81n29, **168**. *See* household rules or codes

heaven (*ouranos*), heavenly
  ascended into, 89n50. *See also* Christ, Christology
  being or angel, 145
  Christ, 123n22, 146. *See also* apocalyptic; Cerinthus
  city, 17
  court, council, 159, 162
  and earth, 1, 22, 52 Tab. 2.6, 108, 162 (and hades)
  future things, 22. *See* also apocalyptic; eschatology
  great sign in, 163n55. *See also* apocalyptic
  home, 25, 73
  journey, 25
  redeemer, 18, 32, 38
  sanctuary, 16
  inheritance kept in, 82
  mediator from, 27n44, 127n30
  queen of, 162, 164

Hebrew language, 24n39, 27, 29–31, 46, 48, 69, 100, 167. *See also* Aramaic; Scriptures, OT

Hebrews, 19–39
  audience, 33–35
  authorship, 10, 31–33
  date and destination, 36–38
  genre, 11–13
  and gnostic writings, 24–26. *See also* gnostic; Nag Hammadi
  and Hellenistic Christ-followers, 27–31
  and the Judean Scriptures (OT), 20–21
  and Philo of Alexandria, 21–23
  and Qumran scrolls, 23–24
  rhetorical function and structure, 14–19

Hebrews and Hellenists, 29–30, 36

Hegesippus (cited by Eusebius), 43nn12–13, 49, 53, 98

Hellenistic, 29–30, 33, 35–36. *See also* Greco-Roman; Greek, Koine; Hebrews and Hellenists

Hengel, Martin, 29–30, 45n18, 48n25, 67n2, 69n5, 72n11

Heracleon (disciple of Valentinus), 6, 131–32, 172. *See* commentary, ancient

heresy. *See* antichrist; false teachers/teaching; opponents

Hermetic writings, 25–26, 83, 130–31, **169**

Hesiod, *Theogony*, 94, 100n16, 150n26. *See* myth, mythology

INDEX

Hippolytus of Rome, 77, 84, **85n36**, 131, 138, 155n37. *See also* patristic; pseudonimity
history, 22, 144–45, 163
   church, 43n10, 91, 100n17, 106n35, 115, 124n23, 138, 168
   Hebrew or Israelite, 5, 21, 95. *See also* Josephus; Scriptures, OT
   of interpretation, 142n2
   redemptive, salvation, 22, 30. *See* salvation, history
holy, 78 Tab. 3.2, 81n30, 86. *See also* cleanse; sanctify
   city, 152. *See also* Jerusalem
   faith, 4. *See also* faith
   law/torah, 50. *See also* law
   nation, 76
   ones, 107. *See also* saints
   prophets, 112. *See also* Prophets
   wars, 162
Holy Spirit, the Spirit, 2, 4, 28, 50, 52, 79, 100, 118–20, 134
homily (sermon), 11, 14, 49n26, 65, 88, 105, 114, **169**. *See also* exhortation, hortatory; paraenesis
honor, 58, 125n25. *See also* values, virtue
   bring honor, 3, 81, 85n38, 137
   dishonor(s), 2, 106, 125n25, 150. *See also* shameful
   honorable behavior, 2, 17, 63, 87n42. *See also* righteousness
hope, 1, 3, 8, 16, 81, 85, 107, 126, 141, 144, 146, 161, 163. *See also* eschatology
Hornblower, Simon, 81n27, 145n10
household rules or codes, 3, 81, 85–86. *See* ethics, ethical; *Haustafeln*; submit
humble, humility (*tapeinos*), 24, 68, 87
   of Jesus, 28n49, 87 (humiliation). *See also* life, of Jesus

   oneself, 2, 61, 62, 68, 87. *See also* ethics; exhortation
   proud and, 45 Tab. 2.2, 47 Tab. 2.3, 59, 79 Tab. 3.2. *See also* righteousness; sin
Hurtado, Larry, 16n22, 39n81, 122n19
hymns, 81, 143, 159. *See* odes

intercalation, 154–55, 158, 164, **169**. *See also* chiasm
intertextuality, 1, 20n31, 38n79, 157n41. *See* allusion/echo; parallels
invective, 58, 95, 106, **169**. *See* denouncements
Ignatius of Antioch, 19n30, 101–2, 122n19, 126–28. *See also* patristic
Irenaeus of Lyons, 26n42, 42, 67, 84, 100n18, 116, 123, 127, 128n32, 148–49, 155n37, **169**. *See also* patristic
Isaiah, 6, 14, 21, 78 Tab. 3.2, 80, 131, 143. *See also* Prophets
Isocrates, 13, 58n46
   Pseudo-Isocrates, 56
Israel, Israelite, 1, 12–13, 19n30, 21–22, etc., **169**. *See also* Judean

James, Epistle of, 40–65
   authorship and authenticity, 42–49
   1 Peter and Hermas, 51 Tab. 2.5; 52 Tab. 2.6
   and Paul, 50 Tab. 2.4, 50–51, *See also* Paul, the apostle(s)
   and Sermon on the Mount, 46 Fig. 5, 47 Tab. 2.3
   genre, 54–55
   historical situation, 63–64
   rhetorical devices, 56–57
   structure, 58–63
Jeremiah, 1, 8, 12, 14, 16, 20, 24, 49, 54, 60, 62, 128, 130, 161–62. *See also* Prophets

INDEX

Jerome (Lat. Hieronymus), 42–43, 64, 68, 97, 156
Jerusalem, 8, 9 Map A, 19n30, 24n39, 29–33, 35–36, 39, 43–44, 51, 54, 66 Map B
   Church, 35–36, 43, 53, 98
   destruction of, 36–37, 44, 49n27, 51, 77, 126
   New Jerusalem, 8, 154, 162–63. *See also* under new, Jerusalem
   temple, 24n39, 30–31, 49n27, 77
Jesus Christ. *See* Christ, Christology
Joachim of Fiore, 131, 141
John, Gospel of, 6, 11, 25, 31, 38–39, 41, 91, 101, 116, 118–21, 124–26, 131–34, 138–39
John, Letters of, 115–39
   authenticity and authorship, 116–22
   the opponents, 122–23
   dates, 125–26
   genres, 128–33
   and Gospel of John, 118 Tab. 5.1, 120–21
   places of composition, 127–28
   rhetorical function, 88
   structures, 129–30, 133–34
Josephus, Titus Flavius, 19n30, 24n39, 27, 32n63, 34n68, 36, 43n13, 53n34, 64n55, 94n3, 102, 104, 109n40, 122n19, **169**. *See also* Essenes; Jerusalem; Judeans; Rome
joy, 6–7, 47, 83, 87, 118, 129–30, 158
Jude, Letter of, 92–114 (with 2 Peter)
   and 2 Peter, 92 Tab 4.1, 93–96
   authorship and authenticity, 98–100
   canonicity, 96–97
   genre, 104–6
   place of composition, 100–101
   rhetorical function and structure, 106–9
Judean, Judeans, 12–13, **19n30**, 20–27, etc., **169**. *See also* law, Judean

judgment, final, 2, 62, 86–87, 89, 93, 95, 103n28, 105n34, 106–8, 111, 114, 120–21, 133, 143, 145, 147, 154, 56, 158–60, 169. *See also* apocalyptic; eschatology; Prophets
justification. *See also* righteousness of faith
   by faith, 41, 50n29
   by works, 50 Tab. 2.4

Kelly, J. N. D., 67n2, 69n7, 71n9, 76n16, 84n35, 90n53
kerygma, 12–13, 41, 46, 80, 105, **170**. *See also* apostolic teaching
   preaching, proclaiming, 3, 11n8, 68, 74, 86, 89, 97n11. *See also* exhortation
Klauck, Hans-Josef, 40n1, 82nn31–32, 83n33, 105n33, 145n12, 150n26
Koester, Craig R., 10n3, 14n16, 25n41, 27n46, 37n74, 38n79, 142nn2–3, 144n6, 146n13, 148n18, 152n30, 153n35, 158n46, 161n52, 162n54, 163nn55, 57, 164n58
Koester, Helmut, 34n70, 101n22, 102n27
Kümmel, Werner Georg, 38n80, 41n7, 42nn8–9

Lane, William L., 10n3, 11n8, 13n11, 28n49, 35n71
Lanham, Richard A., 15n19, 17n25, 56n41, 154n35
law,
   apodictic, 135n49, **137n51**.
   ethical demands of, 50, 60. *See also* ethics
   of God, 30, 47, 49–50, 160–61. *See also* word, of God
   Judean (purity), 17, 29–31, 35, 39, 43–45, 49, **152**. *See also* food laws (*kashrut*)

INDEX

lawless, 113, 122, 165. *See* antinomian; libertine
Mosaic, Pentateuch, **Torah**, 20, 79, 137, **172**. *See also* Moses
unwritten (inscribed on the heart), 22, 60n49, 60–61. *See* covenant, new
letters. *See* epistolary form
libertine, 100n18, 122–23, 136, 139, **170**, *See also* antinomian; gnostic(s)
life,
  afterlife, 104, 170. *See also* eschatology; judgement, final
  and death, 55 (two ways)
  eternal, 4, 6, 16n23, 55, 79, 118–21, 133, 136, 170
  of fullness (spiritual, eternal), 6, 15–16, 55, 79
  of Jesus, 41, 46, 80, 119–20, 133, 170–72. *See also* kerygma
  lifestyle, 85, 87, 165, 168, 170–71. *See also* ethics; exhortation; humble
  of Paul, 51
  realities of, 15, 56, 64
  short span of, 2, 59n47
  situation (context), 21, 24, 56, 64n55, 76
  view of, 57
literary and rhetorical devices, 48, 56–58, 94, 109–10, 153–59. *See also* figures of speech; rhetoric; Lanham, Richard A.
liturgy, **170**. *See also* worship
  baptismal, 73, 82–86, 90, 135n49, 137–38. *See also* baptism
  heavenly, 154–55. *See also* eschatology, visions of the end of time
  Judean, 159. *See also* law; priests; tabernacle
Longenecker, Richard N., 13n14, 20n31, 21n34, 28n47, 29n51, 80
love, 45, 117, 134, 137

beloved (*agapētos*), **44**, 100–101, 106–9, 113, 129
brotherly love, *philadelphia*, **101**, 137
of God, 4, 119, 120n11, 134
mutual love, 2, 4, 79, 139
one another, 24, 50, 61
your neighbor, 81n30, 118–19, 134
Lucian of Samosata, 106
lust. *See* evil, desire
Luther, Martin, 32, 41–42, 50n29, 64–65, 89–90, 91, 95n5, 98n12, 104n30

Malina, Bruce J., 125n25, 144n7, 163n56
  and John J. Pilch, 142n3, 145n10, 152n33, 163n56
Martin, Ralph P., 35n72, 41n4, 54n37, 64n55
Matthew, Gospel of, 47, 49, 68, 102, 170. *See also* Gospels, the
Mayor, J. B., 41n4, 43–44, 48–49, 52–53, 55n39, 56
McDonald, Lee Martin, and James A. Sanders, 41n3, 97n9, 124n24
McKnight, Scot, 14n17, 41n4, 44n16, 46n21
  and Joseph B. Modica, 74n14, 150n27
Melchizedek, 10, 16, 18, **20–22**, 32n63, 39n81
mercy (*eleos*), 3–4, 47 Tab. 2.3, 81, 78, 85–86, 129
metonymy, **16n23**, 27n46. *See also* figures of speech
Metzger, Bruce M., 76n16, 88n45, 122n18, 146n13, 153n34, 156n37, 164n58. *See also* textual variants; comma, Johannine
midrash, midrashic, 6, 13, 21, 29, 80, 131, **170**
Mishnah ('Abot; Sanh.), 43n14, 60n50, 85, 104, 168, **170**

INDEX

misogyny, 8, 76n15, 161. *See also* women; Pippin, Tina
Moses, 1, 15, 18, 22, 30, 143. *See also* law, Mosaic
mystery cults, 82–83
myth, mythology, 94, 102, 150, **162–63**

Nag Hammadi Library, 25–26, 43n13, 97, 99 Fig. 12, 126–27, 132n41, 149n21, 151n31, 168, **170**. *See also* gnostic(s)
Nero, Emperor, 70, 76, 150–51, 155–56. *See also* persecution, Roman
new,
    age, 22, 145. See also apocalyptic; eschatology
    birth, 3, 73. *See also* birth
    born, born anew, 51 Tab 2.5, 73, 81n26, 83, 85–86
    converts, 55, 73, 80, 88
    covenant, 1, 16, 20, 28, 32, 35, 60n49, 170. *See also* covenant
    creation, 163
    Jerusalem, 8, 162–63
    Testament, xxi, 56, 67, 170. *See* Scriptures, New Testament

obey (*hypokouō*). *See also* faith; humble; submit, suborinate
disobedience, 28, 146, 153n33
obedience of Christ. *See also* Christ; life, of Jesus
obedience of faith, 50. *See also* faith
oracles of God, 15, 20. *See also* oracles; word, of God
the Son, 2. *See also* faith, in Jesus Christ
O'Brien, Peter T., 10n3, 12n8, 15n19, 25n40, 28, 32n62, 38n79
odes, 7, 143, 159n49. *See also* hymns
Odes of Solomon. *See* Solomon, Odes of

opponents, 5, 107, 122–23, 126, 138–39. *See also* false teachers; secessionists
oracles
    of seers/prophets, 13n15, 145n10
    of the Lord (God), 15, 20, 21n33. *See also* agrapha; word, of God
    of woe, 143
orations, oratorical, 12–13, 58, 106, 167, 169. *See* rhetoric; speech, speeches
Origen of Alexandria, 31, 34, 42, 44n15, 48, 111, 152

Painter, John, 41n4, 43n11, 49n27, 53–54
    and David deSilva, 107n37, 118n9
Pantaenus of Alexandria, 33, 34n66
paraenesis (*paraklēsis*), 11–12, 14, 64, 88, 104–5, **171**. *See also* exhortation; word
parallelism, inverted, 8, 87n43, 158, 166. *See also* chiasm
parallels, comparisons, x, 2, 6, 44 Tab. 2.1, 45 Tab. 2.2, 83–85, 128–32, 137–38, 143, etc. *See also* allusion/echo; intertextuality
paronomasia, 56n41, **171**. *See also* concatenation
patristics, church fathers, 53, 97n9, 100, 148, 149n21. *See also* Great Church
Paul, the apostle, 28, 73
    anti-Pauline, 42, 44, 70
    deutero-Pauline, Pauline school, 49, 51, 53, 69, 72, 100, 102n25, 122n17, **167**
    and Hebrews, 28–29, 31
    and James, 49–51
    letters/writings of, 1, 3, 5, 28–29, 32, 37, 40, 72n11, 80, 90–91, 102, 117, 124n24, 128, 130.

INDEX

See also Romans, Paul's
Letter to the; epistolary form
and Peter, 41, 70, 76
and 2 Peter, 101, 113
themes/words/rhetoric of, 5, 28,
37, 41, 54, 58, 65, 69, 100,
110
Perdelwitz, Richard, 82n31, 84n35.
See also mystery cults
Pergamum, 9 Map A, 66 Map B, 140
Map C, 147 Fig. 15, 148
Perkins, Pheme, 27n44, 67n2,
85n37, 102n27, 127n30,
132n41, 133n43
peroration, 17, 54, 59, 61–62, 87,
107–9, 112, **171**. *See also*
epilogue
persecution, generic 3, 7, 28, 37, 39,
63–64, 68, 73, 76, 85, 87–88,
150. *See also* suffering; trials
empire-wide (Rome), 4, 8, 66,
71n8, 73–74, 149–51
end-time, 154, 158
imminent, 39, 85
Judean, 36
local, 8, 70–71, 148, 150–51,
154, 158, 164
Roman (sporadic), 35, 37,
70–71, 76, 90
pesher interpretation, 6, 13, 24, 80,
99, 105, 108n39, 131, **171**.
See also commentary; Dead
Sea Scrolls
Peter, apostle, 41, 44, 51n31, 67–70,
72–74, 95, 98n13
Peter, First Letter of, 67–91
authorship and authenticity,
67–73
audience, 73–76
date, 76–77
genre, 80–85
place of composition, 77–80
rhetorical function, 88
structure, 85–88
Peter, Second Letter of, 92–114
(with Jude)
authorship, 101–2
canonicity, 97–98

genre, 109–10
historical situation, 102–4
and Jude, 92 Tab. 4.1, 94–96
rhetorical structure, 110–13
Philo of Alexandria, 13n15, 19n30,
21–23, 32n61, 36n74, 48,
102n23, 122n19, 163n56,
171
philosophical, philosopher,
philosophy, 19n30, 25n41,
55, 57, 103, 128, 131,
167–68. *See also* Aristotle;
Cynics; diatribe; Epicurus;
Epictetus; Essene; gnostic;
Plato; Seneca; Stoics
Pippin, Tina, 161n51, 162n53
Plato, 21, 102n23, 109n40, 128
Platonic dualism or worldview, 2,
22–23, 171. *See also* dualism
Platonist, Platonism, 21–23, 171
Pliny,
the Elder, 148
the Younger, 4, 74n14, 77n19,
151
plot, plot structure, 7–8, 134n46.
See also denouement; Greek,
drama
Plutarch, 57, 60, 103n28, 104
Polycarp of Smyrna, 68, 76, 100n19,
104–5, 116, 122–23, 127–28,
149
post-apostolic. *See* apostle(s), postapostolic
poverty, 8, 148, 150–51, 164
power(s), authority, 28
angelic, 26, 79 Tab. 3.2, 89–90,
93 Tab. 4.1
Christ's triumph over, 3, 89–91.
See also Christ, triumph over
cosmic, 87n43, 90. *See also* evil,
powers
of death, darkness, 25. *See also*
death, eternal
of God, divine, 83, 102n23, 109
human, 125n25
powerlessness, hopeless, 142,
144

INDEX

power(s) *(continued)*
  of Rome, 160. *See also* Rome
  of two beasts, dragon, 151, 161. *See also* evil, powers
praise (*epainos*),
  and censure, 106–7, 112n47, 146. *See also* censure
  of God, laudation of God, 17, 107, 113, **170**. *See also* doxology, encomium
  sacrifice of praise (*ainesis*), 17. *See also* sacrifice
  of virtues, 4, 14, 106. *See also* encomium; rhetoric, demonstrative
prayer(s), 2, 11, 17, 19, 24, 52 Tab. 2.6, 54, 62–63, 81, 85, 88, 146, 167, 169. *See also* faithful, and prayer; worship
pre-announcements, foreshadowings, 156
prolepsis, 15–16, **171**
priest(s), priesthood. *See also* law; tabernacle
  Christ as high priest, 1, 15–18, 24, 28, 31, 34n68, 39. *See also* Christ, Christology
  of Cybele cult, 82–83. *See also* mystery cults
  of Israel, 22, 26, 35, 64n55, 86n39, 152
  Levitical, 18, 26, 29 Fig. 4, 35
  Melchizedek, 16, **18**, 21–22. *See also* Melchizedek
  royal priesthood of believers, 76, 78
  Wicked Priest, 6, 131. *See also* Dead Sea Scrolls
proem, 15, 18, 38, 58–59, 61–62, 107, 109, 111, 127. *See also* exordium; prologue
prologue, 7, 107n38, 132, 159. *See also* epilogue; proem; exordium
Prophets (OT division), 20, 79, 144n6, 169–70

prophets, seers, 3, 24, 30, 47, 61–62, 111–12, 144n6, 146, 153
prophetic forms, 8, 24, 58, 61n51, 105n34, 143–44, 152–53
protasis, 58, 86, **171**. *See also* apodosis
protreptic, 12n10, 14–15, 167, **171**. *See also* exhortation; paraenesis
Proverbs, proverb, 20, 54–55, 79–80, 102 *See also* wisdom
Psalms, psalm, 15, 20–21, 78 Tab. 3.2, 80, 145
pseudepigraphic writing, 113, **171**
pseudonymity, 53, 72n11
Pseudo-Clementine writings, 25–26, 43–44
pure, undefiled, purify, 17n25, 44 Tab. 2.1, 50 Tab. 2.4, 59–60, 62n52, 64, 83, 86. *See also* cleanse; sanctify
Puskas, Charles B., 13n11, 23 Fig. 3, 45n17
  and David Crump, 126n27, 127n31, 134n46, 154n36
  and Mark Reasoner, 88n46, 122n17, 128n33, 137n53, 145n12. *See also* Elliott, Neal and
  and J. Michael Robbins, 30n52, 32n62, 51nn30–31, 100n18, 123n20, 126n28, 139n54, 142n4, 144n7, 159nn48–49

qal wahomer, **13n13**, 16n23, 18n26, 21n34, 80n22. *See also* rabbinic interpretation
Quintilian, 13n11, 58n46, 106n36. *See also* rhetoric
Qumran, 18, 23 Fig. 3, 32n62, 34, 80, 100–101, 106. *See* Dead Sea Scrolls
Quotation. *See* allusion/echo; intertextuality.

rabbinic interpretation, 13, 21, 80, 131, 170. *See also* midrash; Mishnah
redeem, redemption. 16, 86 *See* church, community of the redeemed; Gnostic Redeemer; salvation
repent, repentance, 34, 37n75, 61, 89, 146. *See also* sin, sins
repetition, 56–57, 156
replacement theology *See* supersessionism
rest, God's Sabbath, 1, 13n13
heavenly, 15, 18, 26
resurrection
of Christ, 1, 3, 41, 46–47, 80, 89–91, 170. *See also* kerygma; life, of Jesus
of Christ-followers, 121, 133
spiritual, 26, 103n28
Revelation, Book of, **141–64**
and apocalyptic genre, 144–45. *See also* apocalyptic
authorship, 151–52
the chiastic structure, 158–62
and epistolary genre, 145–47
literary and rhetorical devices, 153–59. *See also* allusions; chiasm
and prophetic genre, 143–44. *See also* Prophets
social and historical context, 148–51
symbolic and mythical language, 162–63
rhetoric, 4, 13–14, 58n46. *See also* Aristotle; Quintilian
deliberative (symboleutic) rhetoric, 12–15, 38, 58, 63, 88n47, 110n44, **167**. *See also* exhortation; paraenesis
demonstrative, display, **epideictic** rhetoric 88–89, 106–7, 110, **167**. *See also* encomium; values, virtues
righteous, 79 Tab. 3.2, 136. *See also* unrighteous
deeds, 8, 134, 162

godly, faithful, 111, 145. *See also* saints; servants, of God
James, 44, 51
people, 79, 144–45
prayer of the, 63. *See also* prayer
righteousness, 112, 139
of faith, 50n29. *See also* justification
Robinson, James M., 25n41, 43n13, 126n28. *See also* Nag Hammadi Library
and Helmut Koester, 98n15. *See also* Koester, Helmut
Roman Catholic, 41n6, 50n29, 89n51
Romans, Paul's Letter to the, 5, 28–29, 37, 40–41, 56–57, 71–72, 91, 102, 124n24. *See also* Paul, the apostle
Rome, 4, 7–8, 30, 33, 36–37, 39, 74, 77, 149–50, 160, 162n53, 164
church at, 9 Map A, 37, 39
empire of, 66 Map B, 70 Fig. 7, 73, 149, 151
local citizens under/of, 4, 74, 150n27
Roman officials, 70–71, 77
symbolized as Babylon, 77, 90, 149, 162
Ropes, James Hardy, 41n4, 43nn10–11, 48n24, 54n36

Sabbath. *See* rest, God's Sabbath
Sacraments, 41n6, 86–87, 90n54. *See also* baptism; Eucharist
sacrifice(s),
atoning sacrifice of Christ, 1, 16, 22, 38n79, 39, 120, 136. *See also* Christ, Christology
of Cybele cult, 82. *See also* mystery cults
Levitical, 22, 24, 35, 83, 86n39. *See also* priests; tabernacle
of praise, 17n25. *See also* doxology; worship

INDEX

Roman imperial, 151n28. *See also* worship, imperial
spiritual, 17, 24, 32. *See also* spiritual, sacrifices; worship
saints (*hagioi*), 4, 30n54, 36, 99–100, 107, 146n13. *See also* Christ-followers; cleanse; holy; sanctify
sanctify, sanctifying, 2, 44 Tab. 2.1, 79 Tab. 3.2. *See also* cleanse; holy; pure; saints
sapiential, **172**. *See* wisdom
Satan (*satanas*), satanic, 162. *See also* devil
   dragon, 149
   satanic trinity, 157
   synagogue of, 152n30
   throne of, 148n18
save, salvation (*sōteria*), 2–4, 26, 29, 34, 83, 86, 107, 113, 120, 132–33, 152n30. *See also* sacrifice, atoning
   and baptism, 3, 89–91
   eschatological, 7, 73, 85, 154–55
   God/Christ to save (*sōzō*) and judge, 52, 109,
   and good works, 50, 65
   history, 22, 30
   and judgment, 105n34, 158–60
   righteous saved, 79
   save a sinner, 2, 51 Tab. 2.5, 63, 79 Tab. 3.2
Schüssler Fiorenza, Elisabeth, 150n23, 160n50
Scriptures, the 2, 7, 21, **172**. *See also* word
   Hebrew, 12, 139n49, 143–44,
   of Israel (Israelite), 1, 12
   Judean, 20–21, 78, 157, **169**
   New Testament (NT), 7, 27–31, 68, 71–72, 92–3, 102, 118, 145–47, **170**
   Old Testament (OT), 7, 45–46, 78–9, 137, 143–45, 157n41, **170**
secessionists, 122–25, 130–34, 139n54. *See also* John, Letters of; opponents

Selwyn, E. G., 67–69, 71, 82n31, 83n33, 86n39, 89n48
Seneca, Lucius Annaeus, 55 Fig. 6, 102n23, 103n29, 105
sensus plenior, 21. *See also* allegory; midrash
Septuagint (LXX), 13, 20–22, 27, 29, 30n53, 33–34, 38, 45, 48, 78, 157n41, 170–71
Sermon on the Mount, 46, 47 Tab. 2.3. *See* James, Letter of
servant(s), 80n22. *See also* household rules
   of God or Christ, 42, 54, 59, 98, 101, 106–7, 110, 152. *See also* apostle(s); disciple(s), elder(s)
   liturgical service. *See* baptism; worship
   practical service, 1, 17, 36, 60, 62n53
Seth, Sethian, 25–26, 27n44, 127n30, 132n41, **172**. *See* gnostic(s)
shameful, 56. *See also* sin, sins; honor
   ashamed, 78 Tab. 3.2
Shepherd of Hermas, 37n75, 42, 49, 52, 62n52, 84
sin, sins, 2, 16, 51, 57, 60n48, 61, 63, 68, 78–79, 95, 105, 119, 122, 134–36, 166
   sinner, 2, 63, 79. *See also* evil; sacrifices, atoning; save, a sinner; unrighteous
Sirach, 23, 27n44, 54n37, 55, 59–60, 127n30, 169, 171. *See also* wisdom
Socrates, 109n40. *See also* farewell address
Solomon. *See also* pseudepigraphic writing
   Odes of, 25–27, 127
   Wisdom of, 23, 65. *See also* wisdom
Sophocles, 159n49. *See also* Greek drama, tragedy

INDEX

Soulen, Richard N., and R. Kendall Soulen, 21nn34–35, 137n51, 153n33
source(s), 25–26, 43, 45, 52, 82, etc.
   critical theories, 94–95, 135–38, 152n32. *See also* Jude, and 2 Peter
   primary, 12n10, 24n39, 25n41, 126n28, 145n9. *See also* Dead Sea Scrolls; Nag Hammadi; Scriptures
speech, speeches, 5, 12–14, 30–31, 44–45, 58, 60–61, 68–69, 93, 106, 109–10, 114, 143, 165. *See also* orations; rhetoric
spirit
   and body, 57, 61. *See also* dualism
   conservative, 3, 51n31, 53
   of courage, 67
   humble, 24. *See also* humble, humility
spirits in prison, rebellious, fallen, 3, 79, 89–90
spiritual
   adultery (idolatry), 8, 34, 57, 161
   being, 166
   household, 76
   milk, 83, 86
   realm, dimension, 25n41, 129, 168
   resurrection, 26, 103n28. *See also* eschatology, realized; gnostic
   sacrifices, 17, 24, 32n63. *See also* worship
   worship, 83
Stoics, 55, 57, 65, 103, 105, 171. *See also* Cynics; diatribe
submit, subordinate (hypotassō), 51 Tab. 2.5, 61, 75–76, 79 Tab. 3.2, 87. *See also* household rules; obey
Suetonius, 70, 150–51. *See also* Nero; Domitian

suffering,
   of Christ, 32, 38, 41, 68, 80–81, 85, 87, 166. *See also* kerygma
   of Christ-followers, 2–3, 36, 38, 54, 62, 73, 75, 68, 80, 87–88, 148 (*thlipsis*). *See also* persecution; trials
superior, better, (*kreittōn*), 15–16, 18, 28, 35, 39. *See also* Christ; covenant, new; supersessionism
supersessionism, replacement theology, 1, 16n23, 18n28, 35n73.
symbols, symbolism, 7, 157–58, 161 Fig. 18, 162–63
synagogue. *See also* diaspora; Judean; worship, synagogue
   and church, 31, 39
   exclusion from, 126n27
   homily, 11, 55
   in James, 45
   leader, 123n21
   liturgy, 85. *See also* Mishnah
   motifs in John, 126, 128n32
   of Satan, 152n30
Syria, 36, 101
   Antioch of, 9 Map A, 33, 127–28, 138, 166. *See also* Ignatius of Antioch
   churches of, 97

tabernacle, wilderness, 20 Fig. 2, 20–22, 29–30. *See also* Israel, Israelite; law; Scriptures
Tacitus, *Annals*, 38, 150n26
taurobolium, 82–83. *See* baptism; mystery cults
teach, teaching, 36, 130–31
   apostolic, 41, 48, 55, 81, 120, 125. *See also* apostle, apostolic; catechesis
   Cynic/Stoic, 15, 57, 103–4. *See also* Cynics; diatribe; Stoics
   false. *See* false teaching; opponents

teach, teaching (*continued*)
    gnostic, 26, 32, 39, 127n30. *See also* gnostic
    of Jesus, 46–47, 68, 120
    Judean, 13n15, 24, 33
    of Paul, 41, 50, 54
    and practice, 15, 24, 142, 149
    teachers, 13n11, 17, 34, 53, 57, 106
Tertullian of Carthage, 31, 34, 42, 70. *See also* patristic
testimonia, biblical catenae, 20–21, 28–29, 80–81, **172**
testimony. *See* witness(es), testimony (*martyria*)
textual variants 20, 27n47, 76n16, 122, 88n45, 153 (evidence). *See also* Comma, Johannine; Greek, manuscripts; Metzger, Bruce M.
Thomas,
    Acts of, 25n41, 26, 109n40
    Gospel of, 98–99, 127
Torah, **170**. *See* law, Torah
tradition,
    bearer, 121n16, 125n26, 129, 133, 138. *See also* apostle(s), post-apostolic
    Judean, 13n15, 17, 21, 29, 33–36, 82, 89, 94, 124n24, 135, 152n30. *See also* Israel; Judean
    prophetic, 8, 114, 161. *See also* Prophets; Scriptures
Trebilco, Paul, 116n6, 126–28, 149–50. *See also* Ephesus
trials (*peirasmoi*) of Christ-followers, 2–3, 47–48, 50–**51**, 55, 59, 70, 73, 88n44. *See also* persecution; suffering
Trinitarian, 122
    satanic trinity, 157
trust. *See* faith; obey
truth, 6, 63, 111, 117–18, 120n11, 123n22, 127n31, 135, 167
    Spirit of, 119–20
    word of, 51, 60
type, typology, 18n26, 22–23, 30n53, 80n25, 108, 124n23, 161
unrighteous, unrighteousness, 111–12, 134, 146 (disobedient). *See also* faithless; sin

Valentinus, Valentinian, 6, 26n42, 131, **172**. *See also* gnostic; Heracleon
values, virtues (upheld by the community), 4–5, 88, 106, 107, 110. *See also* encomium; rhetoric, demonstrative
Vermes, Geza, 13n14, 24n39, 80n23, 127n31, 131n39, 137n52, 145n9. *See also* Dead Sea Scrolls
visions. *See* eschatology, visions of the end time

Watson, Duane F., 88n47, 102n24, 106n36, 107n37, 110n44. *See also* rhetoric
    and Terrance Callan, 110n42
Wilson, Mark, 144n7, 153n35, 160n50
wisdom (sapiential), 2, 14, 23, 25–27, 33, 36, 54–56, 61, 64–65, 69, 79, 127n30, 144n7, **172**
witness(es), testimony (*martyria*), 7, 62, 119 Tab. 5.1, 151, 158. *See also* tradition, bearer
women, 3, 8, 75 Fig. 9, 75–76, 161–62. *See also* misogyny
word
    of apostles, 93 Tab. 4.1, 94. *See also* apostle(s), apostolic teaching
    of Christ, 47 Tab. 2.3, 68n3, 78 Tab. 3.2, 118–19 Tab. 5.1. *See also* agrapha; Christ; Sermon on the Mount
    of comfort, grace, 8, 164. *See also* grace; blessing(s)
    of exhortation, 11, 17, 161. *See* exhortation; paraenesis

of God, 2, 6, 15, 18, 20, 30, 36,
    47, 51, 56, 60–61, 64, 78,
    118–20, 135, 160.
    See law of God; oracles, of God;
    Scriptures; Septuagint
of prophets, 112, 160. *See also*
    Prophets
title of Christ, *Logos*, 120,
    127n31, 133. *See also* Christ,
    Christology
of truth, 51, 60. *See also* truth
worship, 2, 20–21, 56, 81n26, 84–85,
    148, 166. *See also* liturgy;
    spiritual sacrifices

of Christ, 4, 73–74, 151. *See also*
    Christ, Christology
imperial, 71n8, 150n23
Israelite, 16, 20 Fig. 2, 22, 30, 36.
    See also liturgy, Judean
pure and worthless, 60. *See also*
    spiritual, worship
synagogue, 85

Xenophon, *Anabasis*, 150n26

Zeus, 81n27, 94, 147–48, 150,
    162n54. *See* myth,
    mythology.

www.ingramcontent.com/pod-product-compliance
Lightning Source LLC
Chambersburg PA
CBHW031808220426
43662CB00007B/568